SHARI'A, INSHALLAH

Western analysts have long denigrated Islamic states as antagonistic, even antithetical, to the rule of law. Mark Fathi Massoud tells a different story: for nearly 150 years, the Somali people have embraced shari'a, commonly translated as Islamic law, in the struggle for national identity and human rights. Lawyers, community leaders, and activists throughout the Horn of Africa have invoked God to oppose colonialism, resist dictators, expel warlords, and to fight for gender equality – all critical steps on the path to the rule of law. *Shari'a, Inshallah* traces the most dramatic moments of legal change, political collapse, and reconstruction in Somalia and Somaliland. Massoud upends the conventional account of secular legal progress and demonstrates instead how faith in a higher power guides people toward the rule of law.

Mark Fathi Massoud is Professor of Politics and Legal Studies at the University of California, Santa Cruz. He is the author of *Law's Fragile State: Colonial, Authoritarian, and Humanitarian Legacies in Sudan*. He has held Carnegie, Guggenheim, and Mellon Foundation Fellowships.

D0808688

CAMBRIDGE STUDIES IN LAW AND SOCIETY

Founded in 1997, Cambridge Studies in Law and Society is a hub for leading scholarship in socio-legal studies. Located at the intersection of law, the humanities, and the social sciences, it publishes empirically innovative and theoretically sophisticated work on law's manifestations in everyday life: from discourses to practices, and from institutions to cultures. The series editors have longstanding expertise in the interdisciplinary study of law, and welcome contributions that place legal phenomena in national, comparative, or international perspective. Series authors come from a range of disciplines, including anthropology, history, law, literature, political science, and sociology.

Series Editors

Mark Fathi Massoud, *University of California, Santa Cruz*

Jens Meierhenrich, *London School of Economics and Political Science*

Rachel E. Stern, *University of California, Berkeley*

Past Editors

Chris Arup, Martin Chanock, Sally Engle Merry,
Pat O'Malley, Susan Silbey

A list of books in the series can be found at the back of this book.

CAMBRIDGE
STUDIES IN
LAW AND SOCIETY

SHARI'A, INSHALLAH

Finding God in Somali Legal Politics

Mark Fathi Massoud

University of California, Santa Cruz

CAMBRIDGE
UNIVERSITY PRESS

CAMBRIDGE
UNIVERSITY PRESS

University Printing House, Cambridge CB2 8BS, United Kingdom

One Liberty Plaza, 20th Floor, New York, NY 10006, USA

477 Williamstown Road, Port Melbourne, VIC 3207, Australia

314–321, 3rd Floor, Plot 3, Splendor Forum, Jasola District Centre, New Delhi – 110025, India

79 Anson Road, #06–04/06, Singapore 079906

Cambridge University Press is part of the University of Cambridge.

It furthers the University's mission by disseminating knowledge in the pursuit of education, learning, and research at the highest international levels of excellence.

www.cambridge.org
Information on this title: www.cambridge.org/9781108832786
DOI: 10.1017/9781108965989

© Mark Fathi Massoud 2021

First published 2021

A catalogue record for this publication is available from the British Library.

Library of Congress Cataloging-in-Publication Data
Names: Massoud, Mark Fathi, author.
Title: Shari'a, inshallah : finding god in Somali legal politics / Mark Fathi Massoud, University of California, Santa Cruz.
Description: Cambridge, United Kingdom ; New York, NY : Cambridge University Press, 2021. | Series: Cambridge studies in law and society | Includes bibliographical references and index.
Identifiers: LCCN 2021000606 (print) | LCCN 2021000607 (ebook) | ISBN 9781108832786 (hardback) | ISBN 9781108965705 (paperback) | ISBN 9781108965989 (ebook)
Subjects: LCSH: Law – Somalia – Islamic influences. | Law – Somaliland (Secessionist government, 1991–) – Islamic influences. | Justice, Administration of – Somalia. | Justice, Administration of – Somaliland (Secessionist government, 1991–)
Classification: LCC KTK46.7 .M37 2021 (print) | LCC KTK46.7 (ebook) | DDC 349.6773 – dc23
LC record available at https://lccn.loc.gov/2021000606
LC ebook record available at https://lccn.loc.gov/2021000607

ISBN 978-1-108-83278-6 Hardback
ISBN 978-1-108-96570-5 Paperback

Colaad kasta nabadbaa ka danbeysa. (Every war gives way to peace.)
Somali proverb

Shari'a is more advanced than the [state] laws we are working with. It is not just an ideal. It is a revelation from God. It has specificity . . . [But] this is the problem: as soon as you apply shari'a, they say you are a fundamentalist, or an Islamist.

Lawyer and former militia leader in Hargeisa, Somaliland[1]

[1] Interview 100 with Hassan, legal aid attorney and former militia leader and police official in Hargeisa, Somaliland (June 2014). With the exception of historical figures and the most prominent public officials, all names in this book have been changed to preserve confidentiality.

CONTENTS

FIGURES, MAPS, AND TABLES

PREFACE

July 12, 2013. Hargeisa, Somaliland
Barely lucid, I stirred in an old and dusty hospital bed while connected to an intravenous drip. In the pale moonlight, I saw a man sitting at the foot of my bed and I heard his quiet voice. I had arrived in this city weeks earlier not to seek treatment for amoebic dysentery or cholera (doctors later suggested I had contracted both diseases), but to investigate people's attitudes toward the law. I had learned that state laws were largely irrelevant to the Somali people – either long out of date or drafted by temporary aid workers – so I was less interested in what the law said than in the power of the ideal it presented, what drew people to that ideal, and law's potential as an instrument for peace.

When I lifted my head, I saw that the man speaking quietly was my colleague, a local lawyer and law professor. He was holding his head down, reciting verses from the Qur'an in his hands. He was praying to God to sustain me. His faith and the traditions and rituals of Islam guided him in his personal and professional activities, as I would come to understand. A year later, he was appointed to Somaliland's Supreme Court, where adherence to religious tradition with the hope of serving the will of God – in Arabic, *inshallah* – would inform his daily work, just as it motivated his prayers for my recovery.

This book, *Shari'a, Inshallah*, challenges the conventional wisdom in international law and policy that law is the main guiding hand of our societies and their politics, and that writing and enforcing laws is the most essential step toward building peace and stability in war-torn places. While it is true that some figures have invoked religion for their own reprehensible political goals, I show how this account obscures the ways in which religion is used for remarkably divergent ends. Instead, even where state power is weak and local customs are strong, people invoke religion to challenge colonialism, restrain dictators, expel warlords, write constitutions, plant democratic roots, and campaign for gender equality. Their efforts shape a foundation for the rule of law, a way of governing without arbitrary power.

As someone from Sudan, from which my parents fled when I was a boy and to which I later returned to write a book on how law matters in the world's most fragile states, I knew firsthand that differing kinds of people marshalled the law to serve their political or economic goals. Colonial administrators wrote regulations to criminalize aberrant behavior and shore up their foreign domination over diverse and divided groups. Postcolonial state leaders drafted constitutions and hired judges to delineate a path out of colonialism and civil war. Foreign aid workers and local activists invoked human rights to lift up themselves and the oppressed people they represented.

This process of using legal tools to achieve political, economic, and social ends is called legal politics. I had done research asking what law does for the rule of law and I found, disturbingly, that the activities of legal politics did little to realize the rule of law. I learned that law inspires us because we see its potential to do whatever we want it to do – at least so long as it meets our political ambitions and other goals.

But what of religion and religious law? What does religion do for colonial administrators, postcolonial governments, aid workers, and activists? Is there a legal politics of religion?

As a scholar in the United States, for the past twenty years I have read policy papers and academic studies in law and politics that portray religion as a problem that law solves. Only sometimes, and occasionally derisively, do these studies present piety as not so bad as it might at first seem. These assumptions about religion are clearest in Western foreign policy and policy-oriented writing on Islam and shari'a, which is commonly translated as Islamic law. But policy analysts' accounts of religion's role in politics are too thin. Like any religious or legal order, shari'a can be used in many ways, depending on the political proclivities of those who justify their activities as Islamic.

What follows is intended for an audience of legal scholars, social scientists who study law and religion, and policy practitioners. Scholars of Islamic law (*fiqh*) and Islamic legal theory (*usul al-fiqh*) may find the data and arguments presented helpful for understanding the ways that shari'a is conceived and used in politics and activism outside of courts. I have sought to understand efforts to establish national selfhood, and how religion shapes and is shaped by those efforts. Bringing law right down to the people who practice, shape, and use it, this book takes religion seriously as a force that informs those actors' use of the law.

ACKNOWLEDGMENTS

No endeavor like this book, spanning many countries and years, is accomplished alone. First, I owe deep gratitude to the many Somalis who took an interest in this project and went out of their way to help me discover Somali legal history. In particular, I thank Professor (and Chief Justice) Adam Haji-Ali Ahmed, Hamse Khayre, and Nasir Ali of the University of Hargeisa Institute for Peace and Conflict Studies and Faculty of Law, where I affiliated and where I incubated this project. Abdirahman Aw Ali, Somaliland's former Vice President, provided access to his personal papers. Dr. Abdi H. Gass, former President of the University of Hargeisa, supported foreign researchers in Somaliland. Dr. Abdiweli Ali, Somalia's former Prime Minister, shared his experiences with the generosity that a teacher would show his pupil. Abdilahi (Dhere) Ibrahim Habane of Somaliland's House of Elders and Mohammed Diriye Farah helped me learn the importance of the oral transmission of knowledge in the region and in Islam. I also thank my students at the University of Hargeisa, who reminded me that seeking knowledge is a shared activity. I also acknowledge the critical participation of many dozens of lawyers, activists, religious leaders, and aid workers who must go unnamed. Without these people this book would not be possible. *Ashkurukum wa mahadsanid.*

For helpful feedback on draft chapters, I thank audiences at the University of Hargeisa as well as Addis Ababa University; American University of Beirut; American University in Cairo; Cardiff University; Durham University; Graduate Theological Union; Hargeysa Cultural Center; Indiana University; New York University; Oxford University; Princeton University; Simon Fraser University; Stanford University; University College London; the University of California campuses of Berkeley, Hastings College of the Law, Irvine, Los Angeles, Santa Barbara, and Santa Cruz; University of Cape Town; University of Helsinki; University of Konstanz; and at American Political Science Association, Law and Society Association, and Modern Language Association annual meetings. I acknowledge the support and feedback

I received in these places and, in particular, from Zaid Al-Ali, Talal Al-Azem, Nasir Mohamed Ali, Waheeda Amien, Penelope Andrews, Deena Aranoff, Aslı Bâli, Elizabeth Beaumont, Edmund Burke III, Jennifer Bolton, Matthew Cannon, Nick Cheesman, Lynette J. Chua, Patrick Chuang, James Clifford, Vilashini Cooppan, Scott Cummings, Kevin Davis, Jennifer Derr, Susan Derwin, Elsa Devienne, Sara Dezalay, Mahjabeen Dhala, Karim Ennarah, Matthew Erie, Daniel R. Ernst, R. Michael Feener, Ellie Frazier, Mette Frederiksen, Paul Frymer, Leslie Gerwin, Michael Gilsenan, Laura E. Gómez, Camilo Gómez-Rivas, Carol Greenhouse, Isebill Gruhn, Christopher Hadley SJ, Terence C. Halliday, Laura Hammond, Kenedid Hassan, Laura Hubbard, Susan Hyde, Jama Muse Jama, Amaney Jamal, Diane Jefthas, Munir Jiwa, Turan Kayaoglu, Thomas Kelley, Ahmed Khater, Zoe King, Heinz Klug, Dimitry Kochenov, Martin Krygier, Joseph Lehnert, Michael Lienesch, Ronnie Lipschutz, Clark Lombardi, H. Timothy Lovelace Jr., Aila Matanock, Adam Millard-Ball, Kathleen M. Moore, Kelley Moult, Tamir Moustafa, Sherally Munshi, Neil Narang, Eleonora Pasotti, Michael G. Peletz, Tom Pyun, Lotta Relander, Judi Rivkin, Lawrence Rosen, Jeffrey Sachs, Abdirasak Mohamed Saeed, Nousha Saleh, Nahed Samour, Laura Seay, Amr Shalakany, Kim Lane Scheppele, Reuel Schiller, Benjamin Schonthal, Wolfgang Seibel, Perry Sherouse, Nicholas Rush Smith, Dee Smythe, Domna C. Stanton, Rachel E. Stern, Jemima Thomas, Michael Walls, Caryl Woulfe, Tirsit Yetbarek, Xiaoping Yin, Hind Ahmed Zaki, and Noah Zatz.

For access to colonial records and out-of-print volumes, I thank Sam Booth and Jane Hogan of Durham University's Sudan Archive, where extensive collections on British Somaliland are located; the law librarian at SOAS University of London; and the archivists at Oxford University's Bodleian Library. Ambreena Manji of the British Institute in Eastern Africa provided me support and affiliation in Nairobi. Christina Woolner, a scholar of Somali music and poetry, helped me to launch this study and access materials at Cambridge University's African Studies library. Ramzi Ramey helped to design the maps. James Graham, Michelle Niemann, Jim O'Hara, and Alice Stoakley edited the manuscript. Maryam Ahmad, Mohamed Abdilahi Duale, Ingy Higazy, Guleid Ahmed Jama, Audrey Mocle, Hanan Omar, Alicia Roll, Eric Wang, and Nourah Yonous provided valuable research assistance. Bill Maurer and Cory Hodges of the UC Irvine Anthropology Department organized a book workshop on my behalf; Samar Al-Bulushi, Swethaa Ballakrishnen, Bryant Garth, Cecelia

Lynch, Justin Richland, and Carroll Seron served as commentators. I thank my editorial team at Cambridge University Press, including John Berger and Matt Gallaway, for their efficiency and responsiveness.

Some elements of this book are adapted from "The Rule of Law in Fragile States" (*Journal of Law and Society*, 2020). Parts of the Introduction, Chapter 1, and Chapter 7 draw from my article, "Theology of the Rule of Law" (*Hague Journal on the Rule of Law*, 2019) and from "Ideals and Practices in the Rule of Law: An Essay on Legal Politics" (*Law & Social Inquiry*, 2016). Some sections of Chapter 2 expand on material in "Islamic Law, Colonialism, and Mecca's Shadow in the Horn of Africa" (*Journal of Africana Religions*, 2019). I thank the *Journal of Law and Society*, *Hague Journal on the Rule of Law*, *Law & Social Inquiry*, and *Journal of Africana Religions* for permitting me to draw from these works.

Support for research and writing came from fellowships and grants I received from the American Council of Learned Societies, the Carnegie Corporation of New York, the John Simon Guggenheim Memorial Foundation, and the Hellman Fellows Program of the University of California, Santa Cruz, along with visiting appointments at Oxford University (Oxford Centre for Islamic Studies and Nuffield College), Princeton University (Program in Law and Public Affairs), and the University of California, Hastings College of the Law. I am grateful for their generosity and motivated by their confidence. All statements and views in this book are my responsibility, not theirs. A New Directions Fellowship from the Andrew W. Mellon Foundation allowed me to acquire advanced training in theology at the Graduate Theological Union in Berkeley. My colleagues and students in the Politics Department and Legal Studies Program at the University of California, Santa Cruz, provided a welcoming space for me to research, write, and teach.

Each of the hundreds of people I met in my research treated me with dignity. Some of them gave me the nickname *Dalmar* ("traveler" in Somali). Francis, Helen, Jonah, Ken, Makarim, Mathias, and Risto allowed me to feel at home during my travels in Hargeisa. Cabdifataax, Christina, and Kenedid helped me thrive. As an Arab descended from an Eastern Catholic minority in Sudan, I was welcomed by Somalis who called me their cousin. I am grateful for them, for the families of my birth and travels, for Adam, and for God.

NOTE ON PLACES AND LANGUAGES

Shari'a, Inshallah offers a series of case studies from Somalia and Somaliland, in the Horn of Africa (so labeled for its resemblance on the map to a rhinoceros horn). I do not study law among those populations identifying as Somali in Djibouti, northern Kenya, and eastern Ethiopia's Ogaden region, though some writers and policymakers have also labeled those places Somali territories. A contemporary map appears at the end of this section. Icons at the start of Chapters 2–6 denote the region and period of each chapter's focus.

Somalia and Somaliland have been colonized, connected, and divorced. British Somaliland (in the northern Horn) and Italian Somalia (in the southern Horn) refer to the European colonial administrations. They were replaced by an independent Somaliland and Somalia in 1960. After five days, they unified. In 1991, Somaliland reasserted its sovereignty. Though still recognized as a region of Somalia by the United Nations, Somaliland has developed its own independent government. Its capital, Hargeisa, sits 850 kilometers north of Mogadishu. The semi-autonomous Puntland lies in between Somalia and Somaliland and has its own border disputes with both territories.

Arabic

All Arabic translations and transliterations are my own. A simple reverse apostrophe is used to represent the diacritical mark for the Arabic 'ayn, as in *shari'a*. I render nisba endings *-iyya*, as in *Islamiyya* (Islamic), per the *International Journal of Middle East Studies* transliteration system. While standard transliterations exist, some Arabic words, such as names of persons, have several spellings when transliterated into English (inshallah/insha-Allah/enshalla, Mohamed/Mohammed/Muhammad, Omar/'Umr, and so on).

Somali

The Somali language is based on the Cushitic branch of the large Afroasiatic language family, from which Hebrew, Amharic, and Hausa are also drawn. Somali was largely orally communicated until

1972, when Mohamed Siad Barre's government created an official script based on Roman lettering. The Somali "c" denotes a sound similar to the Arabic *'ayn*. Thus, the Arabic *shari'a* is transliterated as *sharica*; the Arabic name 'Abdul is Cabdul; the Somaliland town, Burao, is spelled Burco; and so on. The "x" (as in the name Maxamed or *xeer*, the Somali word for indigenous customs and laws) sounds similar to the guttural "h" in Arabic. Finally, some writers transliterate "q" and "k" interchangeably (for instance, *aqil* or *akil* for a community leader).

I have aimed for clarity, consistency, and accuracy in Arabic and Somali translation, Arabic transliteration, and Somali spelling. I provide English translations alongside Arabic and Somali words; terms that appear several times are italicized and translated in their first usage in each chapter.

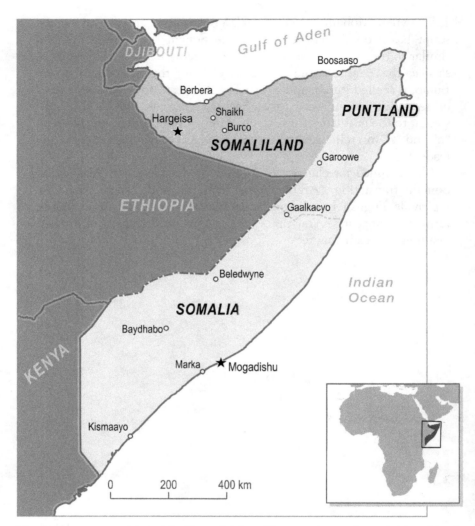

Map 1 Contemporary Map of the Horn of Africa. This map shows inherited colonial borders that Somaliland uses but that Puntland contests. Somalia claims sovereignty over Puntland and Somaliland.
Source: Author, derived from Natural Earth base data.

INTRODUCTION

Only in his twenties, Tayyib was already one of Somaliland's most promising lawyers. I met Tayyib early on a sunny morning, and we sat down on a couple of plastic chairs along the dirt path outside the Hargeisa courthouse. I asked him why he worked in legal aid programs designed to help poor people have free legal representation in court, what cases he was arguing that day, and what events had shaped his career and the broader development of law in Somalia and Somaliland. As we neared the end of our meeting, I invited him to share his professional goals. I wondered if he hoped to enter politics, private practice, or the United Nations system. These paths would provide more stability, renown, and salary than his current position did, and they were often taken by the most prominent professionals. He looked away, toward the dilapidated courthouse and one-story government buildings. Then he turned back to me and said he "would like to stop" being an attorney altogether.

Tayyib had just spent an hour discussing the promise of law, so I was confused about why he would give it all up. And then this: "I want to be a sheikh." Sheikhs are religious leaders. They preach obedience to God, who prescribes ethical and modest behavior. Throughout modern Somali history, sheikhs have used shari'a to resolve disputes like divorce, inheritance, injury, or theft, and to build peace among rival communities over their competing rights. "I want to learn more about the Islamic religion," he continued.[1] Tayyib's ambition was always to build the rule of law in his country. But he wanted to build an Islamic rule of law.

---

[1] Interview 92 with Tayyib, lawyer and paralegal in Hargeisa, Somaliland (June 2014).

The title of this book, *Shari'a, Inshallah*, reflects Tayyib's hope. In the pages that follow I show how state and nonstate actors appeal to shari'a. They imbue shari'a with their political ideals and attempt to do away with rival versions that do not match their interests. Some state officials and militants cite it to justify dictatorship and slaughter. But many others, including Tayyib, embrace shari'a in their struggles for peace, justice, national identity, or women's rights. To them, shari'a supports the rule of law, a style of government that limits the arbitrary exercise of power. Their behaviors demonstrate that the rule of law might not only be reconciled with religion but, counterintuitively, nourished by it.

Shari'a and inshallah must be understood in context. The concepts do not arise in social, legal, or political vacuums. In Islam, the term "shari'a" generally pertains to protecting one's worship of God. Literally, the word shari'a (شريعة) is derived from three Arabic root letters that signify both a beginning and a path to water – taken together, they suggest cleansing, clarity, and purity. In Islamic studies, shari'a sometimes refers to the entire religion of Islam, and sometimes it refers only to the legal or, even more narrowly, penal aspects of Islam. But shari'a is widely understood not as law but as the constitution of Islamic theology, ethics, and spirituality – how best to treat the self, others, and the environment with dignity by minimizing harms to them all. In this way, shari'a is a "living system" that encompasses all aspects of daily experience, not just what Western minds might see as law and order.[2]

To Arabic speakers, the term inshallah – like the term shari'a – has differing uses. It is not normally discussed in connection with shari'a. In common parlance, inshallah denotes uncertainty of the future and hope for God's intercession in it. But saying "inshallah" at the end of a sentence about the future is also not merely "dressing the routine of daily life with religious accessories."[3] In the Qur'an (Islam's holy book), the phrase inshallah sets the limit on human will as the point at which God wills something. The Qur'an employs the active and conditional verb of "until God wills" (إلاَّ أَن يَشَاءَ اللهُ) to define and limit human will. Inshallah recognizes God's unlimited power alongside human beings'

---

[2] Lawrence Rosen, *Islam and the Rule of Justice: Image and Reality in Muslim Law and Culture* (Chicago, IL: University of Chicago Press, 2018), 3; Jonathan A. C. Brown, *Stoning and Hand Cutting: Understanding the* Huduud *and Shariah in Islam* (Irving, TX: Yaqeen Institute for Islamic Research, 2017), 4.

[3] Michael Slackman, "With a Word, Egyptians Leave It All to Fate," *New York Times*, June 20, 2008, https://nyti.ms/2WQuZCF (accessed January 1, 2021).

unpredictability, fallibility, and lack of control, and that human will is conditional upon and restricted by a divine will that judges human actions. Accepting that human will serves God's will – that shari'a is inshallah – sets a limit to human authority that may help recover the rule of law.

Law and religion are unstable and incoherent categories. In this book, law refers to rules, systems, and orders derived from faith in human or state power. Religion refers to rules, systems, and orders derived from faith in higher, divine power. Law and religion take on new meanings as different actors combine the two in varying ways and present their visions to others. People use them to justify violence or propose solutions to that violence. When viewed in the light of people's prayers to God, demands on governments, and daily life experiences, law and religion feel multifaceted and over-lapping. But law does not need to derive its power from the state. Nor does Islamic law need to derive its power from an Islamic state.[4]

Colonial administrators and those resisting occupation, dictators and those opposing tyranny, and activists and aid workers promoting human rights all squeeze law into their politics. They write, challenge, ignore, and bend legal codes and constitutional provisions to build nations and pursue their social, political, or economic objectives. But law is not enough. They also turn to God's will – endeavoring to subsume it, co-opt it, defeat it, reclaim it, and give it new meaning in political practice. They seek out God's bidding, promoting their own versions of shari'a to give themselves hope, attain their goals, and disempower their adversaries.

Consider the British colonial officials who roamed the Horn of Africa in the late nineteenth and early twentieth centuries. Though not Muslims, they presented a version of shari'a to the Somali people, with the support of religious leaders from Mecca and Sudan. Colonial officials hoped that their arguments that shari'a permitted European meddling would counteract another shari'a that prominent Somali activists were using in anticolonial struggles. In the twenty-first century, women activists I met embraced their shari'a too. They used piety and strategy to try to defeat a patriarchal version of shari'a promulgated by religious and cultural leaders. Across the Horn of Africa's various

---

[4] Mark Fathi Massoud, "How an Islamic State Rejected Islamic Law," 66 *American Journal of Comparative Law* (2018a): 579–602.

political epochs – colonial, democratic, and authoritarian – people have appealed to shari'a to build the foundations of peace and the rule of law, or destroy them both.

Shari'a, Inshallah spotlights the many dimensions of law, the resemblances between colonial and postcolonial experiences of law, and the ways that religion seeps into the architecture of modern states. In analyzing the potentials and pitfalls of shari'a – including its practical meanings and the machineries of law incorporating it – I investigate the relationship between two overlapping forms of legal politics: building the rule of law and building an Islamic state. In the process I render visible the religious roots of the rule of law. My findings are based on archival research, ethnographic observations, and personal interviews with Somali lawyers, judges, activists, and religious and political leaders.

This book provides an antidote to those who see religion as an obstacle to peace and a domain to be restricted by law and detached from political life. The world seems to have closed its eyes to the possibility of an Islamic state that protects the rights of indigenous communities, minorities, and migrants, and an Islamic state that might be flexible enough to build the rule of law indigenously, organically, and meaningfully. While some political elites deploy shari'a for their own nefarious purposes, others see the values associated with shari'a and the rule of law as mutually reinforcing social goods.

FEARING SHARI'A

Shari'a has been denigrated. With few exceptions, policymakers, legal scholars, the media, and the public, particularly in the Western world, perceive it as a tool of dictatorial control, and a means for repressive governments to curtail human rights, oppress women, and persecute minorities. Nearly all fifty US states have introduced bills to ban shari'a.[5] In 2020, the Washington, DC-based Center for Security Policy warned that "shari'a-supremacism" was the world's "other pandemic" to Covid-19.[6] Former US Senator Rick Santorum, echoing other conservative policymakers, denounced shari'a as "evil" and

---

[5] Elsadig Elsheikh, Basima Sisemore, and Natalia Ramirez Lee, "Legalizing Othering: The United States of Islamophobia," Report of the UC Berkeley Haas Institute for a Fair and Inclusive Society (2017), https://bit.ly/3glNWpC (accessed January 1, 2021).

[6] Frank Gaffney Jr., "Beware the Other Pandemic – Sharia-supremacism," *Center for Security Policy*, March 11, 2020, https://bit.ly/3lTHeYU (accessed January 1, 2021).

"incompatible" with American law.[7] Associating shariʿa with danger, Donald Trump's 2020 reelection campaign asked voters in 2018 if they were "concerned by the potential spread of Sharia law."[8] Earlier that year, a teacher in Ventura County, California, distributed instructional materials stating that shariʿa allows Muslim men to marry infants and demands that Muslims lie to non-Muslims to get their way. The school district said these statements did not discriminate against Muslims.[9] The Southern Poverty Law Center, a civil rights advocacy group, has described the public anxiety over shariʿa in America as the "mainstream visibility [of] mass hysteria."[10]

Anti-shariʿa attitudes also exist outside the United States. The European Court of Human Rights has twice ruled that shariʿa is incompatible with human rights.[11] Classifying Muslims and shariʿa as "inevitable" threats, Japan's Supreme Court upheld the constitutionality of a government surveillance program that secretly targeted every Muslim and Islamic community group in the country.[12] Regimes in Saudi Arabia, Egypt, and other Muslim-majority countries have derided shariʿa in their own ways. They have labeled anti-regime activists as "stealth jihadis" seeking Islamic law, which has helped leaders of those countries arrest dissidents and build sympathy among Western governments under the guise that they are countering violent extremism.[13] And then-President Doru Costea of the United Nations Human Rights Council silenced a heated debate over shariʿa by declaring that he would interrupt anyone making "judgments . . . of a particular religion," concluding that the Human Rights Council is simply "not prepared to

---

[7] Kendra Marr, "Santorum: Sharia 'is evil'," *Politico*, March 11, 2011, https://politi.co/2WRX3oW (accessed January 1, 2021).

[8] David Smith, "'Are You Concerned by Sharia Law?': Trump Canvasses Supporters for 2020," *Guardian*, March 3, 2018, https://bit.ly/36Pb4JX (accessed January 1, 2021).

[9] Deepa Bharath, "Appeal Filed over 'Appalling, Islamophobic' Teaching Material Distributed in 7th-Grade Social Studies Class," *The Press-Enterprise*, January 11, 2018, https://bit.ly/3gtc P2H (accessed January 1, 2021).

[10] Swathi Shanmugasundaram, "Anti-Sharia Law Bills in the United States," *Southern Poverty Law Center*, February 5, 2018, https://bit.ly/3mTvK97 (accessed January 1, 2021).

[11] *Refah Partisi and Others* v. *Turkey*, Application No. 41340/98, judgment of February 13, 2003, paragraph 128, European Court of Human Rights; *Kasymakhunov and Saybatalov* v. *Russia*, Applications Nos. 26261/05 and 26377/06, judgment of March 13, 2013, paragraphs 99, 100 and 111 (reaffirming *Refah Partisi and Others* v. *Turkey*), European Court of Human Rights.

[12] Matt Payton, "Japan's Top Court Has Approved the Blanket Surveillance of the Country's Muslims," *Independent*, June 29, 2016, https://bit.ly/36PICaX (accessed January 1, 2021).

[13] Ola Salem and Hassan Hassan, "Arab Regimes Are the World's Most Powerful Islamophobes," *Foreign Policy*, March 29, 2019, https://bit.ly/3lXeiiS (accessed January 1, 2021); see also Enes Bayraklı and Farid Hafez, *Islamophobia in Muslim Majority Societies* (New York: Routledge, 2019).

discuss religious matters."[14] Discussions in these global halls of power greet shari'a with either determined contempt or enforced silence.

Some legal scholars have echoed the global critiques of shari'a, arguing that religious fervor begets extremism and populist nationalism, and warning that "The rule of law and the rule of God [are] on a collision course [because] religion offers a credible threat to the liberal constitutional narrative."[15] International policy toward Muslim-majority states is likewise predicated on the notion that, if either dictatorships or shari'a were to be removed, the other would disappear too – paving the way to peace and the rule of law.[16] These characterizations of religion as monolithic, extreme, or detrimental to the rule of law have led aid agencies and international lawyers to fear shari'a, correct it, or avoid it altogether. In short, religion is believed to increase violence, and law believed to reduce it.

But the relationship between shari'a and violence is not fixed, nor can it be presumed, even in Islamic states.[17] Shari'a offers hope to political elites and grassroots activists alike. It also triggers their anxieties. It is contested, fought over, maneuvered around, and reshaped as political situations change. Differing political views are injected into it. In states suffering from legacies of war, law – and shari'a – create expectations and desires. But law and shari'a also induce fear when other actors use them for their own purposes, even among Muslims seeking the stability that legal and religious tools proffer. By positing religious activism as "against the law," scholars and global policymakers miss the ways that law and religion are fundamentally interconnected in the minds of pious activists, lawyers, and officials.[18]

---

[14] "UN Ruling: Islamic Sharia Taboo in Human Rights Council Debates," *UN Watch*, July 1, 2008, https://bit.ly/38IxRXM (accessed January 1, 2021).

[15] Ran Hirschl and Ayelet Shachar, "Competing Orders? The Challenge of Religion to Modern Constitutionalism," 85 *The University of Chicago Law Review* (2018): 425–455, pp. 425, 455.

[16] The state is a governing apparatus of legislative, administrative, and judicial bodies that use, decide upon, and seek to monopolize violent and nonviolent dispute resolution mechanisms. An authoritarian state is one in which political leaders are "intolerant of people or groups perceived as threatening to the regime's monopoly over the institutions of the state." Lisa Wedeen, *Ambiguities of Domination: Politics, Rhetoric, and Symbols in Contemporary* (Chicago, IL: University of Chicago Press, 1996), 26; Rachel E. Stern, *Environmental Litigation in China: A Study in Political Ambivalence* (Cambridge: Cambridge University Press, 2013), 1. On the ambiguities of state institutions, see Akhil Gupta, *Red Tape: Bureaucracy, Structural Violence, and Poverty in India* (Durham, NC: Duke University Press, 2012).

[17] I define an Islamic state as a political institution in which governing authorities intentionally infuse Islamic discourses, ideals, practices, and laws – however they define them – into their efforts to achieve economic, political, and social objectives. In practice, an Islamic state would likely be home to a Muslim-majority polity, but in theory it need not be. In these places political and legal authorities use shari'a instrumentally as a necessary, though insufficient, foundation for lawmaking and dispute resolution activities.

[18] Patricia Ewick and Susan S. Silbey, *The Common Place of Law: Stories from Everyday Life* (Chicago, IL: University of Chicago Press, 1998).

BENDING SHARI'A

Shari'a, Inshallah rejects the one-dimensional view of shari'a as a repressive tool in politics. I expose the ways shari'a is contested and embrace the ways people invoke shari'a to sow the seedlings of peace and the rule of law. Colonial administrators, the local people who worked for and against them, postcolonial governments, and modern rights activists have all worked tirelessly to maintain their own versions of law and Islam – blending them to promote their own aspirations and authority. They have either made shari'a an overt part of the state's foundation, or they have subsumed shari'a like old trees consumed by fire, whose ashes are then incorporated into the state's new growth.

In Islamic legal theory (*usul al-fiqh*), shari'a is divine law interpreted by jurists. But the different meanings that people give it in practice matter also. These diverse interpretations of shari'a derive from each actor who uses shari'a or, at least, something that they label shari'a. In other words, the meaning of shari'a, when put into practice, comes through people's varied interpretations of the content of God's unknowable will. It does not just emerge from religious leaders' interpretations of the Qur'an and the Hadith (records of the Prophet Muhammad's statements, actions, and tacit approvals).

Scholars of law, politics, and religion have discussed shari'a as a form of daily ethics.[19] In postcolonial environments rife with legal pluralism, shari'a is one of many layers of law drawn from an amalgam of European interference, religious proselytization, and indigenous custom, where people often may choose among a few forms of dispute resolution. As ethical guidance for moral behavior, shari'a shapes people's lives more deeply than Western state-based concepts of law do. A study of the depth of shari'a's reach into people's lives and practices is also a study in normative frameworks that function outside of state authority.

But shari'a represents more than God's moral framework for humans. It has become a political narrative, applied in different situations and

---

[19] Shahab Ahmed, *What Is Islam? The Importance of Being Islamic* (Princeton, NJ: Princeton University Press, 2015); Robert Hefner, ed., *Shari'a Law and Modern Muslim Ethics* (Bloomington: Indiana University Press, 2016); Abdullahi An-Na'im, *Islam and the Secular State: Negotiating the Future of Shari'a* (Cambridge, MA: Harvard University Press, 2008); Andrew March, *Islam and Liberal Citizenship: The Search for an Overlapping Consensus* (Oxford: Oxford University Press, 2009).

constantly changing from its varied uses. "Shari'a discourse," for instance, or diverse shari'a-focused "texts, conversations, and institutions," can saturate political debate and law in Muslim-majority societies.[20] State leaders may present their own flattened and rigid system of shari'a to shore up their authority by making religious principles appear to be consistent with narrow state objectives.[21] Activist groups, instead, breathe space into shari'a. They use Islamic discourse as an emancipatory language to create new forms of "lived" religion in daily life that counter state elites' attempts to monopolize principles of faith.[22] In practice, these many versions of shari'a exist. Not all of them are created equal; some versions of shari'a promote values associated with peacebuilding, human rights, and the rule of law more than other versions.[23]

A *Pew Forum* international poll found that 99 percent of Muslims in Afghanistan, 89 percent of Muslims in Palestine, 74 percent of Muslims in Egypt, and 72 percent of Muslims in Indonesia wanted shari'a "to be the official law of the land."[24] Muslims in Somalia and Somaliland, who account for more than 99 percent of the population, are no exception. In practice and politics in all these places, there is no single or pure form of shari'a. It is a consistently revived, transformed, and lived tradition in the daily life of political elites.[25]

Each person – colonial administrator, postcolonial government official, judge, or activist – invokes their own version of shari'a and tries to

---

[20] Morgan Clarke, *Islam and Law in Lebanon: Sharia within and without the State* (Cambridge: Cambridge University Press, 2018); see also Brinkley Messick, *The Calligraphic State: Textual Domination and History in a Muslim Society* (Oakland, CA: University of California Press, 1993).

[21] Mark Fathi Massoud, "The Politics of Islamic Law and Human Rights: Sudan's Rival Legal Systems," in *The New Legal Realism, Volume 2: Studying Law Globally*, Heinz Klug and Sally Engle Merry, eds. (Cambridge: Cambridge University Press, 2016a), 96–112.

[22] Mark Fathi Massoud and Kathleen M. Moore, "Shari'a Consciousness: Law and Lived Religion Among California Muslims," 45(3) *Law & Social Inquiry* (2020): 787–817; see also Elizabeth Shakman Hurd, *Beyond Religious Freedom: The New Global Politics of Religion* (Princeton, NJ: Princeton University Press, 2015); Kristen Stilt, "Islam Is the Solution: Constitutional Visions of the Egyptian Muslim Brotherhood," 46 *Texas International Law Journal* (2010): 74–108.

[23] For a first-person account of how lawyers balance religious and legal principles in shari'a courts, see Huawa Ibrahim, *Practicing Shariah Law: Seven Strategies for Achieving Justice in Shariah Courts* (Chicago, IL: American Bar Association Book Publishing, 2012).

[24] James Bell et al., *The World's Muslims: Religion, Politics, and Society* (Washington, DC: The Pew Forum on Religion and Public Life, 2013), 9.

[25] On religion as a lived tradition in legal history, see H. Patrick Glenn, "Comparative Legal Families and Comparative Legal Traditions," in *The Oxford Handbook of Comparative Law*, eds. Mathias Reimann and Reinhard Zimmerman (Oxford: Oxford University Press, 2006), 421–440.

get others to believe and practice it. They bend shari'a toward many contradictory ends: to facilitate or oppose colonialism; to further or neutralize socialism, clannism, or tribalism; to foster patriarchy or gender equality; and to be the foundation of liberalism or to argue that no such entity as a democratic Islamic state – the "impossible" state – could ever exist.[26] Through shari'a, these varied actors try to change the significance of Islam itself, using shari'a to make Islam into a political force. For some of them, shari'a is not only a transcendent path to the divine. It is also a practical foundation for building the rule of law.

SEPARATING SHARI'A FROM THE RULE OF LAW

Separating law from religion is a political act. When political leaders construct a state, they attempt to replace religion with law. Their effort to build a national legal system – with all its values, documents, institutions, and personnel – is an attempt to create a parallel faith in an authority that, like God, is transcendent and willed. Even in states where political leaders appear to separate them, law and religion remain entangled. Religious faith and knowledge of the power of faith shape the secular laws of state leaders and the legal consciousness of those subjected to those laws.

As shown in studies from Egypt, Iran, Malaysia, and Indonesia, among other places, government officials and citizens struggle to blend the ideals of political liberalism, human rights, and shari'a. These accounts largely focus on the arena of courts.[27] Scholars of Islamic law and society have similarly been preoccupied with the work of courts, scouring records to show how jurists interpret Islamic norms.[28] Anthropologists of religion

---

[26] Wael Hallaq, *The Impossible State: Islam, Politics, and Modernity's Moral Predicament* (New York: Columbia University Press, 2012); but see Guy Burak, *The Second Formation of Islamic Law: The Hanafi School in the Early Modern Ottoman Empire* (Cambridge: Cambridge University Press, 2015) and Andrew March, "What Can the Islamic Past Teach Us About Secular Modernity?" 43 *Political Theory* (2015): 838–849.

[27] Daniel Lev, *Islamic Courts in Indonesia: A Study in the Political Bases of Legal Institutions* (Oakland, CA: University of California Press, 1972); Tamir Moustafa, *Constituting Religion: Islam, Liberal Rights, and the Malaysian State* (Cambridge: Cambridge University Press, 2018); Arzoo Osanloo, *The Politics of Women's Rights in Iran* (Princeton, NJ: Princeton University Press, 2009); Michael G. Peletz, *Islamic Modern: Religious Courts and Cultural Politics in Malaysia* (Princeton, NJ: Princeton University Press, 2002); Michael G. Peletz, *Sharia Transformations: Cultural Politics and the Rebranding of an Islamic Judiciary* (Oakland, CA: University of California Press, 2020); Benjamin Schonthal, *Buddhism, Politics and the Limits of Law: The Pyrrhic Constitutionalism of Sri Lanka* (Cambridge: Cambridge University Press, 2016).

[28] Clark Lombardi, *State Law as Islamic Law in Modern Egypt: The Incorporation of the Shari'a into Egyptian Constitutional Law* (Leiden: Brill, 2006); Intisar A. Rabb, *Doubt in Islamic Law:*

have taken a broader view, looking beyond courts to question the notion that secularism is merely the separation of religion from the state. Secularism, they contend, involves the state's regulation of religious difference.[29] Surveilling and regulating religious activities can lead people to challenge the state. Under these conditions, secular state laws and institutions cause rather than resolve religious strife.

The very concept of the rule of law developed through a historical process that separated religion from the state. As European monarchies and state governments decoupled themselves from the authority of churches during the Enlightenment of the seventeenth through nineteenth centuries, law purportedly abandoned its religious roots and traditions. Secularization and political liberalization were processes by which state authorities created their own "autonomous set of orienting goals" in the law, rather than in religion.[30] By design, the law was kept at arm's length from religious and other nonstate leaders.

The state was designed so that rights and duties would come from a legal order that it could control, not a religious order beyond its control. This singular legal order often treated religion as a competing worldview – even as a threat – to political liberalism and its rule of law. Speaking in different registers about religion and law allowed state leaders to propound a new form of authority built on but not indentured to religious authority. Rhetorically freeing law from religion was purposeful. It caused, according to intellectual historian Rajbir Singh Judge, the "increased encroachment ... by the sovereign state in this world, rather than one adjudicated by the Divine, [to encourage] faith

A History of Legal Maxims, Interpretation, and Islamic Criminal Law (Cambridge: Cambridge University Press, 2015); Kristen Stilt, Islamic Law in Action: Authority, Discretion, and Everyday Experiences in Mamluk Egypt (Oxford: Oxford University Press, 2012).

[29] Hussein Ali Agrama, Questioning Secularism: Islam, Sovereignty, and the Rule of Law in Egypt (Chicago, IL: University of Chicago Press, 2012); Talal Asad, Formations of the Secular: Christianity, Islam, Modernity (Stanford, CA: Stanford University Press, 2003); Mayanthi Fernando, The Republic Unsettled: Muslim French and the Contradictions of Secularism (Durham, NC: Duke University Press, 2014); Katherine Lemons, Divorcing Traditions: Islamic Marriage Law and the Making of Indian Secularism (Ithaca, NY: Cornell University Press, 2019); Ziba Mir-Hosseini, Islam and Gender: The Religious Debate in Contemporary Iran (Princeton, NJ: Princeton University Press, 1999); Saba Mahmood, Religious Difference in a Secular Age: A Minority Report (Princeton, NJ: Princeton University Press, 2015); Noah Salomon, For Love of the Prophet: An Ethnography of Sudan's Islamic State (Princeton, NJ: Princeton University Press, 2016).

[30] Antônio Flávio Pierucci, "Secularization in Max Weber: On Current Usefulness of Re-Accessing that Old Meaning," Special Issue No. 1 Brazilian Review of Social Sciences (2000): 129–158 (trans. Roderick Steel), published originally in 13(37) Revista Brasileira de Ciências Sociais (1998): 43–73.

in the law itself."[31] Religion in the European imagination began to be seen as set apart from and, over time, antithetical to the rule of law.[32]

The early modern European state's organizing principles – seizing or separating local traditions and religion from the state and its law – made their way into colonial administrations in the nineteenth and twentieth centuries. European empires sought to expand their territories and "civilize" the Global South by constructing Western forms of governance beyond Europe's geographic borders. The colonial approach to building the rule of law was designed to subsume the power of religion into the state or, where that was not possible, to excise it from the state entirely. To those who experienced colonialism, the rule of law seemed like just another inescapable imposition. European colonial administrators demanded their subjects see the state and its laws as the central elements of social structure.

In sub-Saharan Africa, colonial administrators dreamed up religion and law as recognizably different political objects. Separating religion from law and custom, they promoted each as a distinct source of authority and subsumed them all to state power. Post-independence political leaders likewise wielded these discursive weapons, and, particularly in times of trouble, some of them claimed the force of law or of God to rationalize their violent impulses.

State-building – the practice of constructing governments and civil societies – can separate law and religion in theory. But in culture and politics, these concepts remain entwined. Political and religious leaders, for instance, regularly cite religious principles, issue commands, and invite God's blessing. For the purposes of state-building, shari'a in Muslim-majority societies is rooted in Islam. Similarly, the legal traditions that built up in the countries of North America and Europe derive from Judaism or Christianity. Put another way, when used as state law shari'a is no more Islamic than the US constitution is Christian. While the religious nature of authority may be important to some people, others care more about the stability, values, order, and ethical sensibilities that religion brings to the political table than about the religion itself. There is also public consensus that Western state legal systems, which regulate religion, are objective or value-neutral in the

---

[31] Rajbir Singh Judge, "Mind the Gap: Islam, Secularism, and the Law," 29(1) *Qui Parle* (2020): 179–202, p. 181.

[32] Giorgi Areshidze, "Taking Religion Seriously? Habermas on Religious Translation and Cooperative Learning in Post-secular Society," 111(4) *American Political Science Review* (2017): 724–737.

11

application of the law, and there is little reason to suggest that, given time, Islamic states would be any different.

In the long term, religion may not disappear from governance in strongly Islamic countries. Indeed, the state's power is often exerted through discourses of religion that pervade daily life – in radio commentary, television programs, architecture, street posters, and political advertisements – even in those places where the state's authority seems weak or illegitimate.[33] Just as it was in North America and Europe, the ideals of justice and dignity in the world's most unstable regions may be built upon long-held religious principles. Justice and dignity take their first steps not in democratic elections and representative governments but instead in law, courts, and religion – when religious leaders, judges, and activists use religious law to help people resolve disputes without resorting to weapons or physical violence.

SHARI'A IN THE HORN OF AFRICA

The making of the state is a process of consolidating a multiplicity of legal orders, systems, and hopes into a single state-controlled system. The state promotes its own authority through this seemingly singular legal system that the state also portrays as flexible enough to accommodate other traditions. This process of trying to build a distinct, unified, and internally coherent state out of the battle to overcome legal pluralism, and the endurance of Islam throughout this process, is exemplified in the Somali case.

In modern Somali history, colonial administrators, postcolonial democratic and authoritarian regimes, lawyers, and women's rights activists – and the people who resisted each of these actors – all seemed to turn toward shari'a, rather than away from it. They turned toward shari'a because, as with other forms of law, it provided a foundation for their political or social views. But shari'a is not simply a tool of law. It is an instrument of divinity. Justifying political activities by their accordance with God's will invests those activities with piety, morality, and restraint. It also gives state and nonstate actors hope that their activities might go unchallenged because God's will does not change and because pious persons would not disagree with what God wills.

As these diverse state and nonstate actors invest their hopes and fears in shari'a, they create new knowledge of Islam, law, and politics, and new

---

[33] Salomon (2016).

understandings of the relationship among them. To many Somalis, foreign aid workers' goals of drafting state laws to promote a more rational, predictable, and singular legal order seem out of place in a context where religious leaders render careful decisions based on each situation's unique facts. But aid workers have come to understand the orally delivered judgments of elders as another form of law because, as one Somali told me, "White people decide[d] to write [them] down."[34]

To most Western observers, the Horn of Africa is not known for any order at all – much less an Islamic legal order. The region is best known to such people for terrorism, piracy, cycles of famine and drought, and *Black Hawk Down* – a bestselling book and Hollywood film about the disastrous October 1993 US military raid in which hundreds of Somalis and eighteen US soldiers were killed in a fifteen-hour battle in Mogadishu. By 2006, following fifteen years of rule by disparate warlords, Somalia was widely recognized as Africa's largest haven for Al Qaeda, the group responsible for regular attacks on civilians and governments, including on the United States on September 11, 2001. Political fragmentation, corruption, and suicide bombings have rocked major towns. Because of civil war, human rights abuses, human flight, and deep political divisions, Somalia has been ranked as the first or second most "fragile" or "failed" state in the world.[35] (Somalia is designated this way despite the relative calm of Somaliland.)

Because of its political disasters and the resultant human suffering, the Horn of Africa is not studied as a space where law might play an important social and political role, and especially not as a place where principles of peace and the rule of law might take root. But one need not dig far below the ruins of war to find shari'a not just surviving but even thriving as a foundation for social and legal order. In the context of a legally competitive environment – where an abundance of laws and regulations have come from colonial administrators, local authorities, foreign diplomats, aid workers, or religious leaders trained domestically or overseas – everyone seems to agree on the importance of shari'a, even if they disagree as to its substantive content or political implications. Shari'a's resilience is a result of its malleability, as people reinterpret God's will for their own circumstances. Shari'a has withstood the

---

[34] Interview 80 with Gul, aid worker in Nairobi, Kenya (August 2013).

[35] Rankings are 2008 through 2020, inclusively. *Fragile States Index*, The Fund for Peace, http:// fragilestatesindex.org (accessed January 1, 2021). On the genealogy and critiques of "state failure," see Jutta Bakonyi, "Failing States and Statebuilding," in *Understanding Global Politics: Actors and Themes in International Affairs*, eds. Klaus Larres and Ruth Wittlinger (New York: Routledge, 2019), 313–328.

unpleasant and deadly politics of colonialism, authoritarianism, and civil war because people, despite their different interpretations of shari'a, agree on its importance and the hope it provides.

Who are these political elites building state power and the persons challenging them? They are a combination of state and nonstate actors, some of them working out of positions created by colonial officials and rededicated by postcolonial groups. Together, they form the key personnel who have made and remade law and religion, presenting their own ideas of right and wrong as objects of religious tradition or legal reform (Table I.1). The goals of these disparate groups are diverse but generally include resolving disputes

Table I.1 Political elites in Somalia and Somaliland

State actors	Nonstate actors
Colonial administrators (colonial officers and their local employees, including qadis working in state Islamic courts)	Sheikhs (religious leaders who use shari'a to resolve disputes like divorce, inheritance, injury, or theft and to build peace among rival communities; called qadis when acting as judges in state Islamic courts)
Postcolonial democratic state officials (politicians and judges working on behalf of government, including political leaders rebuilding after civil war)	Sultans (community leaders, sometimes also trained as sheikhs)
Postcolonial non-democratic state officials (the 1969–1991 authoritarian regime of Mohamed Siad Barre)	Aqils (community sub-leaders or managers, usually overseen by sultans, and sometimes paid by government to resolve people's disputes)
	Elders (ad hoc groups – *guurti* and *odayal* – who resolve disputes, including clashes between large communities)
	Lawyers and paralegals (persons with and without formal legal training who work with state law, typically in state courts, including for legal aid programs supported by United Nations rule-of-law projects)
	Civic groups (e.g., women's rights organizations, environmental protection groups, and youth/educational associations that use legal tools or religious ideals to foster social change)

Source: Author.

and building peace, stability, and order, as they variously define these ideals. In other words, their goals are tied to shaping the building blocks of the rule of law, even if they do not use the term, and even if it is difficult to imagine such diverse actors collectively building a foundation for the rule of law. Each of them – colonial and postcolonial officials, religious and community leaders, lawyers and civic groups – has sought the legitimacy of shari'a, inscribing God's will into their preferred vision of the state.

Colonial administrations learned the lessons of law and religion the hard way. They fought religious insurgencies rooted in an Islamic hope of achieving God's will and in disagreements over whether non-Muslims could be trusted to resolve disputes among Muslims. Similarly, today's foreign policy officials, particularly from Western nations, earmark billions of dollars to military intervention, aid delivery, and reconstruction efforts in the hope of dominating and subsuming religious fervor. And in between, authoritarian regimes and democratically elected governments have had to reckon with Islam, much like earlier colonial administrations and later international aid workers. Like rights, religion becomes a cloak under which varying groups can smuggle in their values and their political proclivities, clad in the authority of the state or the divine – or both. And, like those who invoke rights, activists who invoke religion increase the rhetorical stakes of their struggles against opponents.[36]

Law and religion, woven together, have shaped Somali political history. State actors – colonial, authoritarian, democratic – and non-state actors like women's rights activists have had to contend with shari'a and present their own version of it at every turn in their work to build, destroy, or rebuild the Somali state and civil society. Many of them draw a causal link between shari'a and the values associated with the rule of law, including limited government, political freedom, nonviolence, and gender equality. But others confront and promote more secular notions of law that regulate or subsume religion's power while nominally decoupling it from the state. By examining this history of the Horn of Africa, the book also explores the potential of shari'a to build peace and the rule of law in the most challenging environments.

---

[36] Kristen Stilt, "Constitutional Islam: Genealogies, Transmissions and Meanings," in *On the Ground: New Directions in Middle East and North African Studies*, ed. Brian T. Edwards (Doha: Akkadia Press, 2014).

OVERVIEW OF THE BOOK

Those who use shari'a to achieve their political, economic, or social goals stretch the term in many directions. In Somalia and Somaliland, state and nonstate actors attempting to build legal order – from European administrators in the 1880s to community elders, religious leaders, state politicians, and the aid workers supporting them in the 2010s – have justified their legal activities as consistent with shari'a. They universally fear the threat of offending God's will, as they simultaneously test its boundaries by revising and using it to achieve their goals. They create a dynamic politics of shari'a by using it for diverse and often conflicting ends, including *contesting* its meaning to support and challenge colonialism, *constraining* it to claim postcolonial power, *restoring* it after civil war, *integrating* it into postwar governments and constitutions, and *reclaiming* it to achieve rights and equality.

The chapters that follow demonstrate how different actors across time and place understand the changing relationship between religion and the rule of law. My focus is on Somalia and Somaliland from colonial intervention in 1884 until 2021, thirty years after Somalia's 1991 collapse. In that 137-year period, Somalis were ruled by multiple European colonial masters, saw their governments unite and separate, and fought multiple civil and regional wars. Their famines and droughts have resulted in some of the most massive and rapid human migrations in history, and in some of the world's costliest humanitarian aid programs.[37] Some of the survivors who left have returned to help transform the state and civil society, resulting in tensions with those who never left. But everywhere one turns in modern Somali history, some leader or activist is trying to build the state by promoting or limiting the power of shari'a. This study traces the remarkable elasticity, resilience, and endurance of shari'a amidst considerable political disorder.

Chapter 1, "Embracing Shari'a and the Rule of Law," provides an overview of the concept of shari'a and its relationship with the ideal of the rule of law. It also explains why Somalia and Somaliland provide critical cases for understanding the relationship between shari'a and the rule of law. Chapters 2 through 6 then each investigate a different case

---

[37] Paul D. Williams, *Fighting for Peace in Somalia: A History and Analysis of the African Union Mission (AMISOM), 2007–2017* (Oxford: Oxford University Press, 2018); Alex de Waal, *The Real Politics of the Horn of Africa: Money, War and the Business of Power* (Cambridge, UK: Polity Press, 2015).

of legal development – and whether and how shari'a emerges – to provide a glimpse into the shifting meanings and uses of shari'a across various time periods and locations. Together, the five case studies in Chapters 2 through 6 illustrate how people use shari'a as a tool of politics and, when they do this, how shari'a becomes a source of hope during the chaos of epic political changes and strikes fear into the hearts of dictators and warlords (who also try to control or destroy shari'a to meet their needs). In Part I, Chapters 2 and 3 address the interplay between religion and the rule of law under colonialism (1884–1960) and in the first generation after independence (1960– 1991). Part II examines key moments in the first thirty years following the state's 1991 collapse in Somalia (Chapter 4) and in Somaliland (Chapters 5 and 6).

Contesting Shari'a: Colonialism

In colonial British Somaliland in the late nineteenth and early twentieth centuries, British administrators sought to build a colonial outpost by signing treaties with Somali elders, writing new laws, building courthouses, and controlling how Somalis resolved their disputes. They hoped to create a unified legal system derived from what they saw as three distinct source codes: Islam, European law, and Somali custom. In the early 1900s Sheikh (Sayyid) Mohamed Abdullah Hassan – a poet, nationalist, arbitrator, and religious leader – used what he labeled as shari'a to resolve people's disputes over theft, inheritance, personal injury, and the like. The British were at first happy with the stability the sheikh provided among rival Somali groups, particularly those that had been raiding one another's lands. But as the sheikh became more skilled at oratory, he cited shari'a as his core rationale for what would become an anticolonial struggle that deployed both violent and nonviolent tactics. British colonial officials and newspapers relabeled him the "Mad Mullah."

The British, meanwhile, were busy designing their own competing Islamic courts – they called them "qadi courts" – that promoted another version of shari'a to Somalis who supported British involvement more than Sheikh Hassan's followers did. (The British-instituted qadi courts would later become northern Somalia's district, or lower, courts.) Shari'a offered hope both to the British and to those who fought them that civilization was thriving in the region. It was a source of mutual trust among adversaries. No one, not even British colonial officials, denied its authority. Islam mattered as much to non-Muslim colonial authorities as it did to Muslims resisting colonialism. Chapter 2, "Contesting Shari'a," focuses on this story of British colonialism, and the two-decade war (1899–1920) between the British administration and the followers of Sheikh Hassan. The chapter is set in British Somaliland, located in the northern Horn of Africa, and also draws comparisons with Italian Somalia, located in the southern Horn.

Constraining Shari'a: Colonialism's Aftermath
Later, after independence in 1960, postcolonial governments repeatedly sought to destroy or create Islamic states by writing Islam out of or into their constitutions and other laws. Their efforts in the postcolonial, united Somalia – which encompassed the former British Somaliland and Italian Somalia from 1960 to 1991, when Somaliland broke away – are the focus of Chapter 3, "Constraining Shari'a." During that thirty-one-year period, political leaders in Mogadishu painstakingly created laws designed to contain Islam rather than allow it to flourish, furthering the British experiment of creating a limited Islamic state. Those efforts, however, ultimately resulted in the state's collapse in 1991.

The authoritarian regime of the 1970s and 1980s, while ostensibly socialist during most of its rule, could not escape Islam's power. President Mohamed Siad Barre, a dictator who seized power over Somalia by military coup in 1969, went to great lengths to claim that socialism and Islam were compatible so that Somalis would put nation before tribe. But when a group of sheikhs disagreed with the government's 1975 family law on the grounds that it violated shari'a principles, Siad Barre's regime had those men quickly and publicly executed. To Siad Barre, the sheikhs – and Islam itself – were a threat to nationalism, even as the dictatorship attempted to paint its rule as compatible with Islam.

Chapters 2 and 3, described above, compose Part I of the book and demonstrate how colonial, democratic, and authoritarian rulers fear God's will even as they need it – interpreting and using shari'a publicly in their struggles for authority. Shari'a mattered to Somalia's political leaders trying to build a functioning state and, though their efforts ended in failure in 1991, they all had invoked shari'a to justify their ideologies. Devotion to shari'a, and to Islamic faith more generally, simultaneously animated much of the resistance to colonial and authoritarian rule.

Restoring Shari'a
President Siad Barre fled the country in 1991 during a disastrous civil war, and the government collapsed. Somaliland in northern Somalia,

where many rebels had been based, quickly declared its sovereignty. The rest of the country fell to warlords and their militias. While some of these warlords had once been religious leaders, they focused not on promoting peace or Islamic faith, but on amassing weapons and wealth by installing roadblocks where their militiamen collected arbitrary fees from travelers. The years of violence and human suffering since 1991 have led observers to label Somalia the "world's most dangerous place."[38] Chapter 4, "Restoring Shari'a," explains Somalia's path into and out of the rule of warlords. The chapter is set in the area sometimes labeled "south-central Somalia" to denote its geographic separation from Somaliland.

The first stable peace in the country's warlord-controlled regions would not arrive until 2006, fifteen years after the 1991 collapse. This peace did not come from foreign military intervention or from United Nations relief agencies but from a group of religious leaders who set up courts in and around Mogadishu to resolve business disputes and handle criminal matters. When these courts merged, they called themselves the Islamic Courts Union (ICU). With their own bailiffs and militias protecting them, the judges successfully removed the warlords from power. No longer did people have to travel impeded by the warlords' many checkpoints, and no longer did they live with the fear of extra-judicial disappearance.

But as the ICU grew, so did its factions. Each faction promised to implement its own distinct version of shari'a. They split between extremists who, like the warlords, wanted weapons and war, and moderate judges who preferred peace and stability. This factionalism threatened the ICU's solidarity and Somalia's future. Despite the stability the courts provided to Somali people who accessed them or lived nearby, the idea that an Islamic state was emerging in Mogadishu seemed an affront to the US-led war on terror. A group of warlords joined their forces and then accepted American counterterrorism assistance to battle the Islamic courts. An American-backed invasion by the Ethiopian military then did away with the courts just six months after they had brought peace to Mogadishu. But anyone in Mogadishu will still tell you that the Islamic courts, although they had real problems, did give people hope that they could unlock their doors and go outside again, free from the threats and corruptions of local warlords.

---

[38] James Fergusson, *The World's Most Dangerous Place: Inside the Outlaw State of Somalia* (Boston, MA: Da Capo Press, 2013).

Though short-lived, the ICU was the closest Mogadishu had come to a government since the fall of Somalia's Siad Barre military regime nearly two decades earlier.

The warlords and the judges of the Islamic courts were not the only people who tried to establish stability after the state's 1991 collapse. A fledgling and transitional government, working either in exile or out of a small compound in Baidoa, Somalia, also tried. They liaised with aid workers and international lawyers and drafted new constitutions that carried their hope that putting guiding principles in writing would change the country. Separately, Somaliland too wrote its own constitution. The framers of these postwar constitutions all adopted Islam as the foundation of their constitutional frameworks and declared Islam to be the only official religion – in other words, they created Islamic states. When I asked them why, the men who wrote these constitutions gave me the same answer: they wanted to ensure that extremists had nothing to fight for. If the constitution itself created an Islamic state and promoted shari'a, what could religious extremists rally around? They also told me that, in a climate of fear, religion was the only solution that most people could trust.

Integrating Shari'a
Somaliland's efforts to build an Islamic state after it broke away from Somalia in 1991 are the subject of Chapter 5, "Integrating Shari'a." Somaliland declared independence by reasserting a sovereignty it had for five days (June 26–30, 1960) prior to unifying with then-Italian Somalia. The self-declared state of Somaliland is what much of the world sees as northern Somalia. Its government has made strides to reject authoritarianism by outlawing military courts and adopting a constitution rooted in Islamic human rights principles. Drafters of Somaliland's constitution told me that they gave primacy to shari'a to keep religious extremists at bay. They also told me that guaranteeing fundamental rights to life, liberty, equality, and property would draw international support. Despite being located – in the view of many outsiders – within a collapsed state, Somaliland provides strong evidence of grassroots peacebuilding and political progress in the Horn of Africa. But the strategic intentions behind Somaliland's Islamic legal arrangements are largely invisible to foreign aid officials, who remain focused on delivering aid, constructing courthouses, and training judges and lawyers to apply international law.

Reclaiming Shari'a

Somalia's and Somaliland's judges and constitution writers were not the only ones who sought refuge in Islam. Women activists I met who struggled for gender equality in family life and in political rights and freedoms also turned to shari'a for support. They used Islamic legal principles rhetorically to fight for gender equality, without adopting a strategy of filing lawsuits and seeking redress from state courts. Educated, multilingual, and sophisticated, these activists developed important relationships with government officials and aid workers. They fought for shari'a as they simultaneously tried to minimize alternative views of it. Gender equality is a key principle of international human rights law, and Somali women have been using Islam's foundational sources – the Qur'an and the Hadith – to promote it. But they have had trouble convincing sheikhs to publicly support the women's understanding of Islamic principles. They have sought rights protections that they argue are rooted primarily in shari'a – and secondarily in state law or international law – in order to promote values associated with the rule of law, not the rule of men. Shari'a has been these women's source of hope and frustration too. Their struggle to reclaim shari'a is the subject of Chapter 6, "Reclaiming Shari'a."

Chapters 4 through 6 form Part II of the book and show how aid workers from 1991 to 2021 were preoccupied with building the rule of law while Somalis were preoccupied with building an Islamic rule of law. The chapters reveal how people's experiences of shari'a and the rule of law are shaped by the legacies of colonialism and postcolonial transitions between democratic and authoritarian rule. Somalia and Somaliland had divergent paths – one toward sustained collapse, the other toward a frail peace – but political elites in both places desired and used shari'a as the basis of state law. These postcolonial religious and political legacies continue to shape the region's constitutional development.

Chapter 7, "The Rule of Law, Inshallah," concludes the book by delving more deeply into the rule of law's historical relationship with religion. Activists who invoke religious discourse to demand change provoke anxiety among incumbent officials whose positions such change may destabilize. When activists prioritize the will of God over the will of state officials, they set limits on the colonial or authoritarian inclinations of those officials. Understanding the resemblances between doing God's will and building the rule of law is a step toward lasting peace in societies where people take religion seriously, including

Islamic states as volatile as Somalia. While historically the rule of law
has offered itself as an alternative to theology, many people submit to
faith to advance the values of the rule of law.

RESEARCH METHODS

How are values associated with the rule of law and shari'a formed, and
how do they relate to one another in practice, particularly in war-torn
societies? To what extent are these concepts shaped by colonial rule,
authoritarianism, and interactions with international aid workers and
activists? To answer these questions, I have employed three primary
research methods: archival and documentary-based research, qualitative interviews with key informants, and ethnographic observations of
dispute-resolution activities in courts, legal aid centers, and at workshops sponsored by international and local aid groups.

The purpose of combining these three methods is to trace developments across different historical and political contexts within a single
setting. Such a comparative and inductive approach reveals continu-
ities and changes in how key political actors use the discourse of shari'a
to build up the rule of law or to destroy it. It also creates space for
people's voices and their surviving historical records to speak first,
before developing hypotheses about law or religion. This longitudinal
and multi-method approach is best suited to tracking changes over
time, and it is similar to the methodologies I adopted for my book on
Sudan.[39] This intensive and grounded research process responds to
Clifford Geertz's admonition to scholars to study not just the law but
also the meanings, understandings, and symbols that people give to and
produce from the law.[40]

During an interview in Nairobi, Kenya, a government official from
Mogadishu told me "Everything was destroyed" in Somalia's civil war
and its aftermath. Reflecting on his own survival, he reminded himself,
"Sadly, also, many in the legal establishment ... were killed."[41] Civil
war and terrorism have cut lives short and burned buildings down.
Survivors and their historical records have been scattered. I met key
witnesses to these events and accessed important documents in seven

[39] Mark Fathi Massoud, *Law's Fragile State: Colonial, Authoritarian, and Humanitarian Legacies in Sudan* (Cambridge: Cambridge University Press, 2013a).
[40] Clifford Geertz, *Local Knowledge: Further Essays in Interpretive Anthropology* (New York: Basic Books, 1983).
[41] Interview 86 with Barkhado, retired senior government minister in Mogadishu, Somalia (conducted in Nairobi, Kenya) (August 2013).

cities in four countries: Hargeisa, Somaliland; Addis Ababa, Ethiopia; Nairobi, Kenya; and Cambridge, Durham, London, and Oxford, in the United Kingdom.

I conducted five months of research in the Horn of Africa over three separate trips in 2013, 2014, and 2019. During those periods I made my base primarily in Hargeisa, the hub for courts and legal aid activities in Somaliland. Research there provides insights not only about legal development in the context of state collapse, but also about law in a state that, to much of the rest of the world, does not exist. Lawyers, activists, government officials, and other key informants from Mogadishu sometimes passed through Hargeisa, and I was able to meet with them during their travels.

I also accessed materials and conducted interviews in Nairobi and Addis Ababa. Nairobi has been the nerve center for aid operations to Somalia since the state's 1991 collapse, and I met former Somali government officials who were living or working in Addis Ababa, the headquarters of the African Union. Throughout my research I adopted an ethnographic sensibility toward the documents and persons I encountered. Such an approach involves "listening, participating, witnessing, and reflecting" in order to understand people's lived experiences and how they generate meanings, relationships, and goals around law and religion in local context.[42]

In 2019, I returned to Hargeisa to finalize my fieldwork and present my research in public lectures and in closed meetings with government officials, judges, lawyers, and activists. Sharing my book as I was writing it gave Somalis I met the first opportunity to hear the arguments, reflect, and provide me with feedback.

Historical Research

To evaluate the impact of colonial rule upon law and religion, I conducted research in the United Kingdom – at its national libraries, colonial archives, and university libraries in Cambridge, Durham, London, and Oxford. I supplemented these materials with documents I gathered in Hargeisa and Nairobi, on file with relief organizations

---

[42] Carole McGranahan, "What Is Ethnography? Teaching Ethnographic Sensibilities without Fieldwork," 4 *Teaching Anthropology* (2014): 23–26, p. 24; see also Nick Cheesman, "Rule-of-Law Ethnography," 14 *Annual Review of Law and Social Science* (2018): 167–184; Laura Nader, *The Life of the Law: Anthropological Projects* (Oakland, CA: University of California Press, 2005).

based there or with the library of the British Institute for Eastern Africa, in Kenya.

The decades of violence and instability left few archival records in Somalia and Somaliland. Somalis told me how paper, including government documents, was used as kindling for fires to keep them warm on cold nights during the war. The records that survived are often incomplete or tell only one side of a story. Because I knew that historical knowledge was often passed down orally, I secured interviews with adult children of deceased sheikhs, aqils, and qadis who had worked in British Somaliland. I was also able to meet the last surviving aqil employed by the British colonial administration. Many of these materials appear in Chapter 2, on the colonial period.

Personal Interviews
In addition to obtaining historical evidence in documentary and oral form, I recorded, translated, and transcribed 142 semi-structured interviews, mostly in Hargeisa, Somaliland. Eighteen of these were repeat interviews, and twenty-one were conducted outside Somaliland, during research trips to Nairobi, London, and Addis Ababa. I conducted eighty-seven of these 142 interviews in 2013, forty-six in 2014, three (by telephone) in 2015 and 2016, and six in 2019. Appendix B contains the interview list.

I conducted interviews with lawyers, religious authorities (sheikhs and sultans), community leaders (aqils and sultans), scholars, judges, university administrators, current and former government officials, foreign aid workers, and civil society activists. Collectively, these interviewees worked in Hargeisa, Burao, and Borama (in Somaliland); Mogadishu and Kismayo (in Somalia); and Garowe (in Puntland). Because of instability, many other Somali activists and aid workers remain based outside the region. These include consultants, aid workers, and former government officials whom I met in person or who spoke with me by telephone from their homes or offices in the United Kingdom, Kenya, Ethiopia, Tunisia, Canada, and the United States.

To gather information about the role of religion in legal work and constitutional development, I asked lawyers and officials to share with me why they chose their careers, what they understood to be the defining moments of legal development in Somalia and Somaliland, and whether and how shari'a came up during those periods of personal, national, or legal change. To gather information about the role of religion in civil society development and legal activism, I asked representatives of civic groups to share with me their backgrounds and motivations, the key moments in the development of civil society, and whether and how law and religion came up in their work. I also asked foreign aid workers about the role of shari'a and its relationship to their aid work, and the broader challenges of humanitarian efforts to promote the rule of law in the region. Sultans, sheikhs, aqils, and legal aid attorneys all discussed their experiences as dispute resolvers for their communities, both inside and outside local courtrooms. Interviews ranged from 45 minutes to two hours, with most lasting about 90 minutes.

Best efforts were made to convene a diverse group of interviewees. I decided early on not to ask people about their clan affiliations, if any, to avoid reifying these social categorizations that early European anthropologists and colonial administrators attached to the Somali people.[43] I obtained additional interviews through asking for referrals from current interviewees (snowball sampling) and through my prior work and diverse professional networks.

Despite best efforts to obtain gender balance, only forty-four (31 percent) of my 142 interviews were with women. Not only are government agencies, the legal profession, and civil society in the Horn of Africa dominated by men, but my use of snowball samples likely also propelled me into meetings with men. At the same time, my status as a Sudanese-born man made it inappropriate for me to meet privately with some women, shutting the door to many important women's stories in legal development. Identifying as a man allowed me to enter new territories, but it also closed off other spaces. During my fieldwork, there were no women judges and only a few women lawyers in the entire region. This dearth of women in the legal profession led the United Nations Development Programme and local women's nongovernmental organizations to fund scholarships for women to attend law school in Hargeisa and nearby towns. My interviews with women activists provide the foundation for documenting efforts to diversify the legal profession and to build respect for values associated with the rule of law, discussed in Chapters 5 and 6.

I was able to conduct qualitative interviews in English and Arabic, two languages I have in common with most of the people I met, many of whom had lived overseas as refugees in Arabic-speaking countries prior

---

[43] On the limits of colonial British anthropology, see Cawo Mohamed Abdi, "Somalia," in *Arab Family Studies: Critical Reviews*, ed. Suad Joseph (Syracuse, NY: Syracuse University Press, 2018), 96–110.

to returning to the Horn of Africa in the 1990s and 2000s. During one interview I conducted in Somali, a research assistant simultaneously translated into a combination of English and Arabic for me. I translated, transcribed, coded, and analyzed approximately 1,500 pages of data using qualitative analysis software. More information about this analysis process is in Appendix A.

Ethnographic Observations

Workshops and conferences with elders and religious and political leaders constitute part of international efforts to promote the rule of law in fragile states. Another strategy to build the rule of law is funding legal education and legal aid programs, to encourage people to access state courts to resolve their disputes. I met with and observed meetings between legal aid attorneys and their clients at local legal aid centers near state courthouses, and then shadowed them into courtrooms for their hearings. I also attended rule-of-law workshops organized by Somali organizations and UN agencies, sometimes writing summaries for the organizers in exchange for my attendance.

Practical Limits and Methodological Considerations

The conclusions of this book are based on specific observations, close readings of archival texts, and lengthy conversations with survivors in a fragmented, uneven, and war-torn context. Because the Horn of Africa presents an extreme case of such an environment, the desire to generalize my findings must be tempered with careful attention to context and to the limits of this study. Because of a variety of respon-sibilities in my life, the first limit to the study was that I was unable to devote more than a few months of sustained research overseas at a time. This problem was exacerbated by the number of places I needed to visit for this project. For these reasons, I relied more on documentary evidence and personal interviews with key informants, and less on deep and lengthy fieldwork, than I have done in the past.

The second practical limit of this study is personal security, which prevented me from conducting fieldwork in Mogadishu, Somalia's capital. Mogadishu's government buildings, hotels, and secure airport compound – used for meetings between foreign aid workers, research-ers, Somali activists, and government officials – remain active targets. In 2014, while I was living in Hargeisa, Mogadishu's airport compound was bombed, leaving fifteen people dead and scores more injured. In 2019 while I was in Hargeisa, Mogadishu was rocked by daily suicide bombings. The national courts there have also been targeted. Six years earlier in April 2013, as I was preparing for my first research trip to the region, a particularly destructive bomb attack killed about twenty people, including Somalia's top public interest lawyers and other legal professionals. I therefore conducted all personal interviews and ethnographic observations in Hargeisa, Nairobi, Addis Ababa, and London. Even these sites were not, however, entirely secure: weeks after finishing a round of interviews at Nairobi's upscale Westgate Mall in September 2013, the mall was destroyed in a terrorist attack that killed at least seventy-one people and injured hundreds more.

It is difficult in any interdisciplinary study such as this one to differentiate between fact and recollection, as these are both explained by way of one's memory. This difficulty is no less real when encountering written accounts than it is when listening to oral accounts of events. For this reason, I invited those whom I met to share with me not only their perceptions of shari'a and the rule of law but, more importantly, past behaviors around legal and religious politics. Asking about past behaviors helps to uncover how views change over time, and how accurate accounts of the past might be. Doing so captures the nuances of the ways people invoke shari'a. Where engaging with participants on these questions was impossible (e.g., with deceased authors of historical records), I told survivors about what I found in the archives, to ascertain what the records got right or missed entirely. Turning to an array of sources – though each was incomplete on its own – generated a richer comparative legal history, as did a commitment to an ethnographic sensibility about culture, context, and values.

Colonial legacies, political instability, public health, and the threat of violence have restricted research access to many areas of the Horn of Africa, inevitably making this book, like all writing on the region, feel fragmentary. I offer a series of case studies that collectively illustrate how shari'a and the rule of law fit together, in parallel or in contradictory ways. Asking questions of the documents I found and the people I met afforded me the best chance of peering deeply into the functions of shari'a and practices of the rule of law. Where possible in these chapters, I also provide detailed (or "thick") descriptions of my observations for other readers interested in the broader context of state legal development. No study like this one is ever complete, and I hope the challenges I experienced do not outweigh the stories I was able to gather about the relationship between shari'a and the rule of law in practice.

In a café in Hargeisa, a sultan born during the British colonial administration reflected on his life's work as it related to the region's political history. When I asked him about his hopes for the future, he steered the conversation to religion. "Shari'a was abused," he told me. "People misunderstand it. We should know what shari'a is. Shari'a and common sense and the rule of law," he continued, "if you just think in a proper way, they [all] go together."[44] In the context of the Horn of Africa's deep-rooted political and legal troubles, Somalis I met did not separate religion either from the rule of law or from common sense. From the colonial period to the present day, law, religion, and common sense have worked together to create space for peacebuilding and to foster a more comprehensive understanding of law and society.

AIMS AND MOTIVATIONS

Shari'a, Inshallah marks the first major attempt to study legal politics in Somalia and Somaliland from the nineteenth to twenty-first centuries. It forms part of a growing body of scholarship adopting an ethnographic approach to the rule of law that privileges people's lived experiences and the shifting meanings people give to ideals associated with legal order.[45] In reconstructing Somali legal history, this study uncovers the ways in which legal tools are not enough to build the foundation of a colonial or postcolonial state and not enough for activism within those states. State and nonstate actors also use religious tools – as seen through rival versions of shari'a deployed within and across overlapping legal systems – to build the states they seek. Thus, studying the politics

---

[44] Interview 37 with Sultan Mansoor, sultan in Hargeisa, Somaliland (June 2013).

[45] See, for example, Nick Cheesman, *Opposing the Rule of Law: How Myanmar's Courts Make Law and Order* (Cambridge: Cambridge University Press, 2015); Lynette J. Chua, *Mobilizing Gay Singapore: Rights and Resistance in an Authoritarian State* (Philadelphia, PA: Temple University Press, 2014); Melissa Crouch, ed., *Islam and the State in Myanmar: Muslim-Buddhist Relations and the Politics of Belonging* (Oxford: Oxford University Press, 2016); Matthew Erie, *China and Islam: The Prophet, the Party, and Law* (Cambridge: Cambridge University Press, 2016); R. Michael Feener, *Shari'a and Social Engineering: The Implementation of Islamic Law in Contemporary Aceh, Indonesia* (Oxford: Oxford University Press, 2013); John Hagan, *Justice in the Balkans: Prosecuting War Crimes in the Hague Tribunal* (Chicago, IL: University of Chicago Press, 2003); Jinee Lokaneeta, *Transnational Torture: Law, Violence, and State Power in the United States and India* (New York: New York University Press, 2011); Massoud (2013a); Jens Meierhenrich, "The Practice of International Law: A Theoretical Analysis," 76(3–4) *Law and Contemporary Problems* (2014): 1–83; Victor Peskin, *International Justice in Rwanda and the Balkans: Virtual Trials and the Struggle for State Cooperation* (Cambridge: Cambridge University Press, 2008); Jothie Rajah, *Authoritarian Rule of Law: Legislation, Discourse, and Legitimacy in Singapore* (Cambridge: Cambridge University Press, 2012); Jamie Rowen, *Searching for Truth in the Transitional Justice Movement* (Cambridge: Cambridge University Press, 2017); Stern (2013).

of state-building involves learning what elites enshrine in law as well as how their understandings of God's will shape their political decisions. Autocrats may use religious narratives to serve their own will, but religious narratives also can shape a foundation for the rule of law.

There are excellent general histories of Somalia and Somaliland, and many other works provide an overview of the conflicts, failed humanitarian interventions, and struggles for economic development.[46] Given the region's different countries, colonial legacies, and wars, I do not offer such a political or economic analysis. Instead, I focus on the law and how a competition between legal orders has shaped the region's political ills and its range of policy solutions.

If this book offers one public policy takeaway, it is that scholars and policymakers must not be blind to the power of religion in building, as well as constraining, the rule of law. Recalibrating the moral compass of rule-of-law promotion will require international lawyers, particularly those working in non-Western environments, to ask difficult questions about how faith might provide the moral accountability that law often does not and cannot provide in these places.

Modernizing international rule-of-law development initiatives also entails noticing that "fragile" states may not need more law to stabilize themselves. Rather than pushing religion away or artificially separating religion from the rule of law, aid programs must begin with a recognition of the potential of religious faith to build a foundation for the rule of law. Legal pluralism and religion work together to shape moral accountability, promote fundamental rights, and limit arbitrary powers. There is a dire need for policymakers, human rights lawyers,

---

[46] For general history and overview, see I. M. Lewis, *A Modern History of the Somali: Nation and State in the Horn of Africa* (London: Boydell and Brewer, 2003); Mark Bradbury, *Becoming Somaliland* (Bloomington: Indiana University Press, 2008), Said Samatar, *Oral Poetry and Somali Nationalism: The Case of Sayid Mahammad 'Abdille Hasan* (Cambridge: Cambridge University Press, 1982); David Laitin, *Politics, Language, and Thought: The Somali Experience* (Chicago, IL: University of Chicago Press, 1977a); Brock Millman, *British Somaliland: An Administrative History, 1920–1960* (London and New York: Routledge, 2014). On more recent conflicts, economic developments, and humanitarian interventions, see Mary Harper, *Getting Somalia Wrong? Faith, War, and Hope in a Shattered State* (London: Zed Books, 2012); Michael Woldemariam, *Insurgent Fragmentation in the Horn of Africa: Rebellion and Its Discontents* (Cambridge: Cambridge University Press, 2018); Laura Hammond, "Obliged to Give: Remittances and the Maintenance of Transnational Networks Between Somalis at Home and Abroad," 10 *Bildhaan: An International Journal of Somali Studies* (2011): 125–151; Ken Menkhaus, *Somalia: State Collapse and the Threat of Terrorism* (Oxford: Oxford University Press, 2004); Markus V. Hoehne and Virginia Luling, *Peace and Milk, Drought and War: Somali Culture, Society, and Politics (Essays in Honour of I. M. Lewis)* (London: Hurst Publishers, 2010). On piracy and its relationship with Somali port cities, European insurance companies, and global trade, see Jatin Dua, *Captured at Sea: Piracy and Protection in the Indian Ocean* (Oakland, CA: University of California Press, 2019).

and diplomats to be attuned to the salvific power not only of the law but also of religion.

At root, religious faith and the rule of law matter, not only to faith leaders and lawyers, but also to those seeking to build peace, law, and order out of the most intractable conflicts. Promoting the rule of law in Islamic states involves engaging with religion openly and transparently, rather than avoiding it out of fear that discussing faith may offend deeply held notions of piety or human rights. That is, promoting peace and democracy necessarily involves creating a marketplace for ideas, including religious ones. Democracies daily run the risk of allowing untoward ideas to emerge, and we hope that the most reasonable ideas, rather than the most reprehensible ones, will win over people's hearts.

The rise of extremist, populist, or ultra-fundamentalist views – in politics, law, or religion – does not necessarily mean that such extremism will take hold of state officials, or that they will use extremism or populism to govern. Indeed, quite the opposite may happen when leaders use the threat of extremism to determine the limits their societies should not transgress. In this context, religion and the rule of law offer hope not just for the absence of extremism, but for the presence of justice. These dynamics hold true not just in places with pious Muslims but also in any place where faith is central to most people's lives. (I return to these comparative claims about religion and the rule of law in Chapter 7.)

Tayyib, the talented young lawyer depicted at the start of this introduction – who wanted to abandon his successful legal career to become a sheikh – was not alone in seeing the importance of both law and religious faith in his life and in social well-being. The pages that follow document how, for nearly 140 years, state and nonstate leaders alike have also sought salvation and survival in law and religion.

CHAPTER ONE

EMBRACING SHARI'A AND THE RULE OF LAW

In postcolonial Muslim-majority contexts, particularly in areas struggling with political violence, achieving the ideal of the rule of law is
straightforward neither in theory nor in practice. Plural and overlapping legal orders – derived from the principles of Islam, from the
traditions of indigenous communities, and from the laws and institutions imported by colonial administrators or foreign aid workers and
managed by postcolonial state leaders – shape how citizens come to
understand different values associated with legal order. In these states,
common ideals and shared visions of what law is and how it should
work are scarce. Litigants may shop around among different legal
systems (each one derived from an amalgam of traditions) for
a desired outcome of their disputes, as they are pulled in one direction
or another by family members, religious and community leaders, and
lawyers.

The complicated ways these different legal orders work in parallel are
exemplified in the following case I observed at the district courthouse in
Hargeisa, where judges are expected to use shari'a principles in rendering their decisions. A woman brought suit for damages against her
husband, claiming that he and his other two wives attempted to murder
her. Historically these kinds of family problems, even those involving
criminal allegations like murder, are settled outside of state courts. The
adjudicators are either private sheikhs who use shari'a or community
leaders, called sultans or *aqils*, who use *xeer*. In Somali, xeer literally
means law. But Somalis and foreigners use the word synonymously with
xeer dhaqan, or customary law. It is a broad Somali concept for legal

norms generally derived from a combination of Islamic principles and local practices. Although xeer is unique to each community, it is likely the aggrieved wife here would at best receive a nominal award – *hal kado*, in Somali – such as an apology from her husband for her attempted murder. With such a poor result looming for the battered wife, she was willing to take her chances in a state court, especially with the assistance of a United Nations-funded legal aid attorney.

The judge began the hearing by inviting the plaintiff's lawyer to state her case and bring forward witnesses. Three witnesses were sworn in, each on Allah's name. One by one, these three women each told a similar story. Late one night, they saw a man and two women standing above the plaintiff, who was lying on the road and screaming. Because it had been dark, none of the witnesses was able to identify the man or the two women with him. The judge then questioned the plaintiff directly, asking if she knew additional witnesses. The plaintiff said she did know some other people who witnessed her attempted murder. The judge then asked the plaintiff to bring these additional witnesses to the next hearing and quickly adjourned. As we were filing out of the courtroom, I asked the plaintiff's attorney why the judge had demanded additional witnesses. Were the three women not enough? (I knew that under some interpretations of Islamic law, witnesses are treated differently by gender.) The plaintiff's lawyer told me that such an interpretation did not apply because the judge had merely wanted stronger evidence – someone who had more clearly seen the faces of the people standing above the victim. "Here," the lawyer continued, "a witness is a witness," regardless of gender.

Law is a messy business, especially in societies living with colonial legal legacies and postcolonial violence. Legal systems are plural, layered, incomplete, and open to interpretation by state judges and others who claim the authority – from religion, custom, foreign or international legal interventions, or some combination thereof – to adjudicate.[1] But legal order still exists and thrives, albeit in ways that are sometimes parallel and sometimes contradictory to the goals of the rule of law.[2] Many people engage with, invoke, and are empowered by

---

[1] See, for example, Keebet von Benda-Beckmann, "Forum Shopping and Shopping Forums: Dispute Processing in a Minangkabau Village in West Sumatra," 13(19) *The Journal of Legal Pluralism and Unofficial Law* (1981): 117–159. On the "radical, pervasive legal pluralism [that] is a general feature of modern societies," see Roger Cotterrell, "Still Afraid of Legal Pluralism? Encountering Santi Romano," 45(2) *Law & Social Inquiry* (2020): 539–558, p. 540.

[2] On how legal orders thrive in even the most desolate, unforgiving, and brutal political environments in contemporary human history, including Nazi Germany and apartheid South

law, though the outcomes of their efforts may be far from ideal, for both claimants and observers. Here, a judge working for Somaliland's autonomous government and sitting in a court first conceived by British colonial officials applied his own interpretation of shari'a – an interpretation that may have contradicted the interpretations of others. The legal aid attorney, whose salary was funded by UN rule-of-law projects, lamented that even if she were to bring forward more witnesses, the case might eventually be resolved by the plaintiff's elders. They would rule according to their customs, ostensibly built on decisions from previous marital disputes in their communities and said to be consistent with Islamic principles. Most of these different legal orders – derived from some combination among state laws, local customs, and religious norms – claim to rest upon or be consistent with shari'a. But in practice shari'a means many things to many people, and it is difficult to isolate the law's origins in Islam as if it had some precise, determinable genetic code.

A state of confusion surrounding law in Muslim-majority countries dealing with legacies of legal pluralism and political violence results in the perception among foreign policymakers either that there is no law at all or that whatever law does exist is founded upon the arbitrary will of a judge, sheikh, elder, or other person who claims authority.[3] Somali government officials and the aid workers assisting them, in contrast, see the problem not as a lack of law, but as a lack of harmonization among the different systems – religious law, state law, customary law, international law, and human rights principles.[4]

Africa, see Jens Meierhenrich, *The Remnants of the Rechsstaat: An Ethnography of Nazi Law* (Oxford: Oxford University Press, 2018) and Jens Meierhenrich, *The Legacies of Law: Long-Run Consequences of Legal Development in South Africa, 1652–2000* (Cambridge: Cambridge University Press, 2008). Contemporary authoritarian states similarly use law and courts to achieve their political, economic, and social goals. See, for example, Nick Cheesman, *Opposing the Rule of Law: How Myanmar's Courts Make Law and Order* (Cambridge: Cambridge University Press, 2015); Mark Fathi Massoud, *Law's Fragile State: Colonial, Authoritarian, and Humanitarian Legacies in Sudan* (Cambridge: Cambridge University Press, 2013a); Tamir Moustafa, *The Struggle for Constitutional Power: Law, Politics, and Economic Development in Egypt* (Cambridge: Cambridge University Press, 2007); Jothie Rajah, *Authoritarian Rule of Law: Legislation, Discourse, and Legitimacy in Singapore* (Cambridge: Cambridge University Press, 2012); Rachel E. Stern, *Environmental Litigation in China: A Study in Political Ambivalence* (Cambridge: Cambridge University Press, 2013).

[3] Anthropologist Peter D. Little has critiqued the notion of statelessness – the dearth of governing structures and political institutions – for it does not necessarily correlate with social chaos or economic anarchy. He demonstrates how, in the absence of government during the 1990s, Somalis conducting business transactions with one another created local economic markets that flourished. Peter D. Little, *Somalia: Economy without a State* (Bloomington: Indiana University Press, 2003).

[4] This problem of integrating heterogeneous legal systems began as early as independence from colonial rule. See, e.g., "Integration of the Laws in the Somali Republic: Report on the Work of

The international aid community's efforts to build respect for the rule of law generally involve working with Somalis to smooth out the distinctions among different legal orders based on indigenous, religious, and state authority. Legal development, as aid workers in the Horn of Africa told me, aims to induce Somali people to turn to the state to resolve their private disputes. In order to divert religious authorities' dispute resolution work into the government, aid workers have encouraged successive Somali governments to subsume the religious leaders' efforts under the state legal system. The government would then draw its strength from below, by bringing religious principles and personnel into the state, and from above, by proclaiming the state's adherence to international human rights principles. Such a government would presumably have enough authority to oversee all dispute resolution efforts, including those of religious people, and to ensure that all decisions would fall in line with international human rights. Aid workers hope that keeping state courts and civil servants busy helping people will legitimize the state's authority in a legally competitive space where, in the eyes of the people, the state has historically seemed at best irrelevant or, at worst, unreliable and untrustworthy.

These efforts to control indigenous and religious authority are also designed to minimize the potential for shari'a's hegemony. Aid work commonly treats religion as "natural, irrational, incontestable, and imposed ... Simply put, religion is the 'other' of international law."[5] In Somalia and Somaliland, aid workers devote energy to development initiatives that draw directly upon international law. In the short term, these initiatives render people's shari'a-based systems of governance invisible. In the long term, such international law-based programs undermine public order and "undercut ... existing informal security systems."[6] Aid workers' efforts to shore up the state and fend off shari'a instead erode human security and the state itself. Put more broadly, international legal development activities in Muslim-majority states are designed to promote the rule of law by unifying pre-existing plural

the Consultative Commission for Integration from its Inception Until 31st March, 1964" 8(2) *Journal of African Law* (1964): 56–58. Decades later, in its 2011 "universal periodic review" submission to the United Nations Office of the High Commissioner for Human Rights, Somalia's Transitional Federal Government described "the harmonization between Sharia law, Somali customary law and modern law" as its primary challenge. United Nations Office of the High Commissioner for Human Rights, "Addressing Impunity in Somalia," April 13, 2012, https://bit.ly/37THXpx (accessed January 1, 2021).

5 Madhavi Sunder, "Piercing the Veil," 112 *Yale Law Journal* (2003): 1399–1472, p. 1402.
6 Ken Menkhaus, "Governance without Government in Somalia: Spoilers, State Building, and the Politics of Coping," 31(3) *International Security* (2007a): 74–106, p. 70.

legal orders under a state, rather than under a religion – despite the fact that many citizens see religion as a stronger legal foundation for peace and stability because Islam constitutes the basis of their personal and communal activities.

Shari'a is, however, not a rigid legal doctrine to follow and implement. Rather, shari'a shapes and is shaped by centuries of textual interpretation, local and regional politics, state-building practices, and colonial and postcolonial interventions. As one Somali told me, "No longer does shari'a belong [only] to the sheikh."[7] Shari'a is, instead, the purview of everyone – claimants, judges, colonial administrators, postcolonial government officials, aid workers, and activists – to invoke, enact, or even dismantle as they seek solutions to their problems. Scholars discuss how "rights" serve as a "master frame" that people use and stretch to pursue their varying aims. So, too, do different actors in Somalia and Somaliland manipulate shari'a as a master frame for their political values and goals.[8]

Governments and observers often misread shari'a as the antithesis of modern state law or the unspeakable legal imprint of dictators, pirates, and warlords.[9] These characterizations cause international policy to miss the ways shari'a instead thrives among those who promote respect for peace, community, and the rule of law. Something remarkable has happened to shari'a. While shari'a technically constitutes a path to God's will, derived from the Qur'an and the teachings and actions of the Prophet Muhammad, God's will is also open to human interpretation, uncertainty, and hope. Shari'a has become a malleable basis for political, legal, and rhetorical claims in many areas of social life – a challenge to colonialism and a justification for it, a challenge to authoritarianism and a justification for it, and a challenge to Western views of human rights and a justification for those views. Shari'a's

---

[7] Interview 126 with Dhahir, senior university administrator in Borama, Somaliland (conducted in Hargeisa, Somaliland) (June 2014).

[8] On how activists and movements use frames – of values, beliefs, and meanings – to mobilize people into action, see Robert D. Benford and David A. Snow, "Framing Processes and Social Movements," 26 *Annual Review of Sociology* (2000): 611–639; David A. Snow and Robert D. Benford, "Master Frames and Cycles of Protest," in *Frontiers in Social Movement Theory*, eds. Aldon D. Morris and Carol McClurg Mueller (New Haven, CT: Yale University Press, 1992), 133–155. On shari'a as a frame for Somali law and custom, see Khaled Abou-Elyousr, "Understanding the Somalia Justice Systems: Challenges and the Way Forward," unpublished paper, December 2016 (copy on file with author); Mehari Taddele Maru, "The Future of Somalia's Legal System and Its Contribution to Peace and Development," 4(1) *Journal of Peacebuilding and Development* (2008): 1–15.

[9] On shari'a as a "taboo" of state law, see Matthew Erie, "Shari'a as Taboo of Modern Law: Halal Food, Islamophobia, and China," 33(3) *Journal of Law & Religion* (2018): 390–420.

flexibility allows those who seek peace or stability to use it along the path to their goals.

Some uses of shari'a are more rhetorical, pragmatic, and strategic, while others are more ideologically committed. Nevertheless, all of the different elites in modern Somali history claim that their interpretation of shari'a is the true and correct one. Rather than seeking to find a "right" shari'a, this book exposes its different versions in practice, pointing out the ways that the debates over shari'a help legal politics thrive, sometimes cultivating and sometimes challenging not only the meaning of shari'a but also the different pathways – violent, nonviolent, or both – toward the rule-of-law ideal.

In short, inasmuch as shari'a has led many Somalis to stand up against injustice, and has led many others to defend that injustice, Islam has become a tool of legal politics.[10] Political elites across Somali history have tried to build peace with it, constitutionalize it, democratize it, co-opt it, and silence it. Amidst radical legal pluralism and shattered statehood, shari'a remains a lasting and resilient force for political and legal development.

THE SOMALI EXPERIENCE OF SHARI'A

Shari'a has provided hope to a number of contending parties in Somali history.[11] It has offered them an ideological, practical, and rhetorical justification for their desires. For instance, shari'a offered hope to British colonial administrators who invoked their own interpretation of it, with some support from sheikhs in Mecca, in their communications with Sheikh Mohamed Abdullah Hassan during the early twentieth-century war against him and his followers. The sheikh entered this war with the hope that a deeper respect for shari'a would unite Somali communities against colonial domination. Shari'a was Sheikh Hassan's source of resistance to the military and economic might of the British administration, even as colonial officials also sought to counter him through shari'a.

Later postcolonial Somali rulers similarly relied on shari'a to justify their authority. In the 1970s, President Mohamed Siad Barre went to

---

[10] On the study of legal politics, see Mark Fathi Massoud, "Reflections on the Future of Global Legal Studies," 25(2) *Indiana Journal of Global Legal Studies* (2018b): 569–581; see also Massoud (2013a), 21, 24–27.

[11] On hope as a "common operative" and a method of knowledge production, see Hirokazu Miyazaki, *The Method of Hope: Anthropology, Philosophy, and Fijian Knowledge* (Stanford, CA: Stanford University Press, 2004).

great lengths to claim that his socialist rule was compatible with shari'a, much as the British had done decades earlier. But, when threatened, Siad Barre's regime also put to death sheikhs who called out the regime's new family law for its incompatibility with shari'a. A generation later, in the 2000s, the Islamic Courts Union in Mogadishu and the de facto independent government in Hargeisa both performed what they believed to be God's will by creating Islamic forms of dispute resolution and Islamic governments. Both groups successfully consolidated peace in their communities. But an Ethiopian-led and American-backed incursion in 2006, fueled by concerns about the rise of an Islamic state in Africa, crushed Mogadishu's most forward-thinking Muslim jurists.

Activist women in the Horn of Africa continue to use shari'a to fight for gender equality and political freedoms, particularly when they find other justifications for women's rights to be culturally inaccessible. For example, these activists empower women to go to school, teach, and run for public office by showing how these rights are consistent with Qur'anic verses. Their efforts to ensure people view gender equality as part of Islam are sincere. Championing this version of shari'a is also pragmatic in a polity that largely views the goals of international law with the same skepticism Somalis had of the goals of colonial law. Even Somali elders who claim that customary law is the central feature of Somali communal life tie the importance of the family or of the rules of patrilineal clans to their consistency with Islam, just as modern constitution drafters in Somalia and Somaliland also declared Islam the foundation of their governments.

These myriad actors across historical periods in Somalia and Somaliland – colonial officials, religious leaders, community elders, authoritarian regimes, and activists – could not be more different. But they all have invoked their own interpretations of God's will, and they all also have had to contend with their adversaries' opposing interpretations of it. In the long run, as the elite actors struggle to present their own shari'a, God's will becomes an enduring source of hope, fear, frustration, and law, even as its precise contours are contested. Conflicting interpretations of and contestations around shari'a, as well as its rhetorical, cultural, and social power, create active and divergent forms of legal politics, all in some way involving shari'a.

To bring into sharper focus the relationship between the principles animating the discourses of shari'a and the rule of law, in the sections of this chapter that follow I first define the rule of law and its relationship to religion. Second, I define the essential elements of shari'a in the context of Islam's connection to the rule-of-law ideal. Third, I explain the region's radical legal pluralism and show how and why Islamic principles and the rule of law inform one another. Together, and through the example of Somalia and Somaliland, these sections help to generate a socio-legal theory of shari'a.

INTERPRETING THE RULE OF LAW

Legal scholars have disagreed over how to define, measure, and promote the rule of law.[12] But they agree that the rule of law is about restraining coercive power; it is a structure of governance in which the law limits the arbitrary power of state officials. But the rule of law also has broader appeal for international policymakers: when law and legal systems configure and constrain social, economic, and political relations, people can resolve disputes peacefully, and their societies can become more politically and economically successful.[13] Thus, a country with a deep respect for the rule of law is one in which citizens know what to expect from their governments. Those expectations typically include robust forms of political liberalism, including regular, free, and fair elections; limited and transparent governance; independent courts that are not the lackeys of any officials; and the promotion of human rights, equality, and liberty for all, paying special attention to a society's most vulnerable or marginalized persons, such as women, children, and members of minority ethnic or religious groups.

The World Justice Project says that the rule of law has four domains: government accountability, clear and evenly applied laws, fair processes, and an ethical and independent judicial authority. These four domains are widely viewed as an antidote to authoritarianism and state corruption. Legal scholars and policymakers have also long understood the rule of law as a bulwark against violence or terrorism. Verifying this

---

[12] Martin Krygier, "Four Puzzles About the Rule of Law: Why, What, Where? And Who Cares?" in *Getting to the Rule of Law: Nomos* No. 50, ed. J. E. Fleming (New York: New York University Press, 2011b), 64–104. On the conceptual, normative, strategic, and empirical claims made about the rule of law, particularly in light of the violence against ethnic and religious minorities, see Paul Gowder, *The Rule of Law in the Real World* (Cambridge: Cambridge University Press, 2016).

[13] Massoud (2013a), 21–23. Countries with a robust rule of law offer a "well-functioning, procedurally guided, independent and rights-based legal system." Nicholas Rush Smith, *Contradictions of Democracy: Vigilantism and Rights in Post-Apartheid South Africa* (Oxford: Oxford University Press, 2019), 85.

conclusion empirically, Seung-Whan Choi studied 131 countries from 1984 to 2004 and found that the rule of law, evidenced by fair elections and impartial judiciaries, limited citizens' willingness to participate in political violence, which in the long term reduced the likelihood of terrorist events.[14]

The United Nations General Assembly, gathering in 2012 for its first high-level meeting devoted to the rule of law, declared the rule of law to be the foundation of all "just societies" and "equitable state relations."[15] The administrator of the United Nations Development Programme similarly said that "The rule of law is at the very heart of what is needed for human development."[16] For UN officials, the rule of law is as much an outcome as it is a set of processes associated with building state structures that promote due process, social justice, civil rights, economic development, and the expectation of reasonable state behavior.

In global political history, such a perfect rule of law has been, alas, a "rare achievement."[17] Ideals like the rule of law, however clear or compelling to the mind, do not fit neatly into reality, particularly in the context of colonialism, violence, or human and environmental disaster. The models must be made real by humans who are themselves imperfect, a point emphasized by legal philosophers and historians.[18] To build trust, UN agencies and other aid groups must give a "a local face and local legitimacy" to their projects promoting the rule of law and other international norms.[19] In practice, the rule of law may look "thicker" or "thinner" depending on the political processes and power

---

[14] Seung-Whan Choi, "Fighting Terrorism through the Rule of Law?" 54(6) *Journal of Conflict Resolution* (2010): 940–966.

[15] United Nations General Assembly, "World Leaders Adopt Declaration Reaffirming Rule of Law as Foundation for Building Equitable State Relations, Just Societies," Sixty-seventh General Assembly, GA/11290, 2012, https://bit.ly/38DsDwp (accessed January 1, 2021).

[16] Ibid.

[17] Martin Krygier, "Approaching the Rule of Law," in *The Rule of Law in Afghanistan: Missing in Inaction*, ed. Whit Mason (Cambridge: Cambridge University Press, 2011a), 15.

[18] Douglas Hay, "Property, Authority, and the Criminal Law," in *Albion's Fatal Tree: Crime and Society in Eighteenth Century England*, eds. D. Hay, P. Linebaugh, J. G. Rule, E. P. Thompson, and C. Winslow (New York: Pantheon Press, 1975), 17–64; Morton J. Horwitz, "The Rule of Law: An Unqualified Human Good?" 86 *Yale Law Journal* (1977): 561–566; E. P. Thompson, *Whigs and Hunters: The Origin of the Black Act* (New York: Pantheon Books, 1975); Sanford Levinson and Jack M. Balkin, "Morton Horwitz Wrestles with the Rule of Law," in *Transformations in American Legal History II: Law, Ideology, and Morals: Essays in Honor of Morton J. Horwitz*, eds. Daniel W. Hamilton and Alfred L. Brophy (Cambridge, MA: Harvard University Press, 2011), 483–500; see also Mark Fathi Massoud, "Ideals and Practices in the Rule of Law," 41(2) *Law & Social Inquiry* (2016b): 489–501, p. 494.

[19] Lisbeth Zimmermann, *Global Norms with a Local Face: Rule-of-Law Promotion and Norm-Translation* (Cambridge University Press, 2017), 2.

relations that produce it.[20] Political elites may seek to promote legitimacy, authority, or even repression by building legal institutions associated with some of the rule of law's principles.[21]

Studying the rule of law, then, is both a normative concern of legal philosophy and an empirical concern of social science.[22] As a normative matter, rule-of-law principles nourish the work of legal activists. As an empirical matter, those principles may be studied, and even criticized, when state officials or legal activists try to achieve them.

In this book, I examine the rule-of-law ideal through an empirically grounded lens, by rooting the ideal in a specific history, context, and set of practices. I privilege the stories found along the precarious path toward the rule of law, rather than the perfected, philosophical ideal at the end of that path. These stories include admirable moments when political leaders or activists struggle for the rule of law, as well as lamentable moments when those same people succumb to more tempting, selfish desires. As we shall see, practices associated with the rule of law are as broken, inconsistent, and discordant as individual people.[23] Elusive though it may be, the rule of law is nevertheless the goal toward which aid workers, legal scholars, and policymakers continually strive, particularly when they work in or study societies emerging from civil war.

Policymakers, legal scholars, and the public do not doubt the rule of law's significance. What is less clear is how societies facing legacies of civil war and legal or religious pluralism should begin to implement the rule of law's principles. Typically, legal development projects in conflict and post-conflict settings share a common design: international lawyers, diplomats, and aid workers arrive carrying the mantle of human rights and use it to build up national governments.[24] These foreign

---

[20] William Hurst, *Ruling Before the Law: The Politics of Legal Regimes in China and Indonesia* (Cambridge: Cambridge University Press, 2018).

[21] Frank Munger, "Thailand's Cause Lawyers and Twenty-First-Century Military Coups: Nation, Identity, and Conflicting Visions of the Rule of Law," 2(2) *Asian Journal of Law and Society* (2015): 301–322; see also Massoud (2016b), 493.

[22] Philip Selznick, *A Humanist Science: Values and Ideals in Social Inquiry* (Stanford, CA: Stanford University Press, 2008); Lon Fuller, *The Morality of Law* (New Haven, CT: Yale University Press, 1964).

[23] Henri Nouwen, *The Wounded Healer: Ministry in Contemporary Society* (New York: Doubleday, 1979); Wil Hernandez, *Henri Nouwen: A Spirituality of Imperfection* (New York: Paulist Press, 2006).

[24] On the challenges of implementing international legal reform programs in conflict settings, see David Marshall, ed., *The International Rule of Law Movement: A Crisis of Legitimacy and the Way Forward* (Cambridge, MA: Harvard University Press, 2014); Rachel Kleinfeld, *Advancing the*

officials then encourage new state leaders (themselves oftentimes militiamen) to "harmonize" different legal systems under a single, modern constitutional framework and to construct independent government bureaucracies, judiciaries, law schools, and prison systems that adhere to those constitutional values.[25] The intense focus on achieving the rule of law – through state-building, constitution-writing, and legal training initiatives – obscures from view the problems associated with cultivating the rule of law from the ground up. The failure to pay deep attention to the productive capacity of religious law ranks among the problems disturbingly present in international legal development activities.

British colonial administrations in Muslim-majority societies offer an important empirical example of the relationship between religious power and the rule of law. British colonial officials went to great lengths not to excise religion from the state; rather, they subsumed and regulated it. Colonial officials integrated Islam into the colonial enterprise by limiting Islam's legal jurisdiction to disputes within families, such as divorce and inheritance. Cases were handled by specially designated "Mohammedan" courts whose judges (called qadis) were paid by and answered to the colonial administration, which merged imperial objectives into the process of building legal institutions and turned the rule of law into an instrument of empire. This process of managing religion and imperializing the rule of law showed local officials how to limit state power while it promoted injustices in courts and prisons, the very institutions meant to uphold the rule of law.[26]

Thus, colonial secularism was not the absence of religion as much as it was the active management of religion, as part of a bid to earn people's respect for the rule of law. For at least a short time and for some people, the process did work in the way colonial administrators intended. As a result, in Muslim-majority states transitioning to

---

Rule of Law Abroad: Next Generation Reform (Washington, DC: Carnegie Endowment for International Peace, 2012).

[25] Aid workers and consultants have written numerous reports on integrating what they classify as distinct legal systems. See, for example, United Nations Habitat, "Harmonization of the Legal Systems Resolving Land Disputes in Somaliland and Puntland: Report and Recommendations," HS/007/16E (July 2015); Andre Le Sage, *Stateless Justice in Somalia: Formal and Informal Rule of Law Initiatives* (Geneva, Switzerland: Centre for Humanitarian Dialogue, 2005); Erica Harper, ed., *Working with Customary Justice: Post-Conflict and Fragile States* (Rome: IDLO-International Development Law Organization, 2011).

[26] These injustices are as real in robust democracies as they are in fragile states. Robert M. Cover, "Violence and the Word," 95 *Yale Law Journal* (1986): 1601–1629; Rachel Kleinfeld, *A Savage Order: How the World's Deadliest Countries Can Forge a Path to Security* (New York: Pantheon, 2018).

independence, young democratic-minded political elites who had worked for colonial administrations made the decision to compartmentalize or even reject religious law just as their colonial bosses had done. Many new officials in former British colonies, for instance, saw their states to independence by giving continued priority to English common law and sidelining religious jurists, which stunted the development of progressive versions of religious law and opened up space for more extremist versions.[27]

While colonial elites recognized the need to work with religion, modern policymakers and scholars have largely abandoned the notion that religion can be a part of the rule of law. In fact, protecting religion – much like preserving local "culture" – has often been the preferred justification of dictators seeking to deny rights to women or minorities.[28] In early modern Europe, among other places, protecting religious rights and liberties encouraged racism, homophobia, and the subjugation of women.[29] Some scholars have argued that, even if other religions can help introduce principles associated with the rule of law, Islam is unlikely to help do so. Professors of finance and banking have concluded that the rule of law is more durable in Protestant-majority and Catholic-majority countries – where corruption is lower and economic development is stronger – than in Muslim-majority countries.[30] Economic historians have argued that indigenous and decentralized Islamic legal practices – not European colonialism – held Muslim-majority regions back from achieving long-term political stability, economic growth, and the rule of law.[31]

Contemporary socio-legal scholars have, at best, asked whether courts, constitutions, and the rule of law can resolve religious conflicts.[32] But the

---

[27] On the case of Sudan, see Mark Fathi Massoud, "How an Islamic State Rejected Islamic Law," 66 *American Journal of Comparative Law* (2018a): 579–602. On the case of Israel, see Izhak England, "Law and Religion in Israel," 35(1) *American Journal of Comparative Law* (1987): 185–208.

[28] Autocrats starting in the 1990s, particularly in Asia, launched the idea of protecting local cultural values in a bid to exempt themselves from considerations of international human rights law, which they criticized for its Western origins. See, for example, Michael D. Barr, "Lee Kwan Yew and the 'Asian Values' Debate," 24(3) *Asian Studies Review* (2000): 309–334; Yash Ghai, "Asian Perspectives on Human Rights," 23(3) *Hong Kong Law Journal* (1993): 342–357.

[29] Deborah Orr, "For Human Rights to Flourish, Religious Rights Have to Come Second," *Guardian*, December 27, 2013, https://bit.ly/33RDSzG (accessed January 1, 2021).

[30] Charles M. North, Wafa Hakim Orman, and Carl R. Gwin, "Religion, Corruption, and the Rule of Law," 45(5) *Journal of Money, Credit, and Banking* (2013): 757–779.

[31] Timur Kuran, *The Long Divergence: How Islamic Law Held Back the Middle East* (Princeton, NJ: Princeton University Press, 2010); Jean-Philippe Platteau, *Islam Instrumentalized: Religion and Politics in Historical Perspective* (Cambridge: Cambridge University Press, 2017).

[32] Aslı Ü. Bâli and Hanna Lerner, eds., *Constitution Writing, Religion and Democracy* (Cambridge: Cambridge University Press, 2017); Benjamin Schonthal, Tamir Moustafa, Matthew Nelson, and Shylashri Shankar, "Is the Rule of Law an Antidote for Religious Tension? The Promise

influence can also move in the opposite direction. That is, religion can help resolve legal troubles and prevent provincialism and intolerance. Modern Somali history is, in fact, a case study in the coexistence of religion and the desire to build limited government, justice, and order, even if ordinary Somalis do not always name these desires as the "rule of law." Somali political leaders, however, have long reflected on what the rule of law means, and religion has long been a commonsense component of the meaning of the rule of law. In a 1968 speech to Royal African Society in London, England, the Prime Minister of the Somali Republic, Mohamed Haji Ibrahim Egal, stated that his government promoted the rule of law not through its received European laws but through the people's Somali heritage and grassroots relationships.[33] He used the term "rule of law" in relation to people's shared religious tradition (Islam), shared language and poetry (Somali), and shared culture (in which interpersonal disputes are resolved by community leaders using local norms).

The emotional potentialities of law and religion swing in many directions. In societies facing legacies of political violence, the path to order, stability, and peace may be stained by the blood of victims of political elites who had promoted legal or religious change. But there is little research to suggest that rights and duties that come from religion present, on their own, a direct threat to the rule of law, especially when a consciousness of God can evoke a deeper consciousness of ethics, and vice versa.[34] As with the normative principles of the rule of law, religious principles can just as easily be used to promote human rights, limited government, fairness, dignity, responsibility, and justice.[35]

By more clearly articulating what the rule of law means in strongly religious societies, where it comes from, and its relationship with religion and religious duties, *Shari'a, Inshallah* informs the practice of

and Peril of Judicializing Religious Freedom," 60(8) *American Behavioral Scientist* (2015): 966–986.

[33] Mohamed Haji Ibrahim Egal, "Somalia: Nomadic Individualism and the Rule of Law," 67(268) *African Affairs* (1968): 219–226, p. 219.

[34] Shahab Ahmed, *What is Islam? The Importance of Being Islamic* (Princeton, NJ: Princeton University Press, 2015); Robert Hefner, ed., *Shari'a Law and Modern Muslim Ethics* (Bloomington: Indiana University Press, 2016); Mark Fathi Massoud and Kathleen M. Moore, "Rethinking *Shari'a*: Voices of Islam in California," 5(4) *Boom: A Journal of California* (2015): 94–99. A. Kevin Reinhart, "Islamic Law as Islamic Ethics," 11(2) *Journal of Religious Ethics* (1983): 186–203.

[35] John Witte, Jr. and M. Christian Green, eds., *Religion and Human Rights: An Introduction* (Oxford: Oxford University Press, 2012).

the rule of law.[36] Contemporary conceptions of the rule of law – exported by American or European lawyers to the Global South – are constrained by the belief that religion ought to be governed and managed, while rights become a kind of unmanaged "religion" that can stand on their own self-assertive authority.[37] For this reason, rule-of-law advocacy typically promotes religious freedom within clearly defined limits, by excising religious thought from the public sphere or tacitly treating religion as separate from – or even contrary to – the goals of legal development and human rights.[38] This advocacy obscures how religion may, in fact, be doing some of the very work of the rule of law.

INTERPRETING SHARI'A

A civic activist I met in Hargeisa told me that preventing women from participating in politics was, in her words, "not international-legal and not Islamic-legal."[39] In her mind, international rule-of-law projects that sought to empower women to vote and seek political office were entirely consistent with the Islamic goals of maintaining women's rights and dignity. As shown in these pages, the values of shari'a as understood in Muslim-majority countries share much in common with the values that Western legal scholars and international policymakers associate with the rule of law. To show that, an overview of Islam and shari'a is necessary. Islam comes from the Arabic word, *aslama*, which means "to submit." "Islam" is commonly translated as "submission to God." A Muslim is a person who submits to God's will and the religion of Islam. Muslims trace their lineage through the prophets who carried the message of God (whom Islam labels God's messengers), including the major figures of Judaism and Christianity such as Adam, Moses, David, and Jesus.

---

[36] On the relationship between rights and duties in Islamic and international human rights laws, see Mark Fathi Massoud, "Do Victims of War Need International Law? Human Rights Education Programs in Authoritarian Sudan," 45(1) *Law & Society Review* (2011): 1–32.

[37] Jedidiah J. Kroncke, *The Futility of Law and Development: China and the Dangers of Exporting American Law* (Oxford: Oxford University Press, 2016).

[38] Winnifred Fallers Sullivan, *The Impossibility of Religious Freedom*, 2nd ed. (Princeton, NJ: Princeton University Press, 2018); Elizabeth Shakman Hurd, *Beyond Religious Freedom: The New Global Politics of Religion* (Princeton, NJ: Princeton University Press, 2015).

[39] Interview 125 with Sohir, NGO executive director and women's rights activist in Hargeisa, Somaliland (June 2014).

Islam's Political History

The Prophet Muhammad first received a revelation from God when he was forty years old, while on a personal mountain retreat near Mecca in present-day Saudi Arabia. He continued to have these revelations until he died in the city-state of Medina at the age of sixty-three. God's words to Muhammad were orally preserved during the Prophet's lifetime and later reordered into verses of the Qur'an. After the Prophet's death, this holy book was codified into a single document of 114 chapters (*soorah*) totaling 6,236 verses (*ayat*). The text was preserved by Muhammad's surviving wife, Aisha, whom Islamic studies scholars credit with helping Islam thrive after the Prophet's death. The Prophet Muhammad's statements, actions, and tacit approvals, all carefully documented during the last twenty-three years of his life, are collectively labeled the Sunnah or, when gathered in written form, the Hadith. Today, the Qur'an and the Hadith are the two primary source materials for shari'a.

According to the Prophet Muhammad, as revealed in the Hadith of the Angel Gabriel, Islam is made up of three constituent parts: legal, theological, and spiritual (Table 1.1). Together, these prescribe

Table 1.1 Legal, theological, and spiritual aspects of Islam

Legal Aspects of Islam (*islam*)	Theological Aspects of Islam (*iman*)	Spiritual Aspects of Islam (*ihsan*)
Shahada (testimony of faith that there is one God and that Muhammad is God's final messenger)	Belief in God Belief in God's angels Belief in God's messengers Belief in God's holy books	Living through good works, knowing that one acts – worships, conducts business affairs, participates in family and community, and commits not to injure others and the environment – in order to please God
Salat (prayer)	Belief in the last day of judgment	
Zakat (helping the poor)	Belief that God's will is predetermined (*qatr*)	
Sawm (fasting)		
Hajj (pilgrimage to the ka'bah, considered the first house of God, in Mecca)		

Source: Compiled by the author, from the Hadith of Gabriel.

particular modes of worship as well as beliefs, good works, and treating people and the environment well.

The legal aspects of Islam are collectively labeled *islam*. (Technically, the word "Islam" refers both to the legal aspects of the religion, when discussed in relation to Islam's theological and spiritual aspects, and to the broader religion of the same name.) These are (1) *shahada* (the testimony that there is only one God and that Muhammad is God's final messenger); (2) *salat* (regular prayer, usually at least five times each day); (3) *zakat* (helping the poor); (4) *sawm* (fasting, typically from all food and drink during daylight hours during the holy month of Ramadan); and (5) *hajj* (pilgrimage to the *ka'bah* in Mecca, considered to be the first house of God). These five legal pillars primarily govern worship, but they also reach into political and social life, including business transactions, relationships, and crimes. These pillars constitute Islam's outward-facing posture, or actions that Muslims must take openly in order to accept Islam.[40]

The theological aspects of Islam, according to the Hadith of the Angel Gabriel, are collectively labeled *iman*, or faith. These are belief in (1) God, (2) God's angels, (3) God's messengers, (4) God's holy books, (5) the last day of judgment, and (6) God's unknowable and predetermined will (*qatr*, or a consciousness that life events, behaviors, and choices occur through or are known only by the will of God, or *inshallah*). These six beliefs are Islam's inward-facing posture, for each Muslim to believe on their own.

Finally, the Hadith of the Angel Gabriel explains that there is one spiritual aspect of Islam, called *ihsan*, which refers to participating in social, political, and financial relationships as if God were always observing and judging the goodness of one's actions. That is, Islam calls one to live through honesty and good works in one's business transactions, one's worship of God, one's participation in family and community, and one's commitment to minimizing harm to others and to the environment.

The legal pillars, theological beliefs, and the spiritual notion that God is always watching form the basis of Islam. While the Hadith of the Angel Gabriel separates these aspects, in practice many lay Muslims may make little or no distinction between what Hadith scholars might portray as the legal, theological, or spiritual aspects of Islam. For many of these persons, the legal parts of Islam may be inseparable from faith, honest participation in relationships with others, and good works.

---

[40] On these four areas of social and political life in Islam, see Wael B. Hallaq, *An Introduction to Islamic Law* (Cambridge: Cambridge University Press, 2009a).

Critical to understanding the tenets of shari'a is attaining an awareness of how Islamic tradition spread and of its social and political history during and immediately after the Prophet Muhammad's lifetime. While the Prophet Muhammad was spreading the values of Islam in Mecca (610–622 CE), the religion grew rapidly. During these first thirteen years of Islam, the Prophet united diverse people – many of whom were practicing different forms of idolatry or polytheism – through regular prayers that recognized monotheism, or the oneness of God (*tawhid*). Tawhid denotes God's primary right: to be worshipped singularly, without any partner or co-equal.

The Prophet went further than uniting people in the practice of monotheism. He called the new Muslims of Mecca to practice social, racial, and gender justice in all their affairs. He advocated for equality among the different ethnic and tribal groups of the region (in his words, according to a generally accepted Hadith, equality "between Black and white . . . and between Arabs and non-Arabs"). Promoting this notion of equality was remarkable in a region where many people were either slave-owners or at war with neighboring tribes, or both. Nonviolence, self-defense, and freeing slaves became important parts of Islamic practice and belief. For instance, if a man broke a promise or a fast, or if he harmed another person or God, Islam demanded that the man free a slave as atonement. Over time, as more people accepted Islam and atoned for any harmful actions, more slaves were freed. This form of justice came alongside gender justice through an expanded notion of women's inheritance. Contrary to local practices at the time, the Prophet demanded that women have rights to their husbands' property and finances. Calling for women to inherit, for slaves to be freed, and for ethnic and racial equality were disruptive propositions in Mecca in the 600s, and they were Islam's first steps toward promoting goals like those that contemporary legal scholars now associate with the rule of law.

Monotheism and an understanding of Islamic ethics – social justice, women's rights, and duties owed to God and others – emerged long before any specific legal regulations in Islam. Legal regulations arose in the second phase of Islam's expansion during the Prophet's lifetime, when he moved to Medina at the age of fifty-three, where he lived for ten years until his death in 632 CE. In Medina, the Prophet cemented his role not just as a religious leader but also as political leader and jurist. Each regulation he discussed and each case he adjudicated in Medina had a clear rationale in Islamic theology or practice. One example is the full prohibition of intoxication (e.g., drinking alcohol), which crystallized in Medina after the Prophet spoke of the difficulty of reaching sufficient clarity of mind for daily prayers that are each just a few hours apart.

In the twenty-three years between the Prophet Muhammad's experience of God outside of Mecca and his death in Medina, the Islamic religion and its impact on daily life would spread thousands of miles across southwestern Asia and northern Africa, growing from one person's mountain retreat into a vast religious tradition and political empire. The earliest followers of Islam during this period engaged in at least seventy local battles and regional wars, leading to shari'a regulations on self-defense, warfare, the treatment of prisoners, and a prohibition against torture. In Medina, regulations emerged in other areas, including business transactions, finance, and trusts.

The Indeterminate Nature of Shari'a

Mainstream media and policy debates presume that shari'a is powerful, barbaric, unitary, and unrestrained – "like a wild animal," as one Somali activist put it to me. "And if . . . people hear that," he continued, "of course [they] would be scared of it."[41] Unlike these popular conceptions of it, however, shari'a is broad, interpretive, plural, and flexible, encompassing process as much as substance. It shapes and is shaped by textual interpretation of the Qur'an and Hadith and by the political history of Islamic empires and states.[42] And though shari'a encompasses much of Islam, the word only appears once in the Qur'an. Not as much a body of written laws, shari'a has evolved into a living tradition of interpreting theological texts in history, culture, and context.

Learning what counts as a source of shari'a, and the rules that allow people to discern those sources and use them to derive contemporary legislation, is a key part of studying shari'a. The sub-discipline within Islamic legal studies of determining which sources matter, how those sources matter, and the rules of interpreting those sources, is called *usul al-fiqh*, or Islamic legal theory.[43] Collectively, the first twenty-three years of Islam are the most important period from the perspective of

---

[41] Interview 32 with Axmed, lawyer and university lecturer in Hargeisa, Somaliland (June 2013).

[42] Anver Emon, *Religious Pluralism and Islamic Law: Dhimmis and Others in the Empire of Law* (Oxford: Oxford University Press, 2012).

[43] The four primary methodological areas of inquiry in *usul al-fiqh* are (1) how to use agreed-upon sources of Islam (Qur'an and Hadith); (2) how to use any disagreed-upon sources; (3) how to study legal rulings; and (4) how to decipher who has the right to make legal rulings (these persons are called *mutahideen* and *muqalideen*).

Islamic legal theory. During these twenty-three years the two major sources of shari'a and, thus, the general sources of Islamic studies and Islamic legislation – the Qur'an and the Hadith – emerged. Scholars disagree about the other sources of shari'a, but most would add two more: *qiyas* (deductive analogical reasoning by learned persons) and *ijma* (the consensus of the learned persons of a particular generation).[44] Both of these sources integrate into Islamic ethics and guide how learned persons interpret God's will.

Shari'a's specifically derived regulations – often called legislation, though these rules predate by centuries the modern notion of the state and its legislative bodies – differ widely among Muslim intellectuals and regions of the world. The sub-discipline within Islamic legal studies of determining and parsing regulations and legislation is labeled *fiqh*, commonly translated as "Islamic law," or the practical legal rulings of jurists who apply the sources of shari'a to the facts of individual cases; they "deduc[e] Islamic laws from evidence found in Islamic sources."[45] Major Islamic universities teach fiqh and usul al-fiqh as separate, multi-year courses. Fiqh has four branches; each regulates one of the main components of Islamic political and social life: worship, business transactions, family, and injuries or crimes. In these ways, shari'a is as much about content and sources as it is about methods: how to interpret Islam's source materials and what counts as source material in the first place.

The first major division between legal schools in Islam occurred about 660 CE over the lines of leadership and authority since the Prophet's death a generation earlier. This division crystallized into two groups: Sunni Muslims, who accepted the first four caliphs (*al-khulafa al-rashidoon*) after the Prophet, and Shia Muslims, who believe that the fourth caliph, Ali (the Prophet's son-in-law and cousin) had a "superior claim to leadership" over the three caliphs who preceded him.[46] Unlike the previous three, Ali was a member of the Prophet Muhammad's family lineage, which matters deeply to Shia Muslims. Sunni and Shia legal schools also differ in their approaches to legal reasoning and their interpretation of the Qur'an and Hadith.

---

[44] There are many disagreed-upon sources of legislation in Islam. These include the opinions of the Prophet Muhammad's companions, the rulings of previous religions, the public benefit (*musalah mursala*), and contemporary judges' opinions based on their life experiences (*istihsan*).

[45] Abu Ameenah Bilal Philips, *The Evolution of Fiqh (Islamic Law and the Madh-habs)* (Riyadh: International Islamic Publishing House, 1990), 12.

[46] Mohammad Hashim Kamali, *Shari'ah Law: An Introduction* (London: Oneworld Publications, 2008), 68.

Sunni Islamic law is practiced widely across Africa and southwestern Asia. Across these thousands of miles and the first five centuries of Islam, dozens of schools of law took root. Today, four schools remain among Sunni Muslims: Hanbali, Hanafi, Shafi'i and Maliki. Each school is named after a particular founder or leader (called an imam) and they disagree largely over matters of law found in jurists' decisions, not over matters of faith. The Maliki and Shafi'i schools of Sunni law have been practiced for the better part of a millennium among sheikhs and courts in northern and eastern Africa, including in Somalia and Somaliland.

Although fiqh and shari'a are considered different disciplines in Islamic legal studies, the fact that Islam long accommodated hundreds of legal orders, each with its own forms of interpretation, means that the religion from the start accommodated legal pluralism and scholarly disagreement (ikhtilaaf) in its goal of understanding God's will. Wael Hallaq, a contemporary scholar of Islamic law, argues that disagreement and pluralism are Islamic law's "central feature," which results in its special adaptability and flexibility, contrary to popular notions of Islam as rigid. Legal cases, for instance, may result in a dozen or more contradictory opinions, with no position taking a monopoly.[47] Similarly, the Qur'an and the Hadith, unlike modern statutes, should primarily appeal to individual conscience and morals. They are not to be used as lists of specific commands and prohibitions.[48]

In fact, modern Islamic legal studies scholars agree that shari'a is a "faith and a moral code first" and that its function as "a legal code is relative and subsidiary."[49] Law in Islam is "always ... subservient to theology,"[50] making any separation between law and morality "neither feasible nor recommended" in shari'a.[51] Nevertheless, as Islamic studies scholars have noted, there is a great "tendency to over-legalize Islam ... in the writing of both Muslims and Orientalists ... which does not find support in ... the Qur'an and Sunnah (Hadith)."[52] Treating Islam as more legalistic than it is fails to attend to the ways that law, morality,

---

[47] Hallaq (2009a), 27.
[48] Mohammad Hashim Kamali, *Principles of Islamic Jurisprudence*, 3rd ed. (Cambridge: Islamic Texts Society, 2005), 131.
[49] Kamali (2008), 5.
[50] Wael B. Hallaq, *Sharī'a: Theory, Practice, Transformations* (Cambridge University Press, 2009b), 79.
[51] Kamali (2008), 44.
[52] Ibid., 1.

theology, and faith are inseparable and how a collective notion of law and theology develops social and political principles of justice.

In terms of regulations, shari'a is concerned with and classifies human activity, ranging from the obligatory (*waajib*) to the recommended (*mandoob*), permissible (*mubaah*), reprehensible (*makrooh*), and forbidden (*haram*). These classifications are designed to promote ethical conduct and respect for God, humans, and the earth. Ethical conduct does not always mean that citizens must obey their leaders at all times; shari'a makes room for civil disobedience. People have a responsibility to obey their imams (religious leaders), but they may revolt against imams if revolting against them is not as harmful as living under their oppression. Indeed, religious scholars have argued that Muslims would be obligated to disobey an imam if he orders Muslims to disobey Islamic regulations on, for instance, daily prayer or alcohol consumption.[53]

Shari'a predates the concept of the rule of law and the modern state in which the term developed. But many of the values associated with the modern term also have long existed within practices associated with shari'a. Letting go of the presumption that shari'a cannot build the rule of law, and starting with the possibility that it can, opens new avenues for socio-legal research on the rule of law in Muslim-majority contexts. That is, considering it possible for shari'a to help in building the rule of law allows scholars and policymakers to see neglected phenomena and to ask more useful research questions about law's power and its relationship to society and religion.

A Socio-Legal Approach to Shari'a

The plural nature of shari'a in theory, and the fact that the state as an entity was not envisaged at the time of Islam's founding, makes it all the more important to study how shari'a is put into practice in particular societies. Studying how political elites – state officials, lawyers, educated activists, and international aid workers – use the term helps uncover its changing configurations in politics. A socio-legal study of shari'a becomes a way to address this gap between shari'a in theory and actual practices in Muslim-majority societies.[54] For scholars of law and

---

[53] Shaykh Muhammad Al-Khudari Bak Al-Bajuri, *The History of the Four Caliphs (Itmam al-Wafa'fi Sirat al-Khulafa)* (London: Turath Publishing, 2012), 29.

[54] On the relationship between legal pluralism, legal orders, and legal institutions in Muslim-majority societies, see Ido Shahar, "Legal Pluralism and the Study of Shari'a Courts," 15 *Islamic Law and Society* (2008): 112–141.

society who care about the law's effects, what shari'a does becomes more relevant than what it actually says.[55] That is, the empirical, interpretive, and historical methods of law and society are well-suited to investigating the interplay among shari'a, social structures, political institutions, economic development, and cultural practices.

Like the meaning of the rule of law or the value of rights, shari'a is socially and politically embedded. Socio-legal scholars have long argued that using legal tools or litigation strategies, even when those strategies fail, can still mobilize people into movements.[56] The discourse of rights works for people when they put it, and the malleable symbols of law, into practice to achieve pay equity, gender equality, or economic reform, among other aims. People may appropriate or even come to love human rights ideals, particularly when those ideals provide an alternative to discriminatory legislation.[57] The project of making rights visible has many beginnings; people's views of what rights entail, what hope rights provide, and how to achieve those hopes emanate from personal and political beliefs, class backgrounds, experiences of discrimination, religious observances, or some combination.[58] In other words, religion matters for rights, and Islam is no exception.

Although anti-Muslim organizations often conflate shari'a with extremism, at its core shari'a's radicalism resides in its plurality, not its rigidity.[59] Shari'a accommodates many divergent legal opinions. As in any attempt by political authorities to integrate a belief system or legal system into the state, the intention of the person using the thing they call "Islamic" matters. While they may use Islam to combat the rule of law, they may also use it to build political values that outlast bad leaders and badly designed political institutions. For many contemporary Muslims, the desire for a more Islamic state may reflect a deeper wish to restrain state authorities.[60] Islamism is, thus, not merely a statement

---

[55] Studying what shari'a does, rather than what shari'a says, is consistent with calls in socio-legal studies for "new legal realism," or the study of law and society at close range, using empirical methods. On new legal realism and Islam, see Massoud (2016a).

[56] Michael McCann, *Rights at Work: Pay Equity Reform and the Politics of Legal Mobilization* (Chicago, IL: University of Chicago Press, 1994).

[57] Lynette J. Chua, *The Politics of Love in Myanmar: LGBT Mobilization and Human Rights as a Way of Life* (Stanford, CA: Stanford University Press, 2019).

[58] Mark Fathi Massoud, "Legal Poverty and the Rule of Law in Strife-Torn States," 34(2) *Whittier Law Review* (2013b): 245–259.

[59] On the spread of anti-Muslim organizations and their influence on mass media and public policy, see Christopher Bail, *Terrified: How Anti-Muslim Fringe Organizations Became Mainstream* (Princeton, NJ: Princeton University Press, 2015).

[60] Northern Nigerians, for instance, have hearkened back to early Islam to envision social justice when they feel contemporary governments cannot deliver it. Sarah Eltantawi, *Shari'ah on Trial:*

of one's political leanings as much as it is the infusion of "law, politics, and society with Islamic values."[61] Hegemony in Islam is not presumed or imprinted; it must be cultivated and, with so much internal disagreement among Islamic scholars, is easily resisted. In these ways, the meaning of shari'a changes when it is put into practice, depending on who uses it and their social, political, and economic goals.

Ultimately, like many forms of law – domestic, international, and transnational – shari'a rests on broad principles like justice (*'adl*), being good to others (*ihsan*), and easing people's hardships through moderation and balance (*wasatiyya*).[62] In practice, however, different people – from colonial administrators to state officials and contemporary aid workers – breathe their own meanings of justice, good conscience, and relief from hardship into shari'a, just as they do into the law. Shari'a has endured, though its meanings and uses have shifted across time and space.[63] For these reasons, to many lawyers, activists, and officials, shari'a presents a particular form of legal power that they know they must engage, whether they assert it, constrain it, or challenge it.

In adopting a socio-legal approach to shari'a, this book does not appeal to a nostalgic return to Islam's roots in Mecca or Medina, or to Islamic originalism. The practical uses of shari'a are regularly contested, and even defining the term and the intents with which people use it can be political acts. A socio-legal approach to shari'a entails investigating the social disruptions, discontinuities, and disobediences that emerge when people invoke shari'a to fight for freedom and limit the authority of those holding power. These disruptions existed at the arrival of Islam. They also appear in the development of many Muslim-majority societies and, as the remaining chapters show, throughout colonial and postcolonial Somali history.

LAW AND RELIGION IN SOMALI HISTORY

Somalia and Somaliland present an important case of the versatility of law and shari'a. Their radical legal pluralism amidst the human struggle to

Northern Nigeria's Islamic Revolution (Oakland, CA: University of California Press, 2017); Ebenezer Odabare, *Pentecostal Republic: Religion and the Struggle for State Power in Nigeria* (London: Zed Books, 2018).

[61] Matthew Cavedon, "Men of the Spear and Men of God: Islamism's Contributions to the New Somali State," 28 *Emory International Law Review* (2014): 473–508, p. 476.

[62] Kamali (2008), 23–24.

[63] On the importance of transnational religious ideologies in shaping national security in Muslim-majority countries, see Lawrence Rubin, *Islam in the Balance: Ideational Threats in Arab Politics* (Stanford, CA: Stanford University Press, 2014).

survive political violence makes them even more critical settings for understanding the endurance of shari'a and the hope that it can represent for the rule of law. Given the region's multi-colonial legacies, the legal culture of the Horn of Africa is notable not for its absence of law but for the heterogeneity of its legal systems. In the twentieth century, Britain, France, Italy, Ethiopia, and Kenya each at various times staked ownership claims or possessory rights over the various parts of the Horn of Africa where Somalis lived. They brought with them ideas about laws, legal institutions, and geopolitical borders that Somalis would use or integrate into their own. European administrators departed during the 1950s and 1960s, paving the way for the region's decades-long alternations between democratic, socialist, and authoritarian rule; civil war; and state collapse. Across these political machinations, Somali communities created and used their own forms of dispute resolution – informed in part by religion, tradition, and colonial heritage – to assert local forms of order. Such highly localized dispute resolution further fragmented the law, giving the state much less control over disputes than it has in other societies with stronger and less heterogeneous legal systems.

Both its colonial legacies and its local needs, therefore, inform the Horn of Africa's legal pluralism. This pluralism is matched by the homogenizing actions of colonial administrators, government officials, and foreign aid workers seeking to create a single legal system that the state, even if weak, can control. Despite these efforts, Islam over time has emerged as a centralizing and unifying feature across these diverse ways of maintaining peace and order. That is, Islam and shari'a are the most unifying legal forces in Somalia and Somaliland, despite the fact that colonial administrations, state officials, and aid workers have encouraged the development of state legal systems that subsume and regulate religion. "It is difficult," according to one Somali aid worker I met in Kenya, "for Somalis to recall what legal system existed prior to Islam."[64] To them, Islam is the cornerstone of human life and, thus, woven into society's legal fabric. Despite the different European and African legal legacies infused into Somali society, "there is one legal history ... in common, and that is Islam."[65]

Islam arrived in the Horn of Africa in the seventh century during the caliphate of Abu Bakr, the successor to the Prophet Muhammad.[66] The

---

[64] Interview 80 with Gul, aid worker in Nairobi, Kenya (August 2013).
[65] Ibid.
[66] Michael Shank, "Understanding Political Islam in Somalia," 1(1) *Contemporary Islam* (2007): 89–103, citing H. Hassan, *Intishar al-Islam wa-al-Urubah Fima yali al-Sahra al-Kubra Sharq al-Qarra al-Ifriqiyyah wa-Gharbiha* (Cairo: Matba-at Lujnat al-Bayan al-Arabi, 1957), 127.

religion began to flourish, but it collapsed as the Horn of Africa entered a period of chaos and tribal rule. In the twelfth century, Muslim sheikhs from the Arabian Peninsula arrived as missionaries to revive African Islam and made the earliest known attempts to build what contemporary legal scholars would now call the rule of law in the region. The Muslim missionaries' goal was to unite disparate groups of Africans across the Horn by preaching about how Islam would help them build peace and create stable, non-arbitrary rules to govern relations amongst themselves.[67] Their preaching attracted new followers and, by the fifteenth century, Islam became the major religion in the Horn.[68] Awareness of this early history means that Somalis continue to see Islam as part of the project of building the institutions of the modern state. Islam matters not only as a religion, but also as a deeply ingrained political culture with oral traditions handed down to each new generation. In contemporary practice, many persons I met felt driven to resolve disputes through religious principles out of "simplicity," as one Somali lawyer told me. "There are no lawyers . . . . In shari'a there is a duty on the . . . judge to find the truth."[69]

Although Islam is a central and shared feature among the Somalis of the Horn of Africa, they also have a common language and common social structures in which patrilineal relations create trust and status. Twentieth-century European anthropologists typically called this scheme of trust and status Somalia's "clan" system. The clan system that European anthropologists, who often worked with or on behalf of colonial administrations, attributed to Somalis has remained scholars' and policymakers' primary designator for Somali society. Somalis, international aid workers, and government officials whom I met used it regularly to explain local cultural norms and practices to me and to one another. While one's clan gives one kin with whom to connect, the clan is more than a patrilineal origin or a network tying together a few dozen to a few hundred people. It is also an insurance policy whereby an aggrieved party – for instance, the victim of a vehicle theft or the survivor of a vehicle collision – appeals to the sultan of their clan to negotiate a settlement with the sultan of the clan whose member caused the injury or harm. No settlement is unique or arbitrary; each is based

---

[67] Egal (1968), 221.
[68] Shank (2007), citing Christopher Ehret, "The Eastern Horn of Africa, 1000 B.C. to 1400 A.D.: The Historical Roots," in *The Invention of Somalia*, ed. Ali Jimale Ahmed (Lawrenceville, NJ: Red Sea Press, 1995), 233–256, p. 254.
[69] Interview 32 with Axmed, lawyer and university lecturer in Hargeisa, Somaliland (June 2013).

on precedent between those two communities when similar past vehicle thefts or collisions occurred. If the harm is totally new – such as the theft of an iPad – then its settlement becomes precedent for future similar harms suffered between those two communities. In the long term, like insurance schemes and court systems, the process protects the two groups from retributory violence. The rules of these settlements – collectively called xeer – draw from local custom and from shari'a, which inform one another. The devotion to family lineage is so entrenched in society that Somalis joke that one's clan may be more important than religion, even to the most pious: "*Sheikh tolkiis kama janno tego*," or "Even the sheikh will choose loyalty to his clan over paradise."[70]

The clan system creates some semblance of order between local communities. Islam is a central feature of that social fabric, tying disparate groups to a legacy transmitted across generations and places.[71] That is, while Somalis and many scholars who study the place often emphasize the clan as the central unit of Somali identity, religion is a life-thread of social identity throughout the region. Islam matters in the stories people share about themselves. "If people are not satisfied [or] see injustice," one young lawyer told me, "that drives them to shari'a."[72] Despite their many clans and contemporary family lines, Somalis nevertheless "claim a common descent from Quraish, the tribe of the Prophet Mohammed."[73] More recently, in the wake of the state's collapse in 1991, leaders from diverse clans that sought to return law and order to Mogadishu turned first to Islam, setting up their own shari'a courts in the city. While fragmented clan mechanisms of settling disputes are common, Islam continues to play a lasting and unifying role in society.

---

[70] Robrecht Deforche, "Stabilization and Common Identity: Reflections on the Islamic Courts Union and Al-Itihaad," 13 *Bildhaan: An International Journal of Somali Studies* (2013): 102–120, p. 104.

[71] On the politics of the clan, see I. M. Lewis, *A Modern History of the Somali: Nation and State in the Horn of Africa* (London: Boydell and Brewer, 2003). For a critique of the colonial formation of the clan nomenclature, see Lidwien Kapteijns, "I. M. Lewis and Somali Clanship: A Critique," 11(1) *Northeast African Studies* (2004): 1–23.

[72] Follow-up interview 93 with Caziz, lawyer and human rights activist in Hargeisa, Somaliland (June 2014).

[73] Deforche (2013), 104, citing I. M. Lewis, "Visible and Invisible Differences: The Somali Paradox," 74 *Africa: Journal of the International Africa Institute* (2004): 489–451; Mohamed Haji Mukhtar, "Islam in Somali History: Fact and Fiction," in *The Invention of Somalia*, ed. Ali Jimale Ahmed (Lawrenceville, NJ: Red Sea Press, 1995), 1–28.

A Case in Disaster

Excepting discussions of Somaliland's political stability relative to that of Somalia, rarely do scholars write about the region as exemplifying even minimal political or legal success.[74] Rather, they regard Somalia as the archetype of political disaster. Writing in 1995, four years after President Siad Barre fled Mogadishu and the country descended into warlord rule, political scientist Ken Menkhaus and policy analyst John Prendergast argued that "There was never in Somalia's history a sustainable basis for a viable central state authority."[75] Peter Woodward, a historian of the region, similarly argued that the Somali state and the authoritarian regime of Mohamed Siad Barre had become almost synonymous, such that when that regime collapsed, it took the state with it.[76]

The perspective that Somalia is the world's bastion of lawlessness is underscored by decades of authoritarian and warlord rule, millions of refugees who fled the country, and thirteen failed national peace conferences during the 1990s.[77] As anthropologist Anna Simons writes, disaster was fueled not by any single political party or matter, but by misunderstanding on all sides:

> Expatriates ... misunderstood Somalis, Somalis misunderstood one another, the West misperceived the "state" of Somalia, the regime in Somalia misunderstood its exact place in the world, and all sides mistook the extent to which they could or could not influence events and each other. And the compounded result of all of this misunderstanding has been singular disaster.[78]

Some scholars of Somalia and Somaliland have noted that the region's myriad problems and weak rule of law stem from the political

[74] Somalia's economy improved slightly during its "stateless" years of the 1990s, compared to the period during its civil war of the 1980s. Benjamin Powell, Ryan Ford, and Alex Nowrasteh, "Somalia after State Collapse: Chaos or Improvement?" 67(3–4) *Journal of Economic Behavior & Organization* (2008): 657–670.
[75] Ken Menkhaus and John Prendergast, "Governance and Economic Survival in Post-intervention Somalia," 172 *CSIS Africa Note* (May 1995): 1–10.
[76] Peter Woodward, *The Horn of Africa: State Politics and International Relations* (New York: Tauris Academic Studies, 1996).
[77] A peace conference in Djibouti in 2000 set up Somalia's Transitional National Government (TNG). In 2004, the TNG was replaced by Somalia's Transitional Federal Government (TFG), which political leaders set up in Nairobi. The TFG was based in exile in Baidoa, Somalia, due to insecurity in Somalia's capital, Mogadishu.
[78] Anna Simons, *Network of Dissolution: Somalia Undone* (Boulder, CO: Westview Press, 1996), cited in Abdurahman M. Abdullahi, "Perspectives on the State Collapse in Somalia," in *Somalia at the Crossroads: Challenges and Perspectives in Reconstituting a Failed State*, eds. Abdulahi Osman and Issaka Souaré (London: Adonis & Abbey, 2007a), 40–57, p. 40.

extremes toward which Somalis have been pushed: the fight for secu-larism on the one hand and the promotion of unfettered religious radicalism on the other hand. To these scholars, the tension between these two extremes brought about a moral breakdown, including when Somalis used Islam to pursue nefarious political goals or satisfy personal impulses.[79] However, political elites turn to shari'a even as they dis-agree about it.

The Somali Legal Order

Most people would presume that the Horn of Africa represents an extreme setting where shari'a is the tool of jihadists, autocrats, and warlords seeking to justify irrationality and violence. Amidst political discord and fragmentation, however, Somalis have time and again used shari'a to fight colonialism, challenge dictatorship, and limit the power of militants and warlords.

For example, Somaliland's experimental democracy since 1991 has provided strong evidence of peacebuilding and political progress, and shari'a has been an important part of that transition. Somaliland was unified with Somalia in 1960, days after its colonial independence was granted, but that union was de facto broken in May 1991 when Somaliland reasserted its nationhood. Putting down guns and deliber-ating over peace accords mattered in the short term. But when it came time to consider a long-term solution that would be viable across Somaliland, a national constitution was drafted and put into force in 2001 that framed Islam as the primary source of Somaliland's law. These Islamic provisions of the constitution provide a basis for citizens and interest groups to challenge any laws passed by the government in order to ensure they are consistent with the principles within shari'a of justice and fairness. The constitution also includes a bill of rights, ostensibly rooted in international human rights law, yet constitutional architects I met made clear that both shari'a and international law were working together to create a broader set of political principles to guide the new nation.

Somalis and foreign aid workers often explained to me that the Somali people in the Horn of Africa have three overlapping legal systems – or three pivots of the same legal system. One is based largely on shari'a, a second on Somali custom, and a third on laws created by

[79] Ahmed Samatar, "The Curse of Allah: Civic Disembowelment and the Collapse of the State in Somalia," in *The Somali Challenge: From Catastrophe to Renewal?* ed. Ahmed Samatar (Boulder, CO: Lynne Reinner Publishers, 1994), 129.

the state or by foreign or international entities.[80] As one Somali told me, when he and his family members had disputes, they entered any forum they could – those led by sheikhs, elders, or state court judges – to achieve their desired results.[81] Like many others I met, he was pragmatic about using a variety of legal systems or venues to pursue his goals. Because these diverse systems have coexisted since the nineteenth-century arrival of Western powers to the Horn of Africa, law plays an outsize role in social relations but, as a former senior minister told me, "not in the Western sense."[82]

I asked my interviewees to describe these three Somali legal systems or orders, and the results were remarkable. Collectively they used only a handful of words to define shari'a and custom, seeing these two legal orders as distinct, but fairly unitary. But they defined the third legal system in much more amorphous terms (Table 1.2). Some called it "law," while others referred to it variously as colonial law, Western law, authoritarian law, and international law.

This lumping of terms like "international law," "human rights," and the "rule of law" with colonialism and authoritarianism led Somalis to see the modern concept of the rule of law as, at best, amorphous or, at worst, yet another imposition linked with the problems of foreign military intervention and also as contrary to shari'a.[83] The Somalis I met did not often use the term "rule of law" itself – unless I asked them or they were speaking about a "rule-of-law program" instituted by the local United Nations office. But when they did mention it, they placed it in the same category as authoritarian law, colonial law, and Western law. The term rule of law carried weight for foreign diplomats, aid workers, and the Somalis who worked most closely with these groups. But the principles within it were still important to Somali people who spoke to me about the ideals they wanted to see in society and how they saw Islam fulfilling them. Those ideals included a limited state that responds to people's needs and promotes justice and environmental protection – in other words, they often matched the values

---

[80] Le Sage (2005) adds civil-society and private-sector justice initiatives to these three systems.

[81] Interview 59 with Kalim, former NGO executive director in Hargeisa, Somaliland (July 2013).

[82] Interview 87 with Muuse, retired senior government minister in Mogadishu, Somalia (conducted in Addis Ababa, Ethiopia) (August 2013).

[83] For similar findings on the relationship between religion, humanitarianism, and modernity, see Ann Swidler, "African Affirmations: The Religion of Modernity and the Modernity of Religion," 28(6) *International Sociology* (2013): 680–696.

Table 1.2 Terms for Somali legal orders

Shari'a	Xeer	Law
Islam	Customary	Formal system
"Effective law"	Traditional	Courts
	Informal	Formal law
	Pastoral	State law
	Clan law	Secular law
		Civil code
		Civil courts
		Conventional law
		Rule of law
		Government law
		British law and statutes
		Civil law
		European law
		European colonial legal system
		Indian penal code imported by British colonial administrators
		Constitution
		Codified law
		Statutory law
		Positive law
		Modern law
		National law
		Colonial law
		Western law
		International law
		Continental law
		"The new legal systems of the international community"
		"Laws enacted by Parliament"
		"Socialist law under Siad Barre"
		"Ordinary judicial system"
		"What do they call [this] one? Is it secular? It confuses me sometimes"

Source: Derived from author interviews.

that Western lawyers and international policymakers relate to the rule of law. Somalis I met largely saw shari'a as the "effective law."[84]

When I asked how the notion of human rights fit into the commonly discussed tripartite format of law in Somalia and Somaliland, some said it was part of shari'a and others saw it as operating within the state. Like the term rule of law, "human rights" as a term (rather than as a principle) was something largely foreign or implemented by foreigners, even though shari'a has its own conceptions of rights, protections, and duties derived from the Qur'an and the Hadith. These various ways of talking about custom, religion, and law continue to guide people's habits and views of what is familiar and what is foreign. And these diverse meanings of the legal order exist alongside a broader perception that the "law" itself still resides in the state's texts. As one former judge told me, despite myriad competing and overlapping legal systems, and many legal codes drafted or finalized, "People [still] say there are not a lot of laws here."[85]

Beyond the Horn of Africa

While the conclusions in *Shari'a, Inshallah* are based on Somalia and Somaliland, these are not the only political spaces where shari'a has existed or an Islamic-based statehood has been desired.[86] For example, Sudan has defined itself politically under Islam, saturating state rhetoric and laws with it as well as, more importantly, radio, television, public advertisements, and art.[87] In northern Nigeria, people have come to see shari'a as an alternative system that would curb the excesses and corruption of secular political institutions. Following US-led invasions, the 2004 constitution of Afghanistan and the 2005 constitution of Iraq both put Islamic identity and jurisprudence at the center of the countries' legal development. The first part of the Malaysian constitution designates Islam as the country's official religion. Egypt, Iran, Libya, Pakistan, and Tunisia have similarly constituted themselves on Islamic

---

[84] Interview 4 with Adnan, law graduate from Somaliland in London, England (June 2013).

[85] Interview 58 with Hussein, university lecturer and former judge in Hargeisa, Somaliland (July 2013).

[86] Though the self-declared Islamic State (ISIS) is a different type of nationalistic enterprise, it operates beyond the boundaries of nation-states recognized under public international law. William McCants, *The ISIS Apocalypse: The History, Strategy, and Doomsday Vision of the Islamic State* (New York: St. Martin's Press, 2015).

[87] Noah Salomon, *For Love of the Prophet: An Ethnography of Sudan's Islamic State* (Princeton, NJ: Princeton University Press, 2016).

terms. In diverse contexts in Africa and Asia, people have placed their hopes of ensuring immediate survival and long-term social and political health in their own ideas of an Islamic state.

This phenomenon is not new. In British Somaliland, colonial administrators also found hope in the idea that their vision of Islam would hold back Somali anti-colonial activists, while those activists similarly turned shari'a against the British. Likewise, Siad Barre justified his postcolonial dictatorship by claiming that socialist principles were consistent with Islam, while the sheikhs who disagreed with him did so on religious grounds, and paid for their disagreement with their lives. Muslim activists continue to use religious principles to promote gender justice in politics and daily life in the Horn of Africa and beyond it.

Somali society's different political epochs, diverse as they have been, are marked by extreme forms of competition between distinct legal orders vying for the attention of political elites – state leaders, chiefs, sultans, aqils, elders, and sheikhs – and everyday people seeking to resolve their disputes. Through it all, they agree on the importance of Islam. If there is to be any single state or group of states for Somalis in the Horn of Africa, people consistently told me, these states would have to be Islamic, or at least consistent with Islam in name if not in practice. Somali political elites' attempts at state-building reveal how shari'a has come to mean different things when put into practice, depending on the goals of the actor using shari'a. Ultimately, shari'a matters to all of them, as they invest their private hopes into shari'a, and then work shari'a into the state.

PART I

COLONIALISM AND ITS
AFTERMATH, 1884–1991

The Horn of Africa's European colonial administrations
(this chapter's focus is British Somaliland).

CHAPTER TWO

CONTESTING SHARI'A:
COLONIAL LEGAL POLITICS

> I have sought and found the Prophetic guidance
> To tell the unbelieving white invaders:
> This land is not yours.
> > Sheikh Mohamed Abdullah Hassan, *Dardaaran*
> > ("The Will"), composed during his struggle
> > against British colonialism[1]

On a cool afternoon in Hargeisa, I met with a prominent sheikh. As we shared a pot of tea while sitting cross-legged together on a large rug in his office, I mentioned I had come to see him for a book I was hoping to write about law in Somalia and Somaliland. He nodded, raised a corner of his lips into half a smile, and began by discussing his grandfather. The sheikh called his grandfather "the most prominent sheikh in [colonial]

---

[1] Said Samatar, *Oral Poetry and Somali Nationalism: The Case of Sayid Mahammad 'Abdille Hasan* (Cambridge: Cambridge University Press, 1982), 1.

Somaliland ... famous and very rich."[2] He had sired more than seventy sons and daughters from many wives, I was told. Colonial officials had appointed him to the prestigious post of qadi (judge of an Islamic court). Once a Somali man was brought to his grandfather's court for killing a British soldier, and his grandfather the qadi ordered the killer to pay fifty camels in *diyya* (roughly translated as blood money). A British official asked the qadi why the families of slain Somalis received 100 camels, but this diyya judgment would be only fifty camels. The qadi responded that, under shari'a, the murdered British man was considered *ahl al-kitaab* (a Jew or Christian; literally, in Arabic, "a person of the book"), so the diyya was half of what a Muslim would receive. Had the deceased been neither Jewish nor Christian, the qadi continued, compensation to the British man's family would have been even less – only one-third the number of camels for a murdered Muslim.

Colonial officials and Somalis in the Horn of Africa disagreed over whose law ought to prevail. They each tried to impose a distinct vision of law, including religious law, onto the other and onto society. Radically plural legal practices, institutions, and personnel mediated the delicate balance both parties struck between tradition and modernity, rights and duties, and faith and secularism, as individual actors also sought to fulfill their own desires for political influence, economic wealth, or adherence to the rule of law. This use of legal mechanisms to achieve economic, social, or political goals – that is, legal politics – shaped colonial relationships between British officials and Somalis.

Insofar as British officials were concerned with religion, they were not trying to purge Islam from Somali life so much as change how Somalis used it outside their mosques. British officials sought to update or "modernize" Islam to fit their civilizing and state-building missions.[3] But even as they sought to stem the rise of versions of shari'a with which they disagreed, they seemed to submit to Islamic legal politics themselves by promoting their own version of shari'a. As Somalis attempted alternatingly to benefit from and resist colonial domination, they too turned to a blend of legal and religious discourse. Drawing on the case of

---

[2] Interview 127 with Sheikh Oweis, sheikh and senior university administrator in Hargeisa, Somaliland (June 2014).

[3] These efforts to bring religion into colonial politics are in contrast to the attempts to purge religion from politics in Europe, during the Soviet Union's Bolshevik revolution and through World War II. Adeeb Khalid, *Islam after Communism: Religion and Politics in Central Asia* (Oakland, CA: University of California Press, 2014); Pedro Ramet, ed., *Religion and Nationalism in Soviet and East European Politics* (Durham, NC: Duke University Press, 1989).

the British Somaliland Protectorate (hereafter "British Somaliland"), this chapter documents the colonial legal politics of religion.

British colonial officials and Somalis fought not only by forming militias and killing each other but also by engaging in a battle of ideas over what law means. The war of words concerned which group – Europeans or Africans – was best suited to resolve people's disputes, to interpret and teach law, and ultimately to win the support of the nomadic and pastoral Muslim communities spread across the northern Horn of Africa's grasslands and deserts. This discursive contestation over who had the power to control law, and whose interpretations of shari'a were more legitimate, ran through the colonial project and remains the key legacy that has shaped Somali politics since, including its postcolonial periods of democratic and autocratic rule, the state's 1991 collapse, and the ensuing attempts at reconstruction, resurrection, and constitutionalism.

My research for this chapter draws primarily on colonial records I consulted in the United Kingdom. I have supplemented this documentary evidence with fieldwork and interviews I conducted with Somalis who worked for or lived under the British colonial administration, or with their descendants. The chapter focuses on British Somaliland, though I draw parallels to Italian Somalia (*Somalia Italiana*) where relevant. This chapter shows how both colonial officials and those resisting them expressed their developmental goals, revolutionary hopes, and political fears through legal and religious discourses. Surprisingly, both colonial administrators and anticolonial activists used the same political strategy to pursue their opposing goals of building a governing apparatus or tearing it down: establishing law and courts to help people resolve their disputes. But in neither case was promoting law enough to build the rule of law, nor even to establish stable legal institutions that would someday ensure the rule of law. At the same time, both British administrators and those who fought them used Islam as a tool of legal politics, with each side invoking shari'a against the other in a battle for political power.

Legal pluralism served colonial interests by making Somalis seem ungovernable. It was through colonialism's separation of shari'a, *xeer* (Somali custom), and English common law that a rigid and tripartite form of legal pluralism took shape. In it, three separate legal systems vied for legal power: religious, traditional, and "modern."[4] This legal

---

[4] Somalis have given various names for each of these systems, including the "modern" system introduced largely by the British (cf. Table 1.2 of this book).

pluralism became a tool of colonial authority. The idea that the Horn of Africa was an ungovernable space – in part because Somalis were still applying non-British-approved versions of shari'a and customary law – began to become entrenched. Rigid jurisdictional boundaries between legal systems were further hardened by Somalis and colonial-era anthropologists whose research on dispute resolution and kinship made its way back to the region.[5] Colonialism compartmentalized the people and the procedures of dispute resolution, shaping how Somalis viewed themselves as a clan-oriented people navigating through a troubled legal scene and pulled between the demands of religious law, clan law, and foreign law.

Paradoxically, even as the British attempted to build a secular colonial state, they also waged an Islamic resistance of their own. In particular, the anticolonial nationalist movement led by Sheikh (Sayyid) Mohamed Abdullah Hassan, a Somali leader who had studied in Mecca, had to confront a British colonial administration that deployed its own transnational Islamic discourse – using statements by religious leaders and envoys in Mecca and Sudan – against Sheikh Hassan. Confronting diversity among Muslims in their understandings and practices of Islam, the British became partisans in the battle, promoting some views of shari'a over others and capitalizing on debates between Muslims over whether Sheikh Hassan's actions were consistent with shari'a. Shari'a was an important part of the state, restricted to the Islamic courts that the British had instituted. These courts and written communications from British officials explained dutifully to Sheikh Hassan and his followers the administration's official view of shari'a's meanings, with support from Mecca.

After exploring the Horn of Africa's multi-colonial legacy, the chapter turns first to the law and discusses four essential features of colonial legal politics, with a focus on British Somaliland: (1) drawing up colonial charters or political agreements between colonial officials and local notables designed to allow foreigners to enter the territory; (2) managing disputes by controlling local custom; (3) employing a new class of legal professionals to resolve disputes; and (4) establishing Islamic (qadi) courts. After examining the importance of legal politics in creating the colonial state, the chapter then turns to religious politics, particularly the ways in which British officials and Somali

---

[5] See, for example, I. M. Lewis, *The Somali Lineage System and the Total Genealogy: A General Introduction to the Basic Principles of Somali Political Institutions*, presented March 18, 1958, to the Royal Anthropological Institute, MS 191 (London: RAI Archives, 1958a).

intellectuals took Islam into war by fighting discursive battles over the meaning of shari'a.

The chapter thus illuminates key events in which both law and religion came to matter for colonial officials and their adversaries: the treaties between British officials and Somali elders that forged Britain's coastal outpost in the mid-1880s; the establishment of courts to resolve people's disputes; and the two-decade war (1899–1920) between the British administration and the followers of Sheikh Hassan. That war was among the longest and greatest tests that shari'a ever put on a British colonial administration. Estimates suggest that 200,000 to 300,000 Somalis were killed because of this conflict – that is, nearly a third of the Somali population of approximately one million – which makes it one of the most devastating wars in the region's history.

Sheikh Hassan was not the only Somali to use Islam in the struggle against colonial rule. Other Islamic-oriented anticolonial movements in the region included the struggle that led to the Lafole massacre (1896), the Biimal revolt (1896–1908), and the revolts led by Sheikh Hassan Barsane (d. 1926) and Sheikh Bashir (d. 1945).[6] The shared use of Islam by colonial rulers, by those who struggled against colonialism, and by those who sought to repress anticolonialism was a central and enduring feature of shari'a politics in the Horn of Africa. The chapter concludes by examining the implications of this colonial legal politics for the study of law, shari'a, and state development.

MULTIPLE COLONIAL LEGACIES

The Horn of Africa is home to a population consisting primarily of Muslims of Somali lineage. Colonialism split the Horn into five areas: British Somaliland, Italian Somalia, French Somaliland, the Ogaden area of eastern Ethiopia, and the Northern Frontier District of Kenya. A small number of non-Somalis (mostly Europeans, Arabs, and South Asians) and non-Muslims (Jews and Christians) also lived in the Horn during the colonial period.[7] The region, which "flanks the [trade] route to India," has been colonized by perhaps more foreigners than anywhere else on the continent – first by the Egyptians with Turkish assistance

---

[6] Abdurahman M. Abdullahi, "Perspectives on the State Collapse in Somalia," in *Somalia at the Crossroads: Challenges and Perspectives in Reconstituting a Failed State*, eds. Abdulahi Osman and Issaka Souaré (London: Adonis & Abbey, 2007a), 40–57, p. 41.

[7] Saadia Touval, *Somali Nationalism: International Politics and the Drive for Unity in the Horn of Africa* (Cambridge, MA: Harvard University Press, 1963), 11–13.

through most of the nineteenth century and then, starting in the 1880s, by the Ethiopians, the British, the Italians, and the French.[8] Each of these foreign empires carved up a different part of the Horn for itself. While the Germans never formally colonized the region, their watchful gaze, and rumors of negotiations with Italy to purchase land in Italian Somalia, reemphasized the region's importance to European empires.

As early as 1870 the British government expressed interest in adding the Horn of Africa to its colonial empire. British military records suggest that the army conducted its own reconnaissance of the region around that time to determine which foreign actors controlled the coastline. They found that each Somali group along East Africa's coast had its own sultan. These nobles, who were sometimes also called chiefs, knew Somali and Islamic law. But there was no European presence, which helped the British government justify its plans to secure trade routes to Aden (across the Gulf of Aden) and South and East Asia.[9]

Though Egypt did have some military presence in Somaliland, in 1884 an opening emerged for the British. Egypt had begun to turn its attention to a nationalist and Islamic revolution in Sudan, led by the self-proclaimed Mahdi ("anointed one").[10] Because Sudan is upstream on the Nile River, Egypt's essential source of water for agriculture, the revolution there threatened Egypt's security. As the Egyptian military shifted its focus away from the East African coast, a British constabulary began policing the region. Accounts vary as to the precise rationales for the British entry that year, but colonial communications reveal a desire to maintain Britain's regional dominance.[11] The British probably also sought to be the first Europeans to fill the power vacuum left by the Egyptians; French, German, and Italian competitors were nearby. In addition, the region's strategic location linked Europe and the Suez Canal with South and East Asia, and the Horn offered known resources, including fish, camels, goats, and sheep. Finally, British military officials were cognizant of Sudan's nationalist rebellion, in

---

[8] Untitled cutting, June 18, 1909. *Liverpool Daily Courier*. Sudan Archive, Durham University, SAD 287/3/78.

[9] Colonel Stanton, "Memorandum on Turkish Claims to Sovereignty over the Soumali [sic] Territory," June 3, 1870. Foreign Office Confidential Prints, Bodleian Law Library, Oxford University, document 1949.

[10] Robert O. Collins, *A History of Modern Sudan* (Cambridge: Cambridge University Press, 2008); Mark Fathi Massoud, *Law's Fragile State: Colonial, Authoritarian, and Humanitarian Legacies in Sudan* (Cambridge: Cambridge University Press, 2013a), 51–53.

[11] "Letter from Wilfred G. Thesiger at the British Legation," Addis Ababa, October 11, 1917. Sudan Archive, Durham University, SAD 125/8/21.

which some British generals and soldiers had been killed, and likely wanted to stave off the possibility of another Mahdist rebellion on the Somali coast. Working with Somali sultans and elders would maintain local order and help open trade discussions between Somalis and the British, who needed resources like food and camels for their military outpost in Aden.

A sustained British presence, rendered official by treaties between British officials and Somali elders, began about 1884. From that year through 1960, British officials would stake their claim to the territory along the African coast of the Gulf of Aden not by force, but by signing legal agreements with Somali sultans, giving them official duties, writing new laws, and developing a colonial relationship with shari'a. The British saw Somali sultans as the official representatives of the region's diverse nomadic and kinship communities. Collectively, the treaties established what Great Britain would call the British Somaliland Protectorate. The British promised "friendly tribes" military protection while agreeing not to interfere with Somali affairs, settle on Somali lands, or marry Somali women. In turn, the Somalis promised to allow British people and British coastal vessels to move freely and conduct trade, and pledged not to cede any territory to non-British Europeans. On the one hand, these agreements meant British Somaliland was not an official colony overseen by London's Colonial Office and, thus, merited less attention from the metropole than, say, India or the Gold Coast. The British, particularly early on, were not attempting to create a state in the same way they did in the twentieth century in places like colonial Nigeria, India, or Sudan. On the other hand, Somalis certainly did not escape British meddling.

In the mid-1880s, as the Egyptians were departing the northern Horn and the British were arriving, Italians began to settle the Horn's lush eastern coast, just south of British Somaliland. The British and Italian colonial projects differed in two primary respects. First, the British government ran its colony directly, employing a small network of British district commissioners and military officials, sometimes seconding them to Somaliland for short periods from other overseas colonial postings. The Italian Foreign Ministry, on the other hand, began its colonial project by outsourcing it to charter companies that were under strict instruction to "maintain good relations with ... native[s] ... in order to attract their trade."[12] The Filonardi Company governed areas of southern Somalia

---

[12] Robert Hess, *Italian Colonialism in Somalia* (Chicago, IL: University of Chicago Press, 1966), 39, citing a June 15, 1893 letter from Foreign Minister Brin in Rome to Filonardi, from *Documenti*

from 1893 to 1896. Following a gap from 1896 until 1899, the Benadir Company took over until 1905. (Italy governed Italian Somalia directly from 1905 to 1941, when it fell to British military occupation.)

Second, the British and Italian colonial projects differed in type of settlement. While the British agreed not to settle non-Somalis in British Somaliland, the charter companies of Italian Somalia were busy creating settler colonies for Italians. One of their goals was to ease overcrowding in the young kingdom of Italy, formed in 1861. Italian traders married Somali women, converted them to Christianity, and started families. By the mid-1950s, a few years before independence, about 5,000 Europeans lived in Italian Somalia, while only about 250 Europeans lived in British Somaliland.

However, as neighboring colonial projects, British Somaliland and Italian Somalia were also similar in many respects. Both Britain and Italy sought natural resources, trade, and a foothold in the Horn's strategic location, and both administrations were intent on writing laws and enforcing them. The Filonardi Company in Italian Somalia, for instance, quickly passed laws decreeing all uncultivated lands (*terre incolte*) Italian government property and granting Italy the exclusive right to exploit "minerals or deposits of any sort of metals, minerals, mineral oils, and precious stones."[13] Both colonial administrations also integrated shari'a into their work, promoting it as a form of judicial development – but only insofar as they found Islam to be compatible with their foreign rule and European principles of law and morality.

Of all the colonial projects in greater Somalia, that of the British dominated through its combination of longevity and territorial expanse. It encompassed the northern Horn for seventy-six years, from approximately 1884 until 1960. While Italian Somalia occupied more land, Italian rule ended about twenty years earlier. Mussolini's government integrated Italian Somalia into Italian East Africa (*Africa Orientale Italiana*), which included parts of Ethiopia and Eritrea, in 1936.[14] In 1941, during World War II, the British military captured Italian Somalia

diplomatici italiani presentati al Parlamento italiano dal Ministro degli Affari Esteri (Blanc): *Somalia italiana 1885–1895* (Rome, 1895), doc. 71, p. 121.

[13] Hess (1966), 42, citing "Provisional Ordinance for the Government and Administration of Territory under the Protection of Italy," annexed to the Filonardi Report, No. 171, September 16, 1894. Pos. 75/1, f. 3, *Archivio Storico dell'ex Ministero dell'Africa Italiana* (ASMAI), Rome, Italy.

[14] On the politics of colonialism in Somalia Italiana and Africa Orientale Italiana, see Hess (1966) and Alberto Alpozzi, *Il Faro di Mussolini: L'opera Colonial più Controversa e il Sogno dell'Impero nella Somalia Italiana, 1889–1941* (Turin: 001 Edizioni, 2015).

and controlled it for almost a decade before handing the territory over to the United Nations in 1949. The United Nations, in turn, invited Italian officials to administer ex-Italian Somalia until its independence in 1960.

The other colonial projects took smaller territorial bites out of greater Somalia. Starting in about 1888, the French government settled a tiny bay area, just north of British Somaliland, that they called *Côte Française des Somalis* (French Somaliland). It was renamed *Territoire Français des Afars et des Issas* (French Territory of Afars and Issas) after a failed 1967 plebiscite on independence, and it became Djibouti after gaining independence in 1977. Complex relationships among European, Ethiopian, and Kenyan elites meant that European colonial officials agreed to cede other areas of Somali-occupied land to Ethiopia and Kenya. In addition, Ethiopian power had extended into the Somali-inhabited Ogaden region during the 1880s, under Emperors Menelik and Menelik II.[15] As a consequence of these multiple colonial legacies, today Somalis remain divided into five political regions (Table 2.1).

Prior to the arrival of colonial officials, pastoral communities interacted with one another largely through their elders.[16] There was no single ruler or government. Elders used local custom to make decisions. Custom was informed by shari'a, which arrived in the Horn of Africa from Mecca centuries before European administrators did. Shari'a was also embedded in the template that elders used to mete out punishment and award compensation in cases of personal injury or community harm. Despite their differences in colonial heritage, and the differing laws that various empires brought with them, Somalis I met agreed that their shared legal history was Islamic. Shari'a was "the law," one religious leader told me in Hargeisa, during "the three hundred years before the British" arrived.[17] A Somali aid worker in Nairobi agreed, saying "Somalis were in one territory when they received Islam, [so] the largest reference to any legal system is Islamic."[18] While there was great variation in how Somali people practiced shari'a, Somali leaders gave primacy to orthodox versions of shari'a, according to Islamic

---

[15] Touval (1963), 47–48.
[16] Touval (1963), 31–36.
[17] Interview 52 with Sheikh Zaki, sheikh and former senior judiciary official in Hargeisa, Somaliland, July 2013.
[18] Interview 80 with Karim, aid worker in Nairobi, Kenya (August 2013).

Table 2.1 Somali populations in the five regions of the Horn of Africa

Political region	Colonial name	Occupying power and period of control	Independence
Somaliland	British Somaliland Protectorate	Great Britain, 1884 (approx.)–1960	June 26, 1960 May 18, 1991[19]
Somalia	Somalia Italiana (Italian Somalia, renamed 1950–1960 as United Nations Trust Territory of Somaliland)	Italy, 1885 (approx.)– 1941 Great Britain, 1941–1950 United Nations, 1950–1960 (employ-ing Italian administrators)	July 1, 1960
Djibouti	Côte Française des Somalis (French Somaliland), renamed 1967–1977 as Territoire Français des Afars et des Issas	France, 1888 (approx.)– 1977	June 27, 1977
Northern Frontier District (Kenya)	British East Africa	Great Britain, 1888 (approx.)–1963	December 12, 1963
Ogaden (Ethiopia)	N/A	N/A	N/A

Source: Compiled by the author.

standards in Mecca. Colonization would come to influence people's understanding of Islam. By introducing the notion and institutions of the state, colonization allowed authorities to infuse shari'a into

---

[19] Somaliland was an independent country for five days (June 26–30, 1960) until it united with Italian Somalia on July 1, 1960, forming the Somali Republic. Somaliland reasserted its independence on May 18, 1991, during the civil war after the collapse of the government in Mogadishu. While Somaliland has developed some diplomatic and trade relationships, the United Nations has not recognized its May 1991 reassertion of sovereignty.

the workings of state institutions, fundamentally altering the context and scope of shari'a and making Islamic legal politics possible.

BUILDING A COLONY THROUGH LAW

Colonial administrators and Somalis disagreed about which legal orders
and legal personnel were best suited to govern the Somali people and
resolve their disputes. In British Somaliland, this colonial legal politics
had four central features: (1) composing formal agreements between
colonial officials and Somalis; (2) managing dispute resolution processes; (3) giving power to new classes of legal elites; and (4) establishing Islamic courts and other legal institutions. In general, these colonial
interventions facilitated the emergence of new hierarchies among both
customary Somali methods of dispute resolution and institutions the
British established. Although Somalis had for centuries linked xeer and
shari'a into a single form of dispute resolution, British colonial attempts
to decouple them – by compartmentalizing shari'a into courts that
heard only cases of family law – shaped how Somalis saw Islam not
only as their faith but also as a source of state law, built atop and
separated from religion.

The British reconfigured Somali dispute resolution methods into
a British-controlled hierarchy of legal personnel and institutions,
including Islamic courts, as they sought to create a state-like structure
in Somaliland. Shari'a thus became a tool for the British and the
Somalis who worked for them to alter the division of labor in the
administration of justice. This management of religion – specifically,
indenturing religion to the state – encouraged Somalis to move away
from tradition and toward modernity, separating their Islamic beliefs
from a growing awareness and use of state law. The British sought to
increase their power by granting themselves final authority over shari'a.
With this authority, the British government portrayed itself as the
"ruler" of the world's "greatest Mohammedan empire."[20]

Composing "Legal" Agreements

British colonial officials used techniques of law to enter and govern Somali
territory. Specifically, they designed, drafted, and recorded agreements with

---

[20] "The Pacification of Somaliland," *Egyptian Daily Post*, May 20, 1909. Wingate Collection,
Sudan Archive, Durham University, 287/2/234.

Somali elites. Legal discourse and contractual commitments complemented military prowess as an expedient way to enter a land, advance a colonial enterprise, and lay the foundation for a state system. When the British arrived in the Horn of Africa, they needed to build sufficient trust with the Somali populations to enable trade for sheep and cattle to feed soldiers stationed at the British outpost in Aden. To build this trust, the British adopted a strategy not dissimilar to those they had used in other colonies: give their agreements with Somalis a legal form, while allowing Somalis to continue to govern themselves. Such an "indirect rule" propagates subordinate forms of authority, breaks lines of responsibility, and diffuses resistance.[21]

In 1827, the British government began formalizing occasional agreements with Somali communities, typically following attacks on British ships off the African coast.[22] To earn the support of Somalis facing Ottoman and European imperial scrambles for African territories, British officials in the 1880s promised full protection and order. On August 1, 1884, the British government gave bold public notice of its intent to occupy the Horn of Africa's northern coast by informing ports along the Gulf of Aden that "Unless the Turkish Government takes immediate steps to occupy the coast areas, His Majesty's Government would send a force there to preserve order."[23] British officials had actually begun their occupation months earlier using the art of law. They had been quietly arranging written agreements with Somali sultans, many of whom were trained as sheikhs through their study of shari'a and fiqh.

The sultans, seen as respected members of their communities, were suspicious of foreigners, especially non-Muslims.[24] Somalis suggested privately to me that British government representatives negotiated with sultans in order "to silence" them and, thus, disarm the potential for Islam to grow in local political life.[25] Between 1884 and 1887, the British recorded ten agreements with seven Somali communities. Perhaps to showcase both British authority

---

[21] Luis Eslava, *Local Space, Global Life: The Everyday Operation of International Law and Development* (Cambridge: Cambridge University Press, 2015).

[22] United Kingdom Central Office of Information, "The Somaliland Protectorate," (London: UK Government Overseas Services, undated), p. 3.

[23] "Lieutenant-General Sir Reginald Wingate's Special Mission to Somaliland," dated June 12, 1909. Foreign Office Confidential Prints, Bodleian Law Library, Oxford University, 9507/09.

[24] Interview 62 with Bilan, NGO executive director in Hargeisa, Somaliland (July 2013).

[25] Interview 89 with Sheikh Abdirahman, sheikh and senior government official in Hargeisa, Somaliland (June 2014).

and Somali communities' feeling of independence from British imperialism, the British government labeled each document an international "treaty."

The language of each treaty was formal and the text was short, one to two pages long. They were written in English and recorded on hide. It is unclear whether even the most capable Somalis were able to decipher the legal texts. But those who signed them knew their contents. These local sultans and elders saw themselves as "kings of the land," and Somalis I met who descended from these men recalled to me the essential provisions of the treaties, which had been passed down orally.[26] (There was no official Somali script until the 1970s, and I have been unable to find evidence of the existence of Arabic versions of the treaties, which educated sultans and sheikhs who had studied overseas in Cairo or Mecca would have been able to read.)

Generally, the ten treaties included similar provisions that promoted the contradictory notions that Somalis were both independent from and reliant upon foreign intervention. Though the treaties do not mention Islam, each one legalizes distinct diplomatic moves toward Britain's colonial goals.[27] The Eisa treaty, for instance, which is similar to the other agreements made during this period, includes the following preamble: "We, the undersigned Elders of the Easa [sic] tribe, are desirous of entering into an Agreement with the British Government for the maintenance of our independence, the preservation of order, and other good and sufficient reasons."[28] In the handful of treaty articles that typically followed, the Somali signatories would cede many rights, including agreeing not to "sell or give for occupation" any portion of their territory (Article 1), not to restrict free trade or the movement of British persons and vessels (Articles 2 and 3), not to traffic in slaves (Article 4), and, critically for colonial purposes, to allow the British to establish an "agent" entitled to respect in the territory (Table 2.2).

The British government viewed these agreements both paternalistically and imperially, and bound itself to a single basic promise: to protect Somalis from belligerent attacks. In a memorandum to the Foreign Office in London, a British official shared his view that "Our

[26] Interview 37 with Sultan Mansoor, sultan in Hargeisa, Somaliland (June 2013).
[27] Touval (1963), 36.
[28] Great Britain Treaties with the Tribes on the Somali Coast (Eisa, Gadabursi, Habr-Awal, Habr Toljaala, Habr Gerhajis, and Warsangali treaties), June 1887. Foreign Office Confidential Prints, Bodleian Law Library, Oxford University, file 5453.

Table 2.2 Treaties protecting colonial interests

Treaty date	Treaty parties	Relevant treaty details
British treaties with Somali elders		
May 1, 1884	British government and Mijjertein elders	Not allowing foreign occupation, free trade for British
July 14, 1884	British government and Habr Awal elders	No contact with foreign power without British approval
Dec. 11, 1884	British government and Gadabursi elders	Not allowing foreign occupation, free trade for British
Dec. 26, 1884	British government and Habr Toljaala elders	Not allowing foreign occupation, free trade for British
Dec. 31, 1884	British government and Isa (Eisa) elders	"Maintenance of [Eisa] independence," not allowing foreign occupation, free trade for British
Jan. 13, 1885	British government and Habr Gerhajis elders	Not allowing foreign occupation, free trade for British
Jan. 27, 1886	British government and Warasangli elders	Assisting wrecked ships (Article III)
Feb. 1, 1886	British government and Habr Gerhajis elders	Not allowing foreign occupation, free trade for British
Feb. 1, 1886	British government and Habr Toljaala elders	Not allowing foreign occupation, free trade for British
Mar. 15, 1886	British Government and Habr Awal elders	Not allowing foreign occupation, free trade for British
Treaties among foreign powers		
Sept. 7, 1877	British and Egyptian governments (via Sultan Khedive)	Assurances not to cede authority over the Somali coast to foreign powers; Britain neither recognizes nor refutes Sultan Khedive's claims to sovereignty
Mar. 15, 1883	Italian government and Sultan of Assab	Demarcates Red Sea coastal territory of Ablia (Aussa)
May 14, 1897	British government and Abyssinian Empire	Sets boundary between British Somaliland and Ethiopia

Note: This table includes only the ten treaties that the British Government made with Somali communities and recorded collectively in its Foreign Office Confidential Prints in June 1887, along with three treaties among foreign powers, also available in British colonial records.

Sources: Great Britain Treaties with the Tribes on the Somali Coast (Eisa, Gadabursi, Habr-Awal, Habr Toljaala, Habr Gerhajis, and Warsangali treaties), June 1887, Foreign Office Confidential Prints, Bodleian Law Library, Oxford University, file 5453; "Lieutenant-General Sir Reginald Wingate's Special Mission to Somaliland," June 12, 1909, Foreign Office Confidential Prints, Bodleian Law Library, Oxford University, 9507/13.

Protectorate Treaties amount to an undertaking to intervene actively on behalf of the protected tribes in case of unprovoked attack on them or their territories."[29] It is unclear what kind of "unprovoked attack" the British or their Somali counterparts may have been worried about, but in the imperial race to carve up the African continent in the 1880s, the British wanted access to strategically located coastal regions before other Europeans took them.

By summer 1887, just over three years after signing its first treaty of protection with elders of the Mijjertein community, Britain's legal occupation of the northern coast of the Horn of Africa was complete, and the boundaries of British Somaliland were drawn. The British government duly notified "the [European] Powers that the Somali Coast from Ras Jibuti to Bandar Ziada had been placed under British protection."[30] Great Britain's claims to the northern Horn of Africa were thus rendered official, at least to European competitors, through treaty documents and notifications. To ensure European rivals did not supersede British claims to authority, the British also signed treaties with them. An Anglo-Italian Protocol in the 1890s, for instance, ensured that the British and Italians knew their respective spheres of influence along the coast as well as the spaces controlled by Abyssinians in the interior.[31]

If the treaties were designed to build trust in the British colonial project through promises of protection and non-intervention, did the British keep their side of the bargain? Evidence is scattered, but three points suggest the British sought, at some expense, to ensure that they complied with the treaties they signed. First, the British set up and used militias of British officers and Somali soldiers to protect Somali communities, particularly from raids by other Somali communities seen as hostile. Second, the British did not allow European settlements in Somali areas, just as they had promised – a point repeated, with affirmation and support, by many Somalis I met during my fieldwork. And third, while the British initially allowed a Roman Catholic mission to open in May 1909 in the coastal town of Berbera, this religious institution was eventually shuttered following complaints by Somalis

[29] "Memorandum by Mr. Bertie on Questions Affecting the Somali Coast Protectorate, Harrar, and Abysssinia, August 1892 to October 1893," August 6, 1892. Foreign Office Confidential Prints, Bodleian Law Library, Oxford University, 6410/3.
[30] "Lieutenant-General Sir Reginald Wingate's Special Mission to Somaliland," dated June 12, 1909. Foreign Office Confidential Prints, Bodleian Law Library, Oxford University, 9507/10.
[31] Winston Churchill, "A Minute on the Somaliland Protectorate," May 5, 1894. Colonial Office Confidential Prints, Bodleian Library, Oxford University, 702/73.

who felt that the British were using the school and church to convert Somali Muslims to Christianity.[32]

And what about the Somali elders whose names appear on these treaties? What was their incentive to formalize contracts with foreigners whom they likely did not trust? Somalis could not have known what level of colonial intervention these free trade treaties and a British "agent" would eventually license. The treaties gave Somalis little work to do in exchange for promises of protection, except to refrain from killing British persons. Protection mattered, particularly as camel raids and other offenses between rival communities were common. And Somali elites were already well accustomed to making and respecting oral agreements, as they had done for centuries with one another. The British treaties also reinforced the elders' stature as the key leaders of their communities.

Managing Custom and Dispute Resolution

While political agreements with Somali elders allowed the British government to plant a foothold in the region, British officials turned to law once again to build trust among a skeptical population. This time, they did not use legal documents, but instead co-opted existing mechanisms of dispute resolution. That is, the British hired local agents to serve the colonial administration by resolving everyday disputes. According to this strategy of colonial legal politics, as the administration's paid judges resolve more disputes over time, their work strengthens local trust in the colonial empire and its project of grafting a formal state-like structure over diverse communities, tying local interests to the colonial project.

The British hoped to create new dispute resolution processes among Somalis, but they knew Somalis were already resolving disputes their own way. Somalis had for centuries practiced a bilateral and bottom-up system of dispute resolution known as xeer. In this indigenous system of common law, elders (in Somali, *odayal*) in rival communities resolve each dispute through precedent generated by decisions recognized between those two communities. If a grave offense is committed by a member of one community against a member of another community, that offense becomes collectivized and elders from the two communities meet and discuss it. When sitting in this capacity, the most

---

[32] "Private Correspondence of Sir R. Wingate to Sheikh Abdel Kader in Burao, Somaliland." Sudan Archive, Durham University, SAD 287/2/140.

respected elders are called *guurti*. Compensation is determined by the resolutions of similar past incidents between the communities. If the offense is new, the elders' decision holds precedential value only between those two communities and only for similar future offenses. Xeer is thus divided into two categories: *ugub* (new decisions that set precedent) and *curad* (precedent from prior decisions). A diffuse Somali common law thus emerges bilaterally, organically, and orally in response to disputes. These contractual relationships and precedents form the basis of dispute resolution between Somali groups.

Because xeer varies across dozens of communities known informally as clans and sub-clans, Somalis debate the extent to which religious law forms the foundation of the xeer system. One Somali interviewee explained the difficulty of distinguishing the sources of oral judgments: "I don't know how people resolve disputes – [is it] xeer, Islam, or a blend ... Who are we to decide what they relied on?"[33] The xeer system may be described as prima facie non-religious, though it is similar to and likely draws from religious rules, depending on the two communities involved. That is, religion is neither necessary nor sufficient for xeer. Though Somalis disagree on whether shari'a is the foundation of xeer, no one disputes that shari'a is woven into xeer's fabric, particularly in cases of punishment or compensation. This deep interrelationship between shari'a and xeer is important because the British had other plans for structuring the Somali relationship with shari'a. In particular, by separating dispute resolution principles into those drawn from tradition (xeer) and those drawn from faith (shari'a), British administrators constructed a colonial state with the power to manage religion.

As in other colonies on the continent, the British turned to African elites to mediate people's disputes. Changing Somali dispute resolution procedures aimed to allow the British, in their words, to rule through influence rather than coercion. According to Hargeisa district commissioner (and later British Prime Minister) Winston Churchill, "Political officers must at all times bear in mind that the [Somali] tribes should be managed through influence ... Coercion is a mistake ... Moreover, it would be impolitic to use the relatives of tribesmen to coerce them in a matter deeply affecting the private life and habits of the people."[34]

---

[33] Interview 79 with Karim, aid worker in Nairobi, Kenya (August 2013).
[34] Winston Churchill, "Letter from Hargeisa Commissioner to political officer in Wadamago," March 17, 1905. Colonial Office Confidential Prints, Bodleian Library, Oxford University, 770/12.

Descendants of Somali sheikhs who worked in British Somaliland told me that their ancestors had been powerful and united across the region, despite perceived tribal or ancestral differences. Many of these sheikhs had relied on *Minhaj al-Muslim* (Arabic: *The Way of the Muslim*), an Algerian text based on the Prophet Muhammad's teachings, for dispute resolution. The British tried to create a new elite who would turn away from *al-Minhaj* and instead use the Indian penal code that colonial officials brought with them to the Horn in the early twentieth century. The goal was to reduce sheikhs' social influence by transferring religious authority to personnel and institutions the colonial administration created and managed.

Devolving Power to Local Elites: Hiring Aqils and Formalizing Dispute Resolution

The British were not the first outsiders to attempt to control dispute resolution mechanisms as part of a broader strategy of centralizing a governmental system and imbuing it with self-reinforcing legitimacy. The Egyptians, the Ottoman Empire's representatives in the Horn, had done the same for decades during the nineteenth century, employing "salaried chiefs" called aqils (Somali: *caaqil/caaqilo*; Arabic, "wise person").[35] The British resurrected the aqil as a category in Somali political life, increasing aqils' prominence by hiring them and endowing them with authority to resolve disputes – using xeer – across the British-controlled territory. Both Egyptian and British efforts to devolve power to paid subjects of the administration were designed to enable foreign authorities to enter communities that were accustomed to transferring political and legal power through hereditary lineage.

While some British officials argued it would be unwise to employ "natives" as their agents along the Somali coast, British decision-makers put faith in their aqils and "were interested in maintaining" this Egyptian-founded system, according to aqils I later met.[36] British documents also reveal how they integrated Somali legal structures into their administration:

> [When] we took over the administration of the Somalis from the Egyptians ... we found that they had adopted a method, which we have carried on, of appointing headmen or "aqils" to represent each

---

[35] Mark Bradbury, *Becoming Somaliland* (Bloomington: Indiana University Press, 2008), 100.

[36] Untitled manuscript, February 1880. Foreign Office Confidential Prints, Bodleian Law Library, Oxford University, 4099/18.

small section of the tribes with the aim of destroying the power of the hereditary sultans ... presumably on the principle of "divide et impera" and it has certainly had the effect of dividing[,] for what power of control there ever was has passed from the hands of a few sultans to innumerable petty headmen ... It is however doubtful how much real power these sultans ever had.[37]

Somali sultans and sheikhs I met during my fieldwork made the same point. Aqils as a group were designed to be the go-to source for local, everyday forms of dispute resolution. They also had the painful task of collecting taxes on behalf of the administration and became a police force of sorts for the British.[38] The British also served as a kind of police force for the aqils: "The soldiers of the British [would] arrest ... those who refused our decisions," according to one aqil I met who had worked for the colonial administration.[39] The aqils were subservient to British rule. The British would arrest aqils who refused to comply with directives, in some cases exiling them hundreds of miles away to the Seychelles.[40]

By employing aqils, British administrators formalized dispute resolution roles in a familiar way, thus allowing Somalis to accept, however tacitly, some amount of colonial intervention in daily life. The British codified the work of aqils and other dispute resolvers in the political structures they were attempting to create for Somali populations. These other legal personnel included the guurti, oday, qadis, sheikhs, and sultans (Table 2.3). If a problem was too large for aqils to resolve, such as a conflict or war between rival communities, the aqils would "assign ... it to the guurti to solve."[41] Guurti were ad hoc groups of elders chosen from among the most notable members of their communities to resolve specific disputes.

---

[37] Address by Sir Harold Baxter Kittermaster, 1931. Colonial Office Confidential Prints, Bodleian African and Commonwealth Library, Oxford University, paragraph 6, mss. Afr. s. 2341(1).

[38] Sir Reginald Wingate, in his report of a 1909 mission to Somaliland, mentions meeting with four aqils in Berbera, writing, "I understand that the British Government pays these Akhils a sum of about 10,000 Rupees a year in exchange for the right to levy Customs Dues and take Commerce into the Government Enclosures." "Lieutenant-General Sir Reginald Wingate's Special Mission to Somaliland," unpublished report, June 12, 1909. Sudan Archive, Durham University, SAD 287/3/132.

[39] Interview 114 with Mustafa, senior government official and former aqil of British colonial administration (June 2014).

[40] Ismail Ali Ismail, *Governance: The Scourge and Hope of Somalia* (Vancouver: Trafford Publishing, 2010), 62.

[41] Interview 114 with Mustafa, senior government official and former aqil of British colonial administration (June 2014).

Table 2.3 Somali dispute resolvers in British Somaliland

Title	Legal role	How transformed by the British
Aqil (*caaqil/caaqilo/ ooqal*)	Dispute resolvers and tax collectors	"Aqil" position first used by Egyptian administrators in the nineteenth century. British officials also championed them. Sultans saw aqils as sultans' deputies. British officials saw aqils as the colonial administration's deputies
Oday (*oday/odayal*)	Respected elders	N/A
Guurti (*guurti/ guurtiya*)	Oday who sit together as a decision-making body for large-scale conflicts such as intertribal war (literally, "detective")	N/A
Qadi (*qadi*)	Judge of an Islamic court	Created by British colonial administrators
Sheikh (*sheikh/ shuyukh*)	Leader in the community with superior knowledge of Islam	British officials sought to reduce sheikhs' influence by transferring Islamic authority to qadis in the administration's Islamic courts
Sultan (*sultan/ salateen*)	Leader of a Somali clan or kinship/familial unit	Predated the colonial administration; the British sought to transfer power from what had been a small number of sultans to a larger number of aqils

Source: Author, derived from historical records and in-person interviews.

I met descendants of aqils, sheikhs, sultans, and other dispute resolvers who occupy positions similar to those of their fathers and grandfathers and to whom cases and decisions have been passed down orally. In their words, the British "activated" and "formalized" dispute resolution personnel and "paid them [each] a small salary" as compensation for their work.[42] But the process also entrenched rivalries. When I asked a sheikh whose grandfather was a qadi why his grandfather was not an aqil, he replied curtly that the aqil "was something that [showed] you belonged to those white people who came. People [like us] looked down on [the] aqil. It wasn't something of pride."[43] To dilute the religious authority of people like his grandfather, the sheikh said to me, "The British ... created a new secular elite." Though colonization created the positions of qadi and aqil, it also institutionalized a hierarchy and rivalry between Somalis occupying these two positions within the administration.

The British were so focused on creating competing legal elites that Somalis would come to view dispute resolution as the essence of the colonial enterprise. The British tried to compartmentalize Somalis' legal order, dividing dispute resolution into distinct categories. "We learned from [British colonial officials] what is different between xeer and shari'a, and how [to] run the formal law," the former colonial aqil told me.[44] This British-instituted separation of xeer and shari'a led a sheikh to tell me that sultans and aqils were Somalis' preferred dispute resolvers while, to British officials, "The sheikh was the dirty man in the mosque."[45]

As the British saw it, local legal personnel were a means to forestall violence and instability, though British officers were certainly arming Somali personnel in the event that this legal strategy failed. Somalis I met clearly felt that, although the British had built a military of Somali soldiers, British colonial administrators "were not interested in" creating a stable and powerful local legal profession, as they had been doing in colonies like Sudan or India.[46] After all, the British had signed a "protectorate" agreement whose primary goal was securing the territory rather than settling on or developing it. British administrators fragmented legal power and did not open any higher education institutions or law faculties. And, unlike in other British colonies, few Somalis were sent overseas for training in English common law.

[42] Follow-up interview 70 with Kabir, lawyer and senior university administrator in Hargeisa, Somaliland (July 2013).
[43] Interview 126 with Dhahir, senior university administrator in Borama, Somaliland (conducted in Hargeisa, Somaliland) (June 2014).
[44] Interview 114 with Mustafa, senior government official and former aqil of British colonial administration (June 2014).
[45] Interview 52 with Sheikh Zaki, sheikh and former senior judiciary official in Hargeisa, Somaliland (July 2013).
[46] Ibid.

Somali communities typically had no contact with the protectorate administration except when disputes needed resolution and they turned to its paid representatives for help.[47] But devolving power to a group of local elites did not always work exactly as the British intended. The British government's own reconnaissance missions discussed British administrators' "ineptitude" in understanding the situation of Somalis, particularly because aqils, dependent on British paychecks, felt unable to speak their minds openly.[48] Sheikh Idris Wad Abderrahim, a Sudanese notable whom the British had attached to an intelligence mission to Somaliland, wrote that he was "told that all the Somali employés [sic], such as dragomans, policemen, and even the kadi himself, take bribes when they have a chance." They also "explain things in a misleading manner in order to please [the British] ... This is one of the reasons which makes the British Government unpopular with the people of Somaliland."[49]

Somalis sought out British magistrates in addition to or instead of their aqils, sometimes shopping between different legal institutions for a decision. According to British observers, this forum shopping created new administrative burdens because dispute resolution came to occupy most of a magistrate's time. "It has become the custom for ... disputes to be brought before the district magistrate instead of their being settled by the old tribal method and his time has become completely occupied with bench work instead of being free for constructive administration."[50] Proposals to deal with the influx of complaints varied but generally included not hearing cases below a certain monetary value or delegating all judicial authority to "natives themselves."[51] The British "made a start in this direction by the formation of 'aqils courts' that adjudicate on petty cases. They have worked fairly satisfactorily but their decisions are subject to constant scrutiny of the district officer and, more important, the enforcement of their decisions must lie entirely with him."[52] The administration kept a roster of its aqils, who rotated among the aqils courts of Somaliland's colonial districts.[53]

---

[47] Interview 59 with Kalim, former NGO executive director in Hargeisa, Somaliland (July 2013).

[48] Reginald Wingate, "Lieutenant-General Sir Reginald Wingate's Special Mission to Somaliland," unpublished report, June 12, 1909. Sudan Archive, Durham University, SAD 287/3/146–148.

[49] Ibid., Foreign Office Confidential Prints, Bodleian Law Library, Oxford University, 9507/89.

[50] Ibid.

[51] Ibid.

[52] Ibid.

[53] Ibid.

The British shaped Somali politics not only through dispute resolution, but also through an intricate geopolitical system. This policy
of dividing the Somali interior into districts, each with a political
officer overseeing it, began in 1906.[54] By 1931, about fifty years into
its colonial project in the Horn, the British administration had
divided its territory into five districts, each with a district magistrate
supported by police and the Camel Corps (a military force). In these
five districts were more than 200 aqils.[55] Each of these 200 aqils was
tasked with "representing about one thousand natives."[56] In an
address on the situation of Somaliland, Sir Harold Baxter
Kittermaster argued that the aqils were useful in providing order, as
"No native would dream of listening for a moment to any order or
advice given except by his own particular aqil. This excessive representation," Kittermaster continued, "is to my mind the weak point of
our whole administration."[57] Others argued that letting these "tribal
elders" resolve disputes did not always work because "In the case of
intertribal disputes the invariable consequence of our refusal to
arbitrate is a recourse to arms, the result being that intertribal relations become embittered."[58]

Establishing Two Sets of Courts: Civil and Islamic

The British administration sought to control nonviolent forms of dispute
resolution by establishing courts. Colonial officials were so intent on
controlling the institutions of dispute resolution that protectorate laws
provided for imprisonment of up to one year or a fine of up to 1,000
rupees for anyone "attempting to exercise judicial powers unlawfully or
[to] adjudicate without authority to do so."[59] Colonial administrators
constructed two sets of courts in British Somaliland, divided by their
jurisdictions. First were Islamic courts led by qadis. These "qadi courts"

---

[54] "Note by the Commissioner on Mr. Churchill's Confidential Minute," December 28, 1907.
Colonial Office Confidential Prints, Bodleian Library, Oxford University, African No. 896,
African Print No. 904, p. 2.

[55] Address by Sir Harold Baxter Kittermaster, 1931. Colonial Office Confidential Prints, Bodleian
African and Commonwealth Library, Oxford University, paragraph 6, mss. Afr. s. 2341(1).
Interview 46 with Xabiib, senior government official in Hargeisa, Somaliland (July 2013).

[56] Ibid.

[57] Ibid.

[58] "Letter from Somaliland Commissioner Cordeaux to Secretary of State," September 11, 1909,
in "Affairs in Somaliland, May 1908–December 1909," Colonial Office Confidential Prints,
Bodleian African and Commonwealth Library, Oxford University, 926/115.

[59] "The Laws of the Somaliland Protectorate: Containing the Ordinances, Orders in Council and
Orders of the Secretary of State in Force on the 1st Day of January 1950," prepared by Sir Henry
Webb (London: Waterlow & Sons, 1950), Volume 1, 28.

dealt with those matters that the administration deemed nonpenal. Primarily these were personal status matters, such as marriage dissolution and family inheritance. (The qadi courts would become Somaliland's postcolonial District Courts.)

The non-Islamic courts were called "civil courts" and dealt with matters that the British described as penal. These courts did not use shari'a. The bifurcated system thereby prevented Somalis from using shari'a to address crimes and relegated any formal or specific use of Islamic law to family disputes. Because shari'a had been integrated into xeer prior to British arrival, Somalis were not accustomed to using shari'a in this way – that is, tied to courts that heard only family disputes.

While Somalis used structures they had called *mahakim* (courts) before the British arrived, historical evidence suggests that after they arrived the idea of courts took on a new meaning tied to foreign intervention.[60] To administer the qadi courts, for instance, the British employed some Somali judges but also brought trained judges from nearby Sudan. In the words of one Somali I met, the British thought it was prudent to appoint a judge in each court "who looks like" Somalis and is also Muslim.[61] Setting up qadi courts alongside civil courts allowed the British administration to control religion, limit the power of sheikhs, and promote a specific version of shari'a that was tied to the state. British officials presented the colonial state as an enterprise that could work for shari'a, rather than against it. The importance of institutionalizing Islamic courts to the colonial project led some Somalis to tell me they felt that the British "did not have a war against Islam."[62]

The British created the qadi courts to serve as institutions of justice. They would become sites of contestation, and law and religion became their languages of contestation. The British use of Islamic family courts in particular led some Somalis to tell me they believed that Somalis were "much more secular" before British colonialism, when Somalis first learned how religion could shape a European-inspired judicial structure.[63] By formalizing law into structures they called courts, the British built up Islam not merely as belief (Arabic: *'aqeeda*) – to which

---

[60] Follow-up interview 69 with Axmed, lawyer and university lecturer in Hargeisa, Somaliland (June 2013).

[61] Interview 25 with Raouf, senior United Nations official in Hargeisa, Somaliland (June 2013).

[62] Interview 126 with Dhahir, senior university administrator in Borama, Somaliland (conducted in Hargeisa, Somaliland) (June 2014).

[63] Interview 50 with Caziz, lawyer and human rights activist in Hargeisa, Somaliland (July 2013).

nearly all Somalis already subscribed – but also as state law. Building this political bridge between Islam as a form of faith and Islam as a form of law associated the religion with the colonial state, its legal institutions, and its legitimacy. The British had done this in other places as well.[64]

By defining the jurisdictions of legal institutions, colonialism delineated the boundaries between religion and dispute resolution and sought to keep those boundaries as rigid as possible. Aqils would use their xeer for cases of personal injury, qadis would use their shari'a for family matters like marriages and divorces, and British magistrates would use their own principles of justice for criminal matters while enjoying supervisory and appellate authority over aqils and qadis. Despite these differences, aqils and qadis alike were paid by the British administration.[65] The result of using Somali subjects to graft British-controlled legal structures onto preexisting dispute resolution processes led to a complex and layered system of what became labeled as "formal" dispute resolution (including in Islamic courts that the British set up and used) and what became labeled as "informal" or "traditional" dispute resolution (through aqils and clan chiefs and other elders).

Shari'a traversed these boundaries between formal and informal, traditional and modern. The British saw shari'a as both the modern way to deal with family-oriented disputes and the premodern – and thus unacceptable – way to deal with criminal offenses, for which the British imported their Indian colony's penal code. Xeer and shari'a had been closely linked before the British arrived in the Horn of Africa. The British then decoupled the aqil from shari'a, creating a distinction between the customary law that aqils were to use and the Islamic law that qadis were to use.

The British maintained Somali practices but subsumed them under imperial institutions. And, to showcase British sensitivity, Somalis could appeal to the local government – including the British district commissioner's office in the area – to review a particular situation when problems arose that aqils could not resolve. To some Somalis, the system seemed to function, at least from a distance, and a form of the rule of law existed. Echoing others I met, one former senior Somali

---

[64] On integrating religion into the state by separating beliefs from law in colonial Egypt and Malaya, see Iza Hussin, *The Politics of Islamic Law: Local Elites, Colonial Authority, and the Making of the Muslim State* (Chicago, IL: University of Chicago Press, 2016). On Sudan, see Massoud (2013a), 44–84.

[65] Interview 42 with Faisal, senior government official in Hargeisa, Somaliland (July 2013).

government official said to me, "During the British time, there was [very little] corruption ... Nobody would dare ask for a bribe, because you could always go to the British District Commissioner and say 'this person asked for a bribe.' During the British things were done fairly, squarely, and by the book."[66]

Legal personnel and institutions mattered to British colonial administrators, who encouraged Somali elders, qadis, and district commissioners to use law to resolve people's disputes. The practice of asking Islamic courts and shari'a-oriented judges to resolve disputes, when repeated over time among different communities, was designed to help build colonial legitimacy via Somalis' Islamic faith. This practice took place not only in British Somaliland, but also to the south, in Italian Somalia.

Italian Somalia: Charter Company Shari'a

The law in Italian Somalia was more arbitrary and legal structure even more fractured than in British Somaliland. By the same token, Italian administrators did not restructure Somali dispute resolution processes as thoroughly as the British had done. The primary reason for these differences is that for most of the early colonial period when Italians were setting up a colonial project, Italian Somalia was governed by a charter company.[67] Italian Somalia's first governors came from the Filonardi Company (1893 to 1896), followed by the Benadir Company (1899 to 1905). The Italian government controlled the area directly between 1896 and 1899. The basis for the Somali state legal system in Italian-controlled areas thus came largely from these trade-promoting companies. Both the Filonardi and Benadir charter companies "took advantage" of Somalis' pre-existing social structures by giving them "official recognition" and turning "the elders" into "government agents [who] received monthly allowances from the Italian authorities."[68] According to historian Robert Hess, "In undertaking paragovernmental operations, the Filonardi Company laid the basis for

---

[66] Interview 17 with Amburo, former senior government minister and United Nations official in Hargeisa, Somaliland (June 2013).
[67] Hess (1966), 70.
[68] Alessandra Vianello and Mohamed M. Kassim, *Servants of the Sharia: The Civil Register of the Qadis' Court of Brava, 1893–1900*, Vols. 1 and 2 (Leiden: Brill, 2006), 30–31. The names of fifteen elders and their monthly allowances from the Benadir Company appear in the Archivio Storico del Ministero dell; Africa Italian Fasc. 75/12 (Appendix). Also cited in Giovanni Piazza, "La Regione di Brava nel Benadir," *Bollettino della Societa'Italiana di Esplorazioni Geografiche e Commerciali, Fasc. I & II* (January and February 1909): 7–29.

indirect rule ... Filonardi's judicial system was based on the traditional role of the cadis and on the Shari'a."[69] After the Filonardi Company's demise, the Benadir Company took control of major ports and continued the practice of relying on shari'a, adding another class of dispute resolvers known as "warrant chiefs."[70] The Benadir Company, like the British further north in Somaliland, also allowed appeal from the cadis and *walis* (local governors) to the central administration.[71]

Again like the British, the administrators of Italian Somalia wrote laws that justified and explained their activities. The Filonardi Company, for instance, prohibited the trade of slaves and required Somalis to obtain permission to cut down trees, a critical source of the region's cooking fuel. Vincenzo Filonardi, a navy captain and Italian Somalia's first governor, placed his hope for the territory on a legal foundation: in his private correspondence, he stated that the administration of justice – which he saw as the "repression of abuses, impartiality, and fairness of judgments" – would earn his company "the confidence of the population."[72]

The Italian Foreign Ministry adopted an approach that integrated local norms into the legal fabric of the colony, just as the British had done. The Foreign Ministry dictated to the charter companies that "whereas Italian law was to be applied to Italian nationals, native law was to be honored for the Somali."[73] A contract between the Italian Ministry of Foreign Affairs and the Filonardi Company indicated that the charter company would administer ports and pay all officials, including judges, to "continue to administer justice in the name of the Sultan and in accordance with the shari'a."[74]

The Italians, in a key difference from the British, did not devolve power to local elites so much as subsume "native law," which they also labeled shari'a, into the legal codes the companies created and enforced themselves. Thus how "native" law was defined became an important part of Italian colonial and commercial authority. Somalis I met felt that Italian administrators had a "phobia" of customary law and, thus, fought against

[69] Hess (1966), 179.
[70] Ibid.
[71] Ibid., 72.
[72] Vianello and Kassim (2006), 53, citing Giuseppina Finazzo, *L'Italia nel Benadir: L'azione di Vincenzo Filonardi, 1884–1896* (Rome: Ateneo, 1966), 295–296.
[73] Hess (1966), 39, citing a June 15, 1893 letter from Foreign Minister Brin in Rome to Filonardi, from *Documenti diplomatici italiani presentati al Parlamento italiano dal Ministro degli Affari Esteri (Blanc): Somalia italiana 1885–1895* (Rome, 1895), doc. 71, p. 121.
[74] Vianello and Kassim (2006), 13, citing Gustavo Chiesi, *Law Colonizzazione Europea dell'Est Africa* (Turin: Unione Tipografica Torinese, 1909), 246.

it.[75] Somalis told me they more readily accepted British intervention in the northern Horn because they saw it as minimal, especially when viewed in relation to Italian settlement in the
southern Horn. British officials were "not intervening in our culture," I was told, except to enforce the decisions of aqils, which
aqils and elders had welcomed.[76]

However, like the British, the Italians sought to minimize Islam
while simultaneously and paradoxically making it an important foundation upon which to introduce Italian law and order. As it was
establishing courts, the Filonardi Company created a legal code for
the Somalis. This code declared the charter company's jurisdiction
over "native law." To justify the company's legal code in relation to
local law, the Filonardi Company, through an ordinance decreed by
Filonardi himself, in September 1894 stated that its "law[s] will be
applied according to the standards of the Muslim Shari'a."[77] Among
Filonardi's first acts upon his arrival to the Somali coast was to
introduce and regulate the post of "cadis." The regulations stated
that the only company-approved qadis would be those appointed by
Filonardi himself, that they would apply shari'a and collect taxes and
fees on their judgments, and that qadi decisions would be appealable
to Filonardi (Table 2.4). Qadi courts charged fees to litigants, and
court revenue was divided "among the company (75%), the wali
(10%), and the cadis (15%)."[78]

The Filonardi Company wrote that "justice would be administered by
company-appointed cadis, or judges. Only sentences passed by cadis who
represented the Filonardi Company would be recognized as legitimate."[79]
In practice, direct forms of administration by "young officers [with] no
previous training or experience ... and very little knowledge of local
languages" meant that local officials often "interfered with ... justice

[75] Follow-up interview 70 with Kabir, lawyer and senior university administrator in Hargeisa,
Somaliland (July 2013); Hess (1966).
[76] Interview 114 with Mustafa, senior government official and former aqil of British colonial
administration (June 2014).
[77] Hess (1966), citing "Provisional Ordinance for the Government and Administration of
Territory under the Protection of Italy," Article VI, annexed to Filonardi Report, No. 171,
September 16, 1894, Archivio Storico dell'ex Ministero dell'Africa Italiana (ASMAI), Rome,
pos. 75/1, f. 3.
[78] Hess (1966), 43, citing "Ordinance for the application of the Muslim Shari'a," signed by
Filonardi, October 24, 1893, Historical-Documentary Collection of the Garesa at
Mogadishu, item 33.
[79] Ibid.

Table 2.4 Regulations governing qadis in Italian Somalia

REGULATIONS FOR THE QADIS (Administration of Justice) [Translation from the Italian]

1. Only the decisions issued by qadis appointed by Consul Filonardi, Administrator of the Compagnia Italiana per la Somalia, shall be recognized as valid and shall be enforceable.

2. Appeal against the qadis' decisions shall be made, in the first instance, to the governor, and in the last resort to the Administrator of the Compagnia Italiana per la Somalia.

3. The law shall be applied according to the provisions of the Sharia.

4. All decisions and all notarial acts shall be recorded in the books that have been delivered to the Governor to this effect.

5. Upon request of the parties concerned, the qadis shall release a copy of the acts and of the decisions recorded.

6. A tax of one percent of the declared value shall be levied on all recorded deeds concerning drafts, promises of payment, sales of personal property and real estate, mortgages, and all other commercial or financial transactions.

7. For all deeds concerning criminal cases and for powers of attorney, the tax shall be half a Thaler or one Thaler, as fee for preparing the copy, in accordance with the value of the matter to which the decision and the recording refer.

8. The books to be used for the transcription of the decisions and the notarial acts shall be kept by the Governor. Copy of the decisions and deeds shall be sent monthly to the Administrator of the Compagnia Italiana per la Somalia. At the bottom of each deed and decision, and their copies, the wadi shall specify the amount of tax levied.

9. At the end of the year, the tax paid in accordance with Article 6 shall be divided as follows: 75% to the Company, 10% to the Governor, 15% to the qadis.

Drawn up in Mogadishu, on the 24th of October 1893.
Signed: Filonardi, Administrator of the Compagnia Italiana per la Somalia

Source: Finazzo (1966), 390–391; Vianello and Kassim, Servants of the Sharia, Vol. 1, 53–54.

[by] obliging the qadis to record decisions that ran contrary to the shari'a."[80]

Under the Benadir Company, many different people claimed to be judges. Although the governor instructed his agents to use shari'a to resolve disputes between Europeans and Somalis, residents complained

[80] The qadi in this court record decided to dissolve a marriage contract because "the [Italian] Consul thought it advisable" to separate the husband and wife. Brava Qadi Record (QR) 515.3, dated 26 Shawwal 1316 (approximately March 6, 1899), in Vianello and Kassim (2006), 1121.

to Benadir Company inspectors that judges actually had "no standard for the administration of justice." They expressed dissatisfaction with the company administration because "in the various stations justice [was] administered according to each resident's individual criteria ... In substance there [was] no organization of justice."[81] This legal pluralism, however, may have helped Italian commercial and administrative elites. When shari'a did not work for them, they forum-shopped by turning to other legal systems for help. "It was ... Italian policy not to tamper with the indigenous judicial institutions. Elements of the Italian judicial system were grafted onto the traditional Islamic and Somali systems. The result of this policy was that much of the Somali testur [custom] and the Muslim Shari'a survived the colonial period."[82]

While very few documents from the Italian administration, particularly from its later years, have survived in Somalia, Italian lawyer Alessandra Vianello and Somali historian Mohamed M. Kassim found a treasure trove of cases recorded from 1893 to 1900 in Brava, a town of about 5,000 residents on the Somali coast, governed by the Benadir Company. The two-volume, 2,200-page compilation of these cases does not reveal what was happening throughout all the Italian-occupied areas, but it does showcase how shari'a came to matter in a legally plural colonial Somali context. Judges calling themselves cadis wrote opinions in Arabic and consistently signed their names alongside the phrase, "*khaadim al-shari'a*" ("servant of the shari'a"). As Italy was trying to cement its grip on administrative and legal power, these judges' opinions, according to Vianello and Kassim, "constantly reiterated their reverence for ... Islamic law."[83]

Shari'a mattered not only to Italian and British colonial officials but also to Somalis who accessed aqils, elders, and qadis to have their disputes resolved. Shari'a mattered as well to politically engaged Somali elites. They turned the shari'a principles they had learned in the Arabian Peninsula against colonialism, using those religious principles as the basis of their anticolonial struggles. Colonial officials and Somali elites pulled Islam toward two contradictory political goals; paradoxically, Islam was put to use both shoring up and rebelling against colonial rule. By analyzing British Somaliland's two-decade anticolonial war, the following section shows how the process of

---

[81] Hess (1966), 74, citing communication from "Eduardo Cappa, Brava, to Elia Raicevich, Inspector of the Benadir Company," March 11, 1903. Archivio Storico dell'ex Ministero dell'Africa Italiana (ASMAI), Rome, pos. 75/6, f. 60.

[82] Hess (1966), 184.

[83] Vianello and Kassim (2006), 1.

inventing a colony through legal politics and religion does not lack challengers. Among these colonial critics were Somali sheikhs, still lauded by many Somalis as nationalist heroes, who were concerned about the impact of colonialism on Somali communities.

SHAPING A COLONY THROUGH RELIGION

Studying courts alone does not do justice to the precarious relationships that colonial administrators and Somali elites had with religion and religious law. Shari'a provided them with a basis for dispute resolution, a rationale for their decisions, and an image of piety and control. Both British and Somali elites cared about law and specifically about Islamic law, trying to transform it, control it, and convince their adversaries to cease their own uses of it. Each elite actor – Somali and British – felt more entitled than the other to interpret God's will for Somali people to follow. Deploying legal and religious ideas as a weapon of resistance ultimately fragmented shari'a into different political practices in the contest for power.

To illuminate this conflict between colonial officials and anticolonial activists over the meaning of shari'a, this section turns to the twenty-one-year war (1899–1920) between the British government and Sheikh Mohamed Abdullah Hassan (Somali: Sayyid Maxamed Cabdulle Xasan; hereinafter, "Sheikh Hassan"). This war nearly bankrupted the British Crown's administration in Somaliland. The strength of Sheikh Hassan's religious convictions and of his followers, some of whom were armed militiamen, prompted the British to give Sheikh Hassan the derisive moniker "Mad Mullah" in an attempt to discredit Somali activities against British colonialism.[84] Sheikh Hassan had created his own Islamic courts to resolve disputes and, in part because the British viewed these courts and Sheikh Hassan's militias as a threat to British colonial legitimacy and power, the British waged war against Sheikh Hassan and his followers.

---

[84] I. M. Lewis, *A Modern History of the Somali: Nation and State in the Horn of Africa* (London: Boydell and Brewer, 2003), 72. Some historians place the earliest mention of the "Mad Mullah" moniker at 1899, in an official report in which Somaliland consul-general J. Hayes-Sadler wrote, "the Mullah has gone religious mad." John P. Slight, "British and Somali Views of Muhammad Abdullah Hassan's *Jihad*, 1899–1920," 10 *Bildhaan: An International Journal of Somali Studies* (2011): 16–35, 19. According to historian Said Samatar, the label "Mad Mullah" (Somali: *Wadaad Waal*) was also used by some Somalis, including people in Berbera from the Qaadiriya religious order. Samatar (1982), 183. The meaning of *waal* (typically translated as "mad") is disputed, however, and ranges from insane to reckless to brave. Samatar (1982), 184.

Differing interpretations of Islam and its uses in politics shaped interactions between the Somalis and the British. Despite being non-Muslims, the British were riveted by Islam. It was not merely that shari'a became a rallying cry for those Somalis who wanted to wrest control from the British. It also became an obsession for the British themselves, who felt free to justify their colonial project on Islamic terms. The two groups differed over how best to flatten shari'a discourse to meet each group's primary goal of either colonial control or liberation from it.[85] Pulling shari'a in both colonial and anticolonial directions enriched and complicated it, and exposed Somalis to divergent interpretations of God's will. At root were two distinct versions of Islam and of Islam's place in modernity. One view of shari'a made room for British colonialism and the other rejected it.

Why does this battle over shari'a, fought so long ago, matter to those who care about the relationship between the rule of law and religion, or legal pluralism and state development? British and Somali confrontations over shari'a reveal how the legacies of colonialism permeate and are permeated by debates over legal and religious ideology. The discursive competition between British and Somali elites shows how shari'a can shape war, as its interpretations take on specific meanings that become logics of disagreement. Not only did the British and the Somalis who fought British colonial rule agree on the need to find space for shari'a in the development of their ideal views of the state and society; both sides used their own interpretations of shari'a as a basis for discussion and, ultimately, battle. The issue was one of interpretation and representation: Who had the right to interpret and represent shari'a? Because British and Somali elites both claimed that right, shari'a still shapes Islam's legacies in the Horn of Africa.

Sheikh Hassan's Rise

Mohamed Abdullah Hassan, a Somali man who had studied Islam in Mecca in the 1880s, returned to Somaliland in the 1890s to become a civil society leader and traveling preacher of sorts, whose religious interpretations attracted supporters. News reports suggest that Sheikh Hassan was disillusioned with British rule in part because the British had handed over the western region of Somaliland, where Hassan's

---

[85] Mark Fathi Massoud, "The Politics of Islamic Law and Human Rights: Sudan's Rival Legal Systems," in *The New Legal Realism, Volume 2: Studying Law Globally*, Heinz Klug and Sally Engle Merry, eds. (Cambridge: Cambridge University Press, 2016a), 96–112.

powerful Mijjertain family was connected, to Ethiopian Emperor Menelik.[86]

Sayyid Hassan, as he came to be known among Somalis, gained a reputation as an orator and poet. Oral poetry was the principal medium of persuasion and mass communication in greater Somalia at this time, and, according to historian Said Samatar, "By any standard the Sayyid could be judged an artist of great power and by Somali standards as something of a literary master." The period from 1875 to 1900 was a time of "widespread religious re-awakening" in African Islam which, occurring alongside "the increasing subjugation of Muslims ... to Euro-Christian rule," gave rise to resistance movements like the anticolonial Dervish movement that Sheikh Hassan would eventually start.[87]

Sheikh Hassan was also a dispute resolver with extensive Islamic legal training in Mecca. While not all Somalis trusted him to resolve their disputes, he was widely regarded in British Somaliland as a respected "peace-maker [during a time of] inter-clan strife."[88] Initially, the British administration did not see Sheikh Hassan's work as a threat to colonialism. On the contrary, according to British reports,

> [Hassan's] influence seemed to be exerted for good. He settled disputes amongst those remote tribes, prevented them from raiding each other, and was regarded by the [British] Administration as being on the side of law and order generally. From time to time he corresponded with the Vice-Consul at Berbera about tribal matters, and occasionally sent down prisoners for trial in the Vice-Consular Court. Thus he acquired considerable influence over the tribes, and people were quick to realize that his rough and ready justice was preferable to the long journey to Berbera.[89]

The British had appreciated Sheikh Hassan's work because, under his influence, once "cantankerous tribes" seemed to become more peaceful.[90] But in August 1899, Hassan declared himself a Mahdi (anointed one) and his relationship with the British began to sour as

[86] "The Pacification of Somaliland," *Egyptian Daily Post*, May 20, 1909. Wingate Collection, Sudan Archive, Durham University, 287/2/234.
[87] Samatar (1982), 3, 93, 137. Samatar continues that, "of the 120 poems which have so far been collected and verified as his, almost two-thirds are poetic diatribes attacking colonial infidels and their Somali collaborators." Samatar (1982), 152, citing collection of Sheikh Jaama' 'Umar 'Iise (Aw Jaamac Cumar Ciiseo), *Diiwaanka Gabayadii*.
[88] Lewis (2003), 68.
[89] Sir Geoffrey Francis Archer, *Personal and Historical Memoir of an East Africa Administrator* (Edinburgh: Oliver & Boyd, 1963), 57–58. Archer copied these statements from Wingate's 1909 report on file at the Sudan Archive, Durham University, SAD 125.
[90] Ray Beachey, *The Warrior Mullah: The Horne Aflame 1892–1920* (London: Bellew Publishing, 1990), 39.

he preached an austere view of Islam for the Somali people.[91] He also lost support from some Somalis over his interpretations of zakat (charitable giving governed by shari'a) and the use of religious texts to solve problems,[92] and because he opposed the Somalis' widespread use of qat, a leafy branch that, when chewed, acts as a stimulant drug.[93]

The British, having seen the power of Islamic resistance during Sudan's fourteen-year nationalist rebellion, were wary of another self-proclaimed Mahdi. Therefore they made it a priority to defeat Sheikh Hassan. Violence ensued in the northern Horn between Sheikh Hassan's followers and Somali supporters of the British administration who, according to the British, had their own "fanatical hatred" toward Sheikh Hassan.[94] By 1901, Hassan amassed thousands of soldiers, many carrying spears or other deadly weapons.

The war with Hassan was exacerbated by his raiding Somali communities that British treaties had promised to protect. The British began to sign more treaties with Somali communities in response to violence among them over Hassan's teachings and to what the administration saw as his threats to British interests. Perhaps formal agreements between the British and Somali groups could thwart Hassan's advances. The British hoped "to compel the tribes to enter into agreements with [the British administration] assuring their good conduct in the future and closing the Dolbahanta country to the Mullah should he ever return."[95]

In effect, the British had facilitated and then joined a war that was erupting between Somali communities on different sides of Sheikh Hassan's vision of Islamic-based dispute resolution. As Hassan's authority as a great Muslim liberator of the Somali people grew, particularly between 1900 and 1902, the British were also busy trying to maintain order in their own communities where resistance to colonial rule was also mounting. They did so by passing laws for their administration and its "friendly tribes." These included alcohol,

---

[91] "Lieutenant-General Sir Reginald Wingate's Special Mission to Somaliland," June 12, 1909. Foreign Office Confidential Prints, Bodleian Law Library, Oxford University, 9507/17.

[92] Sheikh Hassan worked within Hanbali traditions of Sunni Islamic law, while many Somalis followed the Shafi'i school of Sunni Islamic law. While practices associated with these two schools were not totally dissimilar, they differed significantly in interpretation, in approaches to solving problems, and in the payment of zakat (Follow-up interview 70 with Kabir, lawyer and senior university administrator in Hargeisa, Somaliland, July 2013).

[93] Beachey (1990), 38.

[94] Africa No. 3, 1902, p. 17. Wingate Collection, Sudan Archive, Durham University, SAD 125/1.

[95] Ibid.

tax, and labor regulations,[96] sporting regulations;[97] firearms regulations;[98] ordinances to preserve game;[99] customs regulations;[100] and marriage regulations. To ensure that colonial administrators, too, complied, the administration passed regulations on the employment of officers in British Somaliland and on the activities of public officials, governing conflicts of interest and preventing commercial pursuits by British officials.[101]

In 1902, the administration's war effort against Sheikh Hassan began to break down, and the British administration considered a policy of complete retreat from the region. London defeated the colonial administration's withdrawal proposal, and the British stayed, albeit befuddled by Sheikh Hassan's motives and the strength of his war against them.[102] Some said Hassan's activities had "nothing to do with any religious movement,"[103] while others argued that it was precisely Hassan's religious views that prompted him and his supporters to fight the British. For example, a footnote in a British report of its military activity in Somaliland says of Hassan's followers: "These men were called Derawēsh, and were under oath to fight for their religion."[104] Historians, too, agree with the explanation that Sheikh Hassan was "inspired by a religious desire to revive Islam in Somalia."[105] His efforts reflected a "rigid interpretation of the Shafi'i school of [Sunni] Islamic law."[106] Seeing the "Mad Mullah" as a threat to the security of

---

[96] Ordinance No. 5 of 1901. Document 7603, Foreign Office Confidential Prints, Bodleian Library, Oxford University.

[97] Sporting Regulations, January 1, 1902. Document 7640, Foreign Office Confidential Prints, Bodleian Library, Oxford University.

[98] Fire-arms Regulations of 1899. Foreign Office Confidential Prints, Bodleian Library, Oxford University.

[99] Preservation of Game Ordinance, July 10, 1901. Document 7665, Foreign Office Confidential Prints, Bodleian Library, Oxford University.

[100] Customs regulations of 1902, 682. Foreign Office Confidential Prints, Bodleian Library, Oxford University.

[101] Regulations for the Employment of Officers in the British Protectorate on the Somali Coast. September 1, 1902. Document 7762, Foreign Office Confidential Prints. Bodleian Library, Oxford University.

[102] Communication of J. L. Baird, Member of the British Parliament for Rugby and Acting Agent and Consul General in Abyssinia (1902). Sudan Archive, Durham University, SAD 296/1/157.

[103] Foreign Office Confidential Prints, Document 9508/7, Bodleian Law Library, Oxford University.

[104] "Dispatch relating to Field Operations" by Lieutenant-Colonel Swayne to Consul-General Sadler." Africa No. 3, 1902, p. 31.

[105] Slight (2011), 22.

[106] Lewis (2003), 81.

British interests in the region, in 1903 the British War Office in London became increasingly involved in Somaliland.[107]

In 1905, another round of skirmishes ended – this time with a treaty with Sheikh Hassan, the Illig Agreement.[108] But that agreement collapsed three years later. British documents claimed Sheikh Hassan's followers were "raiding the Sultans of Obbia and of the Mijjertein … obtaining arms and munitions."[109] In returning to war, the British focused on the illegality of Sheikh Hassan's actions. According to them, the "Mullah had broken the agreements he had come to with us."[110] Sheikh Hassan had been having problems with the British and also with Italian colonialism in the southern Horn and, according to the British, Hassan put pressure on them in order to punish the Italians, a strategy that quickly failed. The British sent cavalries of the King's African Rifles into Somaliland as conflict restarted in 1908.[111] Confidential interagency memoranda between the Colonial Office and the War Office about the Mad Mullah[112] indicate that the key British strategy was dividing Somalis through increased military support from Whitehall and "entering into relations with and subsidizing all the separate and principal chiefs of the coast."[113] Officials spent more than a decade trying to suppress Sheikh Hassan's activities, while continuing to keep supply lines to Aden open by trading with "friendly" Somali merchants and elders and passing laws for those communities.[114]

The year 1909 became a critical juncture for shari'a. The establishment of the Roman Catholic mission in Berbera that year inflamed Sheikh Hassan and his followers, even though the British had taken steps to close the church.[115] The British viewed Sheikh Hassan as

---

[107] Sudan Archive, Durham University, SAD 273/7/6–7.

[108] Lewis (2003), 74.

[109] "Affairs in Somaliland," May 1908–December 1909, Colonial Office Confidential Prints, 926/143. Bodleian African and Commonwealth Library, Oxford University.

[110] Ibid., 926/144.

[111] In December 1908, the King's African Rifles Ordinance created a battalion of people "charged with the defence of the East Africa, Uganda, British Central Africa, and Somaliland Protectorates." Colonial Office Confidential Prints, 919/1–23. Bodleian African and Commonwealth Library, Oxford University.

[112] "Affairs in Somaliland," May 1908–December 1909, Colonial Office Confidential Prints, 926/1–144. Bodleian African and Commonwealth Library, Oxford University.

[113] "Ibid., 926/144.

[114] Winston Churchill, "A Minute on the Somaliland Protectorate," Colonial Office Confidential Prints 896/3. Oxford University Bodleian Library. October 28, 1907, also at Durham University Sudan Archive, SAD 125/1/3.

[115] Private Correspondence of Sir R. Wingate to Sheikh Abdel Kader in Burao, Somaliland. Sudan Archive, Durham University, SAD 287/2/140.

a madman intent on imposing his views of shari'a on the region.[116] Newspaper accounts began to portray the inhabitants of Somaliland along similar lines, as "fervid Mohammedans."[117] Rumors swirled that the British might put their protectorate under Egyptian administration.[118] Instead, the British began a two-part contest – military and discursive – first, to "arm friendlies"[119] and, second, to engage in a full assault of words against Sheikh Hassan, arguing with him in letters over the proper interpretation of shari'a. The next section examines these communications in detail; they reveal how competition to control shari'a discourse played an important role in the fight over the legitimacy of foreign intervention, colonization, and state development.

Bringing Shari'a into Battle

Alongside the war, a discursive battle over the meaning of shari'a was heating up between British officials and Sheikh Hassan and his followers. According to British reports, Hassan fought the British colonial project using words as well as weapons: "The significant thing is that [Sheikh Hassan] repeatedly sought to achieve in verse what he had failed to achieve in arms," which was to inspire Muslims to remove British authority from the region.[120] British administrators grew increasingly concerned about Sheikh Hassan's ability to unite Somalis by promoting Islam, which overcame rivalries tied to familial or clan heritages.[121] And Sheikh Hassan did not fight solely against British colonialism. He had followers in the Ogaden region of Ethiopia, where his family originated; in French Somaliland, where he was known to have been acquiring weapons; and in Italian Somalia.[122] The British shared reports of Sheikh Hassan's activities, and his intercepted letters, with other colonial powers. In these reports, the British called Sheikh Hassan's letters "severe" and "inspired by religious principles in the Quran."[123]

---

[116] Sudan Archive, Durham University, SAD 237/3/140.
[117] Sudan Archive, Durham University, SAD 287/2/134.
[118] Untitled cutting, *New York Herald*, March 15, 1909. Sudan Archive, Durham University, SAD 286/2/26.
[119] Sudan Archive, Durham University, SAD 286/2/27.
[120] Wingate (1909), SAD 287/3/181; see also Samatar (1982), 181.
[121] Lewis (2003), 76.
[122] British intelligence reports suggest Sheikh Hassan was receiving weaponry and support from "Jibuti." Sudan Archive, Durham University, SAD 287/1/196.
[123] The original diplomatic communication uses the French "*passages très sévéres*" and "*inspirée aux principes religieux du Coran.*" See "Reports on Activities of the Mullah as of March 1, 1909." Wingate Collection, Sudan Archive, Durham University, SAD 286/2/3.

Letters that Sheikh Hassan and the British exchanged either directly or via emissaries – largely between 1908 and 1920, at the height of the British Somaliland war – enacted their discursive fight. Both British archives and Somali oral histories record these communications.[124] The British tried to integrate their own social, political, and economic views into Islam and Sheikh Hassan did the same. Shari'a became the reloadable legal weapon in their war.

British officials and Sheikh Hassan argued about who can interpret shari'a, who understands its tenets better, and who can use it for political purposes. British officials directly accused Sheikh Hassan of not following shari'a. They argued that Sheikh Hassan "run[s] the risk of [distancing himself] from Islam if he keeps on killing Muslims, raping their wives, and taking over their property."[125] Hassan, in turn, responded by encouraging the British themselves to uphold shari'a and obey Islam, and accused them of failing to understand the Qur'an:

> From the Servant of The Almighty God ... It is the duty of us both to obey the order of Islam, to repent and to follow the orders of God and the rules of the Holy Mohammedan Law (Shari'a Mohammediya). If you do this we will do the same, but it is a sin to order others to be upright and not to be so yourselves. God says "You order people to be righteous and forget your own selves" and if you are reading God's book, are you not able to understand this?[126]

According to Colonial Office documents, "The Mullah's prestige received a severe blow by ... the head of the Mullah's sect at Mecca, who denounced his brutalities and excesses, and accused him of being a religious imposter."[127] It is unclear whether the British asked religious leaders in Mecca to reject Hassan, or whether they denounced Hassan of their own volition, without British involvement.[128] But the British certainly advertised the contents of these communications. The Mullah's war against British colonialism was also making headlines as far away as North America. The *New York Herald* reported in March 1909 that some

---

[124] Copies of correspondence between British officials and Sheikh Hassan. Wingate (1909), SAD 446/5/301–309.
[125] Ibid.
[126] Ibid.
[127] "Confidential Memorandum Respecting Affairs of Somaliland." March 4, 1909. Foreign Office Confidential Prints – Colonial Office. Bodleian Library, Oxford University.
[128] Muftis and other scholars in Mecca at the time were writing about European powers in Africa and the nature of the Islamic state, particularly as embodied by the Mahdi in Sudan. See Heather J. Sharkey, "Ahmad Zayni Dahlan's Al-Futuhat Al-Islamiyya: A Contemporary View of the Sudanese Mahdi," 5 *Sudanic Africa* (1994): 67–75.

Somalis were deserting Sheikh Hassan "owing to the threat to excommunicate him from the Mohammedan religion which was made in March last [1908] from Mecca and which very possibly may be carried into effect."[129] British reports at this time were also clear about wanting to rid Somaliland of what they saw as a radical or "fervent" Islam: "From a purely military point of view it cannot be doubted that the best and safest policy would be to crush the Mullah once and for all."[130]

In a 1909 letter, Sheikh Hassan again accused British officials of involving themselves in Somali political, religious, and legal affairs by establishing courts, imprisoning wayward Somalis, and interfering in disputes between believing Muslims over shari'a:

> [Both] I and the Tribes of Idowar and Dolbahanta are all your subjects (from the beginning) and when we had a religious difference which you did not have, you interfered among us without reason and helped one against the other and destroyed others without cause as well, although we are all your subjects from the beginning. You are requested to explain the reasons which induced you to act in this way ... You are always insulting your subjects by putting them to death, flogging them, casting them into prison, looting them, inflicting fines on them, cursing and punishing and blaming them.[131]

The British fought shari'a discourse with more shari'a discourse. They told Sheikh Hassan plainly that his actions were "contrary to Sharia Mohammediya." He replied that if the British understood shari'a so well then they should "send ulemas" to argue religious law with him and that if he was found in the wrong, he would "repent and give up all" his arms, horses, and property.[132] Hassan then told British officials that they – not he and his followers – were the ones actually violating shari'a:

> If, after arguing with your learned men (Ulemas) under the Holy Mohammedan Law, we are [wrong], we will truly repent before God and the Prophet and will give back all that we have unlawfully taken, as a repentant man should do; and we will never again fight the Christians, their subjects, or the Abyssinians ... This is on condition that your

---

[129] Untitled cutting, *New York Herald*, March 15, 1909. Sudan Archive, Durham University, SAD 286/2/26.

[130] Wingate (1909), SAD 287/3/181.

[131] July 1909 letter from Sayed Mohamed Ibn Abdullah El Hashmi (Sheikh Mohamed Abdullah Hassan) to the British Government. Wingate Collection, Sudan Archive, Durham University, SAD 288/2/109, also at Sudan Archive, Durham University, SAD 446/5/301.

[132] "Interview with the Messengers who took the letter from the Mission to the Mullah, Sheikh, Somaliland." June 14, 1909. Sudan Archive, Durham University, SAD 446/5/315.

learned men (Ulemas) convince us that we were wrong, and I swear by God (three times), the Faith, the Prophet, the Throne and Seat, the Slate and Pen, the Angels ... On the other hand I must ask you, if we confute your accusations by the Holy Mohammedan Law, what would you do with us, as it is you who have created sedition such as never been seen or heard of before? ... If, however, we defeat you by the Holy Mohammedan Law, you must give us back all our property, such as the dhow, its crew and cargoe [sic], [and] the ninety-five men you killed at Galadi.[133]

The battle took a regional turn when British officials reached out to their counterparts in Sudan, which had become a British holding in 1898. The British administration sent Muslim Sundanese envoys to Somaliland to discuss shari'a with Sheikh Hassan, as he had requested. The British then penned an open response in Arabic to "all Dervishes." The response also raised the issue that Mohamed Saleh, the leader of Sheikh Hassan's tariqa (brotherhood) in Mecca, had told him he was following the "wrong path":

As you, Oh Dervishes, request us to send our learned men (Ulemas) to discuss and argue with you, with the object of discovering whether your actions and hostilities are right and based on the teaching of the Holy Mohammedan Law (Sharia Mohammediya), we must point out to you that we know of no learned men (Ulemas) so well versed in theology and more greatly to be relied upon that the famous Ulemas of Mecca. The celebrated El Seyid Mohammed Saleh himself, the head of the Salehiya Tarika, has written to you on this subject explaining that you are in the wrong and advising you to repent before God the Almighty and follow the right path. If Seyid Mohammed Ibn Abdullah has any objections to make against the statements of El Seyid Mohammed Saleh on this subject, the way to the Holy Mecca is open to him and we have given him the Aman (peace) of God and His Prophet and of the Government in order that he may go to the House of God and return, if he has the intention of so doing. We conclude this letter with Salaams.[134]

Here, the British were offering Sheikh Hassan protection to return to Mecca, talk to Sayyid Mohamed Saleh, and ideally (for the British), to relearn shari'a in a way that would put an end his anticolonial struggle.

---

[133] Letter from Sheikh Hassan. Sudan Archive, Durham University, SAD 446/3/303, also at Wingate Collection, Sudan Archive, Durham University, SAD 125.
[134] Page two of the response from Wingate and Slatin Pasha "to all the Dervishes," June 16, 1909, in the town of Sheikh, Somaliland, Wingate Collection, Sudan Archive, Durham University, SAD 125.

Their bid to get Sheikh Hassan to leave Somaliland was unsuccessful. But the British continued to capitalize on Sayyid Mohamed Saleh's disagreements with Sheikh Hassan, and debates among Muslims over how to interpret shari'a's relationship to colonialism. British officials wrote to Sheikh Hassan's followers that

> Sheikh El Seyid Mohammed Saleh [in Mecca] ... is your Head and Leader. [He] supported you from the beginning, but ... after having watched your doings, [he] has written to you fully explaining that your deeds have been contrary to the Holy Mohammedan Law (Shari'a Mohammediya) and order[ed] you to repent and to ask the forgiveness of God.[135]

In that letter, British envoys from Sudan requested that Sheikh Hassan send his own envoys "who could speak Arabic [to] discuss these matters" and disagreements over how to interpret shari'a for the Somali people.[136] But Sheikh Hassan, according to the letter, did not respond to that request.

Communications continued to sour over the struggle for authority and particularly the issue of who understood God's will better. Self-proclaimed mujtahids (interpreters of Islamic jurisprudence) also wrote letters to British officials using shari'a to justify their decision to rise up against the British government.[137] Some staff members in London's colonial office, in return, offered their services to negotiate with Hassan. One official in particular argued that, despite being based in London, he had "quite an exceptional knowledge of Mohammedan law," indicating that at least in London the dispute with Sheikh Hassan was thought to be over religion, not colonial domination. British officials in Somaliland responded that knowledge of shari'a would be of no use without "knowledge of negotiation and the administration of Oriental countries."[138]

Contemporaneous recollections of discussions British colonial officials had with envoys they sent to meet with Sheikh Hassan indicate that the envoys did indeed try to change Hassan's views of shari'a. They

[135] Letter from Wingate (Governor-General of Anglo-Egyptian Sudan) and Slatin Pasha (Sirdar of the Army) to El Seyid Mohammed Ibn Abdullah. Sudan Archive, Durham University, SAD 125/6/328.
[136] Ibid.
[137] Letter from Hashim El Shafii El Sumii. Wingate Collection, Sudan Archive, Durham University, SAD 288/6/122–25.
[138] Wingate (1909), SAD 287/3/148.

thought Hassan did not understand the Qur'an as the British and their Muslim supporters understood it:

> They [Sheikh Hassan and his aides] further pointed out that the pre-
> sence of Christians ruling over a Mohammedan country was altogether
> unjustified and is contrary to the Mohammedan law. When we [envoys
> from Sudan] explained to them the difference between temporal power
> and religious authority [in shari'a], he failed to understand it, arguing
> that any Moslem who places himself in a position of subordination to
> a Christian must necessarily be acting contrary to the Mohammedan
> Religion, and, being an ignorant man and only knowing how to read the
> Koran without understanding it, we found it practically impossible to
> alter his opinions or views on this point.[139]

When the British and their Sudanese envoys attempted to correct Sheikh Hassan by letting him know that important Somali elders disapproved of his actions, Hassan responded that those elders "have no knowledge or sense or a spark of religion, and in fact know nothing" about Islam.[140] The British acknowledged their discursive battle by referring to Hassan ultimately as "neither a good Mohammedan or Christian."[141] These words reflect British officials' insistence that shari'a, and the Islamic religion itself, were consistent with the pre-dominant European Christian worldview of the time, which supported colonialism.

The British use of shari'a, like Sheikh Hassan's, was rhetorical and strategic. But it was also ideological. The battle of words between Sheikh Hassan and the British colonial administration that began in 1909 continued alongside actual military raids of rival communities that year, and it lingered on and off for another decade. Hassan and the British both had to shift their attention back and forth between mili-tary strategy and shari'a. According to the anthropologist I. M. Lewis, "Although [Sheikh Hassan] never lost sight of his primary [religious] purpose ... the pressure of circumstances made it inevitable that he should become increasingly preoccupied with the organization and military needs of the Dervishes."[142] Sheikh Hassan died in 1920 – presumably of malaria or influenza, historical records are unclear – as

---

[139] Notes from the Interview with the Messengers who took the letter from the Mission to the Mullah, June 14, 1909. Sudan Archive, Durham University, SAD 125/6/337.

[140] Letter from Seyyid Mohamed Abdullahi (Sheikh Hassan) to the British Government. Wingate Collection, Sudan Archive, Durham University, SAD 288/2/109.

[141] Supplement to the Report on Lieutenant-General Sir Reginald Wingate's Special Mission to Somaliland, July 1909, p. 7. Sudan Archive, Durham University, SAD 125/7/2.

[142] Lewis (2003), 81.

the British were still waging war against him. The British colonial administration never regained its footing; the years between Sheikh Hassan's 1920 death and World War II brought continued political and economic stagnation to Somaliland.[143]

CONCLUSION

This chapter has shown how colonial administrators tried to build a state, primarily in British Somaliland, through two primary channels: law and religion. British administrators, the Somalis who worked under them, and those who resisted colonial authority all used their own legal and religious tools – including distinct versions of shari'a – to achieve their goals. The British protectorate scheme was designed to build trust in the colonial enterprise through legal structures that invoked but also carefully controlled religion. The scheme took shari'a seriously as a necessary part of the governing structure and the government's interactions with a Muslim-majority population. But by constructing both qadi courts and civil courts, the British controlled the process of dispute resolution and sought to confine shari'a to family matters.

Understanding state development in the Horn of Africa involves coming to terms with elites' conflicting allegiances to different forms of law, including the ways in which they turn to shari'a to achieve their political, economic, and social goals. Divided as the region was by multiple forms of colonialism, British colonial officials engaged in their own form of legal politics by writing treaties, creating courts, controlling dispute processes and personnel, reinvigorating aqils as a political tool, and fighting over the appropriate uses of shari'a in politics. Somalis in turn either submitted to British control or fought against subjugation using Islamic legal practices and discourses of their own. In this way, colonial shari'a was shaped by both local and transnational practices, relationships, and struggles for political power. Elites attempted to change the meanings of shari'a and people's relationships with law, religion, and the state. In the process, the colonial encounter built up, changed, and politicized religion.

Somalis I met during my fieldwork generally spoke critically of the colonial enterprise. But they also spoke appreciatively of British officials' stated goals not to interfere in Somali society. "When the British

---

[143] Patrick Kitaburaza Kakwenzire, "Colonial Rule in the British Somaliland Protectorate, 1905–1939" (Ph.D. thesis, University of London, 1976).

used to run the state affairs, also the customary people – the chiefs, aqils – would solve problems side by side. British people … never interfered. They didn't have a plan to get rid of customary [law]," said one Somali lawyer I met. "From the British we learned a lot – the modern city, the modern state, and the rule of law based on the courts and structures of the state like police and army. They established it," he concluded.[144]

What does this case study of colonial politics reveal for scholars interested in how building up the law, including religious law, fosters state development?

First, law is an essential component of colonial state-building, particularly during times of fragility and violence. In British Somaliland, colonial officials promoted law to achieve imperial goals by codifying treaties with Somalis along the coast, importing civil and criminal codes from colonial India, creating Islamic courts, passing colonial legislation, and encouraging dispute resolution processes designed to promote British legitimacy. The British restructured Somali society into a hierarchy: people with disputes and people – agents of the British government – trusted to resolve those disputes. Local elites helped monitor other locals in a manner designed to shore up the legitimacy of British officials as protectors of Somalis from each other and from outsiders. In its courts and through its aqils, the colonial administration helped to create a new state elite that would separate the people's Islamic faith from the state's Islamic law.

Second, just as colonial officials used aqils and qadis to promote colonial authority and legitimacy, so too did they resist opposition to their authority by using religious law, employing envoys from Sudan and using statements of leading sheikhs from Mecca to counter local opposition. That is, colonial authorities pretended that their sometimes inhumane actions were both legal and religiously correct, by using shari'a to mask what was otherwise a form of political and social domination. The manipulation of law and religion framed colonialism, as colonizers seemed free to use the religion of their subjects to justify their repression of anticolonialism. Paradoxically, Islamic legal practices were simultaneously created, transformed, and restricted during this time.

---

[144] Follow-up interview 70 with Kabir, lawyer and senior university administrator in Hargeisa, Somaliland (July 2013).

Third, shari'a equally allured elites engaging in state development or resisting it. They used it in their repertoire of political practices. Islam was important enough that both British and Somali elites alike felt the need to engage with it. Their battles did not merely involve weapons. They fought over a specific and layered configuration of law – one that alternated between religious and secular, traditional and modern, local and foreign – that they had created. This discursive contestation occurred both among Somalis and between the different groups of Somalis and colonial officials.

Colonialism and resistance to it elicited different versions of shari'a from Somalis, British administrators and their Sudanese envoys, and Meccan sheikhs. Religious law mattered not only for state-building but also for trying to tear down state structures. Differing messages from local aqils and qadis, and from Mecca and Sudan, were filtered through the war between Sheikh Hassan and the colonial administration. In these ways, colonial rule in the Horn of Africa shaped Islamic religious tradition and Islam's relationship with local custom, foreign intervention, and peacebuilding.

At some level, the British created an Islamic state by formalizing shari'a into state development. But, just as they formalized shari'a, the British also fragmented it by making Islamic courts deal narrowly with family matters. The meanings of religious law changed over time as local elites interacted with colonizers and vice versa. British and Somali elites alike used religious and legal discourse to express their hopes, their fears, and their strategies of resisting one another's authority. In so doing, they capitalized on the seemingly unchanging and immortal idea of God's will, convincing pious populations to follow the shari'a of one of them and not of the other. Divergent understandings of Islam shaped Somalis' views not only about what God's will is, but also about what God's will does.

Somalia: Two former colonies united, until 1991.

CHAPTER THREE

CONSTRAINING SHARI'A:
POSTCOLONIAL LEGAL POLITICS

Somalia's years of postcolonial independence are marked by disputes over how to build a stable, modern, and functioning legal system – and what to do with shari'a. From the start of the transition to independence in 1950 until the disintegration of the Somali state in 1991, state actors adopted an instrumental view of state law and shari'a. As in British Somaliland, postcolonial authorities in the newly independent Somali Republic used law to achieve their political goals. They also shared the view that shari'a – when understood as an independent, fixed, and sacred constraint on political power – would pose a threat to the state's legal order and power. Successive governments treated shari'a as an expedient and flexible tool to use for their own purposes. This Islamic legal politics – how political leaders confronted, asserted, and constrained shari'a to achieve political, economic, and social goals – became a central feature of the state's relationship with its people.

Somalis were not alone in wrestling with the high-stakes question of the role of religion and religious law in a post-independence

110

government. The mid-twentieth century created a period of hope for Africans that colonial rule would be replaced by independence and pan-African or pan-Arab unity. In this context of hope, leaders in the newly independent Sudan, like their neighbors in Somalia, were also asking themselves whether and how to integrate shari'a into the legal system.[1] A similar question had come up in Israel, where officials debated whether and how to integrate Hebrew language and Jewish law to replace British law inherited from Mandatory Palestine.[2] More recently, across Muslim-majority countries transitioning from decades of authoritarian rule, political elites also faced the thorny issue of what to do with Islamic law, including in Iraq after Saddam Hussein, Egypt after Hosni Mubarak, Afghanistan after the Taliban, Tunisia after Ben Ali, and Libya after Qaddafi.

The central argument of this chapter is that the postcolonial state's political genesis is as much about remaking religion as it is about remaking law. First, law plays an important role for political elites seeking to build a postcolonial state. They create and use legal systems to build the kind of postcolonial state they envision. Their efforts saturate society with ideals of law and modernity. British administrators encouraged Somalis to see the legal order as a unified one, but they also fragmented legal power – state, Islamic, customary – in order to contain shari'a. Second, there is no natural or presumed relationship between the colonial categories of religion, law, and custom in the postcolonial state. Postcolonial democratic and authoritarian regimes, each for their own purposes, completed the work of colonial officials by further constraining shari'a and *xeer* (Somali custom, used as a form of common law to resolve disputes) and pushing to unite Somalia's legal orders once and for all.

Establishing a postcolonial state using the power of law also gives rise to an uneasy relationship with religion. Just as colonial administrators had invoked their own forms of shari'a to shore up their rule – by, for instance, establishing religious family courts and bringing envoys from Sudan to convince Somalis that Islamic revolutions against colonialism were not actually consistent with Islam – postcolonial political authorities aligned shari'a with their aims. On the one hand, they insisted

---

[1] Mark Fathi Massoud, "How an Islamic State Rejected Islamic Law," 66 *American Journal of Comparative Law* (2018a): 579–602; Zaki Mustafa, *The Common Law in the Sudan: An Account of the "Justice, Equity, and Good Conscience" Provision* (Oxford: Clarendon Press, 1971).

[2] Izhak Englard, "Law and Religion in Israel," 35(1) *American Journal of Comparative Law* (1987): 185–208.

that their activities were consistent with Islam. On the other hand, they silenced the forms of Islamic legal power that they could not control. But not all uses of shari'a were the same. Elites used shari'a as a legal practice, as a method of argument, as a rhetorical style, and as a politically-invoked power for state-building.

This chapter focuses on Somalia's transition to independence and its first thirty years of postcolonial independence, until the state's 1991 collapse. In particular, it investigates how political officials sought to build the Somali state by promoting law and constraining shari'a during the transition to democracy (1950–1960), the first attempt at independent, democratic government (1960–1969), and the twenty-two-year dictatorship of President Mohamed Siad Barre (1969–1991).

Starting in 1950, colonial administrators and Somalis working under them in British Somaliland and Italian Somalia undertook legal unification as part of the decade-long preparation for sovereignty. They wrote new laws to create a state legal order; restructured the old colonial legal systems to prepare the two colonies for unity; established the region's first law school in Mogadishu; and continued to restrict and formalize the application of shari'a. Late-colonial administrators and the Somalis working with them used the law to push the region toward independence and promote a sense of progress and modernity that Somalis would take with them into the new nation.

Once the two colonies united to form the Somali Republic in 1960, Somali leaders still faced the task of unifying the legal system, which led them to combine the two colonial judiciaries created by the British and the Italians. The 1960s were Somalia's only democratic period, and during that time political elites struggled to put the young nation's future ahead of geographic and clan rivalries. They subsumed shari'a into the state by abandoning the British-instituted system of Islamic family courts and giving jurisdiction over family law to the country's newly combined civil judiciary. Despite abolishing the Islamic courts, public officials called shari'a the basis of the unified country's first postcolonial constitution. They understood shari'a as part of the governing structure, but indentured it to state law.

The Somali Republic's democratic experiment did not last. In 1969, General Mohamed Siad Barre led a military coup that installed him as president. Siad Barre's reign reveals how autocrats use law to uphold their authority. More importantly, Siad Barre treated shari'a as a threat he needed to contain, despite continuously claiming that the regime's version of shari'a was the correct one because, in his view, socialism was consistent with Islam. Siad Barre's relationship to shari'a reveals how shari'a's plurality in practice – its proliferation of interpretations of sources, reasonings, and rulings – is precisely what threatens autocrats and leads them to write more laws.

Investigating how Siad Barre crafted and used an extensive bureaucratic and legal apparatus helps make sense not only of his authoritarian legal politics but also of Somalis' profound lack of trust in the state and the law since that time. Though the regime was initially popular because of its promises to make justice more accessible to ordinary Somalis, it ultimately succumbed in 1991 to a devastating civil war. That civil war had ignited as a result of the regime's catastrophic economic policies, its disastrous effort to annex eastern Ethiopia, and its execution of religious leaders for speaking out against state laws they saw as inconsistent with Islamic teachings.

This period of Somali history, from the transition to independence to the collapse of the government a generation later, reveals how different political leaders – colonial, democratic, and authoritarian – used law and invoked religion to create a national antidote for political disagreements. Taking cues from the colonial administrators who preceded them, postcolonial leaders wrote legal documents and passed many new laws, including a new constitution, to cement authority, centralize state power, and singularize the legal system. Siad Barre's desire to craft a unifying and lasting legal order that subsumed shari'a was not unique to his authoritarian state. It was endemic to different governments, including the administrators of British Somaliland and the democratic government that preceded Siad Barre. Each set of political elites tried to fit law and Islam into its image. Despite the differences in their goals, these colonial, democratic, and authoritarian regimes from 1950 to 1991 were united by a common approach: singularize the law and constrain the power of religion. But God's will and authority provided a baseline from which Somalis would judge each political regime's actions and it became the source of their unremitting resistance to state authority – the seeds germinating an Islamic rule of law.

LAW IN TRANSITION, 1950–1960

In the 1950s, British Somaliland and Italian Somalia remained under the control of colonial administrators preparing for independence. The colonial project of promoting law while compartmentalizing shari'a became a postcolonial project and left Somalia with a legacy of simultaneous "dualism and pluralism."[3] Fractured, layered, and parallel legal orders cut across geographically divided areas of the Horn of Africa. "Dualism" refers to the twin state legal systems inherited from British Somaliland and Italian Somalia. "Pluralism" describes how these different state legal systems overlapped with and had jurisdiction over Islamic and indigenous law, which also rested on their own plural foundations and were shaped by trade, colonialism, and intertribal disputes.

In the transition to independence, courts were important politically but not legally. Setting them up created the illusion of institution-building for the benefit of state elites, though the nascent institutions were not necessarily relevant to people's daily lives. British anthropologists working in British Somaliland suggested that most disputes they witnessed in the run up to independence were settled not through the courts but through the payment of *diyya* (roughly translated as blood money) – itself a dispute resolution process of mixed indigenous and Islamic origin. "Diyya-paying groups" were made up of men, often a few hundred and rarely more than a thousand. Their leaders (who were also aqils) collected monetary or other payments from their members to give compensation to communities harmed by their individual or collective actions. Some estimates suggest there were 300 such groups in British Somaliland alone before independence. The diyya-paying groups were not a form of resistance to new laws and courts as much as an acceptable form of dispute resolution that colonial officials found it easier to allow than to suppress. For all their reshuffling of court hierarchies, late colonial administrators preparing for independence were essentially working around still-functioning forms of customary law. In fact, scholars of the region at the time concluded that there existed a "rule of law" among Somalis – not through attempts to establish a state system, but through diyya-paying groups:

> Outside [diyya-paying groups], disputes are settled basically in terms of self-help and administrative intervention, [but] within them there may be said to be a rule of law, for their members have some powers of punishment with which to impose the terms of the treaty which unites them. They have no constitutionally defined leaders and their affairs are regulated by the component elders in ad hoc councils.[4]

---

[3] Sam Amadi, "Religion and Secular Constitution: Human Rights and the Challenge of Sharia," unpublished research paper, Carr Center for Human Rights Policy (Harvard Kennedy School, 2004), 14.

[4] I. M. Lewis, "Modern Political Movements in Somaliland, Part I," 28(3) *Africa: Journal of the International African Institute* (1958b): 244–261, p. 248.

The courts and legislative activity to set up the state had a limited impact, relative to diyya-paying groups, at least among ordinary people. But the process of constructing this formal legal framework still mattered to foreign colonial administrators. They sought out legal justification for their continued intervention to ensure that the postcolonial Somali state would look and act more like a modern (European) state. They passed laws, established courts, and built Quranic schools and legal education programs: legal techniques and religious frameworks were central to their activities. These changes in the transition to independence shaped the legacy that Somali leaders inherited. In a telling moment in his July 1959 address to the new Legislative Assembly, a year before independence, the first Somali Prime Minister spoke of the importance of maintaining such a juridical approach and a fealty to legal principles, just as colonial administrators had done: "All means must be employed *within the framework of legality*," he advised fellow politicians, "in order to obtain the union of all Somali territories ... under the same flag." He concluded that writing and following laws "constitutes ... a duty ... because it is impossible to distinguish between Somali and Somali."[5]

Italy's failures during World War II and the founding of the United Nations shaped the preparations for 1960 sovereignty. After Sheikh Hassan's death in 1920 and the subsequent demise of his anticolonial movement, British administrators in Somaliland focused on maintaining law and order, as they did in other colonies.[6] To rebuild legitimacy, promote trade, and prevent further resistance, colonial administrators continued to integrate shari'a and xeer into the colonial legal system. According to historian Brock Millman,

> A system of law emerged that recognized [xeer] and [shari'a] – the common law and common sense – as a source of Protectorate law. A judicial system to enforce this legal amalgam gradually developed which withstood all efforts of the legal department to much reform it. For the duration of the Protectorate it was difficult to determine where the justice system stopped and where the administration began. To

---

[5] Haji N. A. Noor Muhammad, *The Development of the Constitution of the Somali Republic* (Mogadishu: Ministry of Grace and Justice, Government of the Somali Republic, 1969), 29, emphasis added.
[6] United Kingdom Central Office of Information, "The Somaliland Protectorate," (London: UK Government Overseas Services, undated), 4.

enforce the law a police force was constructed ... [and] a handy little army which ... was effectively a unit of the British line.[7]

Further south, Italian colonial officials were also using legal techniques to justify their rule over Italian Somalia, the settler colony centered in Mogadishu. Like the British, Italian administrators established a local system of courts that applied local versions of shari'a and xeer.[8] But legal directives always ensured that Italian principles superseded indigenous and religious ones, even in cases where no party was Italian. Qadi tribunals in Italian Somalia applied shari'a and xeer to disputes only "where the parties were of Islamic faith and [only] to the extent that they did not conflict with ... general [Italian] principles of law."[9]

Although Italian forces invaded British Somaliland during World War II, by 1941 Allied forces retook the region and surrounding areas, including south into Mogadishu. Following Italy's defeat, victorious parties had to decide what to do with its colonial holdings, including Italian Somalia. The British chose to administer Somaliland, Somalia, and the Ogaden (later the western region of Ethiopia) until 1950. That year, unable to decide between returning the former Italian Somalia to Italy or ceding it to Britain, the United Nations Security Council put it to a vote of the General Assembly, which decided that Italy would administer what was to be called the United Nations Trust Territory of Somaliland under Italian administration (*Amministrazione fiduciaria italiana della Somalia*). The Trust Territory became the UN's ten-year project to prepare Italian Somalia for its independence in 1960. The trusteeship agreement stipulated that the Italian administration would "foster the development of free political institutions and ... promote the development of the inhabitants of the territory towards independence."[10] Following World War II, rising Somali political leaders organized to establish their political independence from European colonial authorities. They did so largely through law and

---

[7] Brock Millman, *British Somaliland: An Administrative History, 1920–1960* (London: Routledge, 2014), 301.

[8] Federico Battera and Alessandro Campo, "The Evolution and Integration of Different Legal Systems in the Horn of Africa: The Case of Somaliland," *Global Jurist Topics*, April 20, 2001, p. 3, https://bit.ly/3aKa5gF (accessed January 1, 2021).

[9] Noor Muhammad (1969), 14, citing "Judicial Regulations," Decree No. 1638 of June 20, 1935.

[10] Article 3.1, United Nations Draft Trusteeship Agreement for the Territory of Somaliland under Italian Administration, Fifth Session of the General Assembly, Supplement No. 10 (A/1294), January 27, 1950 (adopted as United Nations General Assembly Resolution 442.V, December 2, 1950). Other United Nations trust territories in Africa included areas that would later become Rwanda, Burundi, Ghana, Togo, and Cameroon.

through arguments about the relationship between law, shariʻa, and national identity.

Creating Legal Capacity

Somalis made a variety of arguments to legitimize their claims for independence and justifications for uniting the two colonies. One of their primary arguments was rooted, at least rhetorically, in the law. Creating and enforcing law is central to establishing and maintaining a state, and Somalis did not want law to be a barrier to their own statehood. Specifically, Somali elites saw their inheritance of two colonial legal systems – one from the British, the other from Italians – as a major obstacle to statehood and unity.[11] Forming one state with a single legal system was their solution to that problem. Legal rationales for unification were accompanied by economic ones: free trade of livestock and goods would suffer under the "artificial frontiers" enforced by colonial law, exacerbating cross-border conflict.[12]

Somali political elites as early as the 1940s saw legal reform as a necessary precondition for independence and unity. They wrote legal memoranda to colonial and UN officials to share these arguments and to advocate uniting the two colonies. These memos articulated Somalis' vision of a single Somalia in areas under the control of different colonial powers. Because of multicolonial rule, different Somalis were trained to use different laws and procedures depending on the colonial authority governing their locality. But Somali unity, they said, required combining the various colonial legal systems. In terms similar to those of British colonial administrators, Somali leaders argued that establishing a common set of courts within a single nation would increase people's access to justice and prevent violence:

> In the case of claims between people from different territories the aggrieved party is required to cross the frontier and travel hundreds of miles into a country to which he is a stranger. He has to go to a court the members of which look upon him as an "outsider", and one whose laws and procedure are different from the ones he knows. As a result of the cumbersome obstacles put in his way of speedy legal redress the aggrieved party seldom goes to court. The aggrieved

---

[11] Mohamed Jama, "A History of the Somal," unpublished paper from Mogadishu, Somalia, 1963, pp. 27–28, SOAS University of London, L.VH 967.73, 218.869.
[12] Ibid., 57–77.

retaliates against the next person related to the opposite party who comes within his reach. One raid leads to another counter-raid in ever widening circles and, frequently, result in a tribal feud through which many lives are lost and numerous herds of livestock are looted. Had there been no artificial frontiers it would be possible to obtain direct legal redress against the person or persons concerned in the minimum trouble and delay, and all that harm and damage would have been avoided.[13]

In addition to making these arguments for independence and unity, Somali elites and colonial administrators in the run up to independence reinvigorated the legal hierarchies of the colonial project. Rather than fundamentally changing those hierarchies, they embellished them. They brought law closer to the people than ever before by continuing to devolve power and by training new lawyers to work in the state structure.

Starting in 1950, administrators in the Trust Territory drafted new regulations designed to expand the hierarchy and number of positions allocated to Somalis by appointing chief aqils and junior aqils (Somali: *caaqil/caaquilo*, roughly translated as "clan" leaders). Chief and junior aqils served as head local authorities and assistant local authorities, respectively, on behalf of the colonial administration.[14] District commissioners from Europe, however, continued to retain final administrative and judicial power throughout the region.[15] Meanwhile, in British Somaliland, in addition to employing aqils, district commissioners were appointing another group of paid staff called *illalos*. These illalos worked as armed constables, "preventing crime and apprehending offenders against the peace within the Protectorate."[16] According to the Somali Police Force, illalos protected the public by "bringing offenders to court, guarding prisoners, patrolling townships, and accompanying nomad[s] over grazing areas."[17]

---

[13] Somali Delegation to the Third Session of the United Nations, "Memoranda and Petition from the Somali Peoples on the Future of ex-Italian Somaliland and the Unification of all Somali Territories under UN Trusteeship" (1949), cited in Jama (1963), 57.

[14] Ismail Ali Ismail, *Governance: The Scourge and Hope of Somalia* (Vancouver, British Columbia: Trafford Publishing, 2010), 66.

[15] Ibid., 91.

[16] *The Laws of the Somaliland Protectorate: Containing the Ordinances, Orders in Council and Orders of the Secretary of State in Force on the 1st Day of January 1950, prepared by Sir Henry Webb* (London: Waterlow & Sons, 1950), Volume III, p. 514.

[17] Somalia Police Force, "History," https://bit.ly/2KYoPxF (accessed January 1, 2021).

In addition to devolving power, colonial administrators and Somalis in the 1950s invested in legal education programs. Legal education promised to create a self-perpetuating legal system by training the next generations of lawmakers. In Mogadishu, Italian administrators constructed the Horn of Africa's first university, which was not much more than a law faculty. Established on November 10, 1954, as the Higher Institute of Legal, Economic and Social Studies, it was reorganized in 1956 as the University Institute of Law and Economics. (This institute would, in 1969, become Somali National University.[18]) It began by offering a course of studies "to provide training for the practice of . . . lawyers, judges and administrators" and "to study the special problems of Somalia in the field of political, legal, and economic science."[19] While shari'a was not the focus, Islamic law was taught to first-year students. In the academic year for which data are available (1959–60), the institute enrolled thirty to sixty students per class year in the three-year degree course in law and economics (Table 3.1). Eight of these students were women, one of whom was Somali, and the other women of unknown, likely Italian, origin.[20] Four full-time professors were hired

Table 3.1 Courses at Somalia's first university (University Institute of Law and Economics)

Year One	Year Two	Year Three
Public Law	Criminal Law	Constitutional Law
Private Law	Judicial Law	Labor Law
Islamic Law	International Law	Economic Geography
Political Economy	Administrative Law I	Administrative Law II
History of Political Doctrines	Finance	Economic and Financial Policy
Sociology	Statistics	
Arabic I	Arabic II	
English I	English II	

Source: UNESCO, Public Education in Somalia (Geneva: UNESCO, 1960), pp. 73–77.

[18] UNESCO, Public Education in Somalia (Geneva: UNESCO, 1960), 73; Mohamed Haji Mukhtar, Historical Dictionary of Somalia (Oxford: Scarecrow Press, 2003), 235.
[19] UNESCO (1960), 74.
[20] Ibid., 77.

from Italian universities in Padua, Turin, and Rome, in addition to a number of Somali and foreign lecturers, including three judges, a magistrate from the audit office, an Italian lawyer with the Mogadishu bar, a labor law expert from Italy, a Somali *licencie* trained at Al-Azhar University in Egypt, and a teacher of Somali ethnology.[21]

In British Somaliland, where few resources existed, Britain maintained the region "almost as they found it" nearly a century earlier, still without tap water outside of Hargeisa's government areas.[22] There was no state law school in the region; indeed, the first law school in the northern Horn would not open until 2002. However, Quranic schools that taught Arabic language and Islamic philosophy and law grew in preparation for independence. Before World War II, there were nineteen Quranic schools enrolling 400 students (all boys); most were located in the northern town of Sheikh. By 1958, two years before British Somaliland's independence, the number of Quranic schools had increased to 230. Together with thirty-eight local government authority schools, these programs enrolled nearly 2,000 students (1,746 boys and 221 girls). Thirteen "intermediate courses" enrolled an additional 914 students (856 boys and 58 girls).[23] The twelvefold expansion in the number of Quranic schools in British Somaliland and the establishment of Mogadishu's University Institute of Law and Economics show how administrators sought to ensure that Somalis had at least some legal capacity by teaching them state law and shari'a.

Passing Laws, Establishing Courts, and Compartmentalizing Shari'a

To ensure the success of the new state, colonial administrators turned to law. They spent the 1950s drafting laws to legitimize the great number of governmental changes they were making to prepare Somalis for independence. It was a period of significant legislative activity and state institution-building, taking place in parallel in both British Somaliland and the Trust Territory. These formal legal changes were European attempts not only to create the foundation for a postcolonial judiciary but also to ensure that this judiciary would oversee religion.

New laws restructured the colonial legal systems with an eye toward the independent state to come, and its relationship with religion. Chief

[21] Ibid., 74.
[22] Ismail (2010), 86.
[23] United Kingdom Central Office of Information (undated), 5.

among these was the Trust Territory's 1956 judiciary law.[24] This law removed the opportunity of appeal to Italy and created a domestic supreme court, called the Court of Justice, in Mogadishu. Shari'a was recognized as one of the three substantive sections of this high court (the other two were "ordinary" and "special" accounts).[25] The court's "Shariatic" section would have final authority over all cases involving shari'a. Qadi courts in the Trust Territory would continue to hear disputes between Muslims, and they had jurisdiction over crimes committed by Muslims "to the detriment of Muslims."[26] The 1956 judiciary law also set up a Tribunal of Qadis capable of hearing appeals from the qadi courts. In civil matters, three qadis served as an appellate court. In criminal matters, two qadis and a regional judge (usually an Italian) would sit as an appellate court over a qadi court's decision.[27] Finally, the law created a Higher Judicial Council tasked with "supervision and protection of the rights of judges."[28]

In 1944, British administrators in Somaliland created a law that officially established the courts of qadis and constrained them jurisdictionally to deal only with family (also called "personal status") matters.[29] Other subordinate courts dealt with crimes and civil matters of less than 1,500 rupees.[30] Perhaps legitimizing its role as an overseer of Islamic jurisprudence, the British administration abolished all formal aqils' courts and granted jurisdiction to qadis' courts only in "matters affecting the family life of the Somalis such as marriage, divorce, guardianship, succession, and maintenance."[31] Litigants could appeal to the Court of the Chief Qadi. Further south in the Trust Territory, aqils' courts continued to function, but a 1958 amendment to the 1956 judiciary law similarly restricted qadis' jurisdiction only to cases related to marriage, divorce, and notarial acts.[32] Like colonial authorities in Malaya and Egypt, officials in British Somaliland and the Trust

---

[24] Law on the Organization of the Judiciary of 1956, United Nations Trust Territory of Somalia.
[25] Noor Muhammad (1969), 16.
[26] Ibid., 15.
[27] Ibid., 16.
[28] Ibid., 17, 18. The administration also established a military court in Mogadishu to deal with penal military matters. Law No. 10 of February 20, 1958.
[29] Subordinate Courts Ordinance of July 1, 1944.
[30] Noor Muhammad (1969), 25.
[31] Ibid.
[32] Amendment to Judiciary Law, Somalia Trust Territory, June 8, 1958, cited in Noor Muhammad (1969), 18.

Territory sought to ensure that judges of Islamic law had no jurisdiction over criminal matters.[33]

In the Trust Territory, as nationalism grew and independence approached, officials were supposed to replace Italians with Somalis in administrative and judicial posts in order to achieve a "fuller transfer of judicial power."[34] But three of the six Qadi tribunal judges were non-Muslim Italians and the other three seats lay vacant, which in practice meant that three Italians had supervisory authority over all Islamic-related disputes in the Trust Territory (Table 3.2). The Italians' failed attempts at transferring judicial power undercut Somali elites' desire to create a meaningful justice system that would endure the transition to independence.

Trust Territory administrators were hoping to make it easier for Somalis, particularly in rural areas, to access the courts instead of turning to pre-existing forms of dispute resolution tied to religion and custom. In 1958, administrators expanded the number of districts in the Trust Territory from six to thirty.[35] Each had a district judge with criminal jurisdiction over cases involving punishments of up to three years of imprisonment. Qadis focused on cases involving Muslims only, while the district judges could hear any case involving a non-Muslim.[36]

In sum, the last decade of colonialism left Somalis with two colonial legal legacies – one in British Somaliland in the north and the other in the Italian administration of the Trust Territory in the south. Their geographic limits and their own internal pluralism constrained these two legal legacies. Administrators sought legal solutions to the problem of how to build a state by passing laws, setting up courts, and establishing Quranic schools and a law school. Many Somalis, however, continued to use xeer in daily life. The following decade would see a single, united Somali Republic. Its political leaders would continue to invest in legal techniques to build the state and manage religion. They incorporated shari'a into the state, constraining its social power by subsuming it under the state's authority. Their activities were designed

---

[33] Iza Hussin, *The Politics of Islamic Law: Local Elites, Colonial Authority, and the Making of the Muslim State* (Chicago, IL: University of Chicago Press, 2016).

[34] Noor Muhammad (1969), 18.

[35] In 1955, only one of the Trust Territory's six provincial commissioners was Somali. By 1957, all provincial and district commissioners were Somalis. I. M. Lewis, *The Somali Lineage System and the Total Genealogy: A General Introduction to the Basic Principles of Somali Political Institutions*, presented March 18, 1958, to the Royal Anthropological Institute, MS 191 (London: RAI Archives, 1958a), 121.

[36] Law No. 9 of February 19, 1958; Noor Muhammad (1969), 17–18.

Table 3.2 Courts and judges in the UN Trust Territory and British Somaliland (as of 1959, in reverse hierarchical order)

UN Trust Territory of Somalia[37]	British Somaliland Protectorate[38]
Court of Justice 6 judges – President, Magistrate of Accounts, 2 judges, and 2 qadis sitting in three sections (ordinary, shariatic, special accounts) – all were Italian except for the qadis	High Court Until 1960, appeal from High Court to Court of Appeal for Eastern Africa and Privy Council[39]
Appeal Court of Assize 1 appellate judge – an Italian – and 6 assessors	First-class district courts District officer or assistant district officer sits as judge
Court of Assize 1 regional judge and 6 assessors	Second-class district courts Imprisonment under 6 months; fines under 700 Rupees
Regional Courts 6 regional judges, 3 of them Italian	Subordinate courts (17 judges) and qadis' courts (1 chief qadi and 12 qadis)
District courts 30 judges – 22 non-Somali district commissioners, 7 Somali district court judges, and 1 Italian judge who sat as the district judge in Mogadishu	**Total: 1 Chief Justice; 1 Senior Magistrate; 1 Resident Magistrate; 1 Magistrate (non-professional Somali); 17 subordinate court judges; 1 chief qadi; 12 qadis**
Qadi tribunals 3 Italian judges; 3 seats vacant	
Qadi courts (48 qadis)	
Total: 6 justices of the Court of Justice; 1 Appeal Court of Assize judge; 1 Court of Assize regional judge; 6 regional judges; 30 district judges; 3 judges of the qadi tribunals (all Italian); 48 qadis	

Source: Derived from Haji N. A. Noor Muhammad, *The Development of the Constitution of the Somali Republic* (Mogadishu: Ministry of Grace and Justice, Government of the Somali Republic, 1969).

---

[37] Noor Muhammad (1969), 18–19, 97.
[38] Ibid., 24–26.
[39] Ibid., 26.

to create one legal system under state control. But their new laws and courts would fail to address indigenous Somali concerns beyond the surface level.

UNIFYING LEGAL SYSTEMS, 1960–1969

In 1960, Somali political leaders and colonial administrators in British Somaliland and the United Nations Trust Territory led both regions to political independence within a week of one another (June 26 and July 1, respectively), to create a united Somali Republic on July 1, 1960. The 1960s were the Somali Republic's only period of democracy, and the decade was marked by extreme political turbulence as the nation confronted its multiple colonial legacies. The decade also saw considerable state activity dealing with the law, particularly from 1960 to 1964. Chief among political leaders' concerns was how to unite the legal institutions of Italian Somalia with those of British Somaliland. Of a few dozen trained lawyers in the country in the 1960s, many were foreigners who, with Somali counterparts, helped make changes in the constitution, in legal codes, and in case law.[40] Foreign lawyers, primarily from Europe and North America, worked with Somali government officials to try to create a single, unified, and clearly delineated legal system. These foreigners sought to unify legal systems that they knew little about, changing laws and refining legal orders – including shari'a and xeer – with which they had little experience. According to Somali government documents, this work was meant to instill "law and order"; it was "the core of almost all administrative handlings" during this period.[41]

Given the new nation's legal pluralism, and the many laws added before independence, Somali elites reasonably asked themselves which legal system should govern the country, which laws should remain, and which laws should be abandoned. These questions of how to organize the legal system arose in four key contexts in the early postcolonial period: the drafting of the 1960 constitution, the shuttering of the Islamic courts and the integration of the judicial structure in 1962,

---

[40] Martin R. Ganzglass, "A Common Lawyer Looks at an Uncommon Legal Experience," 53(9) *American Bar Association Journal* (1967): 815–818, p. 817.
[41] Omar Osman Mohamed, *Administrative Efficiency and Administrative Language in Somalia* (Mogadishu: Somali Institute of Development, Administration, and Management, 1976), 36.

political leaders' focus on drafting legal codes, and the Supreme Court's assertion of judicial authority. At these junctures, state officials confronted their colonial past and revised it to suit their purposes. The colonial administration had also set shari'a on an institutionalized path, and postcolonial leaders further institutionalized it, making it part of the judiciary and abolishing the old shari'a courts.[42] The postcolonial democratic government rhetorically embraced shari'a and distanced itself from colonialism, even while carrying forward the colonial project by building on colonial law to create state law. Foreign lawyers contributed to this project, too, by helping to write those state laws and by working to convince Somalis that following shari'a's modes of argument would allow Somalis to subsume shari'a and xeer into the state's legal system.

The 1960 Constitution: "First, an Islamic State"
The question of whether to build the new state on Islamic or Western legal principles, or some combination, became critical in drafting the Somali Republic's first constitution, approved on June 21, 1960, just days before independence. Government officials at the time linked the constitution to the Universal Declaration of Human Rights and claimed that it was "essentially a democratic instrument based on western models, and especially on the model of the Constitution of Italy, and it represent[ed] the culmination of the efforts to evolve a modern political structure for a traditionally democratic society."[43]

But others disagreed with the notion that Western law should be central to the constitution, and over how to integrate Western and Islamic legal orders. Religious law had been taken into account from the start: two religious experts were among the thirty-member constitutional "drafting political committee" appointed by the Ministry of Justice in March 1960.[44] In the end, the 1960 Constitution named Islam as the state's official religion.[45] It also framed Islam as the "main

---

[42] Elisa Giunchi, "The Reinvention of "Shari'a" under the British Raj: In Search of Authenticity and Certainty," 69(4) *The Journal of Asian Studies* (2010): 1119–1142.

[43] Haji N. A. Noor Muhammad, *The Legal System of the Somali Democratic Republic* (Charlottesville, VA: The Michie Company, 1972), 27–29.

[44] Ibid.

[45] Article 1.3 of 1960 Constitution of the Somali Republic, as amended in 1963.

source" of legislation, which required voiding any law contradictory to Islamic principles.[46] Finally, constitutional drafters decided that the Somali president must be Muslim.[47] In its reports to foreigners living and working in Somalia, the government made clear that the Somali Republic's Supreme Court would have the power to review "any legislation which is contrary to the ... constitution and [to] the general principles of Islam."[48] Although the Supreme Court did not initially use this power, the government was giving its courts authority to void some of the laws that had just been passed in the transition to independence, using the name of Islam. The Somali Republic was, according to one of its first Supreme Court justices, "First ... an Islamic State [and] secondly ... a representative, democratic Republic."[49]

Closing the Shari'a Courts and Opening a New Judiciary

From the start, however, postcolonial Somalia was an Islamic state more in name than in practice. Some Somalis, particularly in the former British Somaliland, scoffed at the idea of being governed by shari'a.[50] Despite foregrounding Islam, the nascent Somali government in fact sought to manage the power of shari'a by integrating it into the judicial structure and abandoning the shari'a courts created by colonial administrators.

At its founding, the Somali Republic operated two court systems – one in the south based primarily on Italian law, and one in the north based primarily on British law. Each system had a distinct relationship with Islamic and indigenous law. In 1961, the Somali government decided to draft an Act of Union law designed to set up a single, new, national legal system. The first step in that process, however, was to make both systems – Italian-origin and British-origin – applicable, just as they had been under colonialism, until the single judiciary could be

---

[46] Article 50 of 1960 Constitution of the Somali Republic, as amended in 1963.
[47] Article 71.1 of 1960 Constitution of the Somali Republic, as amended in 1963; see also Haji N. A. Noor Muhammad (1969), 75.
[48] Somali Institute for Public Administration, *Perspectives on Somalia: Orientation Course for Foreign Experts Working in Somalia* (Mogadishu: Somali Institute of Public Administration, 1968), 37.
[49] Noor Muhammad (1969), 35.
[50] Interview 136 with Philip, retired international lawyer who worked in the 1960s–70s in Mogadishu, Somalia (reached via telephone from San Francisco, California) (September 2016).

finalized.[51] The Act of Union law focused on codified laws and institutions of the state, not on shari'a or xeer. It "authorized the continuation of the existing laws and regulations in the respective regions until they were replaced by uniform laws applicable in the entire territory of the Republic."[52] The law came into effect in September 1962 by legislative decree, and even then it affected only the northern area (formerly British Somaliland).[53] The law did not come into effect in the southern area (formerly Italian Somalia) until October 1963, nearly three years after it was drafted.[54] The delay was significant because it meant that the two colonial judicial systems continued to operate after independence, as they had in the colonial period.

One cause of the delay in setting up a single national legal system was tension between Somalia's now united populations of north and south. Seventy percent of the country's northern population rejected a June 1961 referendum on the Somali constitution, saying the government in Mogadishu had "legally abrogated the Act of Union" because, to these northerners, the government favored southern Somalis' priorities, sidelining those of northerners.[55]

A second cause of the delay in uniting the legal systems was the unanswered question of whether and how to integrate shari'a courts into existing civil and criminal court structures in northern and southern areas of the Somali Republic. The full scope of the debates is unclear, but Somali government records suggest that Somali leaders disagreed – just as they had done while preparing the 1960 constitution – over the importance of Islamic legal institutions, while they simultaneously appropriated Islamic legal power for themselves rhetorically and politically. Some Somalis argued that specialized Islamic courts were essential in any Islamic state. But others, including foreigners whose views prevailed, prepared a more careful argument about the legal importance of shari'a. In essence, they argued that because Islam is

---

[51] Law No. 5 of January 31, 1961.
[52] Iqbal Singh and Mohamed Hassan Said, *Commentary on the Criminal Procedure Code* (*Published under the Authority of the Ministry of Justice and Religion*) (Mogadishu: Wakaladda Madbacadda Qaraka – Xamar, 1973), vi; see also Noor Muhammad (1969), 34.
[53] Law on the Organization of the Judiciary, Legislative Decree No. 3 of June 12, 1962.
[54] Noor Muhammad (1969), 135.
[55] Hussain Ali Dualeh, *From Barre to Aideed – Somalia: The Agony of a Nation* (Nairobi: Stellagraphics, 1994), 17.

the basis of all laws in Somalia, and because *qiyas* (analogy) and *ijma* (agreed-upon opinions of scholars) are two of the primary sources of shari'a, then a judge who is trained in multiple legal orders (Islamic, British, and Italian, among others) would be best placed to practice qiyas and ijma. Thus, judges trained in both Islamic and Western sources would better conform to the goals of Islamic jurisprudence than judges who relied solely upon Islamic sources.[56] As in the colonial period, they urged Somalis to practice shari'a principles, paradoxically, by applying European law.

The democratic government shuttered the specialized shari'a courts – which operated primarily in the former British Somaliland – and replaced them with "district courts" that dealt with family matters and applied Islamic family law to Muslim litigants. No state-run courts bearing the title "shari'a" would exist after this time.[57] In other words, to make good on the 1960 constitutional promise to create an Islamic state, postcolonial elites destroyed the shari'a courts, at least in name, and brought non-Islamic sources into their areas of jurisprudence. Colonial officials had compartmentalized shari'a into family courts, and then postcolonial leaders eliminated those courts, continuing and finishing the work of colonial officials to contain shari'a's power.

The small group of European and American lawyers working in Somalia following its independence capitalized on the reasoning behind the 1962 judiciary law as they drafted new codes for the country. Aware that analogy is part of legal reasoning in shari'a and fiqh, these lawyers wrote codes with extensive comments and examples to enable shari'a-trained judges to transfer their methodologies into common law adjudication.[58] In these ways, Western lawyers used tenets of shari'a to convince shari'a-trained legal personnel to turn to non-Islamic sources. They took a broad view of the intellectual and political origins of legal thinking and the use of analogy in order to encourage local judges to do the same. They adopted Islamic modes of reasoning and styles of writing in an effort to prompt judges who would otherwise use shari'a not to do so. This rhetorical co-opting of Islamic styles of argument led to a divergence between the methods of communicating about law and

[56] Noor Muhammad (1969), 135.
[57] The 1962 Law on the Organization of the Judiciary revised the court system hierarchically as follows: a Supreme Court, Courts of Appeal, Regional Courts, and District Courts.
[58] Ganzglass (1967), 817.

the methods of engagement in legal practice, as well as between law's substance and its intellectual and political origins.

Much like colonial administrators in British Somaliland, Somali political leaders wanted judges trained not only at Islamic learning centers but also in non-Islamic approaches to law, commerce, and policy.[59] Together, these political actors created a "perception of the superiority" of the state legal system over shari'a, while justifying state power using Islamic legal precepts and the Islamic notion that judges ought to be conversant in many legal discourses and rules.[60] The legal system was designed to be multi-scalar, multi-systemic, and simultaneously religious and non-religious in order to meet Islam's specific insistence on the universality of learning.

Legal Integration

In addition to drafting the landmark 1960 constitution and 1962 judiciary law, Somali political leaders spent the 1960s passing a range of other state legal codes, and Somali judges generated new case law related to shari'a and xeer through Supreme Court decisions. Such officials clothed the state in law, conscious that citizens would see, encounter, and access the government through law. To make good on the state's promise to integrate the judiciary's British and Italian sources into a single judicial system, political leaders throughout the 1960s focused on legal development. They attempted to weave shari'a and xeer into the legal fabric of the new state.

Independence in 1960 did not abolish colonial law – quite the contrary. The Somali government itself admitted that "legislative provisions [of the 1960s] were enacted to continue the received [colonial] law."[61] The project of drafting new legal codes and making new laws was initially a colonial one, and it extended into the post-colonial state. That is, institutions of the rule of law, and legal rules themselves, were constructed in the context of a particular history. Somali experiences with the colonial legal order, and the ways in which colonial administrators had dealt with Islam and custom, shaped the new legal system. A foreign lawyer who worked in Mogadishu at the time wrote that "all codified law in Somalia originates from a foreign source [but] is

---

[59] Abdulkadir Hashim, "Shaping of the Sharia Courts: British Policies on Transforming the *Kadhi* Courts in Colonial Zanzibar," 38(3) *Social Dynamics* (2012): 381–397.
[60] Barbora Rýdlová, "Civil War in Somalia: A Colonial Legacy?" Research report (Charles University: Institute of Political Studies, 2007), 25.
[61] Noor Muhammad (1972), 45.

subject ... to the influence of Islamic and Somali customary law."[62] Somali lawyers and religious leaders I met likewise told me that lawyers preferred the system in which they were trained and, because Mogadishu had more power as the seat of government than did political elites in Hargeisa, the country's legal system favored a combination of Italian law for civil and criminal matters and shari'a for personal matters, rather than the combination of English common law and shari'a that had prevailed in the north.[63]

Between 1960 and 1964, the national government in Mogadishu busied itself with the daily enterprise of the law. Officials wrote and enacted new laws on nearly every possible topic and governmental institution, including "the organization of the government, the civil service, the judiciary, local government, public order, political elections, citizenship, the penal code, [and] the criminal procedure code."[64] Legal integration, as the government called it, was not easy, as some of these new laws were clearly unconstitutional. The 1963 public order law, for instance, allowed district commissioners to sequester the goods of clans that did not pay diyya. Seizing the possessions of whole groups of people, though, was a violation of the constitutional prohibition on collective punishment. The district commissioner for Hargeisa wrote that he "was keenly aware [that his sequestering of a clan's vehicles] was at once both legal and unconstitutional."[65] The electoral law was also a source of contention for giving district commissioners, whom many Somalis saw as corrupt, the power to appoint electoral officers.[66] Other laws seemed to disfavor certain segments of the population, especially those living in the north. A 1963 taxation law, for example, sought to unify tax laws in the Somali Republic's two regions, but those in the former British Somaliland saw the tax as an intentional form of discrimination against them in particular, leading to demonstrations, injuries, and deaths.[67]

In 1964, to achieve full legal integration, the government created a "consultative commission for legislation."[68] This nine-member integration commission, as it was known, was chaired by an Italian lawyer,

[62] Martin R. Ganzglass, *The Penal Code of the Somali Democratic Republic, with Cases, Commentary, and Examples* (New Brunswick, NJ: Rutgers University Press, 1971), xx–xxi.
[63] Interview 37 with Sultan Mansoor, sultan in Hargeisa, Somaliland (June 2013).
[64] Ganzglass (1967), 815.
[65] Ismail (2010), 191–192.
[66] Ibid., 201.
[67] Dualeh (1994), 18.
[68] Ismail (2010), 129.

and most of its members were either Europeans or Somalis with European legal training. Its task was to integrate the plural colonial legal systems, flattening them into a single legal order. The government also created a separate legislative department in the Ministry of Justice and Legal Affairs that was also tasked with "legal integration."[69]

Attempts to subsume xeer into the state legal order came through the 1962 penal code and the 1963 public order law, which allowed disputes to be resolved using customary law. "The xeer," Somali officials argued, "needed an enforcement mechanism which the Public Order Law of 1963 provided."[70] Once they turned to xeer, officials focused primarily on reconciling the varying colonial criminal and civil codes. The government created a new commission to revise the criminal law by preparing "uniform criminal legislation."[71] The commission decided to define crimes according to the penal code that Italy had created for Somalia. The Somali penal code that came into force in August 1965 was "almost a word for word replica of the Italian penal code."[72] The penal code further integrated shari'a and xeer into the government's criminal laws, so as not to "disregard the people's past reliance on [these] rules and sanctions."[73] Despite borrowing the penal code from the Italian colony, the government adopted its criminal procedure code from British-colonial India, "modified to suit the Somali situation."[74]

Asserting Judicial Authority

Somalia's young legislature was drafting legal codes to integrate the British and Italian legal systems with one another and subsume shari'a and xeer into those codes, and the young Supreme Court was busy compiling case law and asserting its own judicial authority over shari'a and xeer. As in any democratic state, judges were trying to build the state's judicial functions and foster adherence to legal rules. Their decisions speak to how tensions among law, religion, and custom – those overlapping colonial categories – played out in the creation of the postcolonial state. Three Supreme Court cases stand out as examples of

[69] Ganzglass (1971).
[70] Ismail (2010), 193.
[71] Ganzglass (1971), xix.
[72] Singh and Said (1973), vi, xii. The earlier penal code of October 1960 was also largely a "replica" of the July 1931 Italian penal code. Ganzglass (1971).
[73] Irving Kaplan, Margarita K. Dobert, James L. McLaughlin, Barbara Marvin, H. Mark Roth, and Donald P. Whitaker, *Area Handbook for Somalia* (Washington, DC: US Government Printing Office, 1977), 343.
[74] Ganzglass (1971), xix.

the ways in which the young Somali judiciary in the 1960s continued the colonial project of putting artificial barriers between these colonial categories, prizing state law over indigenous and religious law.

The first major case was *Somali National Congress v. the State* (1963), in which the Supreme Court of the Somali Republic created its own authority to review legislative action. In a ruling reminiscent to lawyers at the time of the *Marbury v. Madison* case in the United States, the court held that it had the power to decide the constitutionality of a provision of an electoral law and many other matters: until a separate constitutional court is established, "the ordinary [supreme] court can exercise jurisdiction on constitutional matters."[75]

Once the Supreme Court had confirmed judicial power to review legislative action, it turned its attention to asserting similar constitutional authority over customary law. In perhaps the earliest and most important ruling on the legitimacy of xeer, the Supreme Court held that Somalis must be able to leave their diyya-paying groups, and that the new constitution is a higher legal authority than Somalis' centuries-old indigenous law.[76] The case was brought by Abdullahi Ali – the nephew of a man named Yusuf Boni, who had been killed after being hit by a taxi – against both the taxi driver, Dahir Ahmed Bagan, and his aqil, Gulaid Jama. For his part, the aqil argued that his diyya-paying group was not liable for Boni's death, as the taxi driver who killed Boni had previously left the diyya-paying group. The Supreme Court ruled that membership in a diyya-paying group is granted by birth and on the "basis of Somali social organization maintained by consent between tribes."[77] But the Supreme Court ultimately ruled for the aqil, arguing that his diyya-paying group was not liable for Boni's death. Because the constitution provides for free association, the Supreme Court wrote, Somalis must be able to leave their diyya-paying groups at any time. In other words, the constitutional requirement of free association trumped the xeer requirement that Somalis be members of diyya-paying groups by virtue of their births into those groups.

The third major case asserting the state's constitutional authority over competing legal orders was *Hussein Hersi and Ahmed Adan v. Yusuf Deria Ali* (1964). In this case, a diyya-paying group refused to pay diyya

---

[75] *Somali National Congress v. the State*, November 5, 1963, judgment by Dr. Giuseppe Papale, President, Supreme Court of the Somali Republic, cited in Noor Muhammad (1969), 147.

[76] *Aqil Gulaid Jama v. Abdullahi Ali*, Supreme Court Full Bench Civil Appeal No. 24 of 1964, judgment by Dr. Aldo Peronaci, President, Supreme Court of the Somali Republic, cited in Noor Muhammad (1969), 61–62.

[77] Noor Muhammad (1969), 61–62.

(in this instance, fifty camels) for a girl killed in a traffic collision. The defendants argued that diyya payments violated the constitutional prohibition against collective criminal punishment.[78] The court observed the long history of diyya as a criminal penalty in shari'a but merely a civil penalty in xeer. It then ruled in favor of the girl's clan, ordering the defendant diyya-paying group to compensate for the girl's death. While courts cannot impose criminal penalties on "whole villages," the court judgment argued, there is a longstanding collective responsibility under xeer to pay diyya in the case of homicide.[79] With this judgment, the Supreme Court compartmentalized indigenous law into a distinct legal category, despite its roots in and a relationship to shari'a. Doing so allowed the court to rule that xeer provided the governing rule in this case, delineating the importance of custom not only for Somali society but also for its laws. The court's decision was also its assertion that the state – through its courts – had the constitutional power to create a hierarchy of Somalia's legal orders. In this case, xeer principles were applied over shari'a principles, but the court's involvement in the first place rendered the national constitution, and the court's interpretation of it, supreme over both custom and religion.[80]

With one hand, Somali officials and judges used colonial law as the basis for state law, simultaneously downgrading xeer and shari'a while using them to harness judicial power and build state institutions. With the other hand, they distanced themselves rhetorically from colonialism. In its "orientation course" to foreigners working in Somalia in the 1960s, the Somali government invoked a combination of legal and religious rationales for their rhetorical rejection of colonialism and colonial law. Legal rationales included citing Italian "harsh and oppressive laws ... forced labor ... and discriminatory laws which could not help but breed hatred among the indigenous people" alongside "Ethiopian malpractices."[81] The government's religious rationales against colonial law asserted how "very humiliating [it is] for a Muslim society to accept European or ...

---

[78] Article 43.1 of the Constitution of the Somali Republic, 1960.

[79] Law on the Organization of the Judiciary, Article 82, approved by Royal Decree No. 937, June 11, 1911, British Somaliland Protectorate.

[80] *Hussein Hersi and Ahmed Adan v. Yusuf Deria Ali*, Supreme Court Civil Appeal No. 2 of 1964, judgment by Haji N. A. Noor Muhammad, Vice President, Supreme Court of the Somali Republic. 9(3) *Journal of African Law* (1965): 170–183; see also Noor Muhammad (1969), 73–74.

[81] Somali Institute for Public Administration (1968), 17.

Christian domination."[82] Despite this rhetoric, the democratic
administrations of the 1960s extended rather than curtailed colonial-
era laws and activities, particularly through the process of writing new
laws and trying to dominate shari'a and custom. Domination occurs in
multiple forms, however: the Somali Republic in the 1960s relied
upon foreign aid; by 1969 the biggest donors were Italy (USD
90 million), the USSR (USD 59 million), and the United States
(USD 47 million).[83]

AUTHORITARIAN LEGALITY, 1969–1991

While state leaders worked to create new laws, their democratic government and reliance on foreign aid did not solve Somalis' bigger
economic concerns, especially among the masses of citizens living in
poverty. Politics and law seemed disconnected from everyday life. By
1968, things started to fall apart. That year, the government recorded
a budget deficit of 22 million Somali shillings, met largely through
emergency foreign aid.[84] The economic downturn led government
officials to direct state resources to themselves and their clans, which
in turn caused further decline. Agricultural and livestock exports –
primarily bananas and goats shipped to Italy – also suffered following
the 1967 closure of the Suez Canal.[85]

A dearth of human resources in state and society exacerbated the
economic decline. Education continued to be restricted, which left
little human capacity for government. While a National Teacher
Education Center had been set up by Eastern Michigan University
with support from the United States Agency for International
Development, the only higher education program in Somalia during
the 1960s was that of the University Institute of Law and Economics,
which had reduced its single degree course from the three years to two.
By 1969, there were only forty-six university graduates in Somalia.[86]

[82] Ibid.
[83] See Noor Muhammad (1969), 24.
[84] "Statement by the Minister of Finance, H. E. Hagi Farah Ali Omar, on the Budget Estimates for
Financial Year 1968," *Bollettino Ufficiale Della Repubblica Somalia*, 1968, p. 51.
[85] Ibid., 23–24.
[86] Mohamed (1976), 10. In pointed contrast to the small number of university graduates in
Somalia, hundreds of Somalis were studying for university degrees abroad (451 in the USSR,
268 in Italy, 131 in West Germany, 98 in the United States, 52 in Czechoslovakia, and 33 in
the United Kingdom). See Ministry of Planning and Coordination, *Somalia in Figures*
(Mogadishu: Ministry of Planning and Coordination, 1967), British Library, London, C.S.C.
179/10.(2.).

Tribalism began to take hold in legislative politics too. In the 1969 national election, sixty-four political parties put forward nearly 1,000 candidates to contest the 123 parliamentary seats. But most of these political parties were formed hastily in the run-up to the election, as efforts to ensure that a clan or sub-clan would have some kind of government representation amidst the economic collapse. Political disagreements, clan politics, and the steep economic decline helped to sow discontent with the democratic administration, opening the way for a military takeover. One leading lawyer summarized this period by saying that, although the 1960s were a democratic period, "There was no stability. [There was] crisis, corruption, clannism, nepotism – [and] people were fed up."[87]

General Mohamed Siad Barre – a two-decade veteran (1941–1960) of the Italian colonial police force and a rising member of the post-colonial Somali armed forces – took power by coup in October 1969, one day after the assassination of Somali President Abdirashid Ali Shermarke. Quickly thereafter, Siad Barre suspended constitutional provisions and parliamentary functions. He began to make significant legal changes to build a legal infrastructure subservient to his rule. His government, calling itself the Supreme Revolutionary Council (SRC), dissolved the judicial structure and replaced judges with regime supporters. The SRC passed new "decree-laws" while professing its allegiance to a political philosophy of "scientific socialism" and its alliance with the Soviet Union.[88]

But Siad Barre struggled to convince Somalis of his views, which many saw as denigrating religion. Many people equated socialism with atheism, which was against Islam, and Siad Barre's regime also allowed alcohol consumption, which Islam prohibits. Religious leaders were still involved in resolving people's disputes privately and in brokering peace between rival communities. Many religious leaders thought that Islam and scientific socialism were incompatible, and preached accordingly. But Siad Barre publicly insisted that there were no inconsistencies between Islamic and socialist political teachings, as both are based on classless, egalitarian societies.[89] At a news conference, for instance,

---

[87] Follow-up interview 70 with Kabir, lawyer and senior university administrator in Hargeisa, Somaliland (July 2013).

[88] Ministry of Information and National Guidance, *Somalia Today*, Government of the Somali Democratic Republic (Mogadishu: Ministry of Information and National Guidance, 1975), 58–64.

[89] George James, "Somalia's Overthrown Dictator, Mohammed Siad Barre, Is Dead," *New York Times*, January 3, 1995.

Siad Barre stated, "There is no chapter, not even a single word, in our Koran that opposes scientific socialism. We say, 'Where is the contradiction? The contradiction was created by man only.'"[90] In connecting shari'a with socialism, Siad Barre tried to reframe people's relationship to their faith by promoting his own understanding of shari'a. He bent shari'a to fit his socialist-inspired decrees that conformed to authoritarian rule. He also asserted publicly that "There is no conflict between Islam and socialism, as they both enshrine the principles of human dignity, mutual respect, cooperation, progress, justice and well-being for all."[91] Despite Siad Barre's efforts to promote socialism by linking it with Islam, shari'a had not disappeared from social life. His regime's legacy is characterized neither by socialism nor by shari'a, but by its authoritarian invocations of both.

During the 1970s, Siad Barre took steps to ensure Somalis put nation before both clan and faith – such as abolishing indigenous and religious titles like sheikh and sultan, and employing informants whom the government labeled its "victory pioneers" (Somali: *guul wade*). A Western diplomat in Somalia summarized foreigners' views of this turbulent time of ideological clashes: "Somalia [under Siad Barre] is a country of three M's – Marx, Mohammed and the Mad Mullah."[92] Like the governments that had preceded it, Somalia's military regime was infatuated with creating a unified set of legal solutions to the country's social and political ills. And, in another echo of those colonial and democratic administrations, Siad Barre tried to constrain the power of shari'a by subsuming it under his rule.

To build a new state through law, Siad Barre had to destroy the legal apparatus of the democratic state that preceded him. Like the democratic administration that his coup cut short, his regime also had to publicly embrace its own version of shari'a to legitimize its authority. Siad Barre could not ignore Islam, so he asserted that his actions were consistent with it. Embracing shari'a rhetorically was the essential tone of governance, as it was in the democratic government, repeating the colonial pattern of using shari'a for political ends. The Siad Barre government's efforts to build a socialist state – alongside environmental protection laws to protect forests and grazing lands, improvements to

---

[90] John Darnton, "Somalia Trys [sic] to Live by Both the Koran and 'Das Kapital,'" *New York Times*, October 11, 1977, https://nyti.ms/37Ala0x (accessed January 1, 2021).
[91] David D. Laitin, "Revolutionary Change in Somalia," 62 *Middle East Research and Information Project Reports* (1977b): 6–18, p. 18.
[92] As quoted in Darnton (1977).

higher education, converting to the metric system, and even a motor vehicle insurance requirement – were designed to bring the regime closer to the people's daily experience through its laws and policies.

Law enforcement and courts continued to maintain order after the 1969 coup, which led many Somalis I met during my fieldwork to speak of daily life during the early years of the regime as relatively normal. Indeed, many Somalis "initially supported" Siad Barre for these reasons.[93] Some told me that despite the fact that Siad Barre was a dictator, they felt that "In terms of human capital, investment, [and] decentralization ... the country was on the right track."[94] Siad Barre's own minister of urban planning was known to favor democracy, despite working for an author- itarian administration; he would go on to become a democratically elected president of Somaliland after it broke away from Somalia. Siad Barre's regime also gave refuge to, and allowed Somalia to become a hub for, freedom fighters from other parts of Africa. When I asked one person why he spoke fondly about Siad Barre's dictatorship, he replied, "Because the legal system worked well and was efficient. There was [even] a [state] compensation system in place" to provide redress for injuries to people or their livestock, and the regime expanded labor protections and the right to work.[95] Siad Barre received strong early support from Somalis, given his goal to remove cronyism from a political machine that many Somalis saw as broken. So long as people did not threaten his regime's grip on political power, Somalis who lived and worked under it told me, life seemed to go on as normal – at least until 1975. "It was a strong govern- ment [that] people accepted ... But no one could speak his voice," one person said of her recollection of the period.[96]

Destroying the Law

Siad Barre's government began remaking the state through a sweeping legal assault after the 1969 coup. The regime felt it "had no other recourse open to it" than to destroy the judicial system built during the 1950s and 1960s.[97] In February 1970, the regime abolished the 1960 constitution and took control of legal institutions:

---

[93] Interview 36 with Yasir, senior government official in Hargeisa, Somaliland (June 2013).
[94] Follow-up interview 70 with Kabir, lawyer and senior university administrator in Hargeisa, Somaliland (July 2013).
[95] Interview 109 with Qasim, lawyer and government consultant in Hargeisa, Somaliland (June 2014).
[96] Interview 125 with Sohir, NGO executive director and women's rights activist in Hargeisa, Somaliland (June 2014).
[97] Ministry of Information and National Guidance (1975), 97.

> [Siad Barre] dissolved Parliament, deposed the former civilian govern-
> ment, abolished the Higher Judiciary Council, and assumed all legis-
> lative, judiciary and executive powers ... Thus all functions and
> powers conferred by the then-existing laws were transferred to the
> Supreme Revolutionary Council. The Supreme Revolutionary
> Council then immediately changed all the laws previously
> established ... which were deemed to be incompatible with the spirit
> of the revolution.[98]

The SRC changed the nation's name from the Somali Republic to
the Democratic Republic of Somalia. Judges and other legal personnel
unsympathetic to the regime became targets of the regime's legal
assault. Justices of the Supreme Court were suspended and the court
was reconstituted with regime supporters. Many of those not dismissed
had resigned, among them high-ranking British-trained lawyers and
judges, including two attorneys general, Ahmed Sheikh Mohamoud
and Musa Haji Deria, and the president of the Supreme Court,
Mohamed Sheikh Ahmed.[99] All remaining judges in the country
were "obliged to be committed to the construction of a socialist
state."[100] The judiciary was restructured; the new hierarchy sequestered
shari'a into district courts that were closely monitored by the state
(Table 3.3).

The revolution was written through law and justified with religion.
While the SRC nullified the constitution and most of the country's
laws, it did not leave a legal vacuum. The regime replaced existing laws
with new legal structures and decrees of its own, using law to "turn ...
the state into the people's enemy."[101] The judiciary became, in the
words of a law professor I met, "the hand of the revolution."[102] The
administration governed by military authority through two new charters: the First Charter of the Revolution and the Second Charter of the
Revolution. Together, these two documents served as the Siad Barre
regime's national constitution. But it quickly became apparent to the

---

[98] Ibid., 58.
[99] Ismail (2010), 221.
[100] Girolamo Marotta, "The Active Functions of Judges," 9 *Somali National Reports to the 9th International Congress of Comparative Law* (Tehran, 1974): 15–23, p. 16; see also Ministry of Information and National Guidance (1975), 97.
[101] A. Ibrahim Mohamed (Qoorcade), *A Nation in Tatters: Somalia (Qaran Dumay)* (Liverpool: Somali Education Trust, 2009), 85.
[102] Follow-up interview 11 with Faris, professor and government official in Hargeisa, Somaliland (June 2013).

Table 3.3 Somalia's courts, as structured by the Siad Barre regime

Court	Function
Supreme Court	Appellate jurisdiction over civil cases and revisionary jurisdiction over criminal cases; original jurisdiction over administrative and accounting matters
Court of Appeal and Appellate Assize Section	One Court of Appeal located in each regional headquarters
Regional Court	Two sections (general section for cases valued over 3,000 Somali shillings, except those governed by shari'a; assize section for heinous crimes); one regional court located in each regional headquarters
District Court	Two sections (civil and criminal) handling all cases governed by shari'a

Sources: Derived from Ministry of Information and National Guidance, *Somalia Today,* Government of the Somali Democratic Republic (Mogadishu: Ministry of Information and National Guidance, 1975), 99; Singh and Said 1973, 1–22.

Somali people that the government's socialist structure was not going to serve them as they had hoped.

Siad Barre embraced shari'a, at least rhetorically, during the early years of his revolution, seeking to garner support for socialism by arguing that it was consistent with Islam. The government restructured the judicial system so that new district courts would handle family disputes among Muslims, also using shari'a. Siad Barre made public pronouncements linking progressive socialist teaching with Islamic teaching. During his 1970 Eid al-Adha address, for instance, he stated that

> Our Islamic faith teaches us that its inherent values are perennial and continually evolving as people progress. These basic tenets of our religion cannot be interpreted in a static sense, but rather as a dynamic force, as a source of inspiration for continuous advancement ... Hence the need for our religious leaders to probe within the social reality of our people, and wrest from our religion its practical teachings, thus making available its ideas and actions in the interest of general progress.[103]

---

[103] Statement of Mohamed Siad Barre, as quoted in Laitin (1977b), 18.

If Siad Barre attempted to co-opt Islam and shari'a, his government worked during the 1970s to destroy "tribal" structures. That is, while the regime needed to contain shari'a, it found it easier to attack xeer. The regime framed people's community organization as inconsistent with socialism and issued a law that prohibited "all associations of a tribal nature or whose purpose is to further tribal interests."[104] The government abolished diyya payments, all rights previously granted to clans, and all indigenous titles given to Somalis who serve as dispute resolvers in their communities, including sheikh, sultan, bogar, garad, ogas, malag, iman, and islan.[105] The government also demanded that chiefs, aqils, and other dispute resolvers take on a new regime-created title of "peacemakers" (Somali: *nabadoon*), which would eliminate past references to custom and then tie their work to the new regime's mission and identity.

The SRC argued that these changes were designed to reduce crime and allow the state to help people resolve their disputes with one another nonviolently.[106] The government claimed that most "criminal" cases were against other persons, not against the state. In 1971, the year for which data are available, only about one percent of all recorded crimes were considered political crimes "against the state" (sixty-nine instances, compared to more than 5,000 recorded violations of property, customs regulations, and hunting laws). Regime documents also argued that justice had not been served "by the corrupt practices of the past regimes, to such an extent that even the judges were not ashamed of openly demanding bribes."[107] According to these government reports, by 1969 "people [had] completely lost confidence in the courts of law and one had either to resort to violence against his accused or had to abandon seeking for redress altogether."[108]

Rebuilding the Law

In response to what it claimed was a loss of trust in the state judicial system during the previous democratic administration, the Siad Barre government passed a host of new laws and "circulars" aimed at

[104] Law No. 67 of November 1, 1970.
[105] Noor Muhammad (1972), 31.
[106] Ministry of Information and National Guidance (1975), 99–104.
[107] Ibid., 97.
[108] Ibid.

centralizing its authority and then extending that authority beyond the capital. The regime created national security "salvation courts" (Somali: *mahaakim badbaado*) that did not have the possibility of appeal. The courts were designed both to resolve intercommunal conflicts and to punish dissenters. A law regulating the police force integrated police officers into the national armed forces.[109] The government also formed roving "security committees" (Somali: *guddiyo nabadgelyo*) with the power to imprison people for years at a time. A land registration and reform law in 1975 diverted all land resources, including farms, to government ownership, replacing farmers with renters of limited experience.[110] The government's legal work also included more benign regulations like Somalia's first large-scale environmental resource protection laws and a law unifying weights and measures (Table 3.4).[111] With the passing of these and related laws, the government touted all the legal work it was doing to modernize the state and its citizenry.

As in the earlier colonial and democratic periods, legal pluralism was both the enemy and the friend of the political elite. Pluralism allowed them to promote a public vision of the state's consistency with shari'a while simultaneously limiting shari'a's power to restrain them. Siad Barre's government also claimed that it had the full support of its judges regarding these new laws. "All the blind spots in the Somali Judiciary System have been filled up by the enactment of new laws, sometimes on the recommendation of the annual seminar of the Somali judges," the government proclaimed in 1975.[112]

Siad Barre and his government took legal and psychological change seriously in their efforts to build legitimacy, government infrastructure, and development programs. Government publications complained that previous governments failed to devote resources to help people achieve a "speedy administration of justice," which led to Siad Barre's "famous call" soon after the October 1969 coup for judges to hear cases "even

---

[109] Ibid., 91.

[110] Abdulahi A. Osman, "The Somali Conflict and the Role of Inequality, Tribalism and Clanism," in *Somalia at the Crossroads: Challenges and Perspectives in Reconstituting a Failed State*, eds. Abdulahi A. Osman and Issaka K. Souaré (London: Adonis & Abbey, 2007), 83–109, p. 95.

[111] Law No. 20 of January 15, 1973; see also Ministry of Information and National Guidance (1975), 94.

[112] Ministry of Information and National Guidance (1975), 100.

Table 3.4 Siad Barre increases state power (selected Supreme Revolutionary Council laws)

Law	Function
Law No. 1 of January 10, 1970	Expands the police power of arrest
Law No. 3 of January 10, 1970	Establishes National Security Courts at district, regional, and national levels, to hear political dissent cases (these courts have summary powers and no possibility of appeal; they are subject only to review by the president)
Law No. 14 of February 15, 1970	Creates National Security Service to monitor and stifle political dissent
Law No. 54 of September 10, 1970	Punishes political dissent through "national security" law
Law No. 64 of October 10, 1970	Repeals habeas corpus
Law No. 67 of November 1, 1970	Abolishes tribal titles and defends socialism
Law of November 18, 1972	Protects environmental rights and water resources; regulates well-drilling
Law No. 81 of December 14, 1972	Unifies weights and measures; adopts the metric system
Law No. 38 of April 5, 1972	Expands the Supreme Revolutionary Council's judicial powers
Law No. 23 of January 11, 1975	Comprises hundreds of articles, including family law and women's equality provisions
Law of October 1, 1976	Devolves power to regime affiliates in local governments

Sources: Derived from Ministry of Information and National Guidance, *Somalia Today*, Government of the Somali Democratic Republic (Mogadishu: Ministry of Information and National Guidance, 1975); Ismail Ali Ismail, *Governance: The Scourge and Hope of Somalia*, (Vancouver, British Columbia: Trafford Publishing, 2010), 273.

under the trees."[113] In its first few years after the coup, the government touted its legal development strategies as the country's source of Islamic and socialist modernization. By 1975, the government stated that it

[113] Ibid., 99.

[had] embarked on the provision of proper courts, offices, [and] jail-houses ... throughout the country. Over one hundred university graduates were absorbed into the Judiciary in the past two years ... Qualified clerks [and] registrars ... were also provided; the structure of the courts [was] completed by opening Regional Courts in all regional headquarters and where necessary, the Regional Courts were ordered to tour the towns in their districts frequently and thereby bring justice to the people instead of the other way round.[114]

Although the government spent considerable resources giving teeth to its goal of "bringing justice to the people" by creating courts and writing new legal codes, many of its laws and actions were still aimed at stifling political dissent (cf. Table 3.4). In 1972, Siad Barre survived an attempted coup by two members of his own inner circle, Mohamed Ainanshe Guleid and Salaad Gabayre Kediye. Just as Siad Barre himself had done, they made their own legal justifications for their attempts to overthrow the government. But their speeches about the need for justice landed these men in the national security courts that they had helped to create. The regime left few traces of mercy for those who disagreed, executing the men by firing squad.[115]

The regime demanded people's participation in government in order to transform not only their views of the state but also their values and identities. But the government's scientific socialism policy discouraged the creation of independent civic groups. The regime created state programs to take their place, such as literacy campaigns and development projects in water and sanitation. The regime encouraged people to join these programs through an ideology of government-oriented voluntarism called *iska wax uqabso*. The phrase translates as "do it yourself," and the Siad Barre regime promoted it as a form of community service. "[It was] very much imposed by the state," those involved told me.[116] The state demanded people's involvement not on their own terms as volunteers, but on the state's terms as grassroots promoters of a state ideology. If any nongovernmental civic efforts existed, they "had to have the blessing [of] the regime," according to one women's rights activist I met. These were often restricted to community-oriented

---

[114] Ibid., 99–100.
[115] Ismail (2010), 225. The men were executed alongside a third man, Abdulkadir Dheel.
[116] Interview 78 with Majda, lawyer and human rights activist in Mogadishu and Hargeisa (conducted in Nairobi, Kenya) (July 2013).

income-generation groups with a handful of participants at most. This activist said that her efforts to eliminate the practice of female genital mutilation continued, in a limited way, during the Siad Barre regime because feminist advocacy posed "no threat to the regime" as long as she did not discuss "human rights, freedom of expression," or changing the law.[117]

All the new laws and courts used to suppress dissent were an intrusion that turned people toward Islam, according to Somalis I met. Thus the state, with its attempts to co-opt or eliminate religion and custom, diverged from people who maintained their faith and community practices. Siad Barre's socialism treated the state as a patron, which meant family and community were secondary. Neighborhood committees spied on the state's behalf, which led Somalis to mistrust the state and its program of rebuilding the law, causing some to flee the country for safety. According to a Mogadishu-based lawyer, the "first major exodus of Somalis was in the 1970s [among those] who couldn't stomach the 'Big Brother' state. [Siad Barre] really used the law and legal change. All these things were passed as laws [that] set up certain things."[118] The new laws were publicized through radio channels that were themselves controlled by the government. In addition, the regime continued to marginalize the north, where many people thought that elites in Mogadishu ignored their grievances. But some citizens seemed to appreciate the creation of new legal doctrines; in authoritarian Somalia, new laws were still the hallmarks of a functioning and modern state, as they had been during the late colonial and democratic administrations.

Remarkably, the regime also created the first official Somali script. The Somali language, prior to 1972, was largely oral; writing had been done in Arabic, Italian, and English. That year, Siad Barre's government changed the language of the law from English, Italian, and Arabic into Somali; words like court, judgment, and appeal all had to be translated.[119] New terminology had to be created for banking and finance, education, governing in the ministries, and the law.[120]

---

[117] Interview 55 with Fawzia, women's rights activist and former NGO executive director in Hargeisa, Somaliland (June 2013).

[118] Interview 78 with Majda, lawyer and human rights activist in Mogadishu and Hargeisa (conducted in Nairobi, Kenya) (July 2013).

[119] For instance, "appeal" had been *appello* (Italian); it was then translated into *rafan* (Somali).

[120] Laitin (1977a).

Setting up new terms and a legal vocabulary allowed the regime to control the language of the law. The government either invented new words or adapted words from xeer to create new legal ideas and forms. In creating a Somali script and a new Somali legal language that drew on words from xeer, the regime was also co-opting xeer. It also set up Somalia's first Roll of Advocates to professionalize lawyers[121] and oversaw a major law review, *Majalada Shaariya* (translated loosely as the *Somali Law Journal*).[122] These actions in turn helped the regime control the law and the judicial system more deeply and extend its authority over people.

In order to inspire confidence and align itself with socialist principles, Siad Barre's regime opened new schools and made concerted efforts to improve the educational system. Six colleges were added to Somali National University – agriculture, chemistry, education, engineering, geology, medicine – beyond the Faculty of Law, which was still going by its Italian name, Facoltà di Legge.

By 1980, the socialist experiment was beginning to implode. The economy was collapsing, and people were reeling from the massive loss of life during Somalia's disastrous 1977 invasion of Ethiopia. Perhaps to divert attention from the failing economy and the war, the regime renewed its commitment to higher education. Somali National University added colleges of Islamic studies, journalism, languages, and veterinary science.[123] And the government created an Institute of Evaluation of National Heritage and Mental Decolonization "where students returning from foreign universities and diplomats returning from foreign posts undergo an intensive compulsory three-month course of reorientation."[124]

Shari'a Against the Regime

Although the Somali state would not collapse until 1991, the regime began to crack much earlier. Fissures first opened when the regime

---

[121] "Somaliland Legal Profession," *Somaliland Law* (2020), https://bit.ly/3nUOypl (accessed January 1, 2021).

[122] Interview 5 with Na'im, lawyer and legal consultant in England (conducted by telephone from London, England) (June 2013). Many people referred to the *Somali Law Journal* using the Arabic title, *al-majala* (simply, the magazine).

[123] Mukhtar (2003), 235.

[124] Henry Tanner, "Soviet Giving a Lift to Marxist Junta Trying to Pull Somalis Out of Poverty," *New York Times*, July 15, 1975, https://nyti.ms/36HFIVt (accessed January 1, 2021).

executed a group of sheikhs who disagreed with its policies, and the failed war to annex eastern Ethiopia in a bid to unite the Somali-majority region with Somalia widened them. These two events show how state law and shari'a alone could not save the autocracy. Law was the tool the regime used to raise itself up. But shari'a helped to bring it down.

The feeling of relative social stability, despite restrictions on political activity, changed on Saturday, January 11, 1975, when the regime delivered its new family law. Lengthy and detailed, the law comprised 173 separate articles. Similar to existing laws in the Soviet Union, from which Siad Barre drew his inspiration and financial aid, the law was designed to rearrange the order of society. New rules of succession provided equal inheritance rights to women and men. Previously, women had been entitled only to half of any male heir's inheritance or to none at all when, in the absence of sons, family possessions typically went to other relatives.[125] The law also restricted polygamy, gave women enhanced custody rights and the right to divorce their husbands, and enforced an ex-husband's duty to support his ex-wife and children financially. Article 5 of the law granted women equality in marriage, stating that marriage is a "contract between man and woman who are equal in rights and duties" and that marriage is based in "mutual understanding and respect."[126] While husbands were still seen as the head of the household, there was an added condition that the parties must cohabitate, in part to cut back on polygamy.[127] Finally, marriage could no longer take place without the bride's consent, and the law raised the minimum age of marriage to eighteen.[128]

As with previous legislation, Siad Barre justified this law on a combination of socialist and Islamic grounds: "Islam and socialism supplement each other because both advocate the advancement of the interest of the people, of mankind – justice, dignity, prosperity, and equality."[129] Siad Barre had taken great care to curate his credentials as a Muslim socialist, arguing that "scientific socialism" and gender

[125] Elisabetta Forni, "Women's Role in the Economic, Social and Political Development of Somalia," 19 *Africa Spectrum* (1980): 19–28, p. 24; Iman Abdulkadir Mohamed, "Somali Women and the Socialist State," 4 *Journal of the Georgetown University-Qatar Middle Eastern Studies Student Association* (2015): 2.
[126] Forni (1980), 24.
[127] Abdullahi An-Na'im, ed., *Islamic Family Law in a Changing World: A Global Resource Book* (London: Zed Books, 2002), 81–82.
[128] Forni (1980), 24.
[129] Darnton (1977).

equality fit easily into Islam. The law advanced this project and built on earlier statements and government-run women's programs. Four years earlier, Siad Barre's government had given Somali women a collective "Gold Medal" for their "generous contributions to and boundless sacrifices in the protection of the young revolution."[130] Siad Barre then took it upon his regime to make feminism a state project, announcing that the "women's movement . . . of working class, peasant, and progressive women of Africa must see [itself] as part and parcel of this world-wide anti-imperialist struggle."[131] Siad Barre labeled the feminist struggle a "revolution within this [socialist] revolution."[132] Just prior to the family law of 1975, the administration had released an "Equality Declaration," which prescribed the "complete equality of men and women in their rights and duties in accordance with the Charters of the Revolution."[133]

Siad Barre's family law did not emerge in a vacuum. The legal reforms that Siad Barre implemented in and around the 1975 family law mirrored the rights of women in Islam.[134] Shari'a grants women the right to inheritance and ownership, and provides procedures for settling divorce claims. Perhaps for this reason, some feminist activists would later tell me that Siad Barre promoted women's equality because "he learned it from" religion.[135] Siad Barre's legal reforms also outlined rights later espoused in the Convention on the Elimination of All Forms of Discrimination Against Women (CEDAW), the international women's treaty that entered into force in 1981. The United Nations had labeled 1975 the International Year of Women and the first-ever international women's conference was held two months after Siad Barre announced his law. Sudan had appointed its first woman judge in the early 1970s; Pakistan did so in 1974, while Syria appointed its first woman judge in 1975 and its first woman minister of culture a year later.

Though some Somalis and observers welcomed the legal changes supporting gender equality, opposition to the family law, particularly its

---

[130] Ministry of Information and National Guidance (1975), 53.
[131] Forni (1980), 24.
[132] Ibid.
[133] In one of the many dissonances of the Siad Barre administration, the Equality Declaration also notes that "the husband is the head of the family by law." Ministry of Information and National Guidance (1975), 53.
[134] *Women's Rights in Islam and Somali Culture*, report of UNICEF and the Academy for Peace and Development, December 2002.
[135] Interview 131 with Shamsi, women's rights activist in Hargeisa, Somaliland (June 2014).

section on equal inheritance rights, ran high. Religious leaders criticized the law as "un-Islamic" for going against legal principles found in the Qur'an.[136] For the first time, a government in Somalia seemed to be saying that aspects of shari'a would not apply to family matters, a move even British colonial administrators had not made. While some women appreciated the law, the dominant interpretation of shari'a among Somali religious leaders at this time was that the law was repugnant to Islam. They viewed the presidential decree as anti-Muslim – a blatant attempt to reduce the power of shari'a and of the courts that handled family matters. At the same time, Siad Barre framed the new law rhetorically as a Muslim, and feminist activists regarded it as compatible with shari'a. That is, the law reflected rights granted to women in Islam, but it was considered to be anti-Muslim.

The 1975 family law said daughters and sons must inherit equal shares from a deceased parent, while Islamic law generally provides that daughters inherit only a portion of what their brothers do because it is presumed that many daughters will also inherit from their husbands. (Husbands do not inherit their wives' separate property.) Different Muslim families and societies understand these provisions differently, including in Somalia. But Siad Barre, people felt, simply dismissed Islamic provisions, and Somali people's interpretations of Islam, as "nonsense."[137] Not only did the law attempt a radical alteration of the social order, but it did so by taking decisions "on inheritance and divorce out of the traditional courts" and giving them to the state.[138] For generations, family issues had been settled by sheikhs or elders often using an amalgam of shari'a and xeer. In according equal inheritance rights to women, Siad Barre took the work of family dispute resolution away from nonstate authorities and gave it to the government, which was "unheard of at the time."[139]

On Friday, January 17, 1975, less than a week after the presidential decree, Mogadishu's Cabdulqaadir Mosque was stirring. Starting with the noon prayer and continuing through evening prayer, a group of

---

[136] Interview 5 with Na'im, lawyer and legal consultant in England (conducted by telephone from London, England) (June 2013).

[137] Interview 124 with Najib, former senior government minister in Hargeisa, Somaliland (June 2014).

[138] Brief of Amici Curiae Academic Experts in Somali History and Current Affairs in Support of Respondents (No. 08-155), *Mohamed Ali Samantar* v. *Bashe Abdi Yousuf, et. al.*, Supreme Court of the United States, January 27, 2010.

[139] Interview 6 with Rashida, lawyer in Hargeisa, Somaliland (conducted by telephone from London, England) (June 2013).

sheikhs and imams spoke one by one to crowds about how the new law was a threat to Somali life and tradition, largely for violating shari'a and the historical practices of Somalis.[140] These religious scholars said the family law's references to socialism and equality were contrary to the Islamic laws of succession, inheritance, and post-divorce maintenance that Somalis already used.[141]

Viewing these speeches as a protest against the law and a threat to the government's legitimacy, Siad Barre's regime sent its military police to the mosque. Officers quickly "encircled the mosque from all sides, cut off electricity to silence the [religious] scholars, and arrested hundreds."[142] Those arrested included members of Islamic study circles who had been meeting privately to practice *tafseer* (Arabic: reading and interpreting the Quran). The regime feared that religious leaders were trying to create a *sahwa islamiyya* (Arabic: Islamic awakening).

The regime's views about whether and how to accommodate social change in shari'a conflicted with those of these religious leaders. But the plurality of shari'a itself was part of the threat; the regime wanted to define shari'a only on its own terms. The regime saw itself – not religious scholars – as the final arbiter of the meaning of shari'a. Judges in the country's national security courts sentenced the protesting religious leaders to death for "preaching the Islamic faith falsely" because they opposed socialism and gender equality.[143] Soon after their arrests, ten of the sheikhs were sentenced to public execution, six others to thirty years' imprisonment, and seventeen more to twenty years' imprisonment.[144] The regime then executed by firing squad the ten sheikhs who had preached against the family law – an execution of religious leaders, ostensibly, in the name of gender equality.[145]

It is difficult to know whether Siad Barre's regime executed the sheikhs because they opposed women's rights, because they were seen as a threat to the regime's goals and Islamic credentials, or some combination. Their executions, however, underscore how Somalis,

---

[140] Interview 5 with Na'im, lawyer and legal consultant in England (conducted by telephone from London, England) (June 2013).

[141] These laws came primarily from the Shafi'i school of Sunni Islamic law, which is one of the four schools of Sunni Islamic law, the others being Hanbali, Maliki, and Hanafi.

[142] Mohamed (2015), 6–7.

[143] Laitin (1977b).

[144] Mohamed (2015), 7.

[145] Historical records differ as to the actual number of executed sheikhs; some say ten, others eleven, and others twelve. Darnton (1977). The Siad Barre government claimed these were imposters, not religious leaders. Interview 5 with Na'im, lawyer and legal consultant in England (conducted by telephone from London, England) (June 2013).

especially Somali women, found themselves caught between two visions of Islamic progress – one proffered by the regime's state feminism and the other by dissenting clerics who linked shari'a to Somali customs and practices. Women who witnessed this episode told me privately that "nothing changed" after the 1975 family law, because women "were still beaten and raped."[146] Like the clerics, some of them, too, were critical of the law. They did not believe such a law would achieve women's rights because it politicized them, losing sight of actual women and their concerns, and making women central in a violent debate between elite men's visions of socialism and shari'a.[147]

Military regimes like those of Siad Barre create "unforgivable memories ... of ... state terror."[148] Many Somalis I met regarded the execution of these religious leaders in 1975 as the most unforgivable of memories. Indeed, it was in the wake of these executions that Somalis told me they first understood what it meant to live in an authoritarian state, even though Siad Barre had assumed the reins of power by military coup six years earlier. Things had been, according to one Somali aid worker in Nairobi, "absolutely good," before the executions.[149] People had been "happy" at first, particularly with the government's community development projects and improvements to the legal system's efficiency, said another in Hargeisa,[150] despite the fact that "no one could speak" against the regime.[151] In the years after the sheikhs' executions, people were careful not to raise issues that the government might deem sensitive to its authority. "You better be careful," an activist told me, "so you just would not bother" trying to promote rights in a meaningful way.[152]

The family law may have been as much about restricting the power of religious leaders as about building state forms of feminism.[153] But the

---

[146] Interview 17 with Amburo, former senior government minister and United Nations official in Hargeisa, Somaliland (June 2013).

[147] Interview 55 with Fawzia, women's rights activist and former NGO executive director in Hargeisa, Somaliland (June 2013).

[148] Mohamed Haji Ingiriis, "'We Swallowed the State as the State Swallowed Us': The Genesis, Genealogies, and Geographies of Genocides in Somalia," 9(3) *African Security* (2016): 237–258.

[149] Interview 85 with Ibrahim, NGO program adviser in Nairobi, Kenya (August 2013).

[150] Follow-up interview 96 with Adam, independent researcher and consultant in Hargeisa, Somaliland (June 2014).

[151] Interview 125 with Sohir, NGO executive director and women's rights activist in Hargeisa, Somaliland (June 2014).

[152] Interview 55 with Fawzia, women's rights activist and former NGO executive director in Hargeisa, Somaliland (June 2013).

[153] Mohamed (2015), 8–9.

Siad Barre government's execution of the sheikhs – to protect the regime's commitment to socialism and the legitimacy of its legal authority – was a critical moment, the first fissure in a long series of cracks that would eventually cause its collapse. In the long term, the family law was rarely implemented outside the main towns. In other places, many Somalis continued to rely on the Shafi'i laws of succession and inheritance they had already been using; the family law fell into disuse, especially in rural areas.

The 1975 family law was not popular with Somalis who believed its inheritance provisions contradicted the eleventh verse of the fourth chapter of the Qur'an, which sets out the rules of inheritance. The law was unpopular "even among women," according to activists I met, who saw it as "contradicting shari'a."[154] But, as one Somali government leader told me, "Siad Barre had to kill [the sheikhs], otherwise he was going to lose power."[155] It was "one of the remote causes of [his] fall. Socially, Somalis always mention that. They never forgive him."[156] The executions felt personal, cutting to the heart of people's faith. Senior government officials I met claimed Siad Barre's downfall came when people realized he "was against shari'a."[157] Sheikhs a generation later saw the execution of their own as having long-term consequences: the episode "deeply affected society's loyalty to the state and initiated grave nonconformity between the state and society."[158]

Siad Barre and the sheikhs who despised him fought one another by erecting their own boundaries around Islam, as each attempted to wrest control over its meaning in politics. The family law and stifling of dissent to it does not mean that women's rights are incompatible with Islam; Islamic feminism is precisely what women would later fight for, as Chapter 6 shows. Instead, the executions suggest that Islamic dissent is incompatible with authoritarian rule, even in a situation where there was "clear evidence that Islam was readily misused and ignored by both [Siad] Barre and traditional sheikhs" for

---

[154] Interview 55 with Fawzia, women's rights activist and former NGO executive director in Hargeisa, Somaliland (June 2013).

[155] Interview 85 with Ibrahim, NGO program adviser in Nairobi, Kenya (August 2013).

[156] Ibid.

[157] Interview 87 with Muuse, retired senior government minister in Mogadishu, Somalia (conducted in Addis Ababa, Ethiopia) (August 2013).

[158] Hassan Sheikh Ali Nur Muhammad, Muhammad Danial Azman, and Roy Anthony Rogers, "Before Things Fall Apart: The Role of the Soviet Union in Somalia's Troubled Past (1969–1978)," 25(2) *Intellectual Discourse* (2017): 409–427, p. 417, citing personal communication with a sheikh in Mogadishu, December 2012.

their own political purposes.[159] The executions of the sheikhs also show that Islamic dissent has democratic characteristics, since it involves opening the law to multiple interpretations. Put another way, autocracy could not tolerate the inherently plural ways people use and interpret shari'a.

Resistance and Collapse

After the sheikhs' 1975 execution, the late 1970s and 1980s saw Siad Barre hanging onto power despite disastrous domestic and international policies. Siad Barre's various legal changes, as well as his attempts to enforce a shari'a discourse consistent with his deadly form of socialism, could not last. Recreating the law and trying to control shari'a by declaring his understanding of it the correct one proved insufficient for him to hold onto power. His actions led to political resistance and social unrest – rooted in a different version of shari'a – and, ultimately, to his ouster and the state's collapse.

In July 1977, the Somali military invaded eastern Ethiopia. Siad Barre claimed that Ethiopia's Ogaden region belonged to Somalia, and that Somalia had invaded the Ogaden to protect the majority-Somali population living there and annex it to Somalia. There had long been animosity to the colonial borders that separated Somali people, and this invasion was part of a drive to unify the Horn of Africa once and for all. The two governments defined the war in juridical terms: Somalia's government said that Ethiopia's territorial claims rested on invalid colonial treaties, while Ethiopian rulers claimed that Somalia's invasion violated the principle of national integrity found in the charters of the United Nations and the Organization of African Unity.[160]

Somalia's invasion failed when about one third of Somalia's army, once labeled in the New York Times "one of Africa's finest", was killed within ten months, quickly ending the war.[161] Cold War complexities and mixed alliances also complicated Somalia's ability to win the war because, like Somalia, Ethiopia was an ally of the Soviet Union.[162]

[159] Muhammad et al. (2017), citing Mark Bradbury, *Becoming Somaliland* (Bloomington: Indiana University Press, 2008), 37.
[160] Michael T. Kaufman, "Somalia Announces Mobilization, Dispatch of Its Troops to Ogaden," *New York Times*, February 12, 1978, https://nyti.ms/2IdCakq (accessed January 1, 2021).
[161] John Darnton, "For Many Somalis, It Was a War That Wasn't," *New York Times*, March 19, 1978, https://nyti.ms/343ebwj (accessed January 1, 2021).
[162] When the Soviet Union began supporting Ethiopia, it fell out of favor with Siad Barre, who then reached out to Western nations for support. When Ethiopia turned Marxist, Siad Barre

After the trauma of the failed invasion, Somalis involved told me, militias formed against the regime, and the country's civil war ignited as people turned against one another. By 1980, commentators wrote about Somalia as "more fragile ... than any other country in the world."[163] The Siad Barre government, according to news reports, was combining torture with "widespread arbitrary arrests, ill treatment and summary executions" as part of its strategy to maintain control in the face of widespread protest in the early 1980s.[164] The regime restricted association and movement even more, particularly in areas of the north where opposition groups were forming. Major tax increases on farmland and vehicles only furthered the feeling that the regime was losing support.[165]

To try to hold onto power, Siad Barre engaged in his own clan politics, employing men from his clan in key governmental posts in Mogadishu.[166] In the north, military attacks on Hargeisa and other towns led to massive refugee outflows. According to one former rebel leader of the Somali National Movement, based at the time in and around Hargeisa, "stability, the police, courts, and government" all began to collapse.[167] Lawyers, judges, sheikhs, and others believed to be not on Siad Barre's side became open targets. A trial in Hargeisa in February 1982 resulted in death sentences or long-term imprisonment for a group of physicians, engineers, and teachers who had tried to create local self-help groups. A national security court (Somali: badbaado) found them guilty of attempting to overthrow the government. As one lawyer told me, the ten-year period from 1981 until Somalia's 1991 collapse, particularly in Hargeisa, "was hell. People [either] ran away [or] became fighters against the state."[168]

In Mogadishu, the regime's political authority crumbled when the police arrested a group of religious leaders, leading to widespread demonstrations against the regime on July 17, 1989.[169] About a year later, more

---

sought US support, which brought USD 200 million in aid, largely in weapons deliveries to the Somali military. Kaufman (1978).

[163] Gregory Jaynes, "In Somalia, Every Day's an Emergency," *New York Times*, November 3, 1980.

[164] George James, "Somalia's Overthrown Dictator, Mohammed Siad Barre, Is Dead," *New York Times*, January 3, 1995, https://nyti.ms/3mKxbXJ (accessed January 1, 2021).

[165] *Liberty: Magazine of the Somali National Movement* (No. 1, Spring, January 9, 1986), zc.9. b.1695, British Library, London.

[166] Follow-up interview 70 with Kabir, lawyer and senior university administrator in Hargeisa, Somaliland (July 2013).

[167] Interview 100 with Hassan, legal aid attorney and former police official in Hargeisa, Somaliland (June 2014).

[168] Follow-up interview 70 with Kabir, lawyer and senior university administrator in Hargeisa, Somaliland (July 2013).

[169] H. A. A. Aideed, "The Siyad Barre Regime's Genocide of the Somaliland People," in *War Destroys, Peace Nurtures: Somali Reconciliation and Development*, eds. R. Ford, H. Adam, and E. Ismail (Lawrenceville, NJ: Red Sea Press, 2004).

than 100 religious leaders, business leaders, elders, and politicians who dubbed themselves the "manifesto group" drafted a letter to Siad Barre proposing a neutral "national reconciliation and salvation." Aside from calling for his resignation, their recommendations were largely juridical: constitutional and legal changes to transition the country back to democracy, including terminating all repressive laws and institutions, like the national security courts, that had been established after the 1969 coup (cf. Table 3.3). Siad Barre, himself in his seventies and in poor health, called the manifesto group "destructive" and jailed about half of its signatories.[170] Although he later released them and agreed to multiparty elections, the state self-destructed when Siad Barre was ousted from power and fled Mogadishu on January 27, 1991.[171] He died four years later in exile in Nigeria, on January 2, 1995.[172]

The deep connection between authoritarianism and law, in particular, led to disillusionment with the project of state-building. People came away from Siad Barre's regime calling state law *"xeer jajab"* (literally, "broken law").[173] Siad Barre's uses and abuses of legal systems and techniques shattered the ideal of state law: the building blocks and institutions of the rule of law had become things to be feared. When I asked one Somali about his experience of law at that time, he said that as he witnessed the regime's actions he came to understand that "the law ... is for the man in rule."[174] Law supported the regime, not the ordinary Somali. Likewise, the regime's attempts to limit Islam's power in politics – through its socialist political project, its execution of sheikhs, and military bombardments of its own cities to stamp out what it saw as an Islamic-based threat – facilitated civil war, Siad Barre's ouster, and the Somali government's demise in 1991.

Long after the regime's collapse, Somalis remain divided over Siad Barre's legacy. Many describe him derisively as "one of our warlords."[175] Others claim the regime made social improvements, at least early on: creating the Somali script, improving literacy rates, and expanding educational programs, social services, and sanitation. Some told me that there remains "a great deal of fondness for the Siad Barre regime."[176] At least for

---

[170] James (1995).
[171] Bradbury (2008), 46.
[172] James (1995).
[173] Interview 101 with Ruben, university lecturer and consultant in Hargeisa, Somaliland (June 2014).
[174] Interview 113 with Majed, legal aid attorney in Hargeisa, Somaliland (June 2014).
[175] Interview 129 with Xalwo, women's rights activist in Hargeisa, Somaliland (June 2014).
[176] Interview 109 with Qasim, lawyer and government consultant in Hargeisa, Somaliland (June 2014).

a short time, economic development and law and order came at the cost of the stifling of dissent. Siad Barre did create his own "cult of personality," hanging self-portraits and banners for his Supreme Revolutionary Council along Mogadishu's streets and holding celebratory parades for the informants in the national security service.[177] The regime consolidated its authoritarian legal apparatus through the rulings of its national security courts, which used criminal law to silence dissent. Siad Barre's legacy not only includes executions of religious leaders, the 1980s civil war, and the 1991 state collapse, but also remains hidden in mass graves still under investigation by the Somaliland Genocide Committee. His legacy lies, as well, in varied attempts – ultimately unsuccessful – to legitimize his rule and to constrain shari'a, which in the end proved more powerful to the Somali people than his autocracy.

CONCLUSION

This chapter has shown how late-colonial, democratic, and authoritarian governments in Somalia all sought to unify legal systems and overcome legal pluralism. It has also shown how, in different ways and to varying degrees, both the democratic administration after colonial rule and Siad Barre's authoritarian regime attempted to co-opt shari'a and Islam while making them subservient to state law (in the first case) or stifling their power and generating dissent (in the second).

Across three distinct periods – the transition to independence, the democratic administration, and the Siad Barre regime – public officials created and enforced a centralized legal order to build a postcolonial state. Their attempts to unify the law succeeded instead in further fragmenting it. But law is not enough to give governments the power they seek. Political elites also invoked Islam and tried to contain shari'a during these three periods. They tried to subsume religious power into the government, justify their rule according to it, and overcome the capacity of religious faith to develop nonstate forms of authority. Resistance to state authority, particularly against Siad Barre's authoritarian regime, likewise drew on shari'a principles.

By the time the Somali government collapsed in 1991, Somalis who survived the chaos and destruction had little faith remaining in the state or in the law, after a century of disastrous colonial and

---

[177] Interview 136 with Philip, retired international lawyer who worked in the 1960s–70s in Mogadishu, Somalia (reached via telephone from San Francisco, California) (September 2016).

postcolonial state-building projects. Through the transition to independence in the 1950s, the democracy in the 1960s, and the Siad Barre regime in the 1970s and 1980s, Somalis did not develop an enduring trust in the state project of using law, and limiting shari'a, to create a singular political authority over the Somali people. If anything, law seemed to be in the service of elites and at the expense of Somalis and even of religion, which made people view not only the state but even the law with suspicion.

In the late-colonial period, colonial administrators busily wrote and passed laws in an effort to make the new nation-to-be more "modern," while also transferring (or failing to transfer) positions in the judiciary from Europeans to Somalis. In the democratic period, Somalia's government ironically closed the shari'a courts in its attempt to build an Islamic state, and foreign lawyers used the tenets and rhetorical style of shari'a to encourage judges trained in it to apply Western (non-shari'a) sources of law. Those paradoxes suggest how varied the instrumental uses of shari'a were, and how widely legal practice and legal rhetoric can diverge. And in the authoritarian period, Siad Barre pushed the unification of law to an unsustainable extreme and executed religious leaders for disagreeing with his unconventional interpretation of shari'a. In his push for a unified legal system and a modern state, he, too, carried forward the trajectories that colonialism had set in motion.

Put another way, just as there was never a single, coherent legal and political order in postcolonial Somalia, there was also no single, coherent religious order under government control. During the transitional period prior to independence, British and Italian administrators continued to make shari'a subservient to state law, a practice that postcolonial elites continued when they shut the colonial Islamic courts and divided the judiciary. Siad Barre seemed to promote his socialist ideology through shari'a, using it as a pretext for power. When religious leaders disagreed, religion – like legal pluralism – became a threat to state power rather than a source of it.

As Part II of this book will show, so also goes the story of Somalis' turn to legal and religious solutions to resolve crisis, promote order, or contribute to civil society development after the state's 1991 collapse. They, too, have promoted intensive legal change toward their own view of a single legal system, while each political regime and organization adopts its own instrumental version of shari'a and sets Islam's political boundaries – just as colonial, democratic, and authoritarian governments in Somalia did for decades.

PART II

STRUGGLES OF A BROKEN
NATION, 1991–2021

Somalia (shaded region also called south-central Somalia),
1991–present.

CHAPTER FOUR

RESTORING SHARI'A:
ISLAMIC COURTS IN A SHATTERED SOMALIA

In 2013, I traveled to Addis Ababa, Ethiopia, to meet a senior government minister from Somalia's Transitional Federal Government (TFG). He had recently left Mogadishu and I asked him to reflect on his years working to rebuild Somalia's government, his successes and failures, the country's legal development, and what the Islamic Courts Union and a series of failed international humanitarian interventions had left behind. He spoke about his country's legacies of colonialism, violence, democracy, and authoritarian rule; his political strategies; and his struggle to survive attacks from militants who claimed shari'a as their inspiration. Shari'a inspired him too. He wished to see an Islamic state rise from Mogadishu's ashes – a state that would protect all citizens' political rights and fundamental freedoms. He, the Somalis he represented, and those who fought against them all felt strongly about shari'a; they just defined it differently according to their differing goals. "The Somali people know shari'a will not disadvantage them," he told me firmly. "They trust shari'a more than any other law."[1] Ending our second day of meetings together, he sum-marized his years-long efforts trying to restore the rule of law to his country and to earn the public's trust, saying, "Look ... you have to use Islam to win the hearts and minds of the Somali people, [and] to make the law attractive to [them]."

Somalis seizing control of national institutions, those helping them, and those battling against them have long had their hearts and minds set on the law. All have used what they publicly label "shari'a" to achieve their political, economic, and social objectives. Their efforts to advance either law and order – stability at the cost of repression – or the rule of law bear striking resemblance to one another; both goals lead them toward, rather than away from, religion. Political elites know that their adversaries create or appropriate their own version of shari'a to promote different understandings of legal change, public order, and God's will. Meanwhile, international lawyers and aid workers seeking legal order in Somalia have either compartmentalized or ignored shari'a, defining it as a religious law that, if it is to be integrated into the state at all, must be subordinated to international law.

By analyzing the thirty years following President Siad Barre's 1991 escape from Mogadishu and the subsequent collapse of the Somali government, this chapter shows how shari'a courts were beginning to help build stability and a path toward the rule of law in Somalia. This experiment in grassroots state-building was cut short, however, largely by outside military intervention.

By turning to the law, establishing local courts for self-governance, and then linking individual courts into a legal system, Somalis in the 1990s and 2000s repeated patterns characteristic of pre-democratic and early demo-cratic Western Europe and colonial and early postcolonial North America, where state-building relied upon courts, and judges invoked God's will. Before the founding of the English Puritan movement and modern European states, John Calvin wrote that the law "is the best instrument for [people] to learn more thoroughly each day the nature of the Lord's will."[2] Two centuries later in the American colonies, judges in trial courts – called county courts – constructed the foundation of American independence and democracy on this same principle of God's will. These judges were influential political and religious figures who "believed unswervingly

---

[1] Interview 87 with Muuse, former senior government minister in Mogadishu, Somalia (con-ducted in Addis Ababa, Ethiopia) (August 2013).
[2] John Calvin, *Institutes of the Christian Religion* (ed. J. T. McNeill, trans. F. L. Battles, Philadelphia, PA: Westminster Press, 1960 [1536]), book two, chapter seven, paragraph twelve.

in their right to rule in the name of God and according to [God's] divine plan."[3] Courthouses not only sentenced criminals in God's name. They were also "jack-of-all-trades" administrative bodies, the "workhorse of . . . government . . . They ran the show."[4] Following American independence, nineteenth-century judges and lawyers regularly invoked God's will by perpetuating the legal maxim that "Christianity is part of the common law."[5] Summarizing America's early legal and political development, historian Lawrence Friedman writes that "It would be hard to overemphasize the influence of religion . . . It was the duty of the law to uphold, encourage, and enforce true religion."[6]

Somalia is no exception to this process also found in Western civilization, in which human beings invoke God's will and the law as their state-building partners. Between 1991 and 2021, Somalia was not simply a chaotic and lawless place, as media reports suggest. These "stateless" years are instead a case study in how shari'a courts – like the courts that sprang up in the early history of democracies – are the seedlings of stable governance and the rule of law. As Islam was one of the only credible institutions left when the Somali state collapsed in 1991, it is no accident that the courts that took shape were – in name at least – shari'a courts. As this chapter shows, when these courts merged and became more vocal about national politics, they attracted enemies in high places whose attacks they could not withstand.

This chapter, "Restoring Shari'a," uncovers the long-term legal politics of religion: how political authorities and nonstate actors prioritized or rejected God's will to achieve their political, economic, and social objectives. Their efforts to promote or challenge the rule of law in Somalia drew from how they viewed shari'a and practiced it. (Chapters 5 and 6 also address questions about the interplay between religion and the rule of law over the same thirty-year period in Somaliland, after it broke away from Somalia in May 1991.) Somalia's political authorities have yet to make good on their promises of a stable Islamic state responsive to the needs of all citizens. This chapter is an effort to document a generation of their attempts.

The stereotype of Somalia as a lawless state was never closer to reality than in the years immediately following its 1991 collapse. As people

---

[3] Lawrence M. Friedman, *Crime and Punishment in American History* (New York: Basic Books, 1993), 24.

[4] Ibid.

[5] Stuart Banner, "When Christianity Was Part of the Common Law," 16(1) *Law and History Review* (1998): 27–62, p. 27.

[6] Friedman (1993), 32, 33.

fled the country and state institutions fell apart, militiamen emptied the army's weapons depots and obtained guns on the black market. By amassing this arsenal and recruiting foot soldiers to patrol territory, these militiamen became warlords. They installed checkpoints on key thoroughfares and busy intersections, demanding payment from those who left their homes and villages to meet relatives or trade goods and services; revenue from such tolls enabled the warlords to buy more weapons and recruit more soldiers.[7]

Groups of elders, religious leaders, political elites, and others who survived the civil war tried to promote stability despite the rule of warlords and the lack of functioning state institutions. Some of them were inspired to help by their religious faith alone, others by the possibility of power or wealth, and others by a combination of religion, politics, and profit. They appropriated different versions of what they called shari'a to counter the absence of the rule of law and of the state itself. Their aspirations led to similar responses to the violence, banditry, and warlordism. These strategies included (1) creating courts that used shari'a to deal with business and family matters, crimes, and social or moral decay; (2) forming political organizations, militias, and social movements rooted in Islamic faith and Islamic legal institutions; and (3) rebuilding and reasserting the state's foundation in Islamic law. Together, these three overlapping efforts, discussed in this chapter, reveal how law and religion are tied to building a state. In Somalia since 1991, shari'a emerged as a universalizing legal language among distinct political actors who addressed what they saw as the nation's political, economic, and social breakdowns. As the ubiquitous system that disparate actors already had in common, shari'a also became the unifying force that brought to life people's varying aspirations and allegiances.

Religious leaders who set up shari'a courts in Mogadishu during the 1990s were among the first to respond to the disintegration of state institutions after Siad Barre's ouster. The religious leaders were not seeking national power. Their courts were for neighborhoods, designed for local people – typically from a shared family lineage – to resolve their disputes with one another. As the warlords sought, separately, to control transport lifelines and to implement their own brand of law and

---

[7] Many of the Somali military's weapons initially arrived in the 1980s as part of a 200 million dollar aid package from the US to Siad Barre's regime after he had agreed to give up his allegiance to the Soviet Union. Gregory Sanjian, "Promoting Stability or Instability? Arms Transfers and Regional Rivalries," 43(4) *International Studies Quarterly* (1999): 641–670.

order built on the threat of violence, individual religious leaders turned to the law to create peaceful ways to solve ordinary conflicts. The judges in these courts mainly helped people manage petty crimes like theft or resolve family disputes over marriage dissolution and inheritance. In other words, they helped bring some order to people's everyday problems.

In the 2000s, something remarkable happened in Mogadishu. Each shari'a court had its own unofficial armed police force and, when the courts and their militias united, they fought back against and expelled Mogadishu's most notorious warlords. Western intelligence agencies and governments were caught by surprise by the rise of the Islamic courts; the United States government, for instance, was actually supporting the warlords because they had agreed to help catch terrorists hiding out in Somalia. When acting as a group, the judges and their armed and unarmed staff called themselves Itihad al-Mahakim al-Islamiyya (Arabic: Islamic Courts Union or ICU). Within weeks of the ICU's expulsion of Mogadishu's warlords, grateful and hopeful Somalis began to unlock their doors, clean up their streets, and reopen their schools and hospitals – all in the name of Islam.

The ICU was a diffuse organization, with rival leaders sending conflicting messages about the group's goals. Some of its leaders had national political ambitions, while others wanted to resolve disputes and bring people closer to Islam. The ICU's political successes and the support Somalis gave them did not go unnoticed overseas. Western governments and neighboring Ethiopia deemed the ICU a threat to the American-led global war on terror. Within six months of cleaning up Mogadishu and expelling the city's warlords, the ICU collapsed, in part from its own internal disagreements but also from a US-supported and Ethiopian-led military invasion designed to put an end to what Western political leaders and policymakers labeled Somalia's "armed Islamist" threat.[8] After the ICU was defanged, its politically moderate judges fled to Yemen, Eritrea, and neighboring countries. A military wing that called itself Harakaat al-Shabaab al-Mujahidun, or simply al-Shabaab (Arabic: Youth) remained behind. Since 2006, al-Shabaab militants have used people and weapons – along with the name, discourses, and symbols of Islam – to promote their own punishing version of law and order by ridding the region of anyone else they

---

[8] Bronwyn E. Bruton, "Somalia: A New Approach," *Council on Foreign Relations Special Report No. 52* (New York: Council on Foreign Relations, 2010).

could: the warlords, government officials, aid workers, and everyday East Africans unaffiliated with al-Shabaab's militias.

Through the Islamic courts, nonstate actors attempted to build the rule of law – but they were not alone. Political authorities seeking to rebuild the state also combined law and religion to achieve their goals. At first these efforts were hampered by Somalis' strong mistrust of the state, exhausted as the public was from twenty-two years of Siad Barre's dictatorship. For personal security reasons, those claiming state authority met outside Somalia with international lawyers and Western foreign policy experts who tried to help them. They met north of Somalia, in Djibouti, in 2000 when they founded the Transitional National Government (TNG), and then a new batch of political leaders met south of Somalia, in Kenya, in 2004, this time as the Transitional Federal Government, or TFG. Between 1991 and 2021, these numerous political leaders made at least fifteen attempts to put together a central government in Mogadishu. Transitional Federal Government officials worked in exile or out of a small compound in Baidoa, Somalia. In a 2010 brief to the US Supreme Court, a group of academic experts characterized the TFG as "not a government in any common-sense definition of the term. It effectively administers hardly any territory, and provides no services to the citizens who find themselves in the limited zones where it is even present."[9]

In the face of al-Shabaab's efforts to destroy them, TFG officials renewed their commitment to rebuilding Somalia's political and legal institutions, obtaining support from the United Nations and Western aid agencies and governments. In the 2000s and 2010s, TFG officials quarreled amongst themselves as they waged a taxing, one-step-forward-two-steps-back war with al-Shabaab. But the threats and violence did not stop them from drafting a constitution largely supported by the international development community. When completed in 2012, the constitution declared Somalia an Islamic state whose primary source of law was shari'a. Focusing on the varying political actors who tried to create stability during the first generation after Somalia's 1991 collapse – the

---

[9] Brief of Amici Curiae Academic Experts in Somali History and Current Affairs in Support of Respondents (No. 08-155), *Mohamed Ali Samantar v. Bashe Abdi Yousuf, et. al.*, Supreme Court of the United States, January 27, 2010, p. 23; see also Mohamed H. Mukhtar, "Somali Reconciliation Conferences: The Unbeaten Track," in *Somalia at the Crossroads: Challenges and Perspectives in Reconstituting a Failed State*, eds. Abdulahi A. Osman and Issaka K. Souaré (London: Adonis & Abbey, 2007), 123–130, p. 125, citing International Crisis Group, "Can the Somali Crisis Be Contained?" *Crisis Group Africa Report No. 116* (Nairobi/Brussels: ICG, 2006), 7–8.

local shari'a courts and the Islamic Courts Union, al-Shabaab, and the TNG and TFG – this chapter examines their repeated and conflicting attempts to restore shari'a on their own terms – and to rebuild Somalia or destroy it.

THE GROWTH OF SHARI'A COURTS, 1991–1999

Following the collapse of Somalia's state institutions, the first institutions attempting to provide stability were nonstate religious courts. Lawlessness was expensive, particularly for families and local traders, and in these courts disputing parties could present their claims to neutral judges without resorting to violence. These religious courts earned people's trust because their judges claimed to rule according to God's will. This link with Islam enhanced the perceived stability and sanctity of these new legal spaces. Though it is unclear how much training in shari'a these judges actually had, they used what they called shari'a to bring stability to their locales by resolving disputes and catching criminals.

Those who established, joined, and used these shari'a courts had varying visions of shari'a. Some argued that the courts signaled a new "time ... to employ ... the tolerant form of Islam."[10] Others, instead, wanted to make the courts empower local religious police and enforce strict social mores. Still others wanted the courts to focus only on providing economic security and resolving disputes, paying heed to neither a rigid nor a flexible view of social ethics. With such divergent political goals and viewpoints in play, the courts attracted political activity and fringe groups. This diversity of economic, social, and political goals resulted in some unpopularity, as many people wanted the courts to focus only on their own priorities.[11] Some were also, with good reason, suspicious of attempts by any shari'a court to exercise political power beyond its limited geographic jurisdiction in a country where little political authority remained. But the courts were the earliest attempts to build local stability in the aftermath of the civil war, and they did so by invoking the power of both law and religion.

Some scholars have held that people grew to trust the courts when they saw them as part of a long legacy of Islamic empires in the region and a more recent tradition of Somalis fighting colonial and

[10] Mukhtar (2007), 130.
[11] Oscar Gakuo Mwangi, "The Union of Islamic Courts and Security Governance in Somalia," 19 (1) *African Security Review* (2010): 88–94, p. 92.

authoritarian domination by promoting a shared religious identity.[12]
Others have argued that the courts were more pragmatic than religious –
spaces for building confidence and order.[13] This section of the chapter
shows that the courts were both religious and pragmatic. It should not
surprise legal scholars that the courts invoked religion and pragmatism
to build trustworthy local institutions. Indeed, religious symbols –
Bibles, robes, and courtroom benches reminiscent of church altars –
abound in modern Western courts that are no longer presumed to be
religious. In using religion to build stability, the shari'a courts bear
striking parallels to those courts that played an influential role in the
early development of democratic states.[14]

The Rule of Law Breaks Down

Foreign policy specialists often refer to the decade after 1991 as the
beginning of Somalia's "stateless" period. The government's demise left
no political or judicial power under state control, and no state institution could exercise authority over the Somali people and territory. As
one Somali aid worker told me, "The rule of law broke down. It was
thuggery and warlords."[15] In this chaotic political context, competing
militias, each led by its own military commander, took control of roads,
neighborhoods, and regions, while Somalis turned to those they had
long trusted to resolve disputes: religious leaders and elders in their
extended families or "clan" networks. By 1994, these religious and
community leaders had begun to open and operate their own small
courthouses, affiliated neither with each other nor with any larger
organization. They called themselves judges and they used their interpretations of God's will as the source of their decision making.

These courts were not the first attempt after Siad Barre's fall to use
religious discourse to build respect for law, public order, and peacemaking. In 1990, at the height of the civil war, a group of more than
sixty intellectuals, naming themselves "Islamic Call," had published
a manifesto that used Islamic teachings to reject violence and authoritarianism, calling for peaceful dialogue among warring rivals.[16]

[12] Michael Shank, "Understanding Political Islam in Somalia," 1(1) *Contemporary Islam* (2007):
89–103, p. 95.
[13] Mwangi (2010).
[14] Banner (1998).
[15] Interview 80 with Gul, aid worker in Nairobi, Kenya (August 2013).
[16] Matthew Cavedon, "Men of the Spear and Men of God: Islamism's Contributions to the New
Somali State," 28 *Emory International Law Review* (2014): 473–508, p. 482.

In addition to the scattered shari'a courts, two important political organizations began promoting Islamic faith and Islamic law soon after the government's collapse in January 1991. The first was a decentralized organization called al-Itihaad al-Islamiyya (Arabic: Islamic Union), that opened religious schools and relief clinics in an effort to educate Somalis to replace local customs – corrupted as they were by colonial influences and postcolonial state development projects – with Islamic law. Al-Itihaad al-Islamiyya, which had formed when it broke off from Somalia's chapter of the transnational Muslim Brotherhood, was known for its militancy. Its members claimed responsibility for various deadly attacks, including one in Ethiopia in the 1990s. Taking cues from nearby Sudan's leading lawyer and political operative, Hassan al-Turabi, al-Itihaad al-Islamiyya's leader Sheikh Hassan Dahir Aweys sought power by gaining control of local institutions left behind after the collapse.[17] The second organization was a Sufi movement of the Somali Muslim Brotherhood called al-Islah (Arabic: Reform, sometimes transliterated Al-Islaah). Founded in the 1970s, al-Islah also opened schools and health clinics after the state's collapse. In contrast to al-Itihaad al-Islamiyya's religious militancy, al-Islah publicly called for "restoration of the rule of law" through "respect for Islamic principles" and democratic ideals.[18]

These disparate and divided Somalis all responded to the need for public order and social stability, which there was no government to provide. They also capitalized on Somalis' skepticism of state-building projects and the ongoing fear that government agencies, if they returned, would "appropriate economic resources at the expense of others" and "use the law ... to protect this advantage."[19] As one Somali lawyer told me, Siad Barre's decades of authoritarian rule "made people turn" away from state law and "to[ward] religion," which turned Islam into the preferred solution to local political and legal troubles.[20]

---

[17] Ken Menkhaus, "Political Islam in Somalia," 9(1) *Middle East Policy* (2002): 109–123, https://bit.ly/3aOpM6k. On Turabi's legacy, see Abdullahi A. Gallab, *Hasan al-Turabi, the Last of the Islamists: The Man and His Times, 1932–2016* (London: Rowman & Littlefield, 2018) and W. J. Berridge, *Hasan al-Turabi: Islamist Politics and Democracy in Sudan* (Cambridge: Cambridge University Press, 2017).

[18] Cavedon (2014), 483. A faction within Al-Islah called Damul Jadiid (Arabic: New Blood) helped to organize some Sufi brotherhoods within the organization.

[19] Ken Menkhaus, "State Collapse in Somalia: Second Thoughts," 97 *Review of African Political Economy* (2003): 405–422, p. 408.

[20] Interview 78 with Majda, lawyer and human rights activist in Mogadishu and Hargeisa (conducted in Nairobi, Kenya) (July 2013).

However, these three groups – al-Itihaad al-Islamiyya, al-Islah, and the new courts – could not bring immediate peace to Somalia because of the depth of the country's instability coupled with drought, famine, and forced starvation.[21] According to Physicians for Human Rights, an international relief organization, at least 14,000 people were killed in violence in Mogadishu alone in early 1992.[22] In response, the United Nations constituted its first-ever military intervention for humanitarian purposes in April 1992. It was called the United Nations Mission in Somalia (UNISOM). Because of violence in Somalia, UN operations were based in Kenya: aid workers hoping to promote peace and the rule of law had do so from a distance. In August 1992, the United States joined the effort by providing military transports.

The following year, 1993, is seared into the history of humanitarian intervention. It also cemented Somalia's notoriety as a war zone without legal strictures. In January, a US-led Unified Task Force (UNITAF) began to coordinate operations with UNISOM by bringing approximately 35,000 foreign troops into Somalia. The troops' primary goal was to distribute aid, ensure stability, and protect personnel and supplies from warlords, militias, and bandits. The most infamous of the militia leaders was Mohamed Farah Aideed, a former military general who had helped oust President Siad Barre and whose political faction refused to cooperate in the March 1993 Conference on National Reconciliation, killing what was left of the national peace process. General Aideed rose to prominence in part because nearby Sudan had sent thirty tons of aid to al-Itihaad al-Islamiyya, which harbored Aideed for a time.[23]

In June 1993, an attack on UNITAF killed at least two dozen people, among them Pakistani peacekeepers and American soldiers. The attack confirmed that Aideed and his faction were a threat not only to Somalis but also to UNITAF and the United States. As a result, in October 1993, US special forces tried to capture Aideed and his deputies. But the operation failed disastrously, leaving hundreds of

---

[21] Médecins Sans Frontières, Somalia 1991–1993: Civil War, Famine Alert and a UN "Military-Humanitarian" Intervention (Nairobi: Médecins Sans Frontières, 2013), https://bit.ly/3qCKRX5 (accessed January 1, 2021).

[22] Gérard Prunier, Somalia: Civil War, Intervention and Withdrawal, 1990–1995 (Geneva: United Nations High Commissioner for Refugees, 1995).

[23] Cedric Barnes and Harun Hassan, The Rise and Fall of Mogadishu's Islamic Courts, Chatham House Africa Programme Briefing Paper (London: Chatham House, 2007), 7. Aideed had earlier founded Ahlu Sunna Wal Jamaa in 1991 as a political faction drawn from local Sufi groups that sought to counter religious violence and the spread of Salafi ideologies from Saudi Arabia.

Somalis and eighteen American soldiers dead. Militants were spotted dragging American soldiers' desecrated bodies along the streets around central Mogadishu's Bakaara Market.[24] The event came to be known as the Battle of Mogadishu or Black Hawk Down, named after a book whose title comes from the downing of two US Army Black Hawk helicopters.[25] In the battle's aftermath, the US recalled its troops from Somalia. By the spring of 1995, UN peacekeepers had also retreated, leaving the country and its people to fend for themselves.[26]

Amidst the violence and failed humanitarian interventions, some Somalis focused on trying to restore the national government's authority. A Somali transitional government committee of sixty people drafted a new constitution that included provisions promoting and protecting both Islamic religion and human rights. In November 1993, just weeks after the Battle of Mogadishu, the committee adopted their draft constitution. But as violence was engulfing the nation, the committee's work came to a standstill and the document was never ratified.[27]

Somalia's collapse and the withdrawal of UN peacekeepers left a gap in political power, filled in the 1990s largely by local warlords who commandeered specific areas for themselves. They lined their pockets with payments for goods and services passing through and delivered in their areas. Crime was rampant – and respect for the rule of law absent – as each warlord made his own rules, and as the warlords' militias fought one another. As people tried to survive, theft and other forms of petty crime increased, as did more serious crimes like murder.

Local traders were exhausted. Unmaintained roads prone to flooding made travel difficult. Warlords set up frequent roadblocks where they demanded large sums from traders trying to move goods – such as food, charcoal, fuel, and qat (a shrub with stimulating and appetite-suppressing leaves that many Somalis chewed daily, sometimes for hours) – into place for sale. The country's closed airports and seaports led to the collapse of livestock exports, and Somalia's isolation weakened not only the traders but also the warlords themselves. The traders sought a more stable authority on their side.

[24] Bakaara Market is also transliterated Bukhura Market.
[25] Mark Bowden, *Black Hawk Down: A Story of Modern War* (New York: Grove Press, 1999).
[26] Kenya Human Rights Institute, *Interventionism and Human Rights in Somalia: Report of an Exploratory Forum on the Somalia Crisis* (Nairobi: KHRI, 2007).
[27] "Draft Interim Constitution Handed to Howe; Unosom [sic] to Stay in Interim Period," BBC *Summary of World Broadcasts* (London: British Broadcasting Corporation, November 13, 1993).

Shari'a Courts Spring Up

In 1993 or 1994 – the precise date is unknown – a cleric named Sheikh Ali Dheere (also known as Ali Mohamed Rage) decided to use his training in Islam and his skills in dispute resolution to set up an informal shari'a court that would help local traders and shop owners resolve their disputes, help people arrange legal agreements for large purchases like homes and cars, and try people for crimes. He created one of the first known shari'a courts after the Siad Barre regime's fall.[28] Violence in Somalia at this time resulted in a paucity of oral accounts and written sources of these courts, so it is difficult to know precisely when the courts started and how many there were, particularly in the years immediately following Siad Barre's ouster.

Sheikh Ali Dheere's staff apprehended thieves and bandits and brought them to trial. The court's success led religious and community leaders in the Abgaal sub-clan of the Hawiye clan to establish another shari'a court in northern Mogadishu, also addressing issues from marital disputes to theft and murder.[29] These courts opened at a remarkably tense moment; just as some Hawiye clan members were setting them up, others in their extended families were also rising to power as warlords or working for those warlords.[30] Mogadishu's northern and southern neighborhoods were also deeply divided: each was run by a different sub-clan of the Hawiye lineage group, and the two areas also had their own self-declared national presidents.[31]

The shari'a courts – unlike the 1990 Islamic Call or organizations such as al-Itihaad al-Islamiyya – did not generally take public positions on national political affairs. But they were not mosques, either. Their work focused on institutionalizing Islamic law. The courts provided security and dispute resolution services to businessmen of the same patrilineal groups by employing, in many cases, militias to apprehend bandits on transport corridors.[32] The courts operated for the most part independently of one other and were, at the start, jurisdictionally limited to their neighborhood or sub-clan network.

---

[28] Stanford University Center for International Security and Cooperation (CISAC), *Mapping Militant Organizations: Islamic Courts Union* (Stanford, CA: CISAC, 2016); Lara Santoro, "Islamic Clerics Combat Lawlessness in Somalia," *Christian Science Monitor*, July 13, 1999.

[29] International Crisis Group (2006), 9.

[30] Roland Marchal, "Islamic Political Dynamics in the Somali Civil War," in *Islamism and its Enemies in the Horn of Africa*, ed. Alex de Waal (London: Hurst, 2004), 114–145.

[31] Interview 133 with Stephanie, researcher and author in London, England (July 2014).

[32] Barnes and Hassan (2007), 2.

For this reason, many skeptics saw the courts as disguises for clan authority and *xeer* (Somali custom) – in other words, as Islamic in name only. But the courts were careful to avoid prosecuting people of different clans or sub-clans in order to avoid triggering clan-oriented violence. (Both warlords and Somalia's national governments were also accused of masking clan operatives' attempts to seize authority beyond their lineage group.) The courts accepted financial support from charitable donations (Arabic: zakat) and their own road tolls; the judges' belief in and encouragement of the Islamic pillars differentiated them from warlord-controlled militias that demanded their own tolls from travelers facing their guns. Some of the shari'a courts also accepted money from as far away as Sudan, Saudi Arabia, and Iran. But businessmen who wanted their property protected were the primary backers. The courts relied on those businessmen who, according to one Western observer, did not care whether the courts used "Islamic law or Napoleonic law or common law. Any law [would] do."[33]

Apart from business leaders, other Somalis saw the courts as a mechanism for reforming social mores. Many of these persons blamed Somalia's collapse on moral decay leftover from Siad Barre's socialist regime. As one Somali war survivor told me, the courts were people's alternative to Siad Barre and a new "vision of an Islamic state. How can a country [that is] 100 percent Muslim talk of . . . socialism? [Socialism] is atheism, [and] we cannot accept that."[34] Some of these persons hoped to protect Somalis from further moral degradation, particularly to enforce gender norms and sexual purity, and they turned to the shari'a courts to provide that protection. Some courts worked closely with informal religious police, like the *mutawain* in Saudi Arabia, making sure strict versions of Islamic law were observed, particularly by women.[35] In criminal matters, some courts were known to execute people convicted of murder; there are conflicting reports about whether the courts resorted to amputations.[36] Some Somalis reported that, on

[33] Santoro (1999).
[34] Interview 85 with Ibrahim, NGO program adviser in Nairobi, Kenya (August 2013).
[35] Richard Ellis, "Muslim 'police' crack down on vice in Somalia," *The Sunday Times (London)*, June 27, 1993. Because of their openness, the courts had both "radical and nonradical members." Stig Jarle Hansen, *Al-Shabaab in Somalia: The History and Ideology of a Militant Islamist Group, 2005–2012* (Oxford: Oxford University Press, 2013), 23.
[36] The courts did not impose a standard form of discipline or punishment. Contemporaneous news accounts indicate the courts did not resort to amputation "for fear of becoming unpopular." Santoro (1999). Some persons I met and policy reports I found, however, suggested the courts did amputate the limbs of thieves. See Stanford University Center for International Security and Cooperation (2016).

balance, they supported the judges for "taking responsibility for imposing some kind of rule of law and meting out punishments."[37] To many
Somalis in the 1990s, however, survival was a zero-sum choice: either
alleged criminals had to give up their rights to due process and appeal,
or everyone else had to yield to the rule of the gun.

Somalis across the political spectrum saw the shari'a courts – and
religious law itself – as alternatives to warlord-ruled "fiefdoms," economic standstill, and political impasse. The judges punished thieves,
rapists, and murderers, assisted with public education, welfare, garbage
removal and other social services, and helped both business leaders and
the self-described religious police.[38] The courts often worked alongside
local Islamic businesses and charities. But the courts' procedures were
typically more like mediations (Somali: *masalaxo*) – in which judges
help disputing parties come to a mutual agreement – than arbitrations,
in which judges issue binding rulings.[39]

Most of these Islamic courts appeared in the mid-1990s in northern
Mogadishu. But not all those who set up courts did so for the same
reasons. Militants, particularly those from al-Itihaad al-Islamiyya, who
tended to live in southern Mogadishu, also wanted to establish shari'a
courts. They saw courts not only as dispute resolution schemes but also
as political actors – steps toward a more comprehensive Islamic state.
But General Aideed, who maintained powerful influence over southern
Mogadishu, was critical of this idea.[40] Thus, while shari'a courts were
operating in northern Mogadishu as early as 1993, southern
Mogadishu's first shari'a court did not appear until 1998, two years
after Aideed's death.[41] Ironically, at the same time some of northern
Mogadishu's shari'a courts succumbed to local warlords. Some who
established shari'a courts in southern Mogadishu had no political
ambition at all, while others were former members of al-Itihad al-
Islamiyya who saw shari'a courts as a potential foundation for an
Islamic state.

By 1999, when Somalia was at the bottom of the UN human development index, five active shari'a courts operated independently in or

[37] Interview 133 with Stephanie, researcher and author in London, England (July 2014).
[38] Shank (2007), 92; see also Hansen (2013), 23.
[39] Hanno Brankamp, "Somalia: Not Just Islam – How Somalia's Union of Islamic Courts Used
Local Customs," *ThinkAfricaPress*, July 22, 2013, https://bit.ly/3puC9Zv.
[40] Barnes and Hassan (2007), 2.
[41] Robrecht Deforche, "Stabilization and Common Identity: Reflections on the Islamic Courts
Union and Al-Itihaad," 13 *Bildhaan: An International Journal of Somali Studies* (2013): 102–120,
p. 113.

near southern Mogadishu. They were neither an organized movement nor a government, but they were the closest thing to either that existed. Each court had its own chairperson, its own council of business and religious leaders, and sufficient funds for its own militia. Each court's militia had acquired armored personnel carriers and employed 200 to 250 gunmen known as bailiffs; each bailiff received two meals per day and earned a salary equivalent to 30 US dollars per month.[42] Many of the courts' bailiffs had previously worked for warlords. In the words of one foreign observer I met, these men moved from hitjobs for warlords into "legitimate jobs [that were] no longer shameful. They were not jihadis. They were [still] kids with guns, only now with respectable jobs."[43]

In April 1999, the shari'a courts and their militias came together for the first time and took over Mogadishu's Bakaara Market. By June 1999, they had driven out the warlords and had eliminated the roadblocks between Mogadishu and Afgoi – fifty of them on a thirty-kilometer road.[44] The citizens of Mogadishu, according to policy analyst Stig Jarle Hansen, were "tired of the . . . various ideologies [of] nationalism, fascism, Marxism, and clannism" that led to anarchy.[45] In creating shari'a courts, local religious leaders offered a new route "by which social order [could] be restored" beyond the clan networks that, changed as they were by colonial and authoritarian rule, "failed to achieve a [national] political resolution."[46] Amidst interclan rivalries and a nonfunctioning judicial system, the shari'a courts became Somalia's most durable promise of legal order.

Who worked for this Islamic legal order? Most of the judges and court staff were respected figures, often elders, in their communities. They made decisions by drawing on a mixture (Somali: *barax*) of shari'a and custom, which were entwined and assimilated into one another through decades of decisions.[47] Calling these courts "Islamic" helped them transcend both clan politics and state politics, though few court officials were renowned experts on Islamic law and theology.[48] But

---

[42] Santoro (1999).
[43] Interview 16 with Todd, expatriate consultant and professor, in Hargeisa, Somaliland (June 2013).
[44] Santoro (1999). Afgoi is also transliterated Afgoye.
[45] Hansen (2013), 23.
[46] Mark Huband, *Warriors of the Prophet: The Struggle for Islam* (Boulder, CO: Westview Press, 1998), 33.
[47] Interview 87 with Muuse, former senior government minister in Mogadishu, Somalia (conducted in Addis Ababa, Ethiopia) (August 2013).
[48] Brankamp (2013).

some of them were trained sheikhs who, like Mohamed Abdullah Hassan a century before, used their religious education to promote dispute resolution and their oratorical skills to instill a sense of religious identity in the public. Others, called *wadaad*, advised people on marital matters and performed ritual blessings of sick people and waterholes. Wadaad, who call people to prayer, were as pious as the sheikhs, though typically not as educated. Somalis held both wadaad and sheikhs in high social regard. Custom discouraged people from attacking them. They earned respect, in part, from their commitment to ethical living and nonviolence, including their refusal to eat meat from stolen animals.[49]

The idea of shari'a courts began to spread beyond Mogadishu. Leaders from the Hawaadle clan, in the town of Beledweyne, 350 kilometers north of Mogadishu, also set up a local shari'a court.[50] And about 1,000 kilometers north of Beledweyne, community leaders in Puntland developed their own shari'a courts with their own sets of rules. Puntland simultaneously developed its own national charter, separate from Somalia. The charter prohibited torture "unless sentenced by Islamic shari'a courts in accordance with Islamic law."[51]

International monitoring groups refer to the shari'a courts as one of the few spaces of safe, local governance in Somalia during the 1990s.[52] While most were tied to various lineages of the same Hawiye clan, the majority of the population in the areas where the courts operated claimed these same patrilineal origins; residents thus felt comfortable turning to the courts. The courts' promotion of a shared Islamic identity, moreover, helped people accept the judges' decisions – even when, later, courts began to exercise jurisdiction beyond their specific clan or sub-clan communities.[53]

To Somalis, the warlords seemed to lack moral agency, which made the search for an alternative more urgent. As residents yearned for some kind of order, they also seemed willing, in the words of one aid worker, "to trade [rights] for ... protections of peace and security."[54] As in

---

[49] I. M. Lewis, *Saints and Somalis: Popular Islam in a Clan-Based Society* (Lawrenceville, NJ: Red Sea Press, 1998).

[50] International Crisis Group (2006), 9.

[51] US Department of State, *Country Reports on Human Rights Practices for 2008* (Washington, DC: Government Printing Office, 2010), 524.

[52] International Crisis Group (2006).

[53] Deforche (2013).

[54] Interview 65 with Jen, expatriate aid worker in Nairobi, Kenya (conducted by telephone from Hargeisa, Somaliland) (July 2013).

places like Myanmar, where the judiciary used "law and order" to control citizens and dismantle the rule of law, the threat always existed that radical elements might attach themselves to the courts, and co-opt people's desire for stability, in order to seize power or wealth.[55]

THE ISLAMIC COURTS UNION: COURTS AS POLITICAL ACTORS, 2000–2007

From 2000 to 2007, the remit of the shari'a courts expanded. The courts dealt not only with civil and criminal cases but also united against the warlords. People increasingly trusted and turned to the courts for support. As in the past, leaders of the courts still disagreed about how they should be involved in politics. But when the courts merged and formed the ICU, their militias ultimately expelled the warlords and brought peace to Mogadishu, which the individual shari'a courts of the 1990s had not done.

During this period of growth in the courts' political power, both the international aid community and Somalia's government, such as it was, continued to be mostly absent from the country. Officials came and went by airplane, sometimes on single-day trips. Successive governments in exile – the TNG and then the TFG – were the result of at least a dozen national reconciliation conferences held outside Somalia after 1991.[56] Thus, state-level decisions to promote legal development in Somalia were typically made abroad, with little hope for domestic implementation. Other rebuilding efforts came from the Somali diaspora and their allies as far away as England, the United States, and Canada, or from international lawyers in the boardrooms of UN headquarters in Geneva and New York. Those left behind in Somalia complained that Somalis should make rules for themselves, not adopt those crafted with foreign influence – even if they had to draft their new laws under trees rather than in lavish foreign hotels (Somali: *geedka hoostiisa*).

As the courts merged and became political actors, they had to navigate a complex landscape of power shaped by the government in exile, warlords, and international forces. By consolidating, the courts continued to replicate patterns familiar from the early histories of democracies, in which such unification of individual courts into local

---

[55] Nick Cheesman, *Opposing the Rule of Law: How Myanmar's Courts Make Law and Order* (Cambridge: Cambridge University Press, 2015).
[56] Mukhtar (2007), 125.

governments is a key step. In early modern Europe, for instance, the Catholic Church created one of the West's first consolidated legal systems, known as canon law, which formed a foundation upon which national legal systems would grow throughout Western Europe.[57] Seventeenth-century Christian martyrs would later object to excessive fines, torture, and "royal interference in adjudication" because these were "against the will of God," thus helping to strengthen courts, synthesize their "common law," and limit the "arbitrary power of the king."[58] That is, the next step in creating state institutions that can respect the rule of law is for individual judges to merge their efforts and to become more deeply political actors by fusing law to religion.

Shari'a Courts Unite

In 2000, as the courts began unifying their judges and militias, Somalia's political leaders were engaged in a separate state-building project. In Djibouti, at the Arta reconciliation conference, these leaders focused on creating what would become the TNG and a new parliament. Back in Somalia, there was still no state judicial system, and the nonstate shari'a courts were providing legal services to specific neighborhoods. Al-Itihad al-Islamiyya's former leader, Sheikh Hassan Dahir Aweys, however, had a different plan: he hoped to unite the shari'a courts and construct a national judiciary out of them.

Aweys's first step was to create an Islamic Implementation Council (later renamed the Joint Islamic Courts Council), which was the first iteration of what later would become the ICU. The council's goal was twofold: coordinate the activities of the different shari'a courts and engage in negotiations with the TNG for the courts to join Somalia's government.[59] By combining disparate courts and their militias, the council also created Somalia's first militia united against the warlords. Aweys and his deputies hoped this armed support would help convince the TNG to make the shari'a courts the foundation of Somalia's rebuilt judiciary. When asked at the time about the council's work, one of its leaders, Sheikh Hassan Sheikh Mohammed Adde, told the *Christian Science Monitor* that "Islamic law is the only thing that will save this country."[60]

---

[57] Harold J. Berman, "Religious Foundations of Law in the West: A Historical Perspective," 1(1) *Journal of Law and Religion* (1983): 3–43, pp. 7–8.

[58] Ibid., 33.

[59] Gerrie Swart, "Somalia: A Failed State Governed by a Failed Government?" in *Somalia at the Crossroads: Challenges and Perspectives in Reconstituting a Failed State*, eds. Abdulahi A. Osman and Issaka K. Souaré (London: Adonis & Abbey, 2007), 109–122, p. 112.

[60] Santoro (1999). Adde is also transliterated Addeh.

But the council's initial goal of destroying the warlords and rebuilding Somalia's judiciary was short-lived. Though the TNG absorbed some of the shari'a courts into its fledgling government in 2001, it was suspicious of Sheikh Aweys given his troubled past. He was a suspect in the 1998 bombings of US embassies nearby, in Tanzania and Kenya. In 2001, the US government declared him a terrorist and, later, so did the United Nations.[61] Later, the US banned all contact with Aweys, refusing to negotiate with him even as his political authority grew in Somalia.[62]

While Sheikh Aweys and his deputies wanted to use the shari'a courts to help fulfill their national political ambitions, Somalia's towns, villages, and neighborhoods told a different story. The people knew the shari'a courts would improve public safety, particularly in places where the courts also set up schools and hospitals. Few could argue with the courts' social services and their growing viability as an alternative to the warlords. The courts' diffuse structures comprised judges, Sufi clerics, local politicians, community leaders, traders, shop owners, and elders. The courts earned people's support "because they spoke of rights, and supported" people, according to a Mogadishu-based academic I met who was familiar with their operations in the 2000s.[63] An aid worker in Nairobi told me, "The courts did not just impose justice. They were also the police. If [you had] a problem, you would go to the [shari'a] court."[64] As a human rights activist in Mogadishu related, the courts' legitimacy came "not just because they called themselves courts. They [also] created a sense of new opportunity for Somalia."[65]

It was precisely the courts' Islamic identity that helped Somalis accept them – even those who felt the courts might have been too punitive or might have gone too far to achieve security and stability. For the first time since Siad Barre was deposed, Somalis willingly

---

[61] Andrew Harding, *The Mayor of Mogadishu: A Story of Chaos and Redemption in the Ruins of Somalia* (New York: St. Martin's Press, 2016), 154.

[62] Interview 87 with Muuse, former senior government minister in Mogadishu, Somalia (conducted in Addis Ababa, Ethiopia) (August 2013); see also "U.S. Bans Contact with Islamist Leader in Somalia," *Reuters*, June 26, 2006, https://bit.ly/2JVRtPt (accessed January 1, 2021); Saul Shay, *Somalia between Jihad and Restoration* (London: Routledge, 2017).

[63] Interview 9 with Naqeeb, professor at the University of Mogadishu, Somalia (conducted in person in Hargeisa, Somaliland) (June 2013).

[64] Interview 65 with Jen, expatriate aid worker in Nairobi, Kenya (conducted by telephone from Hargeisa, Somaliland) (July 2013).

[65] Interview 78 with Majda, lawyer and human rights activist in Mogadishu and Hargeisa (conducted in Nairobi, Kenya) (July 2013).

submitted to an institutionalized legal authority. As a UN official told me, even aid workers reluctantly saw the benefit of religious courts: "I myself want to keep shari'a to family law, but . . . the [courts] had a lot of support. People . . . wanted stability, not because of good governance but because [the courts] rose above the tribal divides."[66] Although individual shari'a courts had been devoted to helping people from a single clan or sub-clan group in the 1990s, as the courts merged in the 2000s, judges began to define the courts' jurisdictions regionally rather than by clan, which allowed them to work across hereditary lineage groups. Their multi-clan jurisdictions and shared Islamic identity helped the courts as a whole foster order and stability between rival groups, not just within them.

However, it was also precisely the courts' Islamic identity that led to international concern about their growing influence. The Ethiopian government, in particular, saw the growth and consolidation of Somalia's shari'a courts as a threat, given that former members of al-Itihaad al-Islamiyya had been joining the courts' leadership and rank and file.[67] In trying to unite Somalis, the courts had been encouraging dialogue among "a broad spectrum of religious groups, from moderate to radical Islamists."[68]

From 2002 through 2004, as the shari'a courts were spreading across and outside the capital, peace talks in Kenya – called the Eldoret conference – were creating Somalia's new TFG.[69] (The TFG would move to a small compound in Baidoa, Somalia, in 2005.) Eldoret was Somalia's fourteenth multilateral peace conference.[70] It led to the adoption of a provisional federal constitution and established a parliament of 275 members chosen according to the "4.5" scheme: the four largest family lineages (Darood, Hawiye, Dighil, and Mirilfe confederation, and the Isaaq and Dir confederation) each received sixty-one seats, while minority groups were allocated thirty-one seats in total. Between September and November 2004, parliament chose a president, Abdulahi Yusuf Ahmed, and speaker, Sharif Hassan

[66] Interview 77 with Khadra, United Nations official in Nairobi, Kenya (July 2013).
[67] "Ethiopia Says Somalia 'a Threat'." BBC News, June 28, 2006, https://bbc.in/3hmoMI1 (accessed January 1, 2021).
[68] Religious Literacy Project, The Islamic Courts Union (Cambridge, MA: Harvard Divinity School, 2020), https://bit.ly/38Fufpt.
[69] A. Ibrahim Mohamed (Qoorcade), A Nation in Tatters: Somalia (Qaran Dumay) (Liverpool: Somali Education Trust, 2009), 93.
[70] Abdulahi A. Osman and Issaka K. Souaré, "Introduction," in Somalia at the Crossroads: Challenges and Perspectives in Reconstituting a Failed State, eds. Abdulahi A. Osman and Issaka K. Souaré (London: Adonis & Abbey, 2007), 7–22, p. 17.

Sheikh Adan. President Ahmed, in turn, appointed a prime minister, Mohamed Ali Gedi, and his cabinet ministers. Some Somalis resented these appointments, not least as the president and many of the ministers were themselves former warlords. The TFG also announced that it would set up Somalia's Supreme Court and courts of appeal. But, like the TNG before it, the TFG was a government in exile, as many of its senior officials had deeper connections to aid workers and the Somali diaspora than to ordinary people still in the country.

Soon after the founding of the TFG, around 2005, ten of Mogadishu's shari'a courts united. With unity, they became a more potent political force. They created a new Supreme Council of Shari'a Courts to oversee their work. The new council persuaded additional courts to join a common militia, just as the earlier councils had done.[71] The united courts contributed approximately eighty soldiers each to a shared armed force.[72] Inspired by Islamic faith, they joined into a single movement whose goal was to defeat the warlords entirely and return political order to Somalia once and for all.

It was then that Mogadishu's courts first called themselves Itihaad al-Mahakim al-Islamiyya, or ICU. Other regions followed Mogadishu's lead, including Hiran, Middle Shabelle, Mudug, Nugal, and Bari. These communities were "tired of . . . conflicts and insecurity and . . . saw the shari'a court system as the ultimate remedy."[73] The ICU's purpose was to give the disparate shari'a courts a "superstructure."[74] The consolidation of the shari'a courts into a single ICU was fueled by fears of Ethiopian domination, concerns that a small set of family lineages dominated the TFG, declining loyalty to factionalized warlords, increasing crime rates, and Islamic solidarity.[75] Some scholars have labeled this period of uniting the Islamic courts as Somalia's "golden age."[76] According to journalist Andrew Harding, "a new force had risen up from within Somalia. Organically and from the grassroots. No wonder people were so hopeful about the Islamic Courts."[77]

[71] Swart (2007), 112.
[72] Stanford University Center for International Security and Cooperation (2016).
[73] Deforche (2013), 113, citing Andre Le Sage, *Stateless Justice in Somalia: Formal and Informal Rule of Law Initiatives* (Geneva: Centre for Humanitarian Dialogue, 2005); see also Barnes and Hassan (2007), 1.
[74] Interview 87 with Muuse, former senior government minister in Mogadishu, Somalia (conducted in Addis Ababa, Ethiopia) (August 2013).
[75] Hansen (2013), 31–33.
[76] Barnes and Hassan (2007), 7; Deforche (2013), 102.
[77] Harding (2016), 153.

The Courts Begin Building the Rule of Law

From the 1990s to 2006, Somalia's shari'a courts and then the ICU developed as grassroots mechanisms of self-governance that recall the role courts often played early in the history of democracies. By 2006, it was becoming clear that the courts' strategy of building local security might work on a national scale. According to one news report, the courts' "attempt at justice was welcomed" and led neighborhoods to set up their own courts to find and try accused gunmen, rapists, thieves, and murderers.[78] Echoing Somalis I met who lived through the period, a sheikh told me that ordinary Somalis – "simple people," in his words – spent what little money they had to donate food and weapons to the ICU, begging them to "please protect us from the warlords." The courts were, in his words, "part of the people."[79] They had "popular legitimacy," according to a foreign observer.[80]

In addition, the courts "were ... tools [to] enable the business community to escape plunder by the various warlord militias."[81] Although Somalia remained one of the poorest countries in the world, its economy actually improved between 2000 and 2005, relative to its own past performance and to the economies of neighboring African countries. According to a study in the *Journal of Economic Behavior & Organization*, while the life expectancy of people in Somalia fell by two years during the civil war of the 1980s, life expectancy had "increas[ed] by five years since ... [1991]. Only three [African] countries improved life expectancy as much."[82] Technology also leapfrogged that of neighboring countries; using a mobile phone in Somalia was "cheaper and clearer than ... anywhere else in Africa."[83]

The ICU functioned for a variety of reasons. Demand for more Islamic courts came from businessmen who were not religious extremists or militants.[84] But these business leaders were not the ICU's only backers. Militants on the courts' fringes were amassing weapons for war, and they saw the ICU as a conduit to achieve their own goals of an

[78] Marc Lacey, "In Somalia, Islamic Militias Fight Culture Wars," *New York Times*, June 19, 2006, https://nyti.ms/2MeUs6E (accessed January 1, 2021).
[79] Interview 127 with Sheikh Oweis, sheikh and senior university administrator in Hargeisa, Somaliland (June 2014).
[80] Interview 133 with Stephanie, researcher and author in London, England (July 2014).
[81] Hansen (2013), 33.
[82] Benjamin Powell, Ryan Ford, and Alex Nowrasteh, "Somalia after State Collapse: Chaos or Improvement?" 67(3–4) *Journal of Economic Behavior & Organization* (2008): 657–670, p. 662.
[83] "Somalia Calling: An Unlikely Success Story," *The Economist*, December 20, 2005, https://econ.st/34QtGI3.
[84] "Profile: Somalia's Islamic Courts," *BBC News*, June 6, 2006, https://bbc.in/2WQzvB0.

austere Islamic state. Other Somalis saw the ICU as a hopeful way out of interclan rivalries that were destroying the TFG from the inside and making it, they thought, a puppet government for Ethiopia, Kenya, the United States, and other foreign interests. For traders, shop owners, and other citizens, the ICU, like the disparate shari'a courts before it, offered a way to transport people and goods without warlords' road-blocks and tariffs. The ICU, unlike the warlords, "had a proven track record of restoring security and was associated with the provision of other social services and charitable works."[85] The ICU's social services agencies showed "good organization and accountability," while others were "plagued by corruption and theft."[86] The ICU provided a kind of security that the warlords could not.

Xeer, or locally rooted customary law, was vital to the work of the courts; though the courts labeled themselves Islamic, they were not exclusively Islamic.[87] Like all courts, they were legal assemblages.[88] In resolving family disputes about marriage, divorce, and inheritance, judges drew from a combination of xeer and shari'a. Most of the judges had rudimentary knowledge of Islamic law, and it is unclear which rulings were based on shari'a and which were based on custom, especially given the wide variety of precedents and versions of shari'a and xeer available. Some judges used what amounted to hybrid versions of shari'a, not necessarily tied to any specific school of Sunni Islamic law.[89] Other judges, with limited education, were guided by the hope that what they were doing was consistent with what they believed to be God's will.[90]

Although many ICU staff, particularly early on, were from the same Hawiye clan, the courts' Islamic identity was meant to lessen the impor-tance of the clan in people's lives.[91] The ICU's main consultative council (Arabic: *shura*) was made up of religious, community, and business leaders. The united courts, according to Somalis I met, "were successful because they were listening to the people [and] they were part of the people."[92] The preponderance of the courts' work focused on family matters and crime, including murder, banditry, looting, and roadblocks.

---

[85] Barnes and Hassan (2007), 4.
[86] Deforche (2013), 112, citing Menkhaus (2002).
[87] Brankamp (2013).
[88] Michael G. Peletz, *Sharia Transformations: Cultural Politics and the Rebranding of an Islamic Judiciary* (Oakland, CA: University of California Press, 2020).
[89] Religious Literacy Project (2020).
[90] Brankamp (2013).
[91] Ibid.
[92] Interview 127 with Sheikh Oweis, sheikh and senior university administrator in Hargeisa, Somaliland (June 2014).

Aside from these issues and assisting with contracts, the ICU's other priorities were health care, education, and environmental protection.[93] Because Somalia's trees were rapidly disappearing, burned into charcoal for cooking, the ICU's environmental regulations tried to protect trees from the charcoal trade.[94] The ICU also tried to protect Somalia's coasts: according to policy analysts, piracy was virtually eliminated within six months of the ICU's rise to power in June 2006.[95]

The ICU's "sudden ascendance" seemed, to the outside world, to be a "carefully planned Islamic revolution."[96] But if it was an Islamic revolution at all, it was not a threatening one to most Somalis. The US government, however, worried that the ICU would become a haven for the al-Qaeda militants that a coalition of Western nations had been hunting in their war on terror. It did not help the ICU's moderate judges and nonviolent religious leaders that Osama bin Laden released a tape praising the courts' restoration of stability and saying Somalia's success was due to its embrace of Islam. (Osama bin Laden had earlier funded al-Itihad al-Islamiyya.) In his audio tape, bin Laden said, "We warn all [Western] countries from ... send[ing] international forces to Somalia ... We swear ... that we will fight their soldiers in Somalia and ... punish them on their lands."[97]

Unlike al-Qaeda, however, the ICU was not a global militant organization. Rather, the ICU was as fragmented as the diverse courts and militias that made it up.[98] Various Sufi tariqas (Arabic: brotherhoods) and non-Sufi organizations affiliated with the ICU helped to hire and train new bailiffs and policemen, construct new buildings, hold street cleanups, and encourage local community organization. Others in the ICU's membership disputed whether and how to integrate Islam into a new state. Some talked of democratic elections, while others prepared

[93] Deforche (2013), citing Shank (2007); see also Ken Menkhaus, "There and Back Again in Somalia," *Middle East Research and Information Project (MERIP)* (2007b), https://bit.ly/2WQzIUO (accessed January 1, 2021).
[94] Shank (2007).
[95] Roger Middleton, *Piracy in Somalia: Threatening Global Trade, Feeding Local Wars* (London: Chatham House, 2008); Mary Harper, *Getting Somalia Wrong? Faith, War, and Hope in a Shattered State* (London: Zed Books, 2012), 157–158. Some historians question the extent to which ICU laws reduced piracy. See Awet Tewelde Weldemichael, *Piracy in Somalia: Violence and Development in the Horn of Africa* (Cambridge: Cambridge University Press, 2019), 85–86.
[96] Barnes and Hassan (2007), 1.
[97] Octavia Nasr, "Tape: Bin Laden Tells Sunnis to Fight Shiites in Iraq," *CNN*, July 2, 2006, https://cnn.it/3pvMC72 (accessed January 1, 2021).
[98] Jeffrey Gettleman, "Islamists Calm Somali Capital with Restraint," *New York Times*, September 24, 2006, A1, https://nyti.ms/2KEK3k4 (accessed January 1, 2021).

for religious rebellion and war. Contradictory statements from the ICU revealed its internal political rifts. Some of the leaders, like Aweys, were more radical and emboldened; they looked beyond Somalia to develop links with al-Qaeda. Others, like Sheikh Sharif Ahmed, who would later become Somalia's president from 2009 to 2012, sought peace without violence.

The ICU's ambivalence about whether and how to use violent tactics, combined with financial support it received from Eritrea, Ethiopia's enemy at the time, provoked Ethiopia's hostility toward the courts. As a result, Ethiopia provided financial support both to the TFG and to warlords who secured safe passage for goods from that landlocked country to Somalia's ports.[99] Unexplained killings and disappearances of several of the courts' militia commanders and religious leaders led to retaliatory killings of TFG officials. These retaliations were pinned on the ICU, and foreign embassies began calling it a terrorist group. This led some in the ICU to take a more political stance toward the TFG and the international community.[100] By early 2005 a new splinter group, al-Shabaab, arose "in the shadow of the courts."[101] Al-Shabaab, which had only thirty-three core members at its founding, opened a training camp for its own militia, separate from those of the ICU.

Meanwhile, the TFG was busy drafting a new national constitution. In 2004 in Nairobi, the TFG set up an Independent Federal Constitution Commission (IFCC) tasked with drafting a constitution in line with the "principles of Islam, democracy, and social justice."[102] They did not submit their first draft constitution to the TFG parliament until 2010.

Because of its power in the mid-2000s, the ICU "threaten[ed] to eclipse the fragile TFG."[103] Ironically, while the IFCC was drafting a democratic constitution based on Islam, the courts were already practicing their own interpretation of God's will, and Somalia, particularly in Mogadishu, was changing almost overnight. By the end of 2005, the ICU had a few thousand bailiffs and other gunmen on its payroll who launched a series of offensives against local warlords. The

[99] Andrew Cawthorne, "US says al Qaeda behind Somali Islamists," *Reuters*, December 15, 2006, cited in Barnes and Hassan (2007), 6.
[100] Barnes and Hassan (2007), 3.
[101] Hansen (2013), 31.
[102] Ali Hirsi Ahmed, *Constitution-Making in Somalia: A Critical Analysis, 1960–2013*, MA Thesis, Institute of Diplomacy and International Studies (Nairobi: University of Nairobi, 2014), 46.
[103] International Crisis Group (2006), 1.

battles weakened the warlords, whom American intelligence agencies had been paying to catch terrorists. With the business community's financial support, and a "well-funded and well-motivated militia," ICU leaders decided to take a stand against the warlords in early 2006.[104] Facing this threat, the warlords quickly united under an umbrella group they named the Alliance for the Restoration of Peace and Counter-Terrorism, whose leadership was made up of TFG officials and warlords. The alliance funneled US counter-terrorism funding – for apprehending al-Qaeda suspects – to the warlords.

Ethiopia and the alliance represented the ICU "as a breeding ground for radicalism and a potential haven for jihadi elements."[105] Western officials, particularly from the United States, likewise "seemed incapable of perceiving what was initially a loose alliance of highly localized shari'a courts as anything other than an al-Qaeda-linked threat."[106] Hard-line members of the ICU saw the alliance's actions as an attack on the ICU and "an attack on Islam itself."[107] In the first half of 2006, battles between alliance and ICU militias killed dozens, many of whom were unaffiliated with either group. The warlords "were armed to the teeth," but they "were not a match to the will of the people," Somali politicians told me of this time.[108] By June 2006, most warlords had either died or fled.

The ICU had gained control of Mogadishu, uniting the city for the first time in fifteen years. The BBC News called the ICU Somalia's "strongest fighting force" and its "most popular political force."[109] The ICU reopened the airport and seaports to the public. Diasporic communities slowly began to return. People opened their doors and removed roadblocks and trash.[110] One man told me how, when he came back from Europe in 2006, he and his friends walked Mogadishu's streets for the first time in two decades "without guns ... without fear, [and] without ... harassment."[111] Another exclaimed to me that the

---

[104] Barnes and Hassan (2007), 4.
[105] Harper (2012), 170.
[106] Ibid.
[107] International Crisis Group (2006), 12. Swart (2007), 113.
[108] Interview 87 with Muuse, former senior government minister in Mogadishu, Somalia (conducted in Addis Ababa, Ethiopia) (August 2013).
[109] "Profile: Somalia's Islamic Courts," BBC News, June 6, 2006, https://bbc.in/3rxw7sX (accessed January 1, 2021).
[110] Barnes and Hassan (2007), 4.
[111] Interview 127 with Sheikh Oweis, sheikh and senior university administrator in Hargeisa, Somaliland (June 2014).

peace was so rapid and real that "even Somalilanders [who had seceded in 1991] started to think of a union again!"[112]

The ICU set up special courts to deal with property restitution claims that returnees were bringing against those who occupied the land and homes they had fled. The very building where the warlords had established their alliance became a shari'a court. The warlords found refuge in Ethiopia or Congo or even within the TFG, where some of them became cabinet ministers under President Ahmed. Because the TFG was a government of reconciliation, the warlords "couldn't be fired," which further eroded people's trust in it.[113] As the TFG kept one foot in Somalia – in its small Baidoa compound – and one foot outside, its power quickly faded. For example, the 275 members of the TFG parliament refused to travel into Somalia for a meeting in February 2006 unless the United Nations Development Programme (UNDP) agreed to pay each of them all travel expenses, *dhaadhac daw* (per diems) for hotel accommodations, and a USD 1,800 monthly allowance, which publicly alienated these elites from those whom they represented.[114] At best, many Somalis saw the TFG as just another political faction rather than as a national government.[115] The TFG's judiciary consisted of just eight people, a Supreme Court chairperson and seven novice justices. Limited as it was, the TFG still had the international community's support.[116]

From June to December 2006, the ICU briefly controlled much of southern and central Somalia. During these six months, the ICU claimed unfettered control from Kismayo just north of the Kenyan coast to Galkayo, which lies about 1,200 kilometers further north, near Puntland.[117] It was a "dramatic change" for the country, though Somalis recognized that achieving it was "messy [and] imperfect."[118] According to the *New York Times*, ICU militiamen "allowed soccer games, planned for democratic elections, reopened movie theaters,

---

[112] Interview 85 with Ibrahim, NGO program adviser in Nairobi, Kenya (August 2013).

[113] Interview 87 with Muuse, former senior government minister in Mogadishu, Somalia (conducted in Addis Ababa, Ethiopia) (August 2013).

[114] Mukhtar (2007), 125, citing International Crisis Group (2006), 7–8.

[115] International Crisis Group (2006), 22.

[116] Andre Le Sage, "Somalia's Endless Transition: Breaking the Deadlock," *Strategic Forum No. 257* (Washington, DC: Institute for National Strategic Studies, National Defense University 2010).

[117] Interview 87 with Muuse, former senior government minister in Mogadishu, Somalia (conducted in Addis Ababa, Ethiopia) (August 2013). Like any authority, the ICU did not have total support. It faced opposition in Kismayo, where residents saw the ICU as the disguise of a clan seeking to dominate their own clans. Barnes and Hassan (2007), 5.

[118] Interview 133 with Stephanie, researcher and author in London, England (July 2014).

educated girls in schools, and even permitted commercial activity in front of their headquarters during noon prayers."[119]

The Islamic Courts Union Is Destroyed

This renaissance would not last. In June 2006, ICU chairperson Sheikh Sharif Sheikh Ahmed promised peace with the TFG and rival groups: "The joint Islamic courts do not want continuation of hostilities and will ensure peace and security following the change attained by the victory of the people with the support of Allah."[120] His statement led to a series of peace talks between the ICU and the TFG, the first of which were held in June 2006 in Sudan. The TFG boycotted the next round of talks, claiming that the ICU was still seizing Somali territory. At another round of talks in September, ICU leaders rejected any TFG proposition that foreign troops enter Somali territory, which ultimately led to calling off the final round of talks. Though the ICU and a parliamentary delegation led by speaker Hassan Sheikh Adan did reach a preliminary peace agreement, the TFG rejected it.[121] Thus the back-and-forth negotiations came to a halt in late 2006, and both groups began preparing for military operations. The ICU was emboldened by its victories and recharged with weapons seized from warlords. The ICU militias had their eyes set on Baidoa, the small town where the TFG was based.

An international military invasion to bring down the ICU soon followed. Officials of the TFG were facing a possible invasion of their small compound. The leadership of landlocked Ethiopia felt threatened by the ICU's control of seaports and by Eritrea's support for the courts. And the US government was worried about the rise of an Islamic state in East Africa and possible terror attacks against American interests, as ICU leaders sent conflicting messages about their relationship with al-Qaeda. The ICU had emerged during an era when, from the US perspective, "Islam [had] replaced communism as that which must be cracked down by all means."[122]

---

[119] Gettleman (2006); see also Cavedon (2014), 497.
[120] "Somalia: Mogadishu Islamic Leaders Claim Victory Over Rivals," *United Nations Integrated Regional Information Network (IRIN) News*, June 5, 2006, https://bit.ly/3quIJAq (accessed January 1, 2021).
[121] Swart (2007), 116.
[122] Issaka K Souaré, "Conclusions: Towards a Revived Somali State," in *Somalia at the Crossroads: Challenges and Perspectives in Reconstituting a Failed State*, eds. Abdulahi A. Osman and Issaka K. Souaré (London: Adonis & Abbey, 2007), 209–210.

Ethiopia and the TFG were allied against the ICU and painted the organization "far too simplistically – as a terrorist umbrella, backed by thousands of foreign jihadi fighters."[123] After months of lobbying by the TFG and the Ethiopian government, on December 6, 2006, the United Nations Security Council acted under its powers in Chapter VII of the UN Charter to take all necessary actions to restore international peace and security. Citing the "lack of clarity of the political agenda of the Islamic Courts," the Security Council, in a session that lasted only fifteen minutes, adopted Resolution 1725, which authorized an African Union-led mission to enter Somalia to maintain security in Baidoa, where the TFG was about to come under fire from approaching ICU militias.[124] (That mission, called the African Union Mission in Somalia, or AMISOM, would begin in January 2007.) Resolution 1725 also reasserted the TFG's legitimacy as Somalia's national government and sought to bring the ICU into the UN's peacekeeping agenda by ensuring the free movement of all persons involved in negotiations between the TFG and ICU. However, the intervention of the United Nations Security Council on behalf of the TFG and Ethiopia emboldened the ICU's fringe elements, who felt that there was a growing international conspiracy against them and against the Islamic religion itself.

At the same time, a proxy war between Ethiopia and Eritrea took shape. Eritrea provided support to the ICU while Ethiopia funded the TFG in exile. The TFG essentially gave the Ethiopian military its blessing to invade Somalia. Weak as it was, the TFG relied on foreign support to oust the ICU, which cost it what little local support it still had. In the last two weeks of December 2006, as the ICU's militias inched closer to Baidoa, they were weakened by skirmishes. Ethiopia saw its window of opportunity to invade Mogadishu, sending 15,000 troops alongside hefty support from US air, ground, and naval forces.[125] Unable to face a coordinated, triple onslaught from Ethiopian troops, the alliance's warlord militias, and TFG forces, the ICU collapsed in Mogadishu and across Somalia in just a few days, even more quickly than it had risen to power six months

---

[123] International Crisis Group (2006), 1.

[124] United Nations Security Council, "Security Council Approves African Protection, Training Mission in Somalia, Unanimously Adopting Resolution 1725 (2006)," *United Nations Security Council Press Release* SC/8887, December 6, 2006, https://bit.ly/34PMszi (accessed January 1, 2021).

[125] The US military's goal was to ensure that the ICU cannot "be reconstituted as a political entity." Shank (2007), 90.

earlier.[126] The ICU was no match for an international onslaught led by one of Africa's strongest militaries. The majority of losses were not among militants, however, who "melted back into Mogadishu life" and later regrouped as al-Shabaab.[127]

On December 27, 2006, the ICU leadership resigned en masse. The ICU's moderate judges and politicians fled to Eritrea, Kenya, Yemen, and elsewhere. When they saw the ICU collapsing, some of them joined reconciliation efforts or tried to become part of the TFG itself, to make change from the inside.[128] Those who did not flee Somalia reintegrated either into Somali society or into al-Shabaab, which was emboldened by the Ethiopian attack. Al-Shabaab had been a fringe group that faced the same kind of mistrust that people had of Western aid agencies and the state itself, but support for it increased after the attack.[129] The Ethiopian invasion played "into the hands of the extremists," giving al-Shabaab, with its confiscated weapons and radical agenda, a reason to rise.[130] Thus the intervention paradoxically fed the very nationalistic, Islamist ideals that Ethiopia and the United States sought to defeat.[131]

Violence continued through the early months of 2007. Ethiopian troops and TFG forces clashed with militants, who also clashed with one another, in Mogadishu and areas outside it. More than 1,000 people were killed in this new civil war. Aid agencies and policy analysts estimate that 200,000 people fled the capital city.[132] Over the ensuing months, battles continued to rage throughout Somalia as the TFG tried to take power for the first time. Although distrusted by many Somalis, the TFG had the support of AMISOM troops. The TFG continued to take a hard line against the ICU, firing its own parliamentary speaker, Sharif Hassan Sheikh Adan, because he had earlier called for peace talks with the ICU.

---

[126] Fred M. Shelley, *Governments around the World: From Democracies to Theocracies* (Santa Barbara, CA: ABC-CLIO, 2015), 379.
[127] Barnes and Hassan (2007), 6.
[128] Interview 9 with Naqeeb, professor at the University of Mogadishu, Somalia (conducted in person in Hargeisa, Somaliland) (June 2013).
[129] Harper (2012), 171, citing a blog post by anthropologist Markus Virgil Hoehne, who in turn cites a report of the West Point Center for Combatting Terrorism.
[130] Harding (2016), 155.
[131] Harper (2012).
[132] "Somalia: Escalation and Human Rights Abuses," *AfricaFocus*, April 9, 2007, https://bit.ly/3hqjcEE (accessed January 1, 2021); see also "Help Thousands Displaced, Civil Society Urges Aid Agencies," *United Nations Integrated Regional Information Network (IRIN) News*, April 18, 2007, https://bit.ly/3rsKrTo (accessed January 1, 2021); see also Barnes and Hassan (2007), 6–7.

The ICU, despite the problems associated with its factions, was a broad-based indigenous collective, made up of judges, religious leaders, and businessmen, that had succeeded in bringing stability to Mogadishu and surrounding areas. Many Somalis saw the ICU as a "genuine, apolitical effort" to combat crime and the chaos and uncertainty of daily life under warlord rule.[133] But in a matter of a few weeks in late December 2006 and early January 2007, all of it – the ICU, the shari'a courts, and Somalia's short-lived stability – was destroyed. Somalis told me that, from their perspective, Western governments and Ethiopia "did not want to have an Islamic government that is independent and strong, [and] the reason is religion."[134] The United States and the international community were so focused on destroying Islamic extremism that they also destroyed the shari'a courts, the legal solutions the courts had provided for Somalis, and the path toward stability and the rule of law that the courts had just begun to build.

GOD'S WILL, MILITARIZED, 2007–2021

Since 2007, Somalis trying to exert any kind of political authority have relied on their own distinct versions and interpretations of God's will. These groups include, most notably, al-Shabaab and the TFG. While both al-Shabaab and the TFG have continued to invoke shari'a, neither has come as close to building the rule of law from the ground up as the scattered shari'a courts and the ICU arguably did, first locally and then regionally, from about 1994 to 2006. The international intervention that brought the Islamic courts' experiment to an abrupt end shattered not only shari'a but also the nascent, bottom-up potential for democratic institutions. If history shows that democracies may begin with local courts that, using religious symbols and discourse, unite into legal systems and give rise to other mechanisms of self-governance, Somalia's trajectory from 2007 to 2021 shows the danger of pulling these institutions up by their roots. Such interventions ultimately put long-term democratic development at risk.

In early 2007, capturing Mogadishu for the first time and installing itself as Somalia's national government, the TFG found its capital in

---

[133] Cavedon (2014), 479, citing Menkhaus (2002).
[134] Interview 114 with Mustafa, senior government official and former aqil of British colonial administration (June 2014).

upheaval and instituted martial law. Its support from the United Nations, United States, and Ethiopia meant discouraging the revival of shari'a courts. "Talking about any Islamic courts [was] anathema," one person told me.[135] To survivors, martial law and the non-democratic takeover were reminiscent of Siad Barre's approach to governance. Such moves also seemed deeply anti-Islamic, not least because the shari'a courts, and then the ICU, had enjoyed "fairly consistent support" among Somalis for a decade.[136]

Piracy returned with a vengeance; increasing numbers of container ships were captured after 2007. Somalis I met told me they began once again to feel "threatened by the revival of the warlords with American weapons and money."[137] And rather than eliminating extremism, the ICU's ouster fueled it.[138] Though still uncoordinated in the wake of this disorder, militants from al-Shabaab now began to gather, untethered from the ICU. Some of them had been trained as mujahideen (holy warriors) in Afghanistan. Though al-Shabaab's founding predated the fall of the ICU, it grew stronger after the 2006 Ethiopian invasion. For this reason, aid workers called it a "product of" the war to put an end to the ICU.[139] Indeed, after the collapse of the ICU, Sheikh Ali Dheere, who created Mogadishu's first-known shari'a court in the early 1990s, became a spokesperson for al-Shabaab.[140]

Al-Shabaab took the ICU's place as ruler over Somali areas outside the TFG's control. Al-Shabaab insisted on following legal rules that it, too, linked to shari'a. But its use of popular justice was much more severe than the shari'a of the ICU's moderate judges. Meanwhile, the TFG laid its own claim to God's will and asserted that Somalia would be a democratic Islamic state, drafting a constitution to that effect in 2012. This period after 2007 exposes the strained relations between elites trying to establish a responsive, democratic state and others trying to tear it down, both of them acting in the name of God's will. Not dissimilarly, law in postcolonial nineteenth-century America was animated by local struggles between people driven by religious ardor and "the passions of popular justice" and others, often also informed by

---

[135] Interview 12 with Daniel, expatriate lawyer and NGO program manager in Hargeisa, Somaliland (June 2013).
[136] Barnes and Hassan (2007).
[137] Interview 85 with Ibrahim, NGO program adviser in Nairobi, Kenya (August 2013).
[138] Harper (2012), 172–173.
[139] Interview 85 with Ibrahim, NGO program adviser in Nairobi, Kenya (August 2013).
[140] Deforche (2013).

religious principles, who sought an alternative "idea of the rule of law [that implied] fairness, equality, and consistency."[141]

After examining the legalism that al-Shabaab enforced in areas under its control, the remainder of this chapter turns to the TFG's attempt to reestablish a state judiciary – which was at odds with its constitution's enshrinement of shari'a.

The Legalism of Al-Shabaab

Al-Shabaab used a legalistic version of shari'a as an organizational weapon. Its leaders preached a strict version of Islam opposed to any Western involvement in Somali political affairs. Many of its cadets launched suicide attacks on Somalis and foreigners. Somalis I met told me they felt al-Shabaab saw "international organizations like UNDP [as] agents of the West [that] are not supporting the traditional culture of Somali society."[142] Many Somalis agreed with the idea that United Nations involvement would be bad for Somali politics: as one Somali aid worker unaffiliated with al-Shabaab told me, "I hate UNDP no matter what. Even if they do something good, I find a way to hate it."[143] As a result, al-Shabaab grew its presence, particularly in the southern region of the country, from Jowhar, a town about 100 kilometers north of Mogadishu, south to the Kenyan border.

Al-Shabaab was largely decentralized, but its leaders made every effort to proclaim fidelity to law and avoid any perception of arbitrariness, even while repressing those they deemed enemies of Islam. Despite forcing their rule upon hundreds of thousands of Somalis and being responsible for hundreds of attacks and civilian deaths, al-Shabaab militants spoke publicly about how they did not act arbitrarily and instead followed a strict system of legal rules. Those rules are rooted in a specific vision of Islamic legal order. For example, when questioned by the BBC's Africa Editor, an al-Shabaab leader said his organization does not accept recruits under age fifteen, which would be repugnant to Islamic law, and that women and older persons may "participate in battles . . . because that is allowed in our religion."[144] Another militant recounted that all accused persons are put through a due legal process

---

[141] Samuel Walker, *Popular Justice: A History of American Criminal Justice* (Oxford: Oxford University Press, 1980), 4.

[142] Interview 14 with Maxamed, independent researcher and consultant in Hargeisa, Somaliland (June 2013).

[143] Interview 78 with Majda, lawyer and human rights activist in Mogadishu and Hargeisa (conducted in Nairobi, Kenya) (July 2013).

[144] Harper (2012), 91.

before anyone is punished or executed.[145] Citing a commander from al-Shabaab whom he met in 2009 in Somalia, British journalist Andrew Harding wrote that "Al-Shabaab operated within a system of strict, fair laws that had brought peace to much of Somalia."[146]

Aid workers I met admitted that crime and unrest are "a problem in non-Shabaab areas. There are no trigger-happy people in al-Shabaab areas."[147] While aid workers had clear problems with al-Shabaab's occupation, militancy, and human rights record, they privately explained to me that its "functioning systems" provided services, including courts, health care, education, food, and water, to people who did not cause political trouble.[148] Similarly, al-Shabaab's recruits are often motivated by governance matters like "predictability, structure, law, and order."[149] One government figure I met lamented that al-Shabaab was getting away with a severe form of rules-based repression by capitalizing on many Somalis' perception that "We are [Muslim], [and] this is the law of Allah."[150] But a leading government minister told me that al-Shabaab helped restore stability, notwithstanding their use of publicly administered corporal punishments: "They were harsh ... but they restored order."[151]

To some Somalis and observers, al-Shabaab also transcended clan politics, just as the shari'a courts had done in the 1990s. "If you're talking about the rule of law and being more fair," a researcher who travels to Somalia told me, "Al-Shabaab was certainly more effective in that realm" than the warlords or even the TFG. Areas where al-Shabaab was forced out eventually "had more violence," the researcher acknowledged. In the areas it did control, "even the flow of traffic and law and order [all] improved."[152] During my research I was told of people who fled violence elsewhere to live in Somalia's al-Shabaab areas, feeling safer under al-Shabaab as long as its rules were followed. Al-Shabaab built a repressive order on laws applied regardless of clan

[145] Mary Harper, *Everything You Have Told Me Is True: The Many Faces of Al Shabaab* (London: Hurst, 2019), 107.
[146] Harding (2016), 159.
[147] Interview 82 with Mille, expatriate aid worker in Mogadishu, Somalia (conducted in Nairobi, Kenya) (August 2013).
[148] Ibid.
[149] Harper (2019), 22.
[150] Interview 87 with Muuse, former senior government minister in Mogadishu, Somalia (conducted in Addis Ababa, Ethiopia) (August 2013).
[151] Interview 86 with Barkhado, retired senior government minister in Mogadishu, Somalia (conducted in Nairobi, Kenya) (August 2013).
[152] Interview 133 with Stephanie, researcher and author in London, England (July 2014).

affiliation – in other words, members of majority clans did not receive special treatment. In areas cleared from al-Shabaab, minority clans struggled to gain land and political power from larger lineage groups.

Al-Shabaab's approach to shari'a was characterized by "legalism," or rule-following, formalism, and the pursuit of technical legal details and procedures.[153] But al-Shabaab's fidelity to Islamic legality was not accepted in all sectors. Many Somalis fled al-Shabaab areas, and Western governments labeled it a terrorist group. Even other militant organizations, including al-Qaeda, criticized al-Shabaab for its "heinous" activities and killings.[154] Indeed, as one Somali government official told me, echoing others, al-Shabaab does not have "a monopoly on Islamic interpretation ... The battle is ongoing ... Moderate Islamic scholars ... are fighting al-Shabaab with their own military personnel ... outside of what the government is doing."[155]

From 2008 to 2012, Somalia was perhaps most known to the outside world for suicide attacks within its borders and piracy along its coastline. But some members of al-Shabaab, responsible as their organization was for many deaths in and out of Somalia, actually worked to stop piracy temporarily, much like the shari'a courts and ICU before them. Along with other groups like Hizbul Islam, they tried to drive pirates out of their areas by "accusing them of being un-Islamic."[156] Al-Shabaab operatives were known to condemn piracy publicly as haram (Arabic: forbidden) under Islamic law. However, as al-Shabaab's strength weakened, people I met speculated that some of its members had begun to operate alongside or collect taxes from pirates. As the international community tried to drive al-Shabaab networks out of Somalia, piracy attacks increased from 111 in 2008 to 439 – more than one a day – in 2011.[157] Attacks decreased to 297 in 2012, after

---

[153] Judith Shklar, *Legalism: Law, Morals, and Political Trials* (Cambridge, MA: Harvard University Press, 1964). Legalism is a feature of the democratic societies that Shklar studied as well as colonial administrations, authoritarian states, and militant organizations. See Mark Fathi Massoud, *Law's Fragile State: Colonial, Authoritarian, and Humanitarian Legacies in Sudan* (Cambridge: Cambridge University Press, 2013); Jens Meierhenrich, *The Legacies of Law: Long-Run Consequences of Legal Development in South Africa, 1652–2000* (Cambridge: Cambridge University Press, 2008); Jens Meierhenrich, *The Remnants of the Rechtsstaat: An Ethnography of Nazi Law* (Oxford: Oxford University Press, 2018).

[154] Dominic Wabala, "East Africa: Al Qaeda Criticises Al Shabaab Over 'Heinous and Anti-Islamic' Activities," *STAR*, September 7, 2012, https://bit.ly/3ryCyf8 (accessed January 1, 2021).

[155] Interview 87 with Muuse, former senior government minister in Mogadishu, Somalia (conducted in Addis Ababa, Ethiopia) (August 2013).

[156] Harper (2012), 158.

[157] Jatin Dua, "After Piracy: Mapping the Means and Ends of Maritime Predation in the Western Indian Ocean," 9(3) *Journal of Eastern African Studies* (2015): 505–521; see also Jatin Dua and

a new international marine force formed to patrol shipping lanes along the Horn of Africa.

Al-Shabaab was not the only Somali group trying to rid the coastline of piracy. Further north, in Puntland, a semi-autonomous region of Somalia, there were many attempts to eliminate piracy, including local and federal government interventions. According to an official familiar with the matter, "one man using shari'a" did more to reduce piracy in the region than any other individual or group.[158] The man, Sheikh Abdul Qadir Farah, was a vocal critic of both al-Shabaab and pirates. Sheikh Farah preached that people should neither purchase goods that pirates offered for sale, nor allow pirates to buy goods with their stolen money. He reminded people that Islam prohibits theft and buying stolen property, and that God would judge them for these transgressions on the Day of Judgment. He also told them not to use stolen money for their families and not to rent rooms or homes to pirates. "This is against Islam ... The money you get [from pirates] is haram ... and the penalty in Islam is death," he told them. He also advised fathers not to allow their daughters to marry anyone known to have engaged in piracy. In other words, he used tenets of shari'a – through his interpretation of God's will – to make "life very difficult for the pirates ... Before that, all the power of the state and the international community ... couldn't do it!"[159]

Puntland's semi-autonomous government eventually created its own marine force, which benefitted from the work of Sheikh Abdul Qadir Farah and vocal elders and religious leaders like him.[160] In February 2013, Sheikh Farah was murdered during Friday prayers in his local mosque. Within two weeks, a military court in Puntland sentenced those responsible for his murder to death by firing squad.[161] While Sheikh Farah managed to use Islam to persuade people to mobilize their resources against piracy and put collective social pressure on pirates, al-Shabaab was intent on linking order with a repressive but legalistic version of shari'a. To maintain its version of law and order, in

Ken Menkhaus, "The Context of Contemporary Piracy: The Case of Somalia," 10(4) *Journal of International Criminal Justice* (2012): 749–766.

[158] Interview 87 with Muuse, former senior government minister in Mogadishu, Somalia (conducted in Addis Ababa, Ethiopia) (August 2013).

[159] Ibid.

[160] Robert Young Pelton, "Puntland Marine Police Force Enter Eyl: Force Welcomed by Mayor and Locals but not by UN Somalia-Eritrea Monitoring Group," *Somalia Report*, March 2, 2012, https://bit.ly/3mUyBib (accessed January 1, 2021).

[161] "Somalia: Puntland Court Sentences Al Shabaab Chief Godane and 11 Others to Death," *Garowe Online*, February 27, 2013, https://bit.ly/38DJ8bP (accessed January 1, 2021).

2016 al-Shabaab created its own police force in southern Somalia, which the organization claimed would "carry out harsh punishments including cutting off men's penises as a punishment for adultery."[162] This police force operated in al-Shabaab areas while militants attacked government buildings, hotels, and schools in TFG-controlled areas and neighboring countries. Their attacks in 2019 and 2020 killed, among others, US military contractors and personnel, Mogadishu mayor Abdirahman Omar Osman, and noted Somali journalist Hodan Nalayeh.

The Difficulty of Reestablishing a State Judiciary

As al-Shabaab rose up largely outside of Mogadishu, the TFG was trying to rebuild the Somali state, particularly its judiciary. After seizing Mogadishu from the ICU in 2007, the TFG tried to reestablish a state judiciary. The absence of shari'a courts had meant that there was no institutional space for people to resolve their disputes and to respond to crimes nonviolently. But "People weren't ready for a state judiciary," one official told me. Not only were lawyers and judges in short supply, this official continued, but people "trusted . . . shari'a [more] than the secular laws" of the state.[163] Even if these laws were made by Muslims and ostensibly rooted in Islam, many Somalis did not trust them because they were connected to the state. During this period, according to policy analysts, "Islam was the only belief system in Somalia that had not been discredited, and citizens went to religious leaders with their needs for protection . . . They . . . were seen as upholders of justice and fairness, since they were . . . dedicated to Islam."[164]

Recognizing these difficulties, some remaining members of the ICU joined with members of the TFG to form an opposition party called the Alliance for Re-liberation of Somalia (ARS) in late 2007. The ARS joined the legislature in 2008 with 149 parliamentary seats; its leader Sheikh Sharif Ahmed, formerly a chairperson of the ICU, became president of Somalia from 2009 to 2012. Al-Shabaab stepped up its attacks during and following Sharif Ahmed's tenure, to prevent the government from instituting order. By reestablishing courts and other justice institutions, the government might eventually rebuild people's

---

[162] Jamestown Foundation, "Al-Shabaab Aims for 'Hearts and Minds' with Establishment of Islamic Police Force," Vol. 14, Issue 17, August 19, 2016, https://bit.ly/3pp04cA (accessed January 1, 2021).

[163] Interview 87 with Muuse, former senior government minister in Mogadishu, Somalia (conducted in Addis Ababa, Ethiopia) (August 2013).

[164] Hansen (2013), 23

trust in the state. Al-Shabaab "made reference to the new government trying to destroy shari'a" and attacked courthouses, including the Benadir Regional Court, where leading government officials and lawyers were killed.[165] Al-Shabaab did not want the TFG to succeed in reforming the judiciary; they were fighting for a kind of Islamic legal system that would prioritize al-Shabaab's goals and interpretation of God's will.

Somalia's government leaders had more in mind than simply attracting moderate leaders of al-Shabaab into government positions, as the ARS was trying to do. They also tried to convince religious scholars to speak out, especially against piracy, in order to rebut al-Shabaab's "Islamic narrative [that] portrays government as infidels."[166] These religious scholars also spoke publicly against the desecration of tombs of Sufi saints and others. Some, however, felt the government itself was too beholden to Islamists.[167] But, as one aid worker told me, Islam is the "one legal system" to which everyone in Somalia has been exposed.[168]

After a constitution that enshrined Islam and shari'a as core principles of the state was adopted in 2012, the Somali government turned to building state capacity and institutions to give it teeth. The president made justice one of the key pillars of his agenda, but he needed money to do it. The TFG received donor support from the UNDP, the US and Japanese governments, and the European Union.[169] Additional financial support came from the United Nations-Somalia Integrated Strategic Framework, which governed UN activities in Somalia from 2014 through 2016, and from the ensuing United Nations Strategic Framework Somalia 2017–2020. The UNDP aimed to assist Somalis in writing new laws while rehabilitating courthouse buildings and setting up legal aid programs. In 2014, the UNDP declared that it helped to draft ten new laws for Somalia while also funding ten legal aid

---

[165] Interview 84 with Edith, human rights researcher in Nairobi, Kenya (August 2013).

[166] Interview 87 with Muuse, former senior government minister in Mogadishu, Somalia (conducted in Addis Ababa, Ethiopia) (August 2013).

[167] Harding (2016), 242.

[168] Interview 80 with Gul, aid worker in Nairobi, Kenya (August 2013).

[169] Marcus Manuel, Raphaelle Faure, and Dina Mansour-Ille, *Somalia: Country Evaluation Brief.* Chr. Michelson Institute, Overseas Development Institute, and the Norwegian Agency for Development Cooperation (Oslo: NORAD, 2017), 13. Interview 84 with Edith, human rights researcher in Nairobi, Kenya (August 2013). On the ways donor aid depoliticizes statebuilding programs, see Jutta Bakonyi, "Seeing Like Bureaucracies: Rearranging Knowledge and Ignorance in Somalia," 12(3) *International Political Sociology* (2018): 256–273; Mark Fathi Massoud, "Work Rules: How International NGOs Build Law in War-Torn Societies," 49(2) *Law & Society Review* (2015): 333–364.

organizations that collectively operated sixteen centers with 265 personnel who provided legal aid to nearly 15,000 people.[170] In addition, nearly 9,000 people attended "legal awareness sessions," where they received training on their rights under international law. Similarly, the UNDP reported that approximately 3,000 people received help from the legal aid clinic at Puntland State University in Garowe. The clinic also conducted "rule-of-law trainings" – on case management, family law, criminal law and procedure, and mediation skills – with 239 government officials in Puntland.[171]

The international aid community's extensive engagement in drafting new laws, building courthouses, and promoting legal aid programs was designed to encourage Somalis to come to state courts to seek resolutions to their problems, rather than to religious leaders, ad hoc nonstate entities, or family members. The problem, as aid workers told me, was that Somalia's "justice sector is largely starved of resources and engagement."[172] In other words, people were being encouraged to use a system that struggled to accommodate them. Somalia's government relied on African Union troops for support, and its national justice system was not fully operational. The legal process, moreover, largely eschewed or ignored the Islamic provisions of the constitution – a constitution that the international aid community itself pushed to completion. According to an aid worker from Mogadishu whom I met in Nairobi, "I don't think [UNDP's] donors would ... support the UNDP to work in a proactive, engaged way to improve Islamic laws ... This is anathema to the international community."[173]

The architects of the 2012 federal constitution saw it as Somalia's "overarching legal system."[174] But putting the constitution's shari'a principles into practice was another matter. "The Somali judiciary is not a [series of] religious courts" like the ICU was, I was told.[175] Indeed, even the courthouses were those that were set up by Siad Barre. Government officials and aid workers found that promoting justice put them in the uncomfortable position of inviting people to bring

---

[170] Elizabeth Kang'atta, Christine Fowler, Abdisalam Farah, Abdullahi Yusuf Mohamed, and Magdalene Wanza Kioko, "Access to Justice Project: C.2 Project Annual Report, 2014," *United Nations Development Programme Somalia* (2015).

[171] Ibid.

[172] Interview 78 with Majda, lawyer and human rights activist in Mogadishu and Hargeisa (conducted in Nairobi, Kenya) (July 2013).

[173] Ibid.

[174] Interview 81 with Warsame, lawyer and adviser to the Transitional Federal Government of Somalia (conducted in Nairobi, Kenya) (August 2013).

[175] Interview 80 with Gul, aid worker in Nairobi, Kenya (August 2013)

their disputes into the very courts that last functioned when a dictator used them to oppress dissenters and religious leaders and to destroy the rule of law. Aid workers also admitted the difficulty of being based in Nairobi, far from daily life in Mogadishu, where courthouses were targeted and the most sophisticated lawyers were killed by militants. Such attacks weakened the judiciary and deterred many people from entering a courthouse or using legal aid programs.

Somali society has had to contend with contradictions among local practices, Islam, and international laws. As one person told me, "You can always say shari'a will be the main source [of legislation, but] underground there could be *huduud* [crimes that carry corporal punishments] or FGM [female genital mutilation]. And Somalia is infested with qat. Sheikhs say [qat] is against shari'a, [that] you should prohibit it. But nobody dares."[176] Similarly, journalists have been harassed, arrested, or killed, some of them for their reporting on – or even interviewing – survivors of sexual assault. Between 2010 and 2020, the Committee for the Protection of Journalists reported at least forty journalists killed in Somalia.[177] But, according to one aid worker, a high-profile criminal case against a journalist arrested for interviewing a woman who alleged that she had been raped by government forces "showed us that [Somalia] is still a state where institutions have in some way continued to exist."[178] Although attorneys secured the journalist's release, the lengthy case pitted local norms against international law.

As a result of the country's collapse, sharply differing interpretations of shari'a now coexist in Somalia: some promote corporal punishment while others promote the rights of journalists and women's political participation. Interpretations also differ as to whether Islam allows or discourages the chewing of qat branches. "In Somalia, the law may say something, but on the ground it's very different," I was told.[179] Religiosity, according to political officials I met, is on the rise, with some Somali scholars calling Islam the country's "fountain for social cohesion."[180] Some people believe

---

[176] Interview 134 with Hatim, United Nations official and adviser to the Somali constitution in Mogadishu, Somalia (reached via telephone from Princeton, NJ) (November 2015).

[177] Data at https://cpj.org. For an example, see Committee to Protect Journalists, "Somalia: Journalist Shot and Killed in Mogadishu," June 6, 2016, https://bit.ly/3mTSi9b (accessed January 1, 2021).

[178] Interview 84 with Edith, human rights researcher in Nairobi, Kenya (August 2013).

[179] Interview 82 with Mille, expatriate aid worker in Mogadishu, Somalia (conducted in Nairobi, Kenya) (August 2013).

[180] Abdurahman M. Abdullahi, "Recovering the Somali State: The Islamic Factor," in *Somalia: Diaspora and State Reconstruction in the Horn of Africa*, eds. Abdulkadir Osman Farah, Mammo Muchie, and Joakim Gundel (London: Adonis & Abbey, 2007b), pp. 196–208.

that the calamities of recent decades occurred because people "weren't Islamic enough."[181] In addition, more people have returned from overseas after training with Wahhabi groups in Afghanistan and nearby nations. The combination creates "fertile ground for people to be more fanatic," I was told.[182]

The history of some elders and sheikhs moving into and out of roles as militia leaders and warlords exacerbates anxiety about fanaticism. Officials and aid workers also fear that conservative religious figures might "take ... law in their own hands" when they see people in public – at restaurants and cafes, or on the beach – who are not following their strict interpretations of Islamic dress.[183] The TFG aims to develop state courts so that people will trust and turn to the state rather than to such religious figures or elders with checkered pasts. By reestablishing a state judiciary with UN assistance and adopting a constitution that treats shari'a as a key foundation of the state, Somalia's governmental leaders hope to keep God's will on their side. But they also worry that other interpretations of God's will may breed violent conflict against their own version.[184]

Constitutional Shari'a

Somalia finds itself in a paradoxical situation: its constitution fore-grounds shari'a, but its weak state judiciary, shaped largely by the international aid community and diaspora Somalis, lacks the ability to effectively practice a grassroots Islamic law. This section tells how this situation came about: ironically, the international community helped rush a drafting process that resulted in a constitution that enshrines shari'a. The constitutional drafting process began about 2009, when the Somali parliament adopted shari'a as its "basic source for national legislation."[185] The TFG parliament thus followed up on Article 8 of the 2004 Transitional Federal Charter, which stated that Islam would be Somalia's official state religion. In 2010, a draft con-stitution submitted for review included an article that proclaimed Somalia an Islamic state and required judges to use shari'a in deciding

[181] Interview 87 with Muuse, former senior government minister in Mogadishu, Somalia (con-ducted in Addis Ababa, Ethiopia) (August 2013).
[182] Ibid.
[183] Interview 15 with Evelyn, United Nations official in Garowe, Puntland (conducted by telephone from Hargeisa, Somaliland) (June 2013).
[184] Harding (2016), 245.
[185] "Refounding Somalia: Constitution and Islam," *Pambazuka News*, May 3, 2012, https://bit.ly/2VM8DkX (accessed January 1, 2021).

cases. But a Somali lawyer living overseas explained to me the particular legal difficulties of creating such an Islamic state. He said that *mujtahideen* (persons trained in Islamic legal theory and interpretation, often for decades) would have to interpret various schools of Islamic law, which would result in disagreement and pluralism. In other words, trying to build a nation with a singular Islamic law would paradoxically pluralize state law and render it unintelligible to many people.[186]

In 2011, as negotiations for a national constitution continued, TFG officials still worked either overseas or out of their compound in Baidoa; the TFG controlled only about one square kilometer of Mogadishu. The government and Somalis continued to suffer attacks from al-Shabaab's militants and a growing number of pirates collected their booty offshore.[187] Al-Shabaab would not be expelled from Mogadishu until August 2011, though its operatives' attacks on the city continued after that time.[188]

Members of the TFG had outside help in drafting their constitution. Dozens of Somalis were involved, along with international aid workers, international nongovernmental organizations, UN officials, and local and foreign scholars. According to Somalis and aid workers I met, the writing process was difficult, as they tried to craft a document that represented the competing interests of everyone involved. A group of international lawyers wrote a draft and submitted it to the TFG, which immediately rejected it. Aid workers had felt the TFG's drafts were "too Islamic," while Somalis did not like the idea of approving a constitution written largely by foreigners or on foreign soil.[189] In response to this failed draft, the TFG formed its own committee of experts, with help from UNISOM and lawyers from the UNDP and other humanitarian groups. According to one Somali, "I came in 2011 [and] inherited a draft [constitution] that you can tell was ... written [in] an atmosphere of fear ... The country was ruled by al-Shabaab ... Everything you look at was shari'a."[190]

---

[186] On the legibility of Islamic law in postcolonial politics in Sudan, see Jeffrey Adam Sachs, "Seeing Like an Islamic State: Shari'a and Political Power in Sudan," 52(3) *Law & Society Review* (2018): 630–651.

[187] Interview 86 with Barkhado, retired senior government minister in Mogadishu, Somalia (conducted in Nairobi, Kenya) (August 2013).

[188] "Al-Shabaab in Somalia: US Air Strike 'Kills 60 Militants," *BBC News*, October 16, 2018, https://bbc.in/3hmIhA0 (accessed January 1, 2021); see also "U.S. Troops to Help Somalia Fight al-Shabaab," *BBC News*, April 14, 2017, https://bbc.in/2WPKNFx (accessed January 1, 2021).

[189] Interview 135 with Matilda, international lawyer and adviser to the Somali constitution in Mogadishu, Somalia (reached via telephone from Princeton, NJ) (December 2015).

[190] Interview 86 with Barkhado, retired senior government minister in Mogadishu, Somalia (conducted in Nairobi, Kenya) (August 2013).

The result was a new constitution in which "every article, even if it had nothing to do with shari'a, had to do with it."[191] The growing strength of al-Shabaab, the widespread support of the ICU before them, and officials' fear of being labeled as the lackeys of Western governments made the Somali drafters of the constitution determined that Somalia would continue to call itself an Islamic state. Even "people who seem[ed] to be secular were saying that the constitution had to be based on shari'a," a senior government adviser told me.[192] Collectively, the group considered Somalia's population almost entirely Muslim and thought of religion as the basis of nationhood. "We have the Qur'an and Sunna [Hadith] that . . . provide general principles . . . You cannot now say we are going to confine Islam or shari'a to family issues [as other governments have done]."[193] Pleased with his constitutional drafting efforts, the senior government adviser claimed to me simply, "We do not have legal pluralism. We have one law according to Islam."[194]

But the constitution did more than merely proclaim Somalia an Islamic state. The constitution's framers also aimed to reintegrate Somalia into the international community, so they incorporated international human rights law into the text as well. One of the constitution's key architects said that he told himself, "Don't make mistakes [and] be honest" about these multiple commitments.[195] The result was a constitution "of contradictions" that declared the state's official religion to be Islam at the same time that it guaranteed freedom of religion.[196] "What we meant is that nobody should use shari'a to take away rights of citizens, especially women," another official told me.[197] "That was a tight debate."

In early August 2012, while fasting during Ramadan, 825 delegates in Mogadishu adopted a new national constitution for Somalia. These delegates came from all areas of civic life, among them TFG officials, community leaders, religious scholars, businesspeople, and representatives from youth and women's organizations. It was the biggest step

[191] Ibid.
[192] Interview 81 with Warsame, lawyer and adviser to the Transitional Federal Government of Somalia (conducted in Nairobi, Kenya) (August 2013).
[193] Interview 86 with Barkhado, retired senior government minister in Mogadishu, Somalia (conducted in Nairobi, Kenya) (August 2013).
[194] Interview 81 with Warsame, lawyer and adviser to the Transitional Federal Government of Somalia (conducted in Nairobi, Kenya) (August 2013).
[195] Ibid.
[196] Ibid.
[197] Interview 86 with Barkhado, retired senior government minister in Mogadishu, Somalia (conducted in Nairobi, Kenya) (August 2013).

toward establishing a national government in Mogadishu in the more than two decades since Siad Barre's ouster in 1991. And, not unlike members of al-Shabaab and the ICU, TFG members also envisioned an Islamic state.

How did these constitutional architects enact an Islamic state? First, they articulated a vision of an Islamic state immediately in the preamble, which stated that the constitution itself was informed by shari'a. Second, the constitution declared Islam the official religion of the Somali people. Third, it provided that no person could legally propagate any religion other than Islam in Somalia. These religious components of the 2012 constitution are clear. Article 1 indicates that all power is invested in Allah first and then in the Somali people.[198] Article 2 states that Islam is the state religion, that no other religion may be spread, and that no law may be enacted that is "not compliant with the general principles and objectives of shari'a."[199] Article 3 says that the constitution's foundations are the two main sources of shari'a – the Qur'an and Sunnah – and that its objective is to protect shari'a and social justice.[200] The constitution also proclaims Somalia as "a Muslim country [that] promotes human rights [and] the rule of law."[201] These provisions were "easily accepted" by the 825 delegates, aid workers involved in the discussions told me. One told me, "Of course shari'a would be – if not a source of legislation – the source of the law of the land. It was a non-starter to argue otherwise." She continued, "the SRSG [Special Representative of the Secretary General] wanted to tick off 'we got a constitution,'" which meant picking battles and rushing the constitution out, and not fighting over the Islamic constitution Somalis desired.[202]

The fact that the constitution was based on Islam should not have surprised anyone, either Somalis or the Western governments and aid groups that supported the drafting process. In fact, every previous constitution in Somalia had referenced Islam in one way or another. Somalia's first postcolonial constitution in 1960 had proclaimed Islam the religion of the state.[203] The draft interim constitution of 1993 had

[198] "After Allah the Almighty, all power is vested in the people and can only be exercised in accordance with the Constitution and the law and through the relevant institutions." Article 1, Provisional Constitution of the Federal Republic of Somalia, 2012.
[199] Ibid., Article 2.
[200] Ibid., Article 3.
[201] Ibid., Articles 2, 4.
[202] Interview 135 with Matilda, international lawyer and adviser to the Somali constitution in Mogadishu, Somalia (reached via telephone from Princeton, NJ) (December 2015).
[203] Somalia was not alone in this regard, as legal debates over the place of shari'a had been occurring across the African continent. On the case of Nigeria's shari'a debates in the 1970s,

also included provisions on religion and human rights to give weight to postwar reconciliation agreements signed earlier that year. The TFG's draft constitution in 2010 went even further, requiring that all laws passed be consistent with Islam. There was no way to get around the staying power of Islam in politics and society. Why? As a Somali official told me, the government had to prove itself to "be a better alternative [to] al-Shabaab. The only way to do that is to say we are as good as them, and we also use Islam."[204]

When I asked government officials from Mogadishu who worked on the constitution why it said that each law passed had to be consistent with shari'a, one person told me that they were fighting against Somalis who were labeling the TFG an "infidel government."[205] He recognized in hindsight that, in writing a constitution based on Islam, the TFG had thrust shari'a into the government's state-building priorities. Government officials also told me of their struggle to resist the "secularizing influence" of aid workers. These aid workers included not only international lawyers but also members of the Somali diaspora who wanted the constitution to be the foundation for an improved relationship with the West. Even though foreigners "criticized the constitution," leading TFG officials told me they generally "didn't care ... At the end of the day, the West has to accept the reality of Somalia – that Mogadishu is not San Francisco."[206]

Constitutional delegates I met told me that, in spite of the way the document foregrounded Islam, "People were [still] saying the constitution is not Islamic enough."[207] Such critics pointed out that the government was slow to launch an umma council or structure to institutionalize *ijtihad*, or the interpretation of Islamic law and theology by renowned religious scholars. They also worried that the constitution's various provisions promoting Islamic law were merely the window dressing put on by the 825 delegates. In fact, some religious groups opposed the constitution entirely, arguing that the very writing of a constitution, even one based in Islam, is itself always a "project of

---

see, for example, David D. Laitin, "The Sharia Debate and the Origins of Nigeria's Second Republic," 20(3) *Journal of Modern African Studies* (1982): 411–430.

[204] Interview 87 with Muuse, former senior government minister in Mogadishu, Somalia (conducted in Addis Ababa, Ethiopia) (August 2013).

[205] Interview 86 with Barkhado, retired senior government minister in Mogadishu, Somalia (conducted in Nairobi, Kenya) (August 2013)

[206] Interview 87 with Muuse, former senior government minister in Mogadishu, Somalia (conducted in Addis Ababa, Ethiopia) (August 2013).

[207] Ibid.

the West," and thus that the resulting document could never be Islamic, regardless of what religion its text would espouse.[208]

International aid workers took short trips to Mogadishu or, as one of them put it to me, they traveled "into and out of ... Mogadishu International Airport," where they met local counterparts and rarely left the heavily fortified airport compound because of the city's insecurity.[209] Another told me that he felt that international aid workers he met were "judgmental about" shari'a. "They see it as huduud [crimes that carry corporal punishments]. That's how it's perceived or explained to them by their experts. So they're scared of that. We try to explain to them it's about law, and sources, and how you can [tone] down" extremism.[210] Ultimately, donors reluctantly supported the Islamic provisions of the constitution. "It's not about written law. It's about practices and their interpretation of what shari'a means."[211]

While aid workers' means differed from those of al-Shabaab, their goal – "trying to install law and order" – seemed just the same as al-Shabaab's.[212] Donors and foreign aid workers tried to "build the rule of law on violations of the rule of law," they admitted to me, by "meeting deadlines instead of having debates [and] strong-arm[ing] people" to write a constitution quickly. They also appointed committees of experts and other hybrid structures of government that they felt transgressed both Somali constitutional law and international law. "It's a culture [in the international aid community] of ignoring the rule of law ... when it's convenient. So [the rule of law] is ... not taking root [and] this worries me in terms of future state-building."[213] When I asked why donors felt they were "ignoring" the rule of law, I was told donors were simply trying "to maintain some fidelity to legality" which they hoped in turn would help to build the rule of law.[214] The international aid community continues to engage as many Somalis as it can, perhaps putting them at risk: "If you did engage [with the TFG or aid agencies],

---

[208] Ibid.

[209] Interview 135 with Matilda, international lawyer and adviser to the Somali constitution in Mogadishu, Somalia (reached via telephone from Princeton, NJ) (December 2015).

[210] Interview 134 with Hatim, United Nations official and adviser to the Somali constitution in Mogadishu, Somalia (reached via telephone from Princeton, NJ) (November 2015).

[211] Ibid.

[212] Interview 135 with Matilda, international lawyer and adviser to the Somali constitution in Mogadishu, Somalia (reached via telephone from Princeton, NJ) (December 2015).

[213] Ibid.

[214] Ibid.

you were seen as not a real Muslim. So you were targeted. Activists don't want to be exposed to that risk."[215]

The Siad Barre regime had taken a tough stance against religious leaders – arresting, imprisoning, and even executing them. But in the thirty years from 1991 to 2021, new courts, new leaders, and rising government officials all tried to capitalize on people's trust in Islam to build a new kind of rule of law, under which people can have their disputes resolved through an otherwise barely functioning state. Somalia's contemporary state judiciary has not been especially success-ful at this, inescapably torn between the constitution's embrace of shari'a and support from an international aid community that prefers to ignore it. As one official told me, "In Somalia you can have only two things. Either you have to be powerful enough to devise your own constitution ... and ... implement it using [the] rule of law and force of law. Or you have to use Islam." He continued that Somalis see the state as trying to fight al-Shabaab's version of shari'a by saying, aston-ishingly, "We will introduce Romanic-Germanic law." The "only way to fight" what remains of al-Shabaab, he said, "is to use another religious narrative, [saying that] what they do is not [consistent with] Islam. You have to use another narrative based on shari'a."[216]

CONCLUSION

In April 2013, about a month before my arrival in the Horn of Africa, nine militants disguised as police officers entered the Supreme Court complex in Mogadishu. They started shooting and, by the time two hours of intense gunfighting at the courts ended with their deaths, they had killed at least twenty people. Among these were two of the coun-try's most prominent lawyers – Mohamed Mohamud Afrah, the head of Somalia's bar association, and Abdikarin Hassan Gorod, a human rights lawyer who had "won the release of [a] Somali journalist who [had been] jailed after interviewing a rape victim."[217] These two law-yers had been providing free legal aid to indigent persons, helping them access justice in Somalia's state courts. It was the deadliest attack in Mogadishu in years. The same day, a car bomb detonated outside the

---

[215] Interview 65 with Jen, expatriate aid worker in Nairobi, Kenya (conducted by telephone from Hargeisa, Somaliland) (July 2013).

[216] Interview 87 with Muuse, former senior government minister in Mogadishu, Somalia (con-ducted in Addis Ababa, Ethiopia) (August 2013).

[217] Mohamed Ibrahim, "Coordinated Blasts Kill At Least 20 in Somalia's Capital," *New York Times*, April 14, 2013, https://nyti.ms/2LhsF51 (last accessed January 1, 2021).

Somali security offices, killing ten more people. A suicide attack a month earlier had killed ten others. A spokesperson for al-Shabaab claimed responsibility for the courthouse attack, telling Al Jazeera News that Somalia's courthouses were a "legitimate target."[218]

Rebuilding Somalia's courts – whether through the efforts of local clans and religious leaders or through government programs – has been a priority response to the country's collapse. This chapter has documented the remarkable resilience of shari'a, in its widely varying interpretations, during this process. Many parties have responded to state collapse in Somalia by building legal institutions using religious discourse, giving shari'a new meanings as they do so. Somalis have used law and religion – combining, redefining, and reifying them – to build the stability they seek for their communities.

Like the generation that preceded Somalia's 1991 collapse, the generation that followed never saw a robust rule of law. But, determined not to repeat Siad Barre's authoritarian rule, leaders in Somalia – elders, sheikhs, government officials, and militants alike – emboldened themselves with shari'a. The results included the shari'a courts in the 1990s and early 2000s, the ICU from 2005 to 2006, al-Shabaab's legalism, and the TFG's constitution. Reflecting on Somalia's attempts to rebuild since 1991, Issaka K. Souaré writes,

> Islam is the only authority – if not misused and taken to an extreme – that possesses the essential ingredients to successfully integrate the various elements of the Somali society and provide a stable government capable of meeting the urgent social, political and economic needs of the country. This was the magical stick that the [ICU] members held in their hands ... There was safety, peace and commerce. They reunited the capital, which had been carved up into fiefdoms by various warlords. In other words, they brought Mogadishu back to life.[219]

This chapter has tried to show how the scattered shari'a courts of the 1990s and early 2000s and the ICU were, for all their faults and factionalism, nascent grassroots democratic institutions. Before their experiment in nonviolent dispute resolution based on Islam was cut short by Ethiopia's US-backed invasion, these courts had begun to pave a path toward rule of law in Somalia. Just as Christianity "sustain[ed]

---

[218] "Dozens Killed in Attacks in Somali Capital: Al-Qaeda-linked al-Shabab Claims Responsibility for Two Attacks in Mogadishu That Left More Than 30 People Dead," *Al-Jazeera News*, April 14, 2013, https://bit.ly/33QsWSV (accessed January 1, 2021).
[219] Souaré (2007), 209–210.

modern [Western] society [and] its pervading force furnishe[d] the law," so too has Islam sustained Somalia and furnished Somali law.[220] Islam and God's will were as important to the founding, authority, and self-conception of Somalia's shariʻa courts as Christianity and the Lord's will were, centuries earlier, to the emergence and power of courts in nascent Western democracies.

Militants from al-Shabaab and other groups remain a threat to Somalia's government and to other forms of Islamic activism that try to build the rule of law using shariʻa. Mentioning a revival of Islamic courts outrages not only those in al-Shabaab who adopt a different version of shariʻa but also those in the aid community who know that some members of al-Shabaab trained within the ICU.

Outsiders may see Somalia as a state where Islamic militancy rules. But this chapter has revealed a tense battle over the meaning and practice of shariʻa among Somalis who share a strong sense of Islamic identity. A Somali proverb is telling: *What outsiders' eyes cannot see is still there*. From different sectors – the first shariʻa courts of the 1990s, the ICU, al-Shabaab, and various politicians trying to rebuild the state – emerges a shared cry to rebuild society in the hope of achieving God's will. But Somalis have also dealt with a strong foreign presence that pushed against such efforts to rebuild, saying, in the words of one activist I met, that self-help cannot work and that "No, we [the international community] have to shape Somali society."[221]

No single playbook describes how to construct an Islamic state, let alone a peaceful and democratic one. Chapter 5 reveals how peace-builders and constitutional architects in Somaliland after 1991 created a different kind of Islamic state altogether, one whose leaders and citizens would struggle to unite the values associated with the rule of law, human rights, shariʻa, and democracy.

---

[220] A. H. Wintersteen, "Christianity and the Common Law," 29 *American Law Register* (May 1890), 273–285, p. 285.

[221] Interview 85 with Ibrahim, NGO program adviser in Nairobi, Kenya (August 2013).

Somaliland (national border as claimed by Somaliland),
1991–present.

CHAPTER FIVE

INTEGRATING SHARI'A:
LEGAL POLITICS IN SOMALILAND

> What solves [conflict among] the people is the law ... If there is not
> strong law, there will be no peace.
> *Interview 50 with Caziz, lawyer, in Hargeisa,*
> *Somaliland (July 2013)*

This chapter investigates the endurance of shari'a in Somaliland.
Somaliland declared independence in May 1991, as Somalia was disin-
tegrating, by reasserting the sovereignty it had for five days
(June 26–30) in 1960, prior to unifying with the former Italian
Somalia. Between 1991 and 2021, the self-declared state of
Somaliland made strides to build peace and promote principles associated with the rule of law. Following a series of elders' summits,
Somaliland outlawed Siad Barre's national security courts, held contested elections, developed a government of limited powers alongside
a new currency and economic development programs, and adopted
a constitution rooted in Islamic and international human rights principles. The constitution's architects explained to me their belief that
embedding shari'a into the legal system would keep al-Shabaab

extremists at bay, which southern Somalia was unable to do, while promoting human rights would draw international support. But the strategic intentions behind Somaliland's Islamic legal arrangements have been largely invisible to aid agencies, which remain focused on constructing courthouses and training judges and lawyers to apply non-Islamic law. These aid efforts are predicated on a view of shari'a that connects religious faith to violent extremism – an oversimplified understanding of Islam that undermines the Islamic foundation of Somaliland's stability.

The self-declared nation of Somaliland has provided the Horn of Africa's strongest evidence of progress toward the ideal of the rule of law, despite not being recognized as an independent nation by the United Nations or any country in the world. Practically speaking, Somaliland has been autonomous since 1991, but legally speaking – to Somalia and much of the rest of the world – Somaliland is still part of Somalia.

Somaliland's shari'a-based experiment has lasted much longer than the brief heyday of the Islamic Courts Union in Somalia in the mid-2000s. Somaliland's relative stability shows that legal pluralism is, in itself, not necessarily destabilizing. In fact, shari'a may be the glue that holds Somaliland's plural system together. Somaliland's co-existing legal institutions invoke and use shari'a in four primary ways:

(1) *Shari'a and state institutions.* Judges in Somaliland's district courts (formerly qadi courts under the British Somaliland Protectorate) use shari'a to resolve family disputes.

(2) *Shari'a and customary norms.* Aqils and sultans use *xeer* (Somali custom), which has long been shaped by shari'a and derives legitimacy from it, to resolve disputes between members of different clans outside the state courts, in a system that functions somewhat like a form of collective insurance.

(3) *Shari'a and sheikhs.* In a system that has developed since 1991, individual sheikhs run private offices (*macduum*) where they use shari'a to resolve people's disputes in an ad hoc process that resembles arbitration. The first section of this chapter discusses this system.

(4) *Shari'a and the constitution.* In declaring Somaliland's independence and developing its constitution, Somaliland's state-builders made shari'a their foundational principle. The second section of the chapter recounts this process.

This chapter is based primarily on research I conducted in Somaliland. In addition to fieldwork in legal aid offices, I conducted interviews with Somali lawyers, judges, government officials, scholars, religious leaders, elders (including aqils and sultans), and activists, as well as international lawyers and aid workers. Due to the fragmentary nature of archival and secondary sources on the legal systems in place in Somaliland since 1991, there are few scholarly sources on which to draw. The data I gathered, however, tell the story of law in Somaliland's first thirty years from the perspectives of those who shaped and experienced it.

When Somalis I met discussed Somaliland's legal system, they would often tell me about three systems. When I asked them to name those systems, they were relatively clear about shari'a and xeer, but they offered no fewer than thirty words and phrases to describe the state's legal system, including "courts," "formal law," "secular law," "modern law," "socialist law," "colonial law," "and international law" (cf. Table 1.2). While these different terms may suggest very different legal orders, to many Somalis, they are all the "other" to the core of Islam in people's lives. When I asked an activist I met in 2019 to tell me who is the most politically powerful person or group of people in Somaliland, she did not name government officials, courts, or the police. "The sheikhs," she responded. People see sheikhs, and sheikhs see themselves, as the guardians of shari'a.

Why create an Islamic state? In Somaliland, shari'a was the response to a history of dictatorship, a sincerity of belief, and a strategy of hope. First, introducing Islam into the peacebuilding process in Somaliland in 1991 was a way to limit the arbitrary exercise of power. Elders promoted an Islamic rule of law in their declarations of peace before they turned to Western models of constitution writing. Second, Islam was the most promising path to earning the trust of diverse Somalis in Somaliland's national experiment, because shari'a had already been a central feature of, and largely blended into, Somali customs and traditions (xeer) for centuries after Islam's arrival in Africa. Third, forming an Islamic state was a deliberate strategy to stave off the imminent threat of radical jihadism because, as Somaliland's constitutional architects told me, jihadists in southern Somalia would find little to fight for if they moved north into Somaliland, since Somaliland would already be an Islamic state. An Islamic state provided the foundation that people in Somaliland, despite their political differences, could agree upon.

Western legal scholars and policy analysts presume that governments that use shari'a see it as an expedient tool to control and pacify the population, a muscle that the state flexes to exert unfettered theocratic authority. But the case of Somaliland shows how shari'a laid a foundation for a state of limited authority. Claiming to rule in accordance with God's will can give political leaders authority. But when coupled with democratic intentions, it can also provide a check on state authority. As a civic leader told me in Hargeisa, Somaliland's capital city, "People [here] see a different way of being an Islamic state."[1] This "different way" promotes the rule of law in the name of Islam, preventing potential dictators from using Islam for their own ends. This chapter uses the case of the first thirty years of Somaliland's self-declared nationhood (1991–2021) to investigate the ways elites constructed an Islamic rule of law. The chapter also lays contextual groundwork for Chapter 6, where I analyze how contemporary activists in Somaliland invoke shari'a for women's rights and gender equality.

While attending at a two-day workshop on restorative justice in Hargeisa during my fieldwork in 2013, I witnessed how aid agencies and the Somalis they supported understood shari'a differently. More than thirty sheikhs and aqils who serve as dispute resolvers in their communities traveled from around Somaliland to attend, converging upon a conference hall in the center of town. The United Nations Development Programme (UNDP) and a local nongovernmental organization (NGO) sponsored the workshop, in coordination with the Somaliland Ministry of Justice. The UNDP hired a European Muslim consultant to facilitate the workshop, flying him to Hargeisa for a few days. His remarks focused on getting the participants' support for a UNDP proposal to construct a network of offices across Somaliland where Somalis could seek advice or resolve their disputes. These would be staffed by "paralegals" who are lawyers and nonlaw-yers informally mediating people's disputes. But aqils and sheikhs I had met across Somaliland had told me about their already existing dispute resolution efforts. These religious and community leaders relied on local traditions and practices whose bedrock was what they called shari'a.

During a break on the second day of the workshop, I told the consultant that I was surprised that the word "shari'a" had yet not yet come up. The consultant told me that he knew of shari'a's importance

---

[1] Interview 33 with Salaam, NGO executive director in Hargeisa, Somaliland (June 2013).

both to the attendees and to Somaliland's founding. But, shrugging his shoulders, he said that his UNDP colleagues were "mad" at him "for raising shari'a" before he left Europe to conduct the workshop. "They're scared of it," he reflected. They "didn't want me to use [shari'a], especially Americans. I said, 'I'm just the messenger ... Islam arrived ... in Somaliland long before I did. I didn't make them Muslims!'"

The irony of the workshop was not lost on the consultant: the United Nations had hired him as a Muslim lawyer to convince Muslim religious and community leaders in a Muslim-majority society that "restorative justice" should involve supporting foreign-implemented, non-Muslim dispute resolution frameworks at the expense of pre-existing Islamic efforts. As his superiors had instructed him, he made no mention of shari'a. At the end of the two-day workshop, as the aqils and sheikhs were filing out of the conference hall and walking toward the local mosque for *maghreb* (sunset) prayer, the consultant asked them to "pray to Allah that this [UNDP project] is successful."

Much like colonial, democratic, and authoritarian administrations in Somalia before 1991, state and humanitarian agencies in Somaliland after 1991 promoted an understanding of law that tried to erase versions of shari'a that were unacceptable to them. The workshop I attended took place as Somaliland's Ministry of Justice was drafting a law to formalize private dispute resolution offices, called *macduum*, led by prominent sheikhs. Licensing and regulating these offices would underscore the state's Islamic identity and, thus, increase public support for the state while absorbing competing nonstate authorities. But Somalis typically traveled to these sheikhs' offices to resolve their civil disputes with one another because of their deep trust in Islam and their deep mistrust of state courts and foreign aid agencies. Even the consultant was caught between those in the United Nations who were paying his consultancy fees and those in Somaliland who were attending his workshop. As a European, he was foreign to the sheikhs and aqils. But he was just as foreign, as a Muslim, to his UN supervisors who urged him to leave religious dispute resolution frameworks at the door to the conference hall.

Somaliland's legal arrangements were designed to construct an Islamic state in the wake of the toppled Siad Barre regime. Western powers and aid agencies were largely absent from the creation of Somaliland's Islamic state in the 1990s. But during the 2000s and the 2010s, foreign NGOs and UN agencies slowly began to enter as they

212

saw the territory becoming a haven of regional stability and progress. They opened walled compounds and offices in Hargeisa and began funding local Somali NGOs and community-based groups that carried the banners of human rights, health, girls' and women's education, and community development. Consultants began working with the Somaliland government to write new laws and encourage investment. But foreigners also had to strike a delicate balance between supporting Somaliland's nascent democracy and financing a breakaway Islamic state that neither the world's countries nor the United Nations dared to recognize. Thus aid from UN agencies and international NGOs has not focused on large public infrastructure projects. Rather, these aid dollars have been put to use on lower-cost "soft" interventions, like community development, legal reform, legal education, and legal aid.

Western aid groups and UN agencies do not wish to promote shari'a. Their concern about shari'a comes partly from a long-perceived civilizational divide between Western and Muslim-majority countries and a fear that Islamic states might harbor terrorist organizations or engage in social oppression contrary to human rights. The fear of shari'a comes not only from seeing it as a top-down legal imposition upon a populace. It also comes from shari'a's bottom-up characteristics and ethics, which make shari'a difficult for state authorities to control and give aid groups a collective impression that shari'a runs counter to the rule of law. In promoting Western, secular forms of political development, aid groups seem to demand that shari'a be excised from or at least controlled by the state, just as the British sought to do in their Somaliland Protectorate. To those in Somaliland, however, this approach makes it seem like aid groups and even the United Nations are dismantling not only the precious stability Somaliland created, but also Islam itself.

The contemporary attempts to contain Islam in Somaliland occur via three interrelated activities associated with promoting the rule of law: legal education (building law schools), legal aid (designing programs to help the poor access state courts), and legal reform (writing new laws or revising old ones). These three activities are the primary means by which aid agencies interact with Somaliland's government and people. They are also the three spheres in which aid agencies advance state law and restrain shari'a by subsuming it into state legal institutions or erasing it from public view entirely.

As the previous chapters have shown, building a single, centralizing legal order is essential to building a state, including an Islamic state. Somaliland is no exception. The legal efforts of foreign aid agencies compete with those of Somali sheikhs and aqils, who are also resolving people's disputes to foster social stability. Somaliland has become a competitive legal marketplace in which discursive contests over the sources and meaning of law have overcome the processes and rules that people already use to resolve disputes. People bring their layered colonial, international, transnational, communal, and Islamic institutions and discourses into the legal arena, along with their political alignments and beliefs about how the state ought to function and who or what state law serves.

Somaliland's years of stability offer an important case for studying shari'a's potential to build peace and the rule of law. Somaliland also illustrates the relationship between Islamic and international law in practice. Somaliland's claim to sovereignty, largely unrecognized by the outside world, allows Somaliland to traverse boundaries between Islamic and international law more openly than other Muslim-majority countries. Somaliland is freer from many of the constraints of large-scale donor aid, since donors do not recognize its sovereignty and thus shy away from interfering with its government decisions. During my conversations with lawyers, officials, and activists in Somaliland, I encountered a deep conviction and hope that the world's nations would one day recognize Somaliland as a sovereign state. Without the burdens of state recognition, however, they were making decisions about law, politics, and shari'a relatively free from international scrutiny.

Like other states with democratic roots, Somaliland is far from perfect. Its problems seem only to have increased since I first visited in 2013: presidents have extended their terms, parliamentary elections have been delayed or canceled, and journalists have been prosecuted under spurious anti-terror legislation. Somaliland's politicians seem to think they should have more power than they do, which weakens people's faith in democracy. But Somaliland's politics have remained overwhelmingly nonviolent, even among those who disagree vocally with the actions of individual authorities. Somaliland's political progress, especially when compared to Somalia's, may come more from a commitment to peace and stability than from a commitment to democracy.

This chapter shows, first, how Somaliland's citizens and state-builders have used shari'a as a catalyst for hopeful change since the 1991 collapse of Somalia. Shari'a matters in everyday life as people go to sheikhs' offices to resolve their disputes. But shari'a also has a rich history in Somaliland's founding. The major peacebuilding efforts of the 1990s prioritized shari'a, culminating in Somaliland's 2001 constitution, which proclaimed shari'a the source of Somaliland's laws. Next, the chapter shows how aid agencies, Somaliland's government officials, and civil society groups experience the tensions between Islamic and international law. Efforts to teach new law students, construct new legal aid centers, and write new laws are attempts – not unlike those of colonial and authoritarian administrations before them – to centralize law, co-opt religious power for the state, and strengthen the state's authority while limiting nonstate forms of authority.

BUILDING AN ISLAMIC SOCIETY

Somaliland was built on shari'a. Serving God's will was central to the Somali National Movement's resistance to Siad Barre's regime during the 1980s and its construction of a new state during the 1990s and 2000s. While the second section of this chapter will tell that story, this one tells a parallel story of ordinary people in Somaliland who, by turning to Islamic rules, procedures, and personnel to resolve their disputes, have founded a society on Islamic forms of peacebuilding.

During my fieldwork I learned that many people took this bottom-up approach to shari'a. By turning to shari'a – specifically, to ad hoc tribunals led by sheikhs – people could resolve their disputes quickly and simply. Clan elders and aqils continue to resolve many everyday disputes over identity, theft, and injury, as they have for centuries, and state courts are now available as well. But people told me they trusted the sheikhs for other matters because sheikhs promise to adhere to God's will in rendering judgment. This trust made the litigants bind themselves to a sheikh's decisions before they even entered his office.

Somalis I met in Hargeisa said that they visit the sheikh for many of their problems. When the sheikhs work as dispute resolvers and not in other areas (e.g., validating marital contracts), the sheikhs are called *macduum al-shari'*, or simply macduum (roughly translated as "sheikh's tribunal"). These ad hoc religious courts use shari'a principles. As private dispute resolution offices run by individual sheikhs, they do not function as state-authorized tribunals. But the state has not attempted to shut them down; they provide needed stability within families and between communities. While I was could not observe sheikhs resolving disputes because of their private nature, I met sheikhs who worked as macduum and spoke with Somalis who took their disputes to macduum. Their comments revealed the important role of sheikhs and shari'a in maintaining social stability.

A sheikh accepts a dispute only when he knows that the disputing parties consented to bring their dispute to his office. They typically consent because of the importance of knowing a decision was made in the name of Islam. As in an arbitration tribunal, the parties also must agree to pay the sheikh's fee and to be bound by his decision before he makes it. The conflict must not be so severe that the parties are not speaking to one another, as they need to come together to invite the sheikh to arbitrate. The diverse kinds of disputes that reach sheikhs' offices include disagreements related to divorce, inheritance, and succession; property or financial disputes; theft; and tort claims related to bodily harm, including payments of *diyya* (roughly translated as blood money) after the wrongful death of a family member. These are not major disputes between political parties, but some of the disputes could turn violent if left unresolved.

The most renowned sheikhs are experts in Islamic law. They have memorized many of the primary sources of shari'a – the more than 6,000 verses of the Qur'an, thousands of pages of the Hadith (records of the teachings, actions, and tacit approvals of the Prophet Muhammad), along with the rules of jurisprudence (*usul al-fiqh*) related to using analogy (*qiyas*) and scholarly consensus (*ijma*). The parties presume that the sheikh decides their fates according to these sources of shari'a, which the sheikh has studied and preached in public. Some Somalis call this Islamic dispute resolution process "*al-kitaab*" ("the book") because, in the words of one civil society activist, the sheikh "judges by the Qur'an."[2]

There is generally no way to appeal a sheikh's decision. Parties are free to initiate a separate case in state court if they are unhappy. State courts, however, cannot automatically enforce a sheikh's judgment. Rarely, sheikhs and litigants told me, does a party ignore a sheikh's decision. First, the parties agree in advance to accept it. Second, ignoring a judgment rendered according to God's will is akin to going against religion itself, frowned upon in a pious society. Third, a sheikh's legitimacy comes, not from the state, but from his familiarity with shari'a and his connection to tradition – an asset in a place where state courts are compromised by their colonial foundation and authoritarian legacy.

[2] Interview 59 with Kalim, former NGO executive director in Hargeisa, Somaliland (July 2013).

Somaliland's macduum echo Islam's long history of religiously informed dispute resolution, without the need for time-consuming state court procedures or costly lawyers. It began with the Prophet Muhammad, to whom people in Mecca and Medina turned for arbitration as he was receiving revelations that would be compiled in the Qur'an. Prominent sheikhs since that time have offered their dispute resolution services to local communities. Among the most famous in the Horn of Africa was Sheikh Mohamed Abdullah Hassan, whose religious tribunals and speeches in the late nineteenth and early twentieth centuries united his followers in the struggle against British colonialism (described in Chapter 2).

Sheikhs are not the only nonstate actors who use shari'a to resolve disputes. During the Siad Barre regime in the 1970s, many *wadaad* – leaders of the call to prayer and performers of rituals like weddings, blessings of newborns, and funerary prayers – also began to open their own dispute resolution offices, though they did not have the high-level training of sheikhs. How did these wadaad go from performing religious rites to being trusted arbiters of people's complex personal disputes? Religious men had difficulty finding work as civil servants or judges in Siad Barre's socialist administration, which led many of them into the small private sector. But, as Somalia was collapsing in the 1980s, the state's reach narrowed and trust in its judicial system waned. People increasingly turned to sheikhs and wadaad, asking them to resolve their disputes using shari'a rather than Somalia's state law. After the collapse of the Siad Barre regime in 1991, the Somali National Movement appointed both sheikhs and wadaad "as ... judges ... because they knew ... shari'a."[3] Because "there was no government, no legal system, no rule of law ... they were filling the gap," a civil servant in Hargeisa told me.[4] Sheikhs, like wadaad, attract disputants by becoming well known for preaching on Islamic faith, theology, and law. Their public lectures, radio addresses, and private tutoring earn them legitimacy among ordinary citizens and help them bring paying clients into their offices.[5] One activist told me, "If I went to the University of Hargeisa and gave a speech to 200 or 300 academics, [it would take me] two or

---

[3] Interview 41 with Khalid, lawyer and university lecturer in Hargeisa, Somaliland (July 2013).
[4] Interview 107 with Roble Ali, government agency director in Hargeisa, Somaliland (June 2014).
[5] Follow-up interview 93 with Caziz, lawyer and human rights activist in Hargeisa, Somaliland (June 2014).

three hours [to get my message across]. But one sheikh can change all their minds in five minutes. They are influential."[6]

Some prominent sheikhs have also amassed wealth and power from their work resolving disputes or their engagements in other Muslim-majority countries. But people told me they still turn to sheikhs instead of lawyers or state courts for two reasons: trust and speed. Corruption, mistrust, and slow bureaucracy make the state's courts look unattractive in comparison. A Somali writer in his seventies told me that he felt "religion is spreading [faster] than before" because people are going to sheikhs rather than to state courts for their legal matters.[7] While the parties pay the sheikh a fee to investigate their dispute and come to a conclusion, they also feel that a "bribe is not possible."[8] Even government officials prefer to go to sheikhs: a senior official in the Ministry of Justice told me that when disputes arose in his own family, they went "to macduum" for resolution rather than to the state courts.[9] Women I met said they, too, preferred shari'a-based resolution to their disputes on property claims, divorce, alimony, or maintenance. Even though the sheikhs are men, they are more influential in daily life than government officials and judges, who are themselves almost entirely men. "It's what the religion has said. [Women] are doing the right thing" by resolving disputes using shari'a, one women's rights activist told me.[10] Echoing many respondents, another women's rights activist summarized the role of sheikhs in society and why people turn to them for help: "They are gatekeepers [and] people listen to religion."[11]

Shari'a as "Simplicity"
Over time, the process of turning to sheikhs for dispute resolution also builds trust in them and in Islam, just as regularly turning to state courts would build trust in judges and the state itself. Many people saw sheikhs as embodying the rule of law. "To me as a Muslim ... this is the rule of law," one university lecturer told me. He continued,

---

[6] Interview 125 with Sohir, NGO executive director and women's rights activist in Hargeisa, Somaliland (June 2014).
[7] Interview 21 with Ra'ed, writer and consultant in Hargeisa, Somaliland (June 2013).
[8] Follow-up interview 69 with Axmed, lawyer and university lecturer in Hargeisa, Somaliland (June 2013).
[9] Interview 67 with Omar, senior government official in Hargeisa, Somaliland (July 2013).
[10] Interview 55 with Fawzia, women's rights activist and former NGO executive director in Hargeisa, Somaliland (June 2013).
[11] Interview 125 with Sohir, NGO executive director and women's rights activist in Hargeisa, Somaliland (June 2014).

Because shari'a has everything in it, there's no corruption or bribes or [lack of] transparency. And there is immediacy. They [sheikhs] will not hesitate to make a decision. You know God is watching you. You have to strike a fair decision. But in court, there are lawyers who are not faithful. Judges take bribes and drag things on.[12]

A man with degrees in both shari'a and English common law told me that he prefers shari'a for dispute resolution. To him, shari'a offers "simplicity." Judges who use shari'a find the truth of a matter themselves. They do not rely upon the arguments of lawyers who may be untruthful or who may abuse the procedural protections of "the Western court."[13] Visiting a regional court in Hargeisa, I witnessed a judge request payment from a litigant for his services by using the supplication in Somali, *soo duuce*. The woman next to me, shaking her head, said, "If people ... see [an] injustice [like this], that drives them to shari'a."[14] While the sheikhs also ask for fees, the parties must both agree to pay the same service fee in advance, as opposed to a judge who might demand a payment from only one party, or a higher payment from one party than the other – and who also receives a salary from the state.

In practice, sheikhs are one part of a broader dispute resolution system that includes judges who use state law in state courts and aqils and sultans who use xeer within their communities.[15] While this legal flexibility and pluralism gives people choices of venues and processes, it also can generate confusion and animosity. Somaliland's district courts are descendants of the colonial qadi courts in which judges ruled according to Islamic family law. According to Somalis I met, some district court judges "complained" about sheikhs who seemed to be taking work – and, thus, legitimacy – from the state's courts.[16] But even some judges turned to sheikhs for assistance in their cases. "In the court, when there are complicated cases related to shari'a, the judge may refer to *ulema shuyuukh* [a council of sheikhs] to give their opinion as to what shari'a says about this issue. And sheikhs give their expert

---

[12] Interview 49 with Babiker, university administrator and lecturer in Hargeisa, Somaliland (July 2013).
[13] Interview 32 with Axmed, lawyer and university lecturer in Hargeisa, Somaliland (June 2013).
[14] Interview 104 with Yasmeen, legal aid attorney in Hargeisa, Somaliland (June 2014).
[15] By 2013, 1,600 aqils had registered with the government of Somaliland (1,137 of these receiving a stipend from the Ministry of Interior), an eightfold increase from the 200 aqils in the British Somaliland Protectorate.
[16] Interview 107 with Roble Ali, government agency director in Hargeisa, Somaliland (June 2014).

opinion."[17] Even some lawyers referred to sheikhs' offices as Somaliland's "legitimate courts" in contrast with the state's "non-shari'a ... illegitimate courts." "Normal citizens," this lawyer continued, "call the legitimate courts ... 'shari'a' ... implying that state courts were not doing justice, since ... in [sheikhs' offices], the bribe is not possible."[18]

In addition to trust, the speed of dispute resolution matters. A university administrator I met in Hargeisa told me that "If you want to solve a matter immediately ... go to the sheikh. If you want to continue arguing ... go to the formal courts."[19] Another said of the sheikhs' offices, "Even if you lose ... you still think there was justice."[20] Satisfaction comes from knowing a case was decided not in a state court influenced by colonial law but in a religious office influenced by shari'a.

A foreign consultant told me that Somalis turn to sheikhs because "It's God's law. Verdicts are far easier to reach [than in state court] and the capacity to enforce the verdict is far greater ... Even the person ... on whom a fine is imposed ... says 'This is God's law and I won't disagree with it.' This is a conservative society, so they accept it gladly." He lamented, though, that state courts were "being undermined by a bunch of sheikhs." But he conceded that not everyone can put out a shingle and claim to be a religious authority. It takes years of study, practice, and preaching to be treated as a religious authority in Somaliland. "You have to spend time learning [and memorizing] the Qur'an. Becoming respected [and seen as a person] with a religious background is not easy."[21]

People I met estimated that as many as three out of four disputes they have had or witnessed in their families are not resolved in the courts, with most of those going to sheikhs rather than clan elders. According to those familiar with the process, the most well-known sheikhs in Somaliland have resolved personal and corporate disputes in their private offices. Someone familiar with a multimillion dollar dispute said that the two corporations involved went to a sheikh "because they had greater confidence in getting a fair outcome" than from a state

[17] Interview 100 with Hassan, legal aid attorney and former police official in Hargeisa, Somaliland (June 2014).

[18] Follow-up interview 69 with Axmed, lawyer and university lecturer in Hargeisa, Somaliland (June 2013).

[19] Interview 49 with Babiker, university administrator and lecturer in Hargeisa, Somaliland (July 2013).

[20] Interview 90 with Suleiman, lawyer and paralegal in Hargeisa, Somaliland (June 2014).

[21] Interview 22 with Shahab, expatriate consultant in Hargeisa, Somaliland (June 2013).

court.[22] Occasionally sheikhs resolve real estate disputes – when someone is willing to swear on their religious tradition that a piece of land is theirs – but land issues are otherwise "difficult to arbitrate," especially given that government intervention is typically required to produce accurate measurements.[23]

As a way of encouraging people to understand the state courts as Islamic, sheikhs in the Somaliland Ministry of Religious Affairs have the power to issue fatwas, or religious edicts, and to intervene in district court decisions. If litigants feel a state court judgment was unfair from an Islamic point of view, they may file a complaint with an investigative office of that ministry. The ministry's sheikhs are civil servants who, in addition to advising the government on religious matters, may determine whether a judge incorrectly interpreted shari'a texts related to a case's substance or procedures. Sheikhs from the ministry then meet with the judge to resolve the matter or to encourage the judge to issue a different decision.

Governing the Sheikhs

In the early 2010s, the Somaliland government and the international aid community joined forces to try to "make [the macduum] more formal" by regulating and institutionalizing them under a state ministry.[24] Because the government was aware of people's trust in sheikhs and their ad hoc tribunals, they tried to make them part of the Ministry of Justice by licensing them and, more importantly, having the ability to revoke their licenses, thus controlling and limiting who has the power to use Islam.[25] "If [macduum] were institutionalized under the government ... it [would be] easy to trace their cases and ... have confidence" in them and in the government, the founder of a Somali research organization told me.[26] Some, especially younger men with religious training in Saudi Arabia, suggested that officials should control who is licensed. Others in government said the Ministry of Justice should register sheikhs just as they register lawyers. Others, including aid workers, called for a single case management system that would integrate cases from the courts, sheikhs, aqils, and sultans.

---

[22] Interview 6 with Rashida, lawyer in Hargeisa, Somaliland (conducted by telephone from London, England) (June 2013).

[23] Follow-up interview 98 with Tahir, NGO executive director in Hargeisa, Somaliland (June 2014).

[24] Interview 22 with Shahab, expatriate consultant in Hargeisa, Somaliland (June 2013).

[25] Interview 50 with Caziz, lawyer and human rights activist in Hargeisa, Somaliland (July 2013).

[26] Interview 14 with Maxamed, independent researcher and consultant in Hargeisa, Somaliland (June 2013).

But the government faced resistance from sheikhs who felt institutionalizing their tribunals was "the same [strategy] like the British," as
one sheikh told me.[27] The strategy would put Islam under the state's
control, rather than the other way around – a difference deeply important to those who believe that God's authority is final. Indeed, elites in
Somaliland have long disagreed over the extent to which the government should license, regulate, and oversee sheikhs. Many sheikhs did
not want state oversight of their work. Other Somalis suggested privately to me that macduum offices ought to be taxed or that they were
unconstitutional. Still others saw the sheikhs as a way to relieve
pressure on the state's sluggish and overburdened judicial system. But
the lack of women sheikhs made international NGOs less likely to
support the macduum as a major dispute resolution process. Although
there were no women judges in Somaliland either, such groups thought
that the state system might be more willing to accommodate women
judges in the future.[28]

Somaliland is not alone in the desire to bring sheikhs and their
dispute resolution offices under government control. Puntland's regional Ministry of Justice has registered sheikhs to work as dispute resolvers, with UNDP's support, according to my interviews with aid
workers involved in these efforts.[29] The UNDP officials also initially
wanted Somaliland to adopt macduum-related legislation so that
sheikhs would serve as "mediating bodies" to rehabilitate youth who
might otherwise be sent to prison.[30] But Somaliland's Ministry of
Justice sought broader measures, to register the sheikhs and oversee
all the work they do.

Though sheikhs' macduum tribunals are not state courts, they "are so
strong that . . . they are regarded as courts" by many Somalis.[31] Though
macduum tribunals are unregulated, sheikhs nevertheless benefit discursively and materially from the Islamic state around them, starting
from its constitutional text. In Somaliland, one sheikh told me,
"Muslim scholars . . . are free." He contrasted Somaliland to Somalia's
Siad Barre regime, under which he could not find work or publicly teach

[27] Interview 52 with Sheikh Zaki, sheikh and former senior judiciary official in Hargeisa,
Somaliland (July 2013).
[28] Interview 20 with Akifah, lawyer and university lecturer in Hargeisa, Somaliland (June 2013).
[29] Interview 15 with Evelyn, United Nations official in Garowe, Puntland (conducted by telephone from Hargeisa, Somaliland) (June 2013).
[30] Interview 50 with Caziz, lawyer and human rights activist in Hargeisa, Somaliland (July 2013).
[31] Interview 78 with Majda, lawyer and human rights activist in Mogadishu and Hargeisa
(conducted in Nairobi, Kenya) (July 2013).

his interpretations of shari'a. "The role of sheikhs is increasing," he continued.[32] In Somaliland, shari'a has helped to build an extended period of peace and stability, from the bottom up as well as from the top down.

CONSTITUTING AN ISLAMIC STATE

In the late 1970s, local and diaspora Somalis began meeting to discuss political problems under Siad Barre. Their efforts grew into a transnational political movement, formalized in 1981 as the Somali National Movement (SNM). The SNM included diaspora Somalis in the UK and Saudi Arabia along with Somalis in what was then northern Somalia. In Hargeisa, a group of professionals – among them doctors, engineers, and lawyers – formed a committee to attract foreign donor funding to rebuild the inadequate Hargeisa Hospital. Viewing their search for foreign support as an affront to the regime, Siad Barre's security officers arrested them. They came to be known as the Hargeisa Hospital Group. They were tried in a national security court, called *badbaado*, which targeted and executed dissenters. The arrests and detentions of members of the Hargeisa Hospital Group, many for five years or more, alongside other witch hunts for suspected regime dissenters, helped to catalyze the SNM's growth.

Having experienced the brutalities of authoritarian rule, northern Somalis wanted something better, they told me. Islam was the institution they could trust, and they felt Siad Barre had tried to destroy it. "The revolt against Siad Barre made Islam strong," according to a human rights lawyer.[33] The successful ouster of Siad Barre's authoritarian regime in 1991 strengthened people's resolve to introduce an Islamic state.

From the start the SNM relied upon religious discourse, personnel, and symbols. A lawyer and former SNM militia leader told me that the movement's long-term goal was to "get rid of" Siad Barre and replace the dictatorship "with a better system" rooted in religious faith.[34] Faith inspired the independence struggle. Many SNM leaders had "links with Sufism [and] Islamic teachings."[35] Aqils became the SNM's on-the-

---

[32] Interview 52 with Sheikh Zaki, sheikh and former senior judiciary official in Hargeisa, Somaliland (July 2013).

[33] Follow-up interview 93 with Caziz, lawyer and human rights activist in Hargeisa, Somaliland (June 2014).

[34] Interview 100 with Hassan, legal aid attorney and former police official in Hargeisa, Somaliland (June 2014).

[35] Interview 127 with Sheikh Oweis, sheikh and senior university administrator in Hargeisa, Somaliland (June 2014).

ground support team. Using Islam, the aqils mobilized and inspired people to recruit, feed, and house fighters in the civil war against Siad Barre's regime.[36] Somali National Movement fighters were taught about Islam, told by their leaders that they were fighting the government on behalf of Islam, and given the designation mujahideen (holy warriors).[37]

While Somaliland had no independent government to speak of in the 1980s, the SNM did create its own courts. According to a sheikh I met, the SNM had employed his father – also a sheikh – as a judge: "The SNM used sheikhs as judges," he told me. Not trusting Somali state law made in Mogadishu and inherited from Italian colonialism, the sheikhs instead used *Minhaj al-Muslim* (Arabic, *The Way of the Muslim*), a two-volume guide on practicing creed, righteous character, and good deeds. "When there [was] no government, no established system, the people [went] back to *al-Minhaj*," the sheikh told me.[38] The SNM encouraged sheikhs and disputants to treat Islam as the bedrock of peacebuilding. These became the first steps toward stability in the area that would reassert itself as the nation of Somaliland, a region that Siad Barre's regime was simultaneously trying to destroy.

Throughout the 1980s and early 1990s, the northern region of Somaliland weathered Siad Barre's military assaults and aerial bombardments. After he fled to Nigeria in 1991, Somaliland did not automatically become peaceful. On the contrary, it was devastated. Victims' bodies had been dumped into mass graves. Thousands more had fled as refugees. A decade-long civil war, years of mistrusting Mogadishu, and the Somali state's 1991 collapse all brought survivors to exhaustion. "It was difficult to make [people in Somaliland] reconcile with [the], state, police, courts" in this context.[39] Somalis I met who had returned in the early 1990s found militias controlling major towns and regions.[40] Soon, the SNM's internal rivalries, and clan resentments buried by the civil

---

[36] Interview 45 with Aqil Zaki Yasim, aqil and senior government official in Hargeisa, Somaliland (July 2013).

[37] Mark Bradbury, *Becoming Somaliland* (Bloomington: Indiana University Press, 2008), 64

[38] Interview 127 with Sheikh Oweis, sheikh and senior university administrator in Hargeisa, Somaliland (June 2014). With no state legal institutions, all judgments and decisions of aqils were valid and "sanctioned by religious leaders." Bradbury (2008), 103.

[39] Interview 124 with Najib, former senior government minister in Hargeisa, Somaliland (June 2014).

[40] Interview 18 with Bashir, university administrator in Hargeisa, Somaliland (June 2013).

war against Siad Barre, percolated to the surface, leading to battles in Somaliland until about 1995.

However, as violence was taking hold between communities in Somaliland, and as warlords were controlling southern Somalia, elders and religious leaders in the north were coming together to return stability and autonomy to the region. While Somaliland weathered its own clan-based political violence, warlords did not take over as they did in Somalia. Moreover, elders and religious leaders came together earlier and more regularly in Somaliland than in Somalia, helping to build a more gradual and sustainable peace. They held a series of peace summits between 1991 and 1997; the five largest summits helped to shape Somaliland's nationhood and fortified Islam as its foundation (Table 5.1).[41]

Local norms (*xeer dhaqanmed*) demanded that religious leaders – alongside women, children, and the frail elderly – be spared from violence. A customary practice called *birtu ma gaido* (the iron cannot touch them) protected religious leaders from exposure to violence so they could focus on peacebuilding. As one woman who survived the disintegration of Somalia in 1991 told me in her new hometown of Nairobi, Islam "became very strong because the state [had] collapsed ... Islam [was] the only unifying factor."[42] During the 1990s Somali elders seeking to build peace in the newly independent Somaliland promoted the shared principles of shari'a and human rights, in the words of one diaspora Somali lawyer involved, to "set the proper roots for the reborn state to live peacefully and build democratic structures."[43] Laws inconsistent with shari'a and international human rights treaties were deemed inapplicable. Thus, the legal backstops provided by shari'a and human rights gave Somaliland's elders a foundation for the rule of law – an Islamic foundation – that moved Somaliland, without major foreign aid or intervention, out of Somalia.

By 1991, the SNM's mujahideen had captured most cities in northern Somalia from Somalia's weakening military. The SNM administered the region until 1993.[44] During those two years the mujahideen gave judicial authority to elders, sheikhs, aqils, and sultans most known

[41] Interview 121 with Guleed, senior government ministry staff member in Hargeisa, Somaliland (June 2014).
[42] Interview 77 with Khadra, United Nations official in Nairobi, Kenya (July 2013).
[43] Interview 5 with Na'im, lawyer and legal consultant in England (conducted by telephone from London, England) (June 2013).
[44] Bradbury (2008), 78.

Table 5.1 How shari'a created Somaliland

Event	Date	Outcome
Guurti Summit in Berbera	Feb. 1991	Trust built between rival groups in the Somaliland region, paving the way to a joint statement of independence
Guurti Summit in Burao	April–May 1991	Shari'a described as basis of Somaliland law; independence from Somalia declared May 18, 1991
Guurti Summit in Sheikh	Oct. 1992	Draft national charter, which integrated shari'a and international human rights law, introduced and discussed
Guurti Summit in Borama	Feb.–May 1993	National charter and peace charter debated and adopted; government structure set out; power transferred from SNM to civilian administration; Somalia's laws in place before Siad Barre's 1969 coup declared valid in Somaliland unless inconsistent with shari'a and human rights
Guurti Summit in Hargeisa	Oct. 1996–Feb. 1997	Text of interim constitution settled; constitutional provisions declared shari'a as source of all law; all Somalia's laws before the 1991 collapse declared valid in Somaliland unless inconsistent with "shari'a, individual rights, and fundamental freedoms"
Somaliland Constitution	May 2001	Constitution, based on shari'a principles and international human rights law, finalized and approved by 97.9 percent in national plebiscite

Source: Author interviews with summit delegates; Bradbury (2008).

for their commitments to protecting Islam and building peace. When sitting as ad hoc decision-making councils, these elders were called *guurti*. The guurti were the region's de facto political leadership during the violence. Over time the guurti came to be elected and institutionalized, with representatives of different clans working together. One leading Somaliland government official, who had also been involved in Somaliland's peace negotiations in the 1990s, said that "The guurti were the tool we used to reconcile with those tribes who had been supporting Siad Barre, so people would not take revenge [on one another] or continue the war."[45] Though never formally recognized by Mogadishu or the outside world, the guurti summits, also called conferences, tell the story of Somaliland's separation from Somalia and how elders turned to shari'a for support (cf. Table 5.1).

The first major guurti summit took place in February 1991 in the coastal town of Berbera, two months prior to Somaliland's declaration of independence from Somalia. In Berbera, elders representing the region's rival groups met to end interclan fighting and rebuild trust between their communities. Two months later, in May 1991, they reconvened in the town of Burao (in Somali, Burco) for the second guurti summit. The delegates named this summit the Grand Conference of Northern Clans (Shirweynaha Beelaha Waqooyi). At Burao, the guurti formally declared Somaliland's independence from Somalia.[46] Though no constitution was drafted in Burao, delegates spoke of requiring the future Somaliland government to implement shari'a, according to one of them I met.[47]

Outside of the delivery of international aid to the Somali people and UN assistance clearing landmines, the guurti purposefully avoided foreign help, which they saw as political interference in their work. Just one foreigner – a representative from the British Embassy in Addis Ababa, Ethiopia – attended the 1991 Burao summit. But the delegates gave this British diplomat "a memorandum [saying] that we are the Somaliland community . . . and . . . in solving our peace, we don't need any [foreign] intervention."[48] In contrast to Somalia's peace process, which occurred in foreign countries with the involvement of foreign groups and donors, Somaliland and its guurti seemed to go it on their own.

---

[45] Interview 124 with Najib, former senior government minister in Hargeisa, Somaliland (June 2014).
[46] International Crisis Group, *Somaliland: Democratisation and its Discontents*. Africa Report No. 66 (Nairobi/Brussels: ICG, 2003) 9.
[47] Follow-up interview 68 with Faisal, senior government official in Hargeisa, Somaliland (July 2013).
[48] Ibid.

The third guurti summit – and the first after Somaliland declared independence – took place in October 1992 in the town of Sheikh. There, a few dozen elders and religious leaders brokered a peace deal between rival groups in the coastal town of Berbera and introduced Somaliland's draft national charter. The final national charter would become Somaliland's temporary governing document until a constitution was drafted and ratified. The elders integrated shari'a and human rights into the charter to prevent Siad Barre's authoritarian excesses from recurring.

The fourth major summit, held in 1993 in the town of Borama, was a watershed for the rule of law in Somaliland. The Conference of Guurti of the Communities of Somaliland was also known by its Somali name, Allah mahad leh (Tribute to God).[49] At this summit, SNM mujahideen formally transferred their authority to a civilian administration, and the delegates ratified two legal documents: a peace charter and the national charter, which laid out Somaliland's governing structure and separation of powers. The guurti decided that, rather than write every law from scratch, all laws enacted in Somalia prior to Siad Barre's 1969 coup would be valid in Somaliland, with the important check that any laws contrary either to shari'a or to "fundamental rights" could be voided. In this way, the guurti formalized shari'a principles and human rights law in Somaliland's charter. The civilian administration did pass new laws, but considering whether bills were consistent with Islam was an essential step in writing any legislation. According to those involved, "When we [were] preparing [new] laws, we [had] to look, is there anything against shari'a?"[50]

Somaliland portrayed itself decisively as an Islamic state. On October 14, 1996, a new flag was revealed which, unlike Somalia's, features the central statement of Islamic faith: *La Allah illah Allah, wa Muhammad Rusul Allah* ("There is no God but God, and Muhammad is the Messenger of God"). Islam was literally inscribed on the symbol of Somaliland's sovereignty (Figure 5.1).

In 1997, at their final summit in Hargeisa, the capital of the newly independent Somaliland, the guurti maintained the structures of government – a presidency, a judiciary, and two parliamentary houses (one

---

[49] Bradbury (2008), 98.
[50] Follow-up interview 68 with Faisal, senior government official in Hargeisa, Somaliland (July 2013).

Figure 5.1 Shari'a and the Somaliland flag.
Source: Government of Somaliland, Hargeisa.

House of Representatives and one hereditary house for elders, called the House of Guurti) – which had been laid out in the national charter. They also settled on a text for Somaliland's interim constitution, which would be put to a plebiscite four years later. The constitution's text was at first contentious, with two drafts in circulation. One draft was written by a parliamentary committee. The other was written by Mohammed Ibrahim Khalil, a former minister of justice of Sudan and former dean of the University of Khartoum Law Faculty. Somaliland President Egal had hired Khalil because of his knowledge of Islamic and non-Islamic law and his facility with both Arabic and English.[51] When the final text was settled, the constitution began and ended with references to shari'a and human rights. The preamble declared that shari'a was the primary source of constitutional law, alongside principles about the protection of life and property rights drawn from Islamic jurisprudence and international human rights law. The constitution's final article declared that all of Somalia's laws valid at the time of the 1991 collapse, including laws of the Siad Barre regime, would continue to be valid if they did not "conflict with the Islamic shari'a, individual rights, and fundamental freedoms."[52]

---

[51] Follow-up interview 96 with Adam, independent researcher and consultant in Hargeisa, Somaliland (June 2014); see also Bradbury (2008), 124.

[52] Article 130.5 of the Constitution of the Republic of Somaliland, 2001.

The interim constitution of 1997 did not erase Siad Barre's legacy. Many judges who had worked within the regime continued to resolve disputes over property and inheritance, among others, that emerged as people returned to Somaliland to rebuild their lives. The new civilian administration also retained the regime's criminal and civil procedure codes, though these were in force only to the extent they did not conflict with human rights or shari'a. This exception enabled Somalilanders, according to those involved, to "select the laws we wanted" while any "draconian laws [fell] under the human rights exception."[53] The framers were also "interested in differentiating faith from the state" by creating an Islamic state that they hoped would protect religious freedom. "If I am a Christian," a sheikh involved told me, "I should not be persecuted for that."[54] He said the commission agreed that the constitution of Somaliland must be "against terrorism, and [indicate] that shari'a is the supreme law and that people have freedom and human rights."[55] While there had been disagreement – even amongst religious leaders – about whether to include shari'a in Somalia's first constitution of 1960, Somaliland's 1997 interim constitution was another matter. Sheikhs in Somaliland were "united for the imposition of shari'a," one of them told me.[56] But they differed on what that meant in practice.

The guurti created a state in which Islam would check government authority. That is, the government could pass laws it deemed necessary, but leaders had to ensure that those laws were compatible with Islam. Political leaders aimed to integrate shari'a, custom, and Western notions of the rule of law: "We were trying to reconcile between the notion of the government and its rule of law with the traditional mechanism[s]" rooted in shari'a.[57] In Somaliland's political development, shari'a was interpreted flexibly: "[The constitutional rule that] anything against shari'a is null and void … does not mean that we are taking shari'a exactly [as written in the Qur'an and Hadith]."[58] Shari'a, then, seemed similar to human rights principles. Not only was shari'a

---

[53] Interview 5 with Na'im, lawyer and legal consultant in England (conducted by telephone from London, England) (June 2013).
[54] Interview 52 with Sheikh Zaki, sheikh and former senior judiciary official in Hargeisa, Somaliland (July 2013).
[55] Ibid.
[56] Interview 89 with Sheikh Abdirahman, sheikh and senior government official in Hargeisa, Somaliland (June 2014).
[57] Follow-up interview 68 with Faisal, senior government official in Hargeisa, Somaliland (July 2013).
[58] Ibid.

loosely defined and difficult to enforce, but it also provided a set of discursive resources for legislators to use when making laws and for people to use, later on, when questioning legislation.

Somaliland's founders thus used Islamic tools to construct principles of the rule of law. The state's 2001 constitution embodied its Islamic foundation. In 2000, the civilian administration made some final amendments to the 1997 interim constitution and put the legal document to a plebiscite. On May 31, 2001, the constitution was approved, winning 97.9 percent of the more than one million votes counted, according to the Somaliland government.[59] As of 2021, this constitution remains in force.

According to a senior official involved in the process, Somaliland officials were proud of their work. "The absence of [Western] intervention [in the constitution] was a blessing. It was our own indigenous ... people" who drafted it, one former government minister said.[60] Civic activists agreed. Echoing others I met, one activist said, "The constitution was a local project ... not internationally funded."[61] While the guurti made sure that there was little or no legal, political, or financial interference from the West, Somaliland's constitution was not entirely an indigenous creation. First, a government official from Sudan helped to draft one version, whose text aiming to create a democratic Islamic state was integrated into the final constitution.

Second, as a former university administrator in Hargeisa told me, "The colonial [process] still operates" in Somaliland's constitution.[62] Western forms of government shaped Somaliland's governing structure. The social – but not legal – separation of Somaliland's communities into groups known as clans crystallized during the British colonial administration. The colonial policy of indirect rule – employing local Somali leaders rather than British officials themselves ruling directly – entrenched this clan-based social order.

Even though there was little Western intervention in the 1990s as Somaliland was constituting itself as a nation with its own state agencies, government buildings, schools, police, and currency, past foreign interventions and an awareness of parliamentary and presidential systems overseas still made their way into the constitution, while shari'a

---

[59] Bradbury (2008), 133.
[60] Interview 124 with Najib, former senior government minister in Hargeisa, Somaliland (June 2014).
[61] Interview 103 with Garaad, political activist in Hargeisa, Somaliland (June 2014).
[62] Interview 99 with Shermarke, former university administrator and United Nations official in Hargeisa, Somaliland (June 2014).

served to balance or check the government's power. The constitution "borrowed some things from" the United Kingdom (including a hereditary upper chamber of parliament called the House of Guurti, more resembling the UK House of Lords than the US Senate) and the United States (a Supreme Court with constitutional and appellate authority).[63]

When I asked people about the constitution, their responses revealed the importance of Islamic political debates. A civic activist told me that, in her experience, "People [in Somaliland] saw what [al-Shabaab] did in the south: cutting ... hands, strong laws, manipulating people. People [began] questioning what does religion mean in the Somali context, because of what happened in the south."[64] People were also "fed up with ... secular leadership [and] we need[ed] Islam, shari'a," recalled one lawyer.[65] A sheikh, one of the constitution's drafters, agreed with this sentiment. He and his colleagues made shari'a prominent in order to forestall extremism. "I had a fear [that] if those extremists come in, [Somaliland] would change. I wanted a balanced view of Islam" in the constitution, which led to "introduc[ing] Islam in accordance with [our] customs," he told me. He concluded that creating an Islamic state meant that "we won" over jihadists.[66] The constitution went a step further by promising to maintain religious and political freedoms.

Western groups and governments have largely been absent from Somaliland's political and legal progress, in part because they decided not to recognize Somaliland's independence so as not to encourage further fracturing in the region. But Somalilanders told me that they also did not want them around, to avoid the mistakes they felt Somalia was making. Somaliland, people told me, had "no [meetings] in Nairobi and no fancy lawyers" in hotels drafting constitutional text, as in Somalia's peace process.[67]

When I asked Somalis about the rule of law and what it means, many immediately cited Islam and shari'a. "The supremacy of the constitution is grounded by shari'a. Any act of government is null and void if it's

[63] Interview 5 with Na'im, lawyer and legal consultant in England (conducted by telephone from London, England) (June 2013).

[64] Interview 33 with Salaam, NGO executive director in Hargeisa, Somaliland (June 2013).

[65] Interview 50 with Caziz, lawyer and human rights activist in Hargeisa, Somaliland (July 2013).

[66] Interview 52 with Sheikh Zaki, sheikh and former senior judiciary official in Hargeisa, Somaliland (July 2013).

[67] Interview 6 with Rashida, lawyer in Hargeisa, Somaliland (conducted by telephone from London, England) (June 2013).

against shari'a," a former judge reminded me.[68] Imams have used
political conflicts between the government in power in Hargeisa and
opposition parties as opportunities to preach that the constitution itself
is "un-Islamic" or not Islamic enough because the Western concept of
the state, in their view, threatens Somaliland's stability.[69] During my
fieldwork, parliament was debating a commercial banking system; many
parliamentarians and sheikhs spoke out against it, advocating instead
for an Islamic finance system. Some of them did so by citing Article 130
of the Somaliland constitution that all new laws must be consistent
with shari'a.[70]

State officials I met had no clear understanding of who would decide
whether and how a law is consistent with shari'a. The idea was that
legislators as a group would police themselves, protecting the sanctity of
shari'a or risking God's judgment. Some people instead argued that the
task should be formalized through a commission of ulema (called *majlis
al-ulema*), or scholars of shari'a who could review proposed bills for their
consistency with Islam and also oversee local sheikhs who resolve
disputes. Some early drafts of the constitution included such
a council, but were rejected by the president and ultimately never
implemented. When I asked one sheikh about his hopes, he said he
wished for the establishment of an ulema commission with the power to
review legislation prior to enactment.[71] No one knows how much the
political attitudes of any such commission might dictate its findings,
much as rulings of high court justices in other countries are correlated
with political preferences, ideology, and strategy.[72] An ulema commission would be designed, like the constitution itself, to limit the arbitrary
exercise of power by legislators through a religiously informed rule of
law.[73]

Following the successful constitutional plebiscite in 2001, the
Somaliland parliament passed laws to protect judicial independence.

[68] Interview 58 with Hussein, university lecturer and former judge in Hargeisa, Somaliland (July 2013).
[69] Follow-up interview 93 with Caziz, lawyer and human rights activist in Hargeisa, Somaliland (June 2014).
[70] Interview 118 with Ismaciil, NGO executive director in Hargeisa, Somaliland (June 2014).
[71] Interview 89 with Sheikh Abdirahman, sheikh and senior government official in Hargeisa, Somaliland (June 2014).
[72] Lee Epstein, William M. Landes, and Richard A. Posner, *The Behavior of Federal Judges: A Theoretical and Empirical Study of Rational Choice* (Cambridge, MA: Harvard University Press, 2013).
[73] Interview 110 with Kahlil, lawyer and government consultant in Hargeisa, Somaliland (June 2014).

The Organization of the Judiciary Law of 2003, in particular, aimed to ensure that the judiciary does not become a tool of autocrats. It reiterated constitutional provisions to guarantee judicial independence from the government in power.[74] The law also clarified that, while individual disputants may turn to mediation and other dispute resolution mechanisms among community and religious leaders, the government may not create any special or emergency courts with the power to issue criminal penalties.[75]

The decision to link shari'a with "individual rights and fundamental freedoms" in constitutional law did not come easily. Some religious leaders and elders disagreed. They adopted the "attitude . . . that everything comes from the Qur'an, that the Qur'an [alone] should be the constitution."[76] A constitution was itself a form of secularism incompatible with their version of shari'a. Though different interpretations of the Qur'an caused leaders to disagree about how Islam ought to be integrated into the state, they still agreed on the principle of an Islamic state. As constitutional architects told me, "The role of shari'a is increasing. We are going the way of Islam, rather than [the] secular" way of state-building.[77]

CONTAINING THE ISLAMIC STATE

This section examines the international aid community's relationship with shari'a through aid workers' three main activities promoting the rule of law in Somaliland: legal education, legal aid, and legal reform. Though they need not do so, each of these programs seems to work against shari'a by codifying competing legal orders and undermining shari'a's indigenous democratic development. That is, legal education, legal aid, and legal reform are attempts to build state structures familiar to outsiders and make them trustworthy to locals, while restricting the role of shari'a.

Just as the colonial and authoritarian administrations in Somalia centralized the legal system, so too has the international aid community sought to centralize law in Somaliland. United Nations agencies, particularly UNDP, have led efforts to fund and staff legal education,

---

[74] Somaliland Law No. 24 of 2003; see also Article 97.2 and Article 99.2 of the Constitution of the Republic of Somaliland, 2001.

[75] Article 2.3, 2.4, and 2.5 of Somaliland Law No. 24 of 2003.

[76] Interview 33 with Salaam, NGO executive director in Hargeisa, Somaliland (June 2013).

[77] Interview 52 with Sheikh Zaki, sheikh and former senior judiciary official in Hargeisa, Somaliland (July 2013).

legal aid, and legal reform projects that thwart the local potential of shari'a. These agencies have supported successive governmental efforts to create a single state law in the face of legal pluralism. The irony of UN support has not gone unnoticed by Somalilanders and aid workers alike: "On the one hand, they ... do not recognize Somaliland as sovereign. On the other hand, they support the government to draft [new] laws that augment its 'stateness'."[78]

A new era of legal confrontation has emerged between aid agencies delivering legal assistance and ordinary people who continue to turn to shari'a and other mechanisms of dispute resolution. As in earlier colonial and authoritarian administrations, law and religion exist in tension in Somaliland, as elders, officials, and aid workers search for order. Through this process, shari'a has become a force in legal politics, something to be controlled rather than promoted.

The hallmark of state-building is the creation of legal orthodoxy out of legal heterodoxy. The international aid community takes three interrelated approaches to centralizing Somaliland's legal system. Legal education involves establishing law schools. Legal aid refers to programs that help the poor access state courts. And legal reform includes training legal personnel and drafting bills for passage into law. In order to build the rule of law as they envision it, aid groups seek to separate religion from law and subordinate Islam to state law, tethering shari'a to the ideals they find satisfactory.

Legal Education
In 2013, I met with a senior law professor at the University of Hargeisa. As we walked on the sand between dilapidated buildings he told me that one positive consequence of Somalia's civil war was the development of legal education in Somaliland. When I asked him to explain, he said, "The war helped create legal development, because we had to create a building. You know, the buildings were destroyed. This tree is famous ... in the history of Somaliland. It is under this tree that the law faculty began."[79] The destruction of Somaliland, he continued, had led to the creation of its first law school. Today this law faculty – and other law faculties around Somaliland – are centers of learning that teach students how to navigate the state's legal orders and give primacy to state law.

[78] Interview 22 with Shahab, expatriate consultant in Hargeisa, Somaliland (June 2013).
[79] Follow-up interview 11 with Faris, professor and government official in Hargeisa, Somaliland (June 2013).

The Horn of Africa's first modern law school was opened by Siad Barre in 1970 at the University of Mogadishu. It became fully operational by 1974, teaching a curriculum focused largely on Italian jurisprudence. Legal pluralism was a challenge from the start; English common law still prevailed in the north because of its distinct colonial heritage. Many Italian professors arrived in the 1970s and 1980s, but the law school collapsed with the regime in 1991. No state law school operated outside of Mogadishu until 2002, when the University of Hargeisa, founded in 1998, opened its Faculty of Law. The curriculum was dictated in part by UNDP, which hired foreign consultants to work alongside Somali scholars. Those involved had a diversity of legal training from jurisdictions in North America, Europe, South Asia, the Middle East, and elsewhere in Africa.

I asked university administrators and teachers why they wanted to open a law faculty in the war-torn region. They told me they hoped to assuage people's concerns about state power. According to one professor, "People respected traditional laws and . . . shari'a a lot," but they had a "phobia" of state law.[80] A senior university official told me that the University of Hargeisa launched its law faculty in part through UN involvement: "UDNP intended to develop the rule of law and security." The law faculty would be a pipeline to government service. "Injecting" people into government as advisors and prosecutors, he continued, would strengthen the state and people's trust in it.[81] (Although the state budget did not allow for massive hiring, many students received post-graduation internships in government ministries.)

Not all the founders of the University of Hargeisa Faculty of Law (also called College of Law) agreed with the curriculum dictated by UNDP, but their objections were overruled. According to those involved, "Most of people here wanted shari'a and Arabic language," but an American consultant with experience in Kenya who led the effort on behalf of UNDP wanted the University of Hargeisa's curriculum to match those of Nairobi and Kenyatta universities.

> We discussed it. We said, 'We must be wider [than the Kenyan curriculum] and consider the culture of Somaliland.' Arabic is important. Since judges will be using *ahkam* [Arabic: rulings], fiqh, and the Qur'an, we wanted the name, 'Faculty of Law and Shari'a.' But [the American

---

[80] Follow-up interview 64 with Khalid, lawyer and university lecturer in Hargeisa, Somaliland (July 2013).
[81] Interview 58 with Hussein, university lecturer and former judge in Hargeisa, Somaliland (July 2013).

consultant] said, '[No,] the curriculum should be compatible with Nairobi.'[82]

The four-year curriculum's emphasis was on English common law, taught in English. Three courses were taught in Arabic and Somali: Islamic jurisprudence (usul al-fiqh), Islamic succession and inheritance, and Arabic language. The curriculum confined shari'a to family law disputes, just as colonial and Somali state law had done. A senior professor at the university told me that the Faculty of Law is purposely not called a "Faculty of Shari'a and Law," as in other Muslim-majority contexts, in part because its curriculum is mixed – dealing with domestic and international law – and in part because the university had already opened a faculty of Islamic studies.[83]

Somalis I met mentioned that three legal orders co-exist in Somaliland – shari'a, state law largely derived from European colonialism and interactions with contemporary aid agencies, and the locally binding rulings of elders, aqils, and sultans. At the University of Hargeisa, the law faculty largely trains students in state law derived from colonial sources, while minimizing the study of Islam and ignoring the local rulings of elders and aqils. The four-year undergraduate law degree curriculum is approximately 30 percent general education (e.g., courses in Somali literature, English language, and computer skills). The remaining 70 percent is devoted to the law major, split between domestic law and international law (60 percent) and shari'a (10 percent). All first-year students must take an Introduction to Laws course that provides historical background on the Somali legal system and its diverse sources – laws and rulings made by government, elders, and sheikhs. Students then take a range of courses related to English common law, including criminal law and procedure, civil law and procedure, contract law, maritime law, commercial law, and constitutional law. Students may also take up to three courses in shari'a – al-dhamaan (Islamic tort), al-ahwal al-shakhsiyya (personal status/family law), and al-mirath (succession).

Following four years of coursework, a one-year internship is required to register as a practicing lawyer with the Ministry of Justice, which keeps an official roll of licensed lawyers. A one-year internship with the judiciary is necessary to register as a judge. The result is that many new lawyers are better prepared to practice in state courts than to understand

---

[82] Interview 58 with Hussein, university lecturer and former judge in Hargeisa, Somaliland (July 2013).
[83] Follow-up interview 11 with Faris, professor and government official in Hargeisa, Somaliland (June 2013).

the intricacies of Islamic law. One person lamented to me that "Many lawyers ... are lacking the shari'a component" in their understanding of procedures and traditions.[84] Resort to Somaliland's district (lower) courts, which use shari'a for family matters, is more common than to the regional, appellate and supreme courts, which means that law students are trained best for the rarer work even within state courts. Students' lack of training in shari'a is also remarkable because of the prominence of shari'a in other parts of Somaliland's pluralistic legal system.

While the University of Hargeisa's first class of law students included some fresh out of secondary school, many men in their fifties and sixties working in Somaliland's government also enrolled. They were politicians building the nascent state while attending law school. According to one of the class members, the law school "was ... for Parliamentarians."[85] Their fees were paid by UNDP. Courses taught political leaders to learn global legal norms and limit potential government excesses, thus creating bulwarks for the rule of law. According to one professor, "Most of our [early students] learn[ed] the law to participate in [state] politics. If you are a lawyer, you will be a successful politician [and] you know you cannot go beyond the laws."[86] By the time of its 2006 graduation, the inaugural class included people who were also senior government ministers, judges, and elders.

After 2002, UN agencies began replicating the University of Hargeisa's legal education program by helping launch new universities and law faculties across Somaliland, including in Ammoud and Burao. Private universities were also established, as more Somalis sought higher education. Once other law faculties were built, they needed students. A culture of skepticism and mistrust endured, as state courts used criminal and civil codes inherited from colonial rule. To counteract prejudices about the legal system and attract students, the University of Hargeisa law faculty began to hold "legal awareness" trainings and seminars for judges on the new legal programs.[87] As UNDP increased its funding of scholarships, law school class sizes increased. Law degrees helped graduates secure jobs in government

[84] Follow-up interview 69 with Axmed, lawyer and university lecturer in Hargeisa, Somaliland (June 2013).
[85] Interview 113 with Majed, legal aid attorney in Hargeisa, Somaliland (June 2014).
[86] Follow-up interview 64 with Khalid, lawyer and university lecturer in Hargeisa, Somaliland (July 2013).
[87] Follow-up interview 11 with Faris, professor and government official in Hargeisa, Somaliland (June 2013).

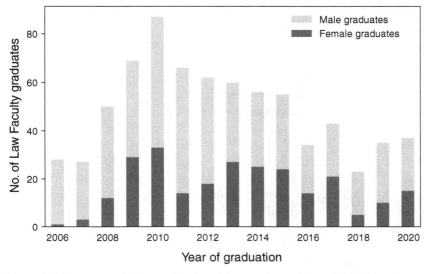

Figure 5.2 University of Hargeisa Faculty of Law graduates (through 2020).
Source: Compiled by the author using data from the University of Hargeisa Faculty of Law.

and with aid agencies. By 2020, the University of Hargeisa had graduated 732 law students – 481 men and 251 women (Figure 5.2).

Law graduates I met in Somaliland offered diverse reasons for going to law school. One person said that he realized that law and courts were not just about crimes and "bad people," but about helping "the state."[88] Others saw Somaliland's politicians work to stabilize society and the economy after the civil war, so they studied law because of its relevance to politics.[89] (University of Hargeisa does not offer a degree in politics, but in 2013 it launched a master's degree in international relations, in which I taught research methods as a visiting professor in 2014.) Others told me they chose law school to help the poor or become human rights activists. Some of them would have preferred to study medicine, psychology, or sociology, but found these degree programs neither feasible nor cost-effective. Such programs were still emerging and required more years of study; their graduates were also less employable given that work for aid groups was generally most

---

[88] Follow-up interview 70 with Kabir, lawyer and senior university administrator in Hargeisa, Somaliland (July 2013).
[89] Interview 4 with Adnan, law graduate from Somaliland in London, England (June 2013).

lucrative. Such students saw law as the best option for getting a job or consultancy with an aid group.[90]

One person said his motivation to attend law school was to learn the Islamic and Western origins of Somaliland's legal system in order to integrate shari'a and law.[91] Others said they studied law because of the UNDP scholarships they received; the organization gave most of these scholarships to women to increase their numbers in the legal profession. As aqils, sheikhs, and sultans, men are the main dispute resolvers in Somaliland, and UNDP sought to give women a way into state courts. Others chose to attend law school precisely because they felt Islam demanded it. "Shari'a says you should learn every subject," one law graduate told me, contrary to public perceptions that studying law means disrespecting "traditional laws and Islamic shari'a."[92]

Somali law students face challenges that reveal the tense relationship between shari'a and state law. The decision to study law was rarely easy. Many saw a troubling disconnect between "legitimate" dispute resolution in Islam and "non-legitimate" dispute resolution in state courts, seeing law school as pro-Western and, thus, anti-Muslim. Many consider state law anti-religious because of its colonial and authoritarian legacies and its connections to Western aid organizations. One law graduate admitted to me that people see him as "among those thinking [with] a Western brain."[93] Others were asked if they were studying the Bible or importing Christian law into Somaliland to curtail Islam. "They said you either study shari'a, or not. [My decision to study law] made people uncomfortable," said one graduate from the first graduating class.[94] Another said that people asked him, "There is shari'a, [so] why are you going to secular law?"[95] At the extreme, some students encountered people who saw "the legal [profession] as a way of going to hell" because they think lawyers defend criminals in a way that is inconsistent with the Islamic tradition.[96]

---

[90] Interview 31 with Fadl, lawyer in Hargeisa, Somaliland (June 2013); Interview 113 with Majed, legal aid attorney in Hargeisa, Somaliland (June 2014); Interview 118 with Ismaciil, NGO executive director in Hargeisa, Somaliland (June 2014).

[91] Interview 41 with Khalid, lawyer and university lecturer in Hargeisa, Somaliland (July 2013).

[92] Follow-up interview 64 with Khalid, lawyer and university lecturer in Hargeisa, Somaliland (July 2013).

[93] Follow-up interview 69 with Axmed, lawyer and university lecturer in Hargeisa, Somaliland (June 2013).

[94] Interview 4 with Adnan, law graduate from Somaliland in London, England (June 2013).

[95] Interview 58 with Hussein, university lecturer and former judge in Hargeisa, Somaliland (July 2013).

[96] Interview 31 with Fadl, lawyer in Hargeisa, Somaliland (June 2013).

Women have faced particular obstacles. Women's education has long been limited in Somaliland. In the 1950s and 1960s the two secondary schools in the region were reserved for boys. Hargeisa had one elementary school for girls, and Burao had one intermediate (pre-secondary) boarding school for girls. Girls could not get a secondary education in Somaliland for many years, which prevented many women from attending university.

While some young women lawyers told me family members or friends encouraged them to attend law school, others said they faced a culture that saw law as Western, anti-Muslim, or immoral. Tradition, they said, prevents women from "talking before men," by appearing in court before a judge.[97] People say women "don't have *akhlaq* [Arabic: morals]" if they study law and that women lawyers are abandoning their "culture, [which means] you do not have dignity."[98] Another woman, who told me she studied law to become a human rights activist, said that many people questioned her decision to go to law school: "It's Western law [and] you are a Muslim. That's not good for our country." She said she had to remind those people that the primary sources of shari'a – the Qur'an and the Hadith – encourage education. She summarized why she studied law: "I want to support my Islamic religion [and] I want to be an educated woman . . . Our Islamic religion encourages us to learn."[99]

The problem of legal pluralism that plagued the University of Mogadishu Faculty of Law curriculum decades earlier continued to plague the law school curriculum in Somaliland. Retention of old laws, including from the era of Siad Barre, exacerbated this problem. One professor told me, "The criminal procedure I'm teaching here is from 1960, but everything has changed."[100] Because of Somaliland's vestiges of British colonial rule, many law books are from the UK and long since outdated. Perhaps for these reasons, students and graduates I met refer to shari'a as "more advanced" than state law.[101]

The question of whether to teach students shari'a, state law, or a combination presents acute challenges. Newer law schools in Somaliland are adopting a different approach – teaching shari'a together with state law in an attempt to co-opt shari'a. An administrator from Borama University in Somaliland told me he felt "UNDP

---

[97] Interview 38 with Fatima, lawyer and aid worker in Hargeisa, Somaliland (July 2013).
[98] Interview 43 with Khadija, legal aid attorney in Hargeisa, Somaliland (July 2013).
[99] Interview 47 with Jamila, NGO executive director in Hargeisa, Somaliland (July 2013).
[100] Interview 20 with Akifah, lawyer and university lecturer in Hargeisa, Somaliland (June 2013).
[101] Interview 100 with Hassan, legal aid attorney and former police official in Hargeisa, Somaliland (June 2014).

prefers these things together, like our Faculty of Law and Shari'a."[102] The goal of combining Western forms of state law with shari'a is to "establish ... a rule of law where [state] law is supreme," a senior government official and University of Hargeisa law graduate admitted.[103] Some lamented that it was "a pity" that UNDP backers did not consider teaching shari'a as important as teaching state law.[104]

Some Somalis wished to integrate shari'a more fully into legal education because "You must know [both] shari'a and formal law" to resolve disputes in Somaliland.[105] Others hoped that the UN officials would be convinced of the local importance of shari'a: "We are one hundred percent Muslim. [Shari'a] is good for us. Our judges and young professionals need to know about [both] the codified legal system and shari'a."[106] A sheikh said he aimed to "teach [university students] Islamic and secular studies together."[107] One person's hopes for Somaliland rested with its law faculties, that, over the long term, would graduate people who "will be conversant with shari'a ... and ... have ... a better understanding of statutory laws."[108]

Legal Aid

During my fieldwork, I spent time with legal aid organizations that help the poor access state courts or file claims; I observed lawyers and paralegals in their organizations' offices and court appearances. I found remarkable the ways in which lawyers trained in Somaliland's law schools tried to harmonize state law, shari'a, and local custom in their minds and practices. Some legal aid lawyers took cases before regional courts, which rule according to state law in contract, crime, and personal injury. But many of the legal aid lawyers I met also took cases before district courts, where their clients sought to resolve family disputes and judges were meant to rule according to Islamic family law. Legal aid lawyers told me the majority of their clients

---

[102] Interview 126 with Dhahir, senior university administrator in Borama, Somaliland (conducted in Hargeisa, Somaliland) (June 2014).

[103] Follow-up interview 68 with Faisal, senior government official in Hargeisa, Somaliland (July 2013).

[104] Follow-up interview 69 with Axmed, lawyer and university lecturer in Hargeisa, Somaliland (June 2013).

[105] Follow-up interview 64 with Khalid, lawyer and university lecturer in Hargeisa, Somaliland (July 2013).

[106] Interview 58 with Hussein, university lecturer and former judge in Hargeisa, Somaliland (July 2013).

[107] Interview 127 with Sheikh Oweis, sheikh and senior university administrator in Hargeisa, Somaliland (June 2014).

[108] Interview 5 with Na'im, lawyer and legal consultant in England (conducted by telephone from London, England) (June 2013).

in the district courts were women bringing cases against spouses and former spouses on behalf of themselves and their children, since these women felt they had little chance of success in customary dispute resolution practices dominated by men.

The University of Hargeisa Faculty of Law and a handful of local lawyers' associations organized legal aid programs. By encouraging people to take their disputes to state courts rather than to elders or sheikhs, such programs were making the courts into a separate and parallel system, partially linked to shari'a and partially abandoning it. The University of Hargeisa's legal aid clinic opened in 2003, with an office on campus and another across the road from Hargeisa's courthouses. The name was changed to "legal aid services" after Somalis complained that the word "clinic" suggested the clients were sick people. In 2007, on the recommendation of a consultant from Harvard University visiting on behalf of the United Nations, legal aid became a permanent part of the law faculty's curriculum. The legal aid course became mandatory in students' third year so they would gain practical experience before returning to their remaining coursework in the final year.[109]

Many returned to the clinics after graduation to work as paid professionals in legal aid, where their salaries were funded by UN agencies and they could realize humanitarian impulses by helping the poor. One person said, "I knew my people [were] poor [and did not] know the law. Also there were vulnerable groups [who] don't have anyone to help them [and] look [out] for their rights."[110] The opportunity to help vulnerable persons access legally guaranteed rights – particularly people who had been convicted of minor crimes but kept in prison for long periods of time without legal support – was crucial for such legal aid workers. Though state law seemed to dominate legal aid programs, I even met sheikhs who moonlighted as legal aid lawyers.

United Nations agencies have funded legal aid programs throughout Somaliland to build trust in the court system, particularly among the poor, because "there is no confidence in the courts," as one attorney told me.[111] United Nations activity reports from Somaliland explain that legal aid attorneys were trying to solve this problem by holding judges to high standards of legal training while providing legal

---

[109] Interview 58 with Hussein, university lecturer and former judge in Hargeisa, Somaliland (July 2013).
[110] Interview 43 with Khadija, legal aid attorney in Hargeisa, Somaliland (July 2013).
[111] Interview 14 with Maxamed, independent researcher and consultant in Hargeisa, Somaliland (June 2013).

representation to those who could not afford it.[112] In practice, the state courts become just another forum for dispute resolution, competing with the activities of nonstate actors like sheikhs, aqils, and community leaders. If people are not happy with a result and they have the time, finances, and energy, they may go elsewhere for a better result.

The new legal aid offices that opened in the 2000s faced important challenges. First among these was Somaliland's proliferation of bar associations that competed with one another to attract new graduates and aid dollars channeled into the legal aid programs. Very few lawyers entered private practice. Another challenge has been the fragmentation of the legal profession along gender, age, and training lines. Younger lawyers trained primarily at the University of Hargeisa were most active in the university's legal aid clinic, while older lawyers were most active in the Somaliland Lawyers Association legal aid clinic and women worked largely with the Somaliland Women Lawyers Association legal aid clinic. Legal aid efforts funded by UN agencies or international NGOs have thus not only widened the gap between state courts and nonstate forms of dispute resolution, but also entrenched a generational and gender divide among lawyers.

Legal aid attorneys experienced the tensions between shari'a and state law in multiple ways. The attorneys I met felt that Somalis thought the legal aid programs were "spreading secular law" because of UN agencies' involvement.[113] But people also told me that "As long as these people [in UN agencies] are not intervening in Islam or religion, it's okay for them to be here" to help.[114] Aid organizations did not try to denigrate Islam, although some individuals might have. Rather, aid agencies' promotion of state courts aimed to ensure that dispute resolution remained as much as possible in the hands of the state, restricting interpretation of shari'a to the district court judges and separating them from aqils, sultans, and sheikhs.

One young attorney justified her work by saying that it was "the right thing" in Islam to help "people who cannot access justice," consistent with UN prescriptions. But there were boundaries to these sentiments. In this attorney's case, when she saw her supervising attorney defend a person who had murdered someone, she "felt sorry, upset, [and]

---

[112] United Nations Development Programme, "Quarterly Update – July 2005," Report of UNDP Somalia, July 31, 2005, https://bit.ly/39RRP4x (accessed January 1, 2021).

[113] Interview 58 with Hussein, university lecturer and former judge in Hargeisa, Somaliland (July 2013).

[114] Interview 89 with Sheikh Abdirahman, sheikh and senior government official in Hargeisa, Somaliland (June 2014).

shameful."[115] From that day onward, she stopped attending court cases, worrying that Allah would not forgive her, either in this life or in *al-akhirah* (Arabic: the afterlife), for offending Islam. For many legal aid attorneys, what mattered was that they were working with Islamic legal principles. One legal aid attorney told me she preferred to work on shari'a-oriented cases in the district courts "because we are a Muslim country and we have to apply what our God says and . . . solve it in our daily life."[116]

Legal Reform

Echoing earlier efforts to "harmonize" Somaliland's legal systems, legal reform projects have focused on building the rule of law through three channels: reforming and rebuilding the courts, writing new laws, and training government officials to apply those new laws. These projects also face the challenges posed by people's distrust of state-sponsored dispute resolution. Like legal aid and legal education, legal reform efforts cut against Somali versions of shari'a that see it as God's pre-existing limit on state authority.

Legal reform focuses primarily on the judiciary. Somalis and expatriate aid workers are familiar with Siad Barre's political interest in the judiciary; he had set up special national security courts (Somali: bad-baado) to try people whom the regime accused of attempting to overthrow it. International aid workers are trying to build formal courts but, as one activist told me, "Many people do not trust in these institutions [and their] competence."[117] Others avoid the courts not only because of their political history but also because they might have direct access to state officials who might "happen to be my cousin or my relative or my friend."[118] Legal reform projects aim to counteract this lack of trust in the courts as well as to synthesize the pluralistic legal system by keeping all forms of dispute resolution – shari'a, custom, and state courts – in line with international human rights law.

As under the Siad Barre regime, court reform in contemporary Somaliland is also designed to contain shari'a. Such efforts are no less political than authoritarian projects to align laws with a regime's wishes. A Somali consultant to aid groups in Hargeisa told me that

---

[115] Interview 66 with Aaliyah, independent researcher and former government attorney in Hargeisa, Somaliland (July 2013).

[116] Interview 74 with Ibtisam, legal aid attorney in Hargeisa, Somaliland (July 2013).

[117] Interview 10 with Tahir, NGO executive director in Hargeisa, Somaliland (June 2013).

[118] Interview 33 with Salaam, NGO executive director in Hargeisa, Somaliland (June 2013).

international aid agencies, like UNDP, focus on the "capacity building" of judges precisely to "encourage . . . the courts, not [the] traditional or religious institutions."[119] United Nations agencies proffer an alternative form of dispute resolution centered on the state and human rights. Shari'a is to be made into a separate and subordinate alternative to the courts, if it is to be an alternative at all. Precisely because Somaliland declared itself an Islamic state in its 2001 constitution, it cannot act like one if it wishes to generate foreign support. That is, "because of regional and international issues" – not least the Islamic Courts Union and al-Shabaab in Somalia – Somaliland's courts cannot be seen to be strengthening the state's Islamic foundation, I was told.[120] A proposed legal and judicial reform commission aimed to identify "gaps," including separating "tradition" from the courts and merging Somaliland's different dispute resolution systems under the state's authority.[121] Somaliland toes the line between allowing local, Islam-informed forms of dispute resolution to continue while not embracing Islam too enthusiastically.

While UN agencies and international NGOs have held workshops and commissioned reports on Somaliland's legal system, including the role of religion and tradition, these groups have not sponsored any laws that would advance shari'a. Most aid workers are "not Muslims," and they want Somalis to know "about their rights in international conventions."[122] Similarly, "the ruling elite . . . in Somaliland will not accept" strengthening shari'a, some people told me, because they "want the support of the international community."[123] Although "many are supportive of . . . Islam," they are also worried about "what happened in the south with al-Shabaab."[124]

Legal reform projects limit the power of shari'a by ensuring that courts focus on developing English common law. "British law is not outside these courts," one lawyer told me. He continued, "Outside the courthouses, the [people] use shari'a."[125] If the courts also used shari'a

[119] Interview 14 with Maxamed, independent researcher and consultant in Hargeisa, Somaliland (June 2013).
[120] Interview 119 with Abubakr, NGO finance manager in Hargeisa, Somaliland (June 2014).
[121] Interview 102 with Cabdelcaziz, government agency director in Hargeisa, Somaliland (June 2014).
[122] Interview 62 with Bilan, NGO executive director in Hargeisa, Somaliland (July 2013).
[123] Follow-up interview 96 with Adam, independent researcher and consultant in Hargeisa, Somaliland (June 2014).
[124] Interview 33 with Salaam, NGO executive director in Hargeisa, Somaliland (June 2013).
[125] Follow-up interview 69 with Axmed, lawyer and university lecturer in Hargeisa, Somaliland (June 2013).

directly, then the judiciary "would seem . . . .like a religious institution," which these court reformers want to avoid.[126] According to a foreign aid worker on a UN-funded project, "Donors are not comfortable with shari'a. You cannot appear to be supporting it."[127] Some sheikhs told me about a conference in Somaliland in the mid-2000s to which UNDP invited global experts on Islamic and international law to meet with Somali sheikhs. The delegates agreed by the end of the conference that UNDP and other international actors should help "advance . . . shari'a in Somaliland." Because that call was never implemented, delegates felt UN officials refused to acknowledge shari'a's importance. "UNDP invited experts [here] from all over the world [who agreed] the best thing is to support . . . shari'a. But UNDP is not doing that . . . It is the same like . . . British [colonialism]."[128] Even aid workers told me that projects to reform the judiciary "merely pay lip service to local sensitivities or trying to integrate shari'a."[129]

Legal reform also involved training lawyers, particularly government prosecutors, to work within a judicial system that respects the rule of law. During my fieldwork I observed a training session, led by diaspora Somali lawyers educated overseas, for new prosecutors appointed by the Somaliland Attorney General's office. At the training, a British Somali consultant began by telling the Somalis that "What's going on in the courts is not adequate." With little attention to the procedures and institutional constraints of Somaliland's courts, he invited them to apply British prosecutorial standards for presenting a case and calling witnesses. Prosecutors "must use their responsibility . . . honestly and respect the rights of individuals," one senior government official told me. "If there's no crime, the [accused] must be released."[130] But financial constraints prevented prosecutors from investigating cases. One aid worker who facilitated the training sessions conceded to me that, under Siad Barre, prosecutors "would go to police stations and look at the files," but now they "don't have money to make phone calls . . . How can [they] go to police stations if [they] have no money for petrol?" The courtroom advocacy skills taught in legal reform workshops focused on

[126] Interview 14 with Maxamed, independent researcher and consultant in Hargeisa, Somaliland (June 2013).
[127] Interview 12 with Daniel, expatriate lawyer and NGO program manager in Hargeisa, Somaliland (June 2013).
[128] Interview 52 with Sheikh Zaki, sheikh and former senior judiciary official in Hargeisa, Somaliland (July 2013).
[129] Interview 19 with Jeff, aid worker and consultant in Hargeisa, Somaliland (June 2013).
[130] Interview 67 with Omar, senior government official in Hargeisa, Somaliland (July 2013).

the English common law system with little regard for Somaliland's reality. When I asked the facilitator about it afterward, he explained that he was told to "be careful . . . not [to] tamper with the shari'a."[131]

Another legal reform strategy is writing new laws, including those meant to update outdated laws. Whenever a problem emerges, people told me, a new law about it is drafted. This strategy is not surprising; it was also adopted by the British colonial administration, the early democratic Somali Republic, and Siad Barre's regime. As one government official told me of the treaties between the British and Somalis in the nineteenth century, "The British put . . . agreement[s] on paper [but] the guurti [elders] didn't believe in paper."[132] Siad Barre's regime passed many new laws, including laws to curtail speech and assembly. According to one Somali lawyer, the Siad Barre regime "was a dictatorial system [that] propagated a lot of laws" to enforce its rule.[133] Many people in Somaliland saw law through this historical lens – as a means for the state to shore up its colonial or authoritarian power against the people and against Islam. People thus mistrusted the very process of law writing.

In Somaliland, law-writing involves drafting bills with the assistance of foreign consultants, who sometimes work of their own volition, but mostly at the urging of government officials. The bills they put forward in the 2010s included a land tenure code, a veterinary law, child labor and child protection laws, an NGO registration law, banking and corporate codes, a macduum law, and draft laws on electrical energy, taxation, juvenile justice, parliamentary procedures, presidential elections, local councils, business transactions, electronic transactions, youth and child rights, police, gender and women's rights, licensing lawyers, and legal aid. One Somali told me, "When it comes to formal law, well, there are too many laws."[134] A foreign aid worker agreed, "There's so much law. The solution [to any problem in Somaliland] is to write laws, write laws, write laws." It's an "aesthetic" solution.[135]

---

[131] Interview 109 with Qasim, lawyer and government consultant in Hargeisa, Somaliland (June 2014).

[132] Interview 35 with Cabdulmajid, senior government official in Hargeisa, Somaliland (June 2013).

[133] Follow-up interview 70 with Kabir, lawyer and senior university administrator in Hargeisa, Somaliland (July 2013).

[134] Follow-up interview 93 with Caziz, lawyer and human rights activist in Hargeisa, Somaliland (June 2014).

[135] Interview 19 with Jeff, aid worker and consultant in Hargeisa, Somaliland (June 2013).

Why draft all these laws? Paradoxically, it comes from a perception that there is a lack of law and the state is weak. As one Somali judge told me, people feel "There are not a lot of laws here."[136] According to a consultant whom I met for lunch one day at a Hargeisa hotel frequented by foreign officials and aid workers, "Forty factories have failed in the last two years mostly because of the cost of electricity, and that's directly tied to no [electricity] laws."[137] The idea was that new laws would create predictability, and that predictability would encourage foreign investment.

Aid groups "basically ... parachute in laws," an expatriate lawyer working in Hargeisa told me.[138] Ministries and NGOs work hard to pass these laws because of financial assistance from UN agencies or international NGOs, but that assistance often means the "agenda was set by someone else."[139] In one case, I was told, "The priority least important to the citizens of Somaliland," particularly rural and pastoral communities, "was selected as the priority for donors," which made the effort feel like "a waste of time."[140]

Many aid workers and government officials in Somaliland saw legal reform as necessary because Article 130 of the Somaliland constitution requires the state to apply existing laws – even laws from the Siad Barre regime – until new ones come into force.[141] "Even the monetary value [of criminal penalties] hasn't changed since the 1960s," a foreign consultant told me.[142] The director of a civic organization agreed, in particular about laws that affect women, which "are outdated and need to be changed."[143] New laws, activists felt, would help bring Somaliland in line with the international community. One notable example was the 2018 passage of Somaliland's first law criminalizing rape, though it was later put on moratorium pending review following an outcry by conservative religious leaders.[144]

[136] Interview 58 with Hussein, university lecturer and former judge in Hargeisa, Somaliland (July 2013).
[137] Interview 23 with Rafiq, expatriate consultant in Hargeisa, Somaliland (June 2013).
[138] Interview 30 with Zack, expatriate lawyer in Hargeisa, Somaliland (June 2013).
[139] Interview 33 with Salaam, NGO executive director in Hargeisa, Somaliland (June 2013).
[140] Interview 22 with Shahab, expatriate consultant in Hargeisa, Somaliland (June 2013).
[141] Interview 132 with Cabaas, senior government attorney and minister in Hargeisa, Somaliland (June 2014).
[142] Interview 110 with Kahlil, lawyer and government consultant in Hargeisa, Somaliland (June 2014).
[143] Interview 55 with Fawzia, women's rights activist and former NGO executive director in Hargeisa, Somaliland (June 2013).
[144] Nita Bhalla, "Somaliland Elders Approve 'Historic' Law Criminalising Rape," *Reuters*, April 9, 2018, https://reut.rs/37KZsXS (accessed January 1, 2021).

Although the goal of drafting legislation was to strengthen Somaliland's democracy, lawmakers had little intention of actually implementing the many complex laws imported by foreign consultants. Once bills are passed into law, little happens to raise awareness about them or enforce them. "Many NGOs hire consultants to write a law. The consultant gets paid, then leaves. [But] the Ministry doesn't understand it [and] Parliamentarians weren't consulted. So [the draft law] just sits there," a consultant told me.[145]

Writing laws also includes parallel efforts to codify the decisions of aqils and sultans resolving intercommunal disputes under the rubric of xeer and the decisions of sheikhs and macduum offices. These attempts began as early as the 1970s under Siad Barre, and the international aid community continues them. But many Somalis do not buy it: "You cannot respect the rule drafted by a person over the rule of Allah. They are not the same."[146] They recognize that shari'a rests upon differing and competing interpretations of key texts, rather than on a body of written precedents that remain in force until judges overturn them.

A sheikh I met felt that the efforts of Western aid groups are designed "to destroy Islam." He paused, and looked around him, reflecting on the instability of the region, saying, "You see the result."[147] A university lecturer and consultant told me, "Shari'a is more advanced than the laws we are working [to reform]." Shari'a is "not just an ideal, it is a revelation from God. It has specificity."[148] But the challenge, I was told, is being labeled a "fundamentalist" or an "Islamist." An American aid worker agreed, telling me that "Shari'a is the one [legal order] that gets minimized the most [by aid workers]." He concluded, sarcastically, "That's the easiest to do ... besides the little detail that everyone believes in it."[149]

While the aid community and their supporters work to revise or write new laws, Somalis are also reframing existing laws to show how they are consistent with Islam. A legal aid attorney told me that Somaliland did not have far to go, as "Most of the articles [in civil law] are ... even based on [shari'a, including] the family law, inheritance, rent, and

---

[145] Interview 23 with Rafiq, expatriate consultant in Hargeisa, Somaliland (June 2013).

[146] Interview 14 with Maxamed, independent researcher and consultant in Hargeisa, Somaliland (June 2013).

[147] Interview 52 with Sheikh Zaki, sheikh and former senior judiciary official in Hargeisa, Somaliland (July 2013).

[148] Interview 100 with Hassan, legal aid attorney and former police official in Hargeisa, Somaliland (June 2014).

[149] Interview 19 with Jeff, aid worker and consultant in Hargeisa, Somaliland (June 2013).

business transactions."[150] Among the first laws passed by Somaliland was the Environmental Conservation and Protection Act of 1998, which is the foundation of the work of Somaliland's Ministry of Environment. Senior government officials told me that this law is based on Islamic principles, not state principles.

> Shariʿa will never tell you to cut [down] a forest. It's illegal in shariʿa [to cut down trees unless] you . . . replant. People should know that if you cut a tree you should plant another . . . The forest belongs to God . . . and our natural resources are God-given, *hamdillah* [Arabic: thank God]. You cannot cut [trees] indiscriminately and transport charcoal from Sanaag [the forested region of Somaliland] to Arabia and . . . Turkey.[151]

Sheikhs also have spoken about protecting the environment in their sermons, referencing verses from the Qur'an rather than the 1998 law.

Somalis are also working on enforcement of the rule of law through Islamic mechanisms related to hopes and fears about the Day of Judgment. For Somalis, UN-funded efforts to build the rule of law cannot stand up to the power of Islam to limit corruption and hold government actors to account. Even though "there is no confidence in the courts," one young civic activist in Hargeisa told me, "if you say a verse [of the Qur'an] to the most corrupt person [in government], he will stop."[152] To these Somalis, the principles that Western legal scholars would associate with the rule of law, to limit corruption or abuse of power, derive from shariʿa, not from government.

Legal reform projects in Somaliland caused confrontations over the relationship between Islamic law, state law, and international law. The major flashpoints according to those I met were differences between Islamic and international law on freedom of expression, women's rights, and criminal penalties. "If you want to transplant a Western state into Somaliland, [it] will create a conflict in terms of law . . . The problem [is that] the West doesn't understand shariʿa."[153] The result is confusion about the different aspects or pivots of Somaliland's legal orders, how to name them, and the meaning and sources of law. The Somaliland government's proposals for creating a "shura council" or "ulema

---

[150] Interview 100 with Hassan, legal aid attorney and former police official in Hargeisa, Somaliland (June 2014).
[151] Interview 122 with Xidig, government minister in Hargeisa, Somaliland (June 2014).
[152] Interview 14 with Maxamed, independent researcher and consultant in Hargeisa, Somaliland (June 2013).
[153] Interview 32 with Axmed, lawyer and university lecturer in Hargeisa, Somaliland (June 2013).

commission" that would review legislation for consistency with shari'a aimed at building an Islamic state. But they, too, would ensure that Islamic authority is vested in the state rather than outside it, thereby earning state law some legitimacy.

Some Somalis wanted a different kind of court reform altogether, one that encouraged judges to learn shari'a more deeply. Better knowledge of shari'a would hold to account "lawyers who are unfaithful [and] judges [who] take bribes," I was told.[154] "If the constitution is based on shari'a [then] judges should be interpreting shari'a, of course," one lawyer said of his hopes for legal reform.[155]

Despite investments in Western-style legal education, many young women and men in Somaliland told me they would like to work more directly with Islamic and traditional sources. Despite investments in legal aid projects, many people continue to seek out sheikhs in mac-duum offices to resolve their disputes. Finally, despite investments in legal reform, many people I met did not understand the purpose of building state law when shari'a already encompassed these matters and Somaliland already defined itself as Islamic.

CONCLUSION

The history of colonial, authoritarian, and humanitarian interventions in Somaliland reveals a space fragmented not only by warfare and slaughter, but also by a discursive battle between different approaches to law, between foreign law and Islamic law, between customary law and human rights law, and between international law and Islamic law. In the short term, many tried to create an Islamic state that paradoxi-cally sidelined Islam. In the long term, these battles are in part about whose visions of tradition, modernity, and shari'a will prevail. They are also about the repeated imposition of state power in the lives of Somalis.

In this context, an array of actors sought to build the law in the 2010s. International aid workers tried to construct dispute resolution offices across Somaliland and convince Somalis to use them. The government drafted a bill to put sheikhs' private macduum offices under its purview. Aqils and sultans continued to use a combination

---

[154] Interview 49 with Babiker, university administrator and lecturer in Hargeisa, Somaliland (July 2013).

[155] Interview 81 with Warsame, lawyer and adviser to the Transitional Federal Government of Somalia (conducted in Nairobi, Kenya) (August 2013).

of custom, precedent, compensation schemes, and shari'a to keep peace after disputes within their communities. All these actors contended with Somaliland's radical legal pluralism as they tried to promote their own versions of legal progress. The result is a fragmented set of legal reform projects in which foreigners and state representatives try to keep the power of law in the hands of the state while others maintain that law is for all, including those sheikhs who interpret and apply shari'a to resolve people's disputes with one another.

This chapter has revealed how few have done more to promote shari'a in Somaliland than those whom Western observers might typically deem its least likely allies – people fighting dictatorship and trying to build peace and constitutional democracy. From the start, Somaliland's state-builders in the 1990s saw shari'a as a source of hopeful change from God. Somalis continue to turn to sheikhs every day, particularly when they consider state courts slow or untrustworthy. "The people," as one lawyer told me, "would like to see a state that is based on shari'a."[156] After all, as a sheikh recounted, "The whole of Hargeisa [was] demolished [in the 1980s civil war because] the people were asking for something. They were using 'Allahu Akbar' [God is great] and ... shari'a when they were fighting Siad Barre." Not to base the state on shari'a would destroy people's hope for a sustainable peace, he continued, "steal[ing] the feeling of the people."[157] Shari'a remains a powerful force in daily life and in government as Somaliland establishes and develops its own Islamic state.

Somaliland's political elites – state officials, elders, and sheikhs – fight for legitimacy by promoting their own versions of shari'a. Given their religious training, sheikhs are perhaps the most prominent among them. But relationships among sheikhs have also broken down over their wealth, ideologies, and how to interpret text and tradition, causing some people to lose trust in them. Most sheikhs follow some variation of the Shafi'i school of Sunni Islamic law, long established in the Horn of Africa. Some belong to Sufi *tariqas* (brotherhoods) that promote spiritual practices and a closeness with God. Others, particularly younger sheikhs trained by Salafi groups in Saudi Arabia, disapprove of Sufi mysticism and call for narrow or literal interpretations of religious texts. Some sheikhs also have ties to the Muslim Brotherhood,

---

[156] Interview 32 with Axmed, lawyer and university lecturer in Hargeisa, Somaliland (June 2013).

[157] Interview 127 with Sheikh Oweis, sheikh and senior university administrator in Hargeisa, Somaliland (June 2014).

a political and religious movement founded in Egypt. By preaching publicly, advising government officials, or helping people resolve disputes, each sheikh hopes that his own views will win over Somaliland's communities and the state itself. But, in practical terms, sheikhs do not have a monopoly over the interpretation of God's will. Building on the descriptive data provided here, the Chapter 6 shows how contemporary activists in Somaliland also champion their own ideal shari'a, one that is consistent with their hopes of achieving women's rights.

Somaliland (national border as claimed by Somaliland),
1991–present.

CHAPTER SIX

RECLAIMING SHARI'A:
WOMEN'S ACTIVISM IN SOMALILAND

For centuries men have dominated Somali families, states, and the law, serving as the aqils, the sultans, and the leaders of the colonial and state governments, militant groups, clans, elders' councils, and religious orders described in the previous chapters. Taking up and using the same religious and legal tools as those men, women activists struggling for rights have sowed a different understanding of shari'a that they hope, inshallah, Somalis will follow. Certainly some women have been involved in co-opting law and religion to reinforce patriarchy or militancy – as informants, foot soldiers, or security agents. But other women have been fighting male domination too. Their efforts combine sincerity, strategy, and symbolism and, like other state and nonstate actors in this book, they have turned shari'a into a form of legal politics.

In 2019, I met with Asha, a university lecturer in her forties who volunteers with civic groups, in a hotel lobby in Hargeisa. Asha had memorized the Qur'an at a young age and, during her adulthood, she taught herself Islamic philosophy and memorized volumes of the Hadith (detailed records of the Prophet Muhammad's statements, actions, and tacit approvals). In other countries, Asha would have held the title of *sheikha* (female sheikh), but local norms prevented women like her from becoming publicly visible religious leaders like men with similarly extensive knowledge of Islam. As we sipped our tea, Asha expressed disappointment over misogynistic interpretations of shari'a that restricted women's roles. She recounted how some politicians in Somaliland have used a statement attributed to the Prophet Muhammad – "A people [or nation] assigning a woman to handle their affairs will not prosper" – to argue that shari'a prohibits women from serving as political leaders. But Asha interpreted this Hadith differently. The Prophet was not speaking about all women, Asha told me, but instead about the narrow context of one monarch, the Queen of Kisra, who had ordered the execution of Muslims. Asha added that one of the Prophet Muhammad's last actions before he died was entrusting the distribution of the Qur'an and the message of Islam to a woman, Aisha, his wife. Such interpretations of religious texts suggested to Asha that it is acceptable for Muslim women to enter politics and lead nations.

Women in Somaliland have joined a long struggle in Islamic discourse over the meaning of shari'a. Islam's decentralization has demanded that people study the sources of shari'a, including the Qur'an and the Hadith. Debates abound over which interpretations are valid. By showing that a given theological text may be interpreted in less patriarchal ways, Somali women shatter myths that men own shari'a and its analysis. But they face the inflexibility of political and religious leaders and everyday Somalis who see women as spectators, not participants, in the interpretation of shari'a.

Some Somali women are generating feminist and religious knowledge, which is not uncommon in Islamic history and other Muslim-majority societies. Islamic history, for instance, counts women sheikhs as among the most important and well-regarded transmitters and preservers of the Hadith, from Islam's earliest days, when women delivered their own lectures and issued their own *ijazat* (Arabic: diplomas) to students. But because women's perspectives have become marginalized, their knowledge is no longer authenticated. Somali feminist activists must position their work so that they do not antagonize either Somalis who see feminist work as anti-religious or Western feminists and aid workers who see religious work as anti-feminist. According to some activists I met, Western feminists seem to fight patriarchy and religion, but Somali feminists fight only patriarchy.

Activists in Somali society must carefully navigate a historical mem-ory in which feminism is closely associated with authoritarian power and thought to be against Islam. Their repertoire of activism is built on piety but also on a strategy of survival given their knowledge of the political context in which they operate. They are creating space for feminist discourse to filter into Islam and Islamic discourse to find its way into feminism. Women activists have also found themselves caught between two disparate groups: the contemporary (foreign) fun-ders they need for financial support and the male sheikhs they need for scholarly support. Understanding how these women move – strategi-cally, symbolically, and piously – in that fraught terrain is crucial for illuminating how feminist activists in Muslim-majority states organize.

What are the implications of this argument that women activists in Somaliland have promoted an Islamic feminism that casts aside Western discourses of human rights? It means that women activists are not only turning to Islam out of piety to build notions of equality and dignity. They also do it out of strategy. This does not mean they do not believe. On the contrary, many of them are putting their beliefs to work, reclaiming shari'a because they recognize the inability of political leaders and international aid groups to come up with the solutions women need. For these women activists, belief and strategy are not mutually exclusive or even inconsistent.

In legally plural contexts, war can disrupt gender hierarchies and create space for women to access state law.[1] In Somaliland, the devel-opment of a new state after the civil war also created space for women activists to promote a post-patriarchal version of shari'a. These activists are sophisticated, educated, urban women who work on a paid or voluntary basis, primarily in Hargeisa. They are knowledgeable and skilled enough to engage with Islamic texts and to promote a shari'a consciousness that reflects women's concerns. Such activists constitute a minority of women in Somaliland, most of whom live in poor, rural areas where *xeer* (Somali custom) is the controlling law and who thus do not have full access to discourses of shari'a. Since Somaliland's reassertion of sovereignty in 1991, women activists have adopted a strategy oriented toward, rather than away from, shari'a.

Activists' efforts to recast women's rights as a core concern of shari'a counter the interventions of international lawyers, foreign diplomats,

---

[1] Egor Lazarev, "Laws in Conflict: Legacies of War, Gender, and Legal Pluralism in Chechnya," 71 (4) *World Politics* (2019): 667–709.

and Western feminists who see Islam as regressive or bad for women and who, instead, promote secular human rights law. But Somali women activists' have a vision of shari'a redemptive and flexible enough to accommodate women's needs in society, law, and politics and built on the goal of achieving equality and dignity for women, which they see as the starting point for any promise of limited government and the rule of law. Their strategy involves educating people that shari'a allows Muslims to take different positions on the same issues, and it resembles the strategies of women's groups in other Muslim-majority areas. In Malaysia, Sisters in Islam has invoked shari'a since its founding in 1987, despite facing lawsuits and a fatwa (religious ruling) against the organization. According to Tamir Moustafa, embracing shari'a was the activists' acknowledgment of the "limitations of ... courts."[2] In Egypt, sophisticated activists also advanced new readings of shari'a that challenged patriarchal interpretations of family law. According to Hind Ahmed Zaki, framing women's activism with shari'a rather than with international human rights conventions helped expand women's access to divorce in Egypt.[3]

While the activists I met in Somaliland have not succeeded in displacing patriarchy, they are the deep thorns that pierce patriarchy's side. They accept the historical reality of men's political and religious power. But they also understand that men have attained their authority from patriarchal laws of the state, custom, and Islam that those same men have long declared inflexible. Though women activists advocate with government officials, they also know that any laws passed in their favor are unlikely to be implemented or followed on a wide scale, given the state's weaknesses. And xeer, based on centuries of precedents by men, will also be slow to change. But the malleability of religious principles and shari'a's multiplicity of interpretations have drawn activists to advocate for their understanding of God's will in order to change society from its roots. Activists struggling for the rights of women have thus allocated their labor and discursive resources to promoting an alternative narrative of shari'a that adequately reflects women's concerns.

This chapter draws on fieldwork and a subset of 52 of my 142 qualitative interviews in Somaliland during my visits in 2013, 2014,

---

[2] Tamir Moustafa, *Constituting Religion: Islam, Liberal Rights, and the Malaysian State* (Cambridge: Cambridge University Press, 2018), 136.

[3] Hind Ahmed Zaki, "Law, Culture, and Mobilization: Legal Pluralism and Women's Access to Divorce in Egypt," 14(1) *Muslim World Journal of Human Rights* (2017): 1–25.

and 2019. These interviews provide a way of seeing into the experiences and efforts of women activists since the 1990s. I met with women lawyers and civic activists, along with sheikhs, government officials, and elders targeted by their activism. My efforts to get to know their stories form a case study of how and why activists use shari'a to fight patriarchy. Activists often cycle through multiple discourses, or frames, for their contestation – rights-oriented, religion-oriented, or a combination – and women in Somaliland are no exception. Over the years they have brought their concerns to colonial, democratic, socialist, and authoritarian leaderships, shifting tones under each political context. Since Somaliland's 1991 reassertion of sovereignty, they have, at different times, championed shari'a for varying, and sometimes overlapping, reasons, primarily (1) to distinguish themselves from the former Siad Barre dictatorship, which executed sheikhs opposed to the regime's women's rights legislation; (2) to obtain the support of male sheikhs, especially those whose preaching is widely heard and trusted; (3) to limit the influence of customary law, which makes fewer resources available to women than to men and results in harsher judgments than shari'a for women seeking rights; and (4) to express a sincere belief in God's will. Just as with male authorities, shari'a activism for women's rights emerges from a combination of piety and strategy. In the process, activists reserve the discourses of international law and principles of human rights largely for their communications with and reports to foreign donors.

Activists fighting for women's rights in Somaliland see God's will as both a source of hope and a source of frustration – for men in power often call upon shari'a to oppose women's rights, while international feminists and lawyers abandon it to promote secular versions of rights. To make this argument, this chapter proceeds in three parts. The first part explains feminism's fraught place in Somali political history, and how a turn to international law has provided important material and financial resources to women's groups but not the discursive legitimacy necessary for challenging patriarchy. The second part describes why women activists see shari'a as supporting their social and political goals. The third part details how the activists use shari'a to advocate for educating girls, setting a minimum quota for women in parliament, and ending female genital mutilation, forced marriage, and sexual violence. While shari'a has long been a tool for male domination of Somali politics, women activists in Somaliland have used that same tool in their struggle against patriarchy.

LEGACIES OF PATRIARCHY

Modern history in the Horn of Africa is marked by attempts and failures to build the rule of law or even a lasting, recognizable state. Across this history, men have been the dominant actors. Colonial administrators, authoritarian leaders, judges from the Islamic Courts Union, the war-lords they fought and the militant groups that emerged from their demise all used shari'a discourse to achieve their goals. International donors armed with aid and foreign militaries armed with weapons have also seen shari'a as religious law largely incompatible with their goals. Somaliland's state officials, sheikhs, and elders, too, have promoted their own versions of shari'a to build stability, peace, and a sovereignty that they hope one day will be recognized internationally. In calling God's will to their sides, and in largely denying political leadership to women, these men also reinforced patriarchy and made Islam the dominant expression of their patriarchal system.

Somalis I met often mentioned the treatment of women as an important difference between British and Italian colonial rule. While British officials were trading in livestock, Italians were settling, creating an Italian Riviera of sorts on the Horn of Africa's lush eastern coast. According to Somalis, Italian men "came with their mafias"[4] and "intermingle[d] ... and married Somali women."[5] Because the British did not "intermingle" with Somali women, many Somalis I met felt the British, particularly through the treaties they signed with Somali elders, had "respected the culture" in a way that Italian colonists had not.[6] Echoing others I met in the region who spoke of the legacies of Italian colonialism, one Somali activist said simply: "They came, they married, and they had [mixed-race] babies."[7] These sentiments gesture to women's long being seen not as bearers of rights and liberties but as a kind of politicized possession or medium for colonial contestation between Somali men and foreigners.

Although women were involved in the struggle for decolonization in the 1950s, as in other transitional states women's concerns largely took second place as men focused on building national unity.

---

[4] Interview 35 with Cabdulmajid, senior government official in Hargeisa, Somaliland (June 2013).
[5] Interview 124 with Najib, former senior government minister in Hargeisa, Somaliland (June 2014).
[6] Interview 45 with Aqil Zaki Yasim, aqil and senior government official in Hargeisa, Somaliland (July 2013).
[7] Interview 22 with Shahab, expatriate consultant in Hargeisa, Somaliland (June 2013).

Somalia's first constitution, ratified in 1960, provided that men and women would have equal rights and duties.[8] But, according to those I met, few things changed for women during Somalia's democratic period (1960–1969). Somalia received more aid per capita than any other African state, but "Nine years of development projects led to . . . no visible improvement in the standard of living – apart perhaps from the creation of the first generation of millionaires," which left many Somalis with the impression that state authorities focused on lining their own pockets.[9] Thus, "Where some Western observers saw democracy, many Somalis saw corruption, tribalism, indecision, and stagnation," which did not improve women's access to rights.[10]

Siad Barre's military regime promoted women's rights in theory but inhibited their development in practice. On the one hand, in the 1970s and 1980s, Somali women faced grave difficulty discussing politics or engaging in any form activism that could be seen as opposing the regime. As an activist I met said of her experience as a young civil servant at the time, "We did not raise things that would raise problems with government. We could not do that."[11] On the other hand, the regime's 1975 family law, drawn from its professed socialist ideology, promised women inheritance equal to that of their brothers and then executed ten sheikhs who disagreed with the state's position on theological grounds – thus doing long-term damage to the cause of women's rights. The regime's mass execution of religious leaders in the name of gender equality is not lost on contemporary women's rights activists in Somaliland. The episode is seared into their memories; activists I met spoke of the difficulty of addressing women's concerns given a historical and political context in which women's rights were a feature of authoritarian rule and of interventions to build adherence to foreign – Western or socialist, rather than Islamic – principles.[12]

Following Somaliland's 1991 declaration of independence from Somalia, women's groups had to confront the omnipresent memory of the Siad Barre regime. Women I met who were involved in equality

[8] Article 3 of the 1960 Constitution of the Somali Republic provides for this equality: "All citizens, without distinction of race, national origin, birth, language, religion, sex, economic or social status, or opinion, shall have equal rights and duties before the law."
[9] David D. Laitin, "Revolutionary Change in Somalia," 62 *Middle East Research and Information Project Reports* (1977b): 6–18, p. 7.
[10] Ibid.
[11] Follow-up interview 139 with Fawzia, women's rights activist and former NGO executive director in Hargeisa, Somaliland (March 2019).
[12] Interview 17 with Amburo, former senior government minister and United Nations official in Hargeisa, Somaliland (June 2013).

activism said Somalis viewed feminist campaigns with suspicion, as if the campaigners were "working for what ... that [Siad Barre] regime [did]," in other words, advocating for the killing of religious men.[13] These accusations are met with further charges that, by promoting women's concerns, Somali women act as the accomplices of foreign aid groups imposing their Western agenda. Not wishing to risk being seen as shills for anti-Muslim ideologies, women's rights activists have instead been using religious discourse, often by encouraging sheikhs to speak publicly in support of the activists' version of shari'a. Somaliland's women activists have been caught between sheikhs whose support they feel they need, state leaders who do not support feminism, and an international aid community whose views of feminism either sideline or eschew Islam entirely to achieve a secular rule of law.

Activists struggling for women's rights in Somaliland did not always adopt an Islam-first approach. Such an approach evolved organically, over a generation, out of the ashes of civil war. According to a long-time activist I met, women like her first got involved in providing services to war survivors displaced to encampments in the 1980s and 1990s, as the regime collapsed and warlords seeking territorial control rose in the government's place. Women, largely from educated and middle-class backgrounds in Hargeisa or Mogadishu, formed "self-help groups" in desert encampments to assist wounded persons and "collect money for sick people."[14] As more wounded and sick arrived, more self-help groups emerged, gradually becoming more organized. What began as community service shifted toward advocacy for women's rights in education, politics, and society. International NGOs arrived, too, hoping to alleviate poverty exacerbated by massive drought. Somali women I met learned how these groups were "seek[ing] funds" to help with girls' education and other local needs.[15] With the assistance of these international NGOs, then, the self-help groups conducted their own trainings on how to form organizations; they shared with one another what they learned about "how to [write] a constitution, how to organize meetings," and how to obtain funding from the international aid groups that came to help.[16]

[13] Interview 55 with Fawzia, women's rights activist and former NGO executive director, in Hargeisa, Somaliland (June 2013).
[14] Ibid.
[15] Interview 62 with Bilan, NGO executive director in Hargeisa, Somaliland (July 2013).
[16] Interview 55 with Fawzia, women's rights activist and former NGO executive director, in Hargeisa, Somaliland (June 2013).

But women faced substantial obstacles in daily life, let alone in efforts to organize and participate. First came the 1991 stoning of a woman in Hargeisa for alleged sexual offenses.[17] Later, in 1993, an armed group arrested and charged five women with prostitution and adultery; an ad hoc religious court condemned them to death sentences by stoning. Although the Somali National Movement, which had been in charge at the time, arrested the religious leaders, many Somalis also demanded their release.[18] In addition to these threats to life and liberty, women were being shut out of politics in the newly independent Somaliland. Somaliland's reconciliation summits during the 1990s reserved delegate places almost entirely for men who were elders and community and religious leaders. By 1997, when Somaliland formed its own House of Representatives, women were excluded from office. According to activists I met, Somalis at the time felt women had already achieved their rights under Siad Barre's family law of 1975, which touched off the country's long, slow collapse. An activist recounted that people told her, "You ladies became liberated [under Siad Barre]," in order to stop her activism.[19] The statement implied to her that women's rights had already been tried with devastating results, blaming women for the regime's heinous acts.

Organizing Against Patriarchy

Despite women's long-term political exclusion, the self-help groups they organized in Somaliland grew into more than thirty NGOs by the late 1990s, many of which had their roots in the refugee camps. These groups formed an umbrella organization that coordinated activities and requested and dispersed aid dollars. Proposing international treaties as guides, Western-based aid organizations increased their efforts to support the self-help groups and NGOs in bringing to light Somali women's concerns, including their exclusion from politics. These projects were undertaken with similar zeal in Somalia. As one international lawyer told me, "Frankly speaking, the international community [has] their own checklist and their own perception of democracy and priorities . . . When you work in a post-conflict country,

---

[17] Judith Gardner and Judy El-Bushra, eds., *Somalia – The Untold Story: The War through the Eyes of Somali Women* (London: Pluto Press, 2004), cited in Mark Bradbury, *Becoming Somaliland* (Bloomington: Indiana University Press, 2008), 181.

[18] Amnesty International, "Report 1994 – Somalia (1 January 1994)," https://bit.ly/2WV524I; see also "Human Rights Brief: Women in Somalia" (Immigration and Refugee Board of Canada, 1 April 1994), https://bit.ly/3rC5MK6 (accessed January 1, 2021).

[19] Interview 55 with Fawzia, women's rights activist and former NGO executive director, in Hargeisa, Somaliland (June 2013).

the first thing you want is elections and constitutional development and parliament and ... empowering civil society [on] gender issues."[20]

But leaving Somali women alone was a hallmark that Somalis had used to separate British from Italian colonialism, when Italian settlers had taken Somali women as their wives. To many Somalis, Western aid groups seemed hyper-concerned with Somali women and their bodies, livelihoods, and rights. Such perceptions of Western aid groups' "taking" Somali women, much as Italian colonists had done, affected people's trust in aid agencies. The aid groups became part of an "unbroken chain" – including early Christian missionaries and colonial administrators – in which outsiders and state authorities seek to change Somali women and, by extension, Somali culture.[21] Women activists, then, slide from being vocal advocates for women to being political objects, pawns, and guarantors of local "culture."

Echoing the words of other activists I met, one civic activist told me that Europeans "brought this language of human rights [and] impos[ed]" it upon Somali people.[22] The ideal of gender equality is a key feature of this imposition. As one activist told me, "There are many organizations that work on human rights [and] they [all] emphasize ... gender." "But," this activist continued, "human rights issues are broader than just" gender.[23] Another male activist similarly complained that large donors, including the UNDP, "want women in law, not [in] medicine or [other areas]."[24] Aid workers are seen to be excessively focused on linking gender to the law, just as colonial administrators and the Siad Barre regime were, thus diminishing the work of women's groups by consigning contemporary women's rights activists to a larger "anti-Muslim" category.

A local sultan confirmed what activists were telling me: that the distrust of aid groups comes from their work with women and their shunning of shari'a and local norms. "The only [thing] that we are afraid of is that [foreign aid workers] are intermingling with women," he said. This unease about potential impropriety is directed at aid organizations and the women activists with whom they have professional

---

[20] Interview 134 with Hatim, United Nations official and adviser to the Somali constitution in Mogadishu, Somalia (reached via telephone from Princeton, NJ) (November 2015).

[21] On the unbroken chain of intervention in Africa, from missionaries to colonial administrators and contemporary aid workers, see Makau Mutua, *Human Rights: A Political and Cultural Critique* (Philadelphia, PA: University of Pennsylvania Press, 2002).

[22] Interview 62 with Bilan, NGO executive director in Hargeisa, Somaliland (July 2013).

[23] Interview 119 with Abubakr, NGO finance manager in Hargeisa, Somaliland (June 2014).

[24] Interview 14 with Maxamed, independent researcher and consultant in Hargeisa, Somaliland (June 2013).

relationships. The sultan continued that he felt aid workers' attention to women's issues also disempowered community elders and religious leaders, just as Siad Barre had tried to do. Aid workers "put together traditional and religious," he said, and then they "sideline" them.[25]

Because Western-based NGOs were seen as suspicious at best or anti-Muslim at worst, civic activists I met worried that encouraging women's rights was synonymous with expressing a distaste for Islam. One activist said that Somalis suspicious of Western aid workers believe that because women's organizations "work with international [funding], we are not Islamic."[26] The UNDP's encouragement of principles associated with international human rights law means, to Somalis, that aid groups are discouraging principles associated with shari'a. A Somali consultant in Hargeisa gave me the example of how the aid groups with whom he works "want to ... downplay [the Qur'an] in the administration of justice" by changing the crime-witness requirement that two male witnesses are the same as one male and two female witnesses. In "encouraging gender equality ... [UNDP officials] don't want to see shari'a ... in the courts," he said.[27] Once Somali NGOs picked up these themes, they were tainted with the same anti-Muslim bias that affected aid workers. As one sheikh told me, international aid groups were simultaneously "sidelining shari'a [and] encouraging law."[28] While international law and Western feminism challenged patriarchy, to these Somalis they also seemed to challenge religion.

Aid Workers Stay "On the Safe Side"

When I asked about differences between international law, shari'a, and xeer, most people responded by discussing the problem of sexual assault. According to many xeer precedents, a rape survivor's clan or sub-clan – not the survivor herself – is compensated for the injury. The survivor is then forced by precedent to marry her perpetrator, because her defilement makes her unfit to marry any other man. A European aid worker explained that "Women's rights are ... not respected" because survivors cannot participate in xeer hearings. "It is not individual justice ...

[25] Interview 37 with Sultan Mansoor, sultan in Hargeisa, Somaliland (June 2013).
[26] Interview 125 with Sohir, NGO executive director and women's rights activist in Hargeisa, Somaliland (June 2014).
[27] Interview 14 with Maxamed, independent researcher and consultant in Hargeisa, Somaliland (June 2013).
[28] Interview 52 with Sheikh Zaki, sheikh and former senior judiciary official in Hargeisa, Somaliland (July 2013).

This is completely against human rights," she told me.[29] According to another aid worker, diplomats and aid workers are "not comfortable getting involved in the shari'a thing ... They say it's not gender sensitive."[30] For these reasons, donors "cannot appear to be supporting" shari'a, said an aid worker.[31] Sheikhs also felt that donors from the West promoted anti-Islamic ideas. People who "don't understand shari'a" and Muslim intellectuals "trained with a Western mindset [who] take the Western argument easily," one lawyer and sheikh in his thirties told me, both fall into the same trap of misinterpreting shari'a as sexist.[32]

According to aid workers, international NGOs generally "do not want to interfere [with shari'a], to be on the safe side."[33] But UN agencies like UNICEF and UNDP have also not hidden their interest in understanding shari'a, instead commissioning studies and programs related to women in Islam. When I asked why, a Somali human rights activist who worked with the United Nations in Mogadishu and Hargeisa told me her colleagues "see Islam as backward and hostile to women." While some of them want to learn more about shari'a, "I don't think their donors would accept to support [UN agencies] to work in a proactive, engaged way to improve Islamic laws. They think this is anathema to the international community," she concluded.[34] United Nations agencies' "studies" of women in Islam and their reluctance to engage with shari'a contribute to the perception, even among activists, of aid groups as anti-Islamic.

Aid workers' attempts to work with Islam continue to be met with skepticism. In addition to worries about neocolonialism and mistrust of aid workers, Somalis have life-and-death reasons for their reluctance to associate with Western aid groups. According to an aid worker in Nairobi, "If you did engage [with Western aid agencies] you are seen as not a real Muslim, so you are targeted [by militants]. Activists don't want to be exposed to that risk."[35] There is a widespread perception in

---

[29] Interview 15 with Evelyn, United Nations official in Garowe, Puntland (conducted by telephone from Hargeisa, Somaliland) (June 2013).

[30] Follow-up interview 94 with Jeff, aid worker and consultant in Hargeisa, Somaliland (June 2014).

[31] Interview 12 with Daniel, expatriate lawyer and NGO program manager in Hargeisa, Somaliland (June 2013).

[32] Interview 32 with Axmed, lawyer and university lecturer in Hargeisa, Somaliland (June 2013).

[33] Interview 62 with Bilan, NGO executive director in Hargeisa, Somaliland (July 2013).

[34] Interview 78 with Majda, lawyer and human rights activist in Mogadishu and Hargeisa (conducted in Nairobi, Kenya) (July 2013).

[35] Interview 65 with Jen, expatriate aid worker in Nairobi, Kenya (conducted by telephone from Hargeisa, Somaliland) (July 2013).

the region that UN agencies do not support shari'a because of a fear amongst aid workers that Islamic law does not promote women's rights in the same way that international law does. Likewise, Somali men holding political and social authority tend to portray UN agencies as anti-Muslim specifically because of feminism, because aid workers portray Islam as unsupportive of women's rights. In this context, women activists find themselves backed into a political and rhetorical corner. Their work with Western aid groups risks branding them as anti-Muslim or making them the targets of extremists even though they also try to appeal to shari'a and work with sheikhs.

What happens to international law in this context, as it sits precariously sidelined in relation to the various versions of shari'a in Somali discourse? While international law provides Somali women with a discourse for obtaining financial support from UN agencies and international NGOs, international law fails to provide women with the discursive potential to challenge the domination of men who feel they have God's will on their side. International law is meant to limit the actions of states but – to the United Nations, Somalia, and much of the rest of the world – Somaliland is not a sovereign state. That limits the effectiveness of any argument that the Somaliland government should commit to and abide by international law, since Somaliland is not a UN member-state and is unable to ratify and be held accountable to multilateral treaties like the Convention on the Elimination of All Forms of Discrimination Against Women (CEDAW). While an appeal to international law provides women activists with important material resources for their organizations and activism, it does not provide them with resources appropriate to their political context.

Somali women continue to work with local and international NGOs to implement a shared vision for women's rights. But, as one staff member of an international NGO told me, "We are . . . pushing for change, but what does change mean for local people? I really do not know." Fearing reprisal from her employers, she asked me to turn off the recorder and then she discussed Somalis' widespread mistrust of the Western NGOs with whom she worked. She ended our conversation with a sigh, "We always find a way to come up with a very nice report."[36]

---

[36] Interview number removed for anonymity.

DISCURSIVE RESOURCES: WHY ACTIVISTS USE SHARI'A

A combination of institutional and historical pressures – the influential authority of sheikhs and a legacy of domestic authoritarianism and international intervention by colonial administrators and aid workers with their own plans for feminist progress that limited or did away with Islamic power – channeled women into an Islam-first strategy. More importantly, as scholars of Islam have pointed out, shari'a provides its own scriptural basis for the rights of women.[37] Rather than feeling oppressed by shari'a, women have come to embrace it as a source of rights. When activists put shari'a into practice, it proves more malleable than expected by observers who see it merely as a divine law that jurists interpret. In the Horn of Africa, broken down by decades of civil war and state collapse, shari'a has become a basis of modern constitutional law and a rallying cry for women seeking the values that aid workers associate with liberal democracy: women's suffrage, women's participation in government and decision-making (including the ability to stand for office, be appointed as judges, or be seen as capable religious leaders), and the rights to be protected from assault, discrimination, genital mutilation, forced marriage, and child marriage.

Women activists adopt an Islam-first strategy, educating themselves about the major sources of shari'a and then teaching others about how these sources provide a basis for women's rights. Activists I met and documents they gave me show that they have adopted a multipronged strategy that includes education and advocacy for public health and criminal justice. They consider female genital mutilation (FGM, also called female genital cutting, or circumcision), sexual assault, forced marriage, and child marriage as predominant issues. Activists also work on encouraging women to run for political office and getting more women to vote for them. Many activists I met affirmed that Islamic faith guides these activities rather than any desire to achieve justiciable

---

[37] Asifa Quraishi-Landes, "Secular Is Not Always Better: A Closer Look at Some Women-Empowering Features of Islamic Law," Policy Brief No. 61 (Washington, DC: Institute for Social Policy and Understanding, June 2013); Tamir Moustafa, "Islamic Law, Women's Rights, and Popular Legal Consciousness in Malaysia," 38(1) *Law & Social Inquiry* (2013): 168–188; Asifa Quraishi-Landes, "Who Says Shari'a Demands the Stoning of Women? A Description of Islamic Law and Constitutionalism," 1(1) *Berkeley Journal of Middle Eastern and Islamic Law* (2008): 163–178. On the relationship among culture, law, rights, and feminism, see Cyra Akila Choudhury, "Beyond Culture: Human Rights Universalisms Versus Religious and Cultural Relativism in the Activism for Gender Justice," 30 *Berkeley Journal of Gender, Law & Justice* (2015): 226–267; Mark Fathi Massoud, "Rights in a Failed State: Internally Displaced Women in Sudan and Their Lawyers," 21 *Berkeley Journal of Gender, Law & Justice* (2006): 2–12.

rights in courtrooms. When I asked an NGO executive director why she works for women's rights, she replied directly, "Because I am Muslim. Every step I can take is based on my Islamic religion. It's part of my motivation. If I am a Muslim woman, and I want to go to my job and have a normal life, it's [all] based on Islamic religion."[38] Another said she is "simply trying to [remind] people ... that we [women activists] are Muslim."[39]

Motivated by the sources of shari'a, women also connect with international groups for financial support. These groups bring additional discourses with them, typically of human rights.[40] In the process, activists in Somaliland have been extricating Islam from their country's authoritarian past, from aid agencies bearing alternative discourses of justice, and from xeer, which women see as less protective of their interests than the sources of shari'a. The work of women's activists shows how, when they put shari'a into practice, they – like colonial and authoritarian administrations, the ICU, and the sheikhs and elders who tried to build peace in Somaliland before them – engage in its interpretation, challenge its political uses, and redraw its boundaries.

Western policy and scholarship on law and courts, largely based on the analogy of legal cases in the United States, would suggest that marginalized groups should turn to national courts to protect their rights when legislators are unable or unwilling to enforce them. That is, many advocacy groups seek to secure rights through constitutional review of private action or state legislation.[41] One might expect this kind of legal activism to prevail in Somalia and Somaliland, where women's rights are written into national constitutions. (Somalia's 1960 constitution, Somaliland's 2001 constitution, and Somalia's 2012 constitution all prescribe women's rights and gender equality.[42]) A lawyer

---

[38] Interview 47 with Jamila, NGO executive director in Hargeisa, Somaliland (July 2013).

[39] Interview 128 with Omera, NGO project manager in Hargeisa, Somaliland (June 2014).

[40] On aid groups' legal reform strategies, see Alejandro Bendaña and Tanja Chopra, "Women's Rights, State-Centric Rule of Law, and Legal Pluralism in Somaliland," 5(1) *Hague Journal on the Rule of Law* (2013): 44–73.

[41] On the extent to which constitutional judicial review promotes social activism and protects minority rights in the United States, see Robert A. Dahl, "Decision-Making in a Democracy: The Supreme Court as a National Policy Maker," 6 *Journal of Public Law* (1957): 279–295; Alexander M. Bickel, *The Least Dangerous Branch: The Supreme Court at the Bar of Politics* (New Haven, CT: Yale University Press, 1986); Gerald N. Rosenberg, *The Hollow Hope: Can Courts Bring About Social Change?*, Second Edition (Chicago, IL: University of Chicago Press, 2008).

[42] The equality clause of the 2012 Provisional Constitution of the Federal Republic of Somalia indicates that the state "may not discriminate ... on the basis of ... gender" (Article 11.3). The equality clause of the 2001 Constitution of the Republic of Somaliland indicates that "all

and activist in Somaliland, educated at the University of Mogadishu, told me, "When we have an argument with the [Somaliland] government, they say you [women already] have all your rights in the constitution."[43] The words "gender" and "women" appear nine times in the constitutions of Somaliland and Somalia. These documents provide gender-related protections in labor, the military, and other areas. On the books, Somali women have access to constitutional protections. With all this constitutional law protecting women's rights, they nevertheless adopt a shari'a-first strategy. Why? Three principal reasons follow.

First, Islam is technically the basis of all law, including constitutional law. All three major constitutions proclaim Islam the religion of the state – in Article 1.3 of the 1960 Somalia constitution, Article 2.1 of the 2012 Somalia constitution, and Article 5.1 of the 2001 Somaliland constitution. The Somaliland constitution further prohibits the passage of any law contrary to shari'a.[44] Understanding shari'a to be the basis of all state law and less susceptible than it to political swings, women have focused on promoting the sources of shari'a – the Qur'an and the Hadith – rather than constitutional protections that may come and go.

Second, even if the courts were to adjudicate constitutional issues around Islam, there is no culture of "impact" litigation. Courts and civil society have been slow to regain their footing since the state's 1991 collapse – including in Somaliland, which began running its own political affairs at that time. According to one Somali staff member with an international NGO in Hargeisa, whom I met in 2013, the idea of impact litigation was still "quite new." Somaliland's first law school did not graduate its first students until 2006 (cf. Figure 5.2). While a strategy of constitutional litigation may eventually be attempted as the state and civil society grow stronger, Somaliland, in his words, lacked "experienced legal people who can really challenge the government [by taking] cases . . . to the constitutional court."[45]

Third, institutional pressures on successive constitutional courts mean that judges, who are not appointed for life, may likely rule for the government that appointed them in order to protect their positions.

---

citizens . . . shall enjoy equal rights . . . and shall not be accorded precedence on grounds of . . . gender" (Article 8.1).

[43] Interview 33 with Salaam, NGO executive director in Hargeisa, Somaliland (June 2013).

[44] "The laws of the nation shall be grounded on and shall not be contrary to Islamic Sharia." Article 5.2, Constitution of the Republic of Somaliland, 2001.

[45] Interview 34 with Cabdi, former political prisoner and retired NGO executive director in Hargeisa, Somaliland (June 2013).

Judges are perceived as first and foremost "loyal to the President."[46] "They would lose their jobs," one observer said of Somaliland's Supreme Court judges if they ruled against the political party in power.[47] When I spoke with activists, most told me they would not take cases before the constitutional court because they saw the court as a space for battles between major political parties, for instance over contested elections. Instead, "To change the law," one lawyer told me, "you go to Parliament."[48]

The authority of sheikhs, the primacy Somalis grant to shari'a, the nascent state of the legal profession, and an inability or unwillingness to take high-impact cases before the courts have all pushed women toward Islamic versions of rights. To the women activists I met, gender roles in Islam differ in meaningful ways from gender roles in Somali culture, which led the activists to promote knowledge of Islam so that women would know their rights according to the Qur'an. Activists told me that many "women ... are illiterate [and] don't know which is religion and which is culture. So, they don't know their rights written in the Qur'an. If a person knows the meaning of the Qur'an, [they] will know a lot of rights of women."[49]

Because many Somalis view the government and aid agencies with skepticism, women's rights activists have forged another path toward legal progress: promoting Islam itself. Rather than alienating sheikhs as Siad Barre once did, activists bring religious leaders into the advocacy process, inviting them to forums and workshops to discuss what the sources of shari'a say about women. Their efforts transform shari'a from a threat to women's activism into a resource for it. Not only do women activists express religiosity through their engagement with sheikhs, but they also design and practice their own strategy of using religious texts and symbols to foster social acceptance of their struggle against patriarchy.

Through creativity and reflection, women activists promote an Islamic discourse of rights, disassociated from Siad Barre's legacy and from the strains of Western intervention. As one woman told me, "you can find support for almost everything" in the Qur'an. While her comments may be read as strategic or even cynical, Islam's flexibility

---

[46] Interview 33 with Salaam, NGO executive director in Hargeisa, Somaliland (June 2013).
[47] Interview 3 with Sam, professor in London, England (June 2013).
[48] Interview 5 with Na'im, lawyer and legal consultant in England (conducted by telephone from London, England) (June 2013).
[49] Interview 125 with Sohir, NGO executive director and women's rights activist in Hargeisa, Somaliland (June 2014).

of interpretation, particularly in relation to xeer's rigidity of precedents, made many women I met prefer Islam to xeer in family disputes, divorce, or cases of sexual violence. International NGOs, for their part, support the efforts of women's NGOs, such as initiatives to work with elders to remove precedents from xeer that contradict shari'a. These groups purposefully strive to separate religion from local culture, a strategy the British colonial administration in Somaliland also employed. As an activist told me, "Sometimes the line between culture and religion becomes so blurred that they tell you it's Islamic that a woman should [stay in the home to] cook and clean ... but it's not Islamic!"[50]

ORGANIZING STRATEGIES: HOW ACTIVISTS USE SHARI'A

Women's rights are sensitive to discuss in Somaliland, let alone to implement. "We always look like the villains ... because we try to give women their own voice," an NGO project manager told me.[51] For this reason, women activists foreground male sheikhs, who are seen as the experts on shari'a, often because of their education overseas in Islamic institutes and universities. Somalis recognize the intensity of study necessary to earn the title of sheikh, so activists want these scholars to construct a public narrative of shari'a that is more supportive of women's concerns. "When it comes to Islam or religion, I think it should be left to people who have received foreign, Islamic educations," one activist told me.[52] The most prominent Somali sheikhs have deep cultural influence through their own radio or television programs, Facebook pages, YouTube lectures, and Twitter handles. Somalis I met also listen to sheikhs from Egypt and Saudi Arabia but, as one person told me, they "give priority to" sheikhs from Somaliland.[53]

In Somaliland's context where sheikhs exercise authority, women activists have found that the most plausible way forward is to try to get the sheikhs to change the narrative of women's rights with the hope of

[50] Follow-up interview 139 with Fawzia, women's rights activist and former NGO executive director in Hargeisa, Somaliland (March 2019).
[51] Interview 128 with Omera, NGO project manager in Hargeisa, Somaliland (June 2014).
[52] Interview 125 with Sohir, NGO executive director and women's rights activist in Hargeisa, Somaliland (June 2014).
[53] Interview 138 with Asha, university lecturer and independent consultant in Hargeisa, Somaliland (March 2019).

changing society's views on women's issues.[54] To meet this goal, women's groups have organized forums with sheikhs to discuss issues related to women's and girls' lives, including education, forced marriage, rape, and female genital mutilation, which affects nearly all Somali women. They have invited sheikhs to lead these sessions, whose audiences consist of other sheikhs. Though women's rights NGOs organize these workshops and sheikhs facilitate them, the NGOs are not religiously affiliated organizations. The civic activists do not sit at the main table and sometimes do not participate at all, because the sheikhs are seen as the "people who can speak authoritatively on shari'a and who can work out the tension" between shari'a, custom, and Somali laws like the penal code.[55] One woman said, "Sheikhs do not lie to us. They are honest [and tell us] what religion says."[56] Another said simply, "Not many women know the Qur'an properly. We do not know the Qur'an, the meaning, and what shari'a ... says. If a sheikh says 'this is so and so,' then we believe him."[57] When women activists do not see themselves as capable of interpreting the sources of shari'a publicly, they direct their activism at male religious authorities, hoping to induce them to change their interpretations. For these women, promoting equality and dignity as starting points for the rule of law means dealing first with the rule of men.

Other women activists spoke more resignedly: "We had to invite [sheikhs]. Otherwise we would be in a problem [because] they [would] say we are following Western ideas. The [sheikhs] say all of the rights of women are in the Qur'an ... so we are fighting for these rights, for our Islamic rights, [to show] how these [Islamic rights] are being violated [in Somaliland]."[58] Working with and through sheikhs to achieve these Islamic rights seemed to be the only discursive option for these women activists. Another said that women tread carefully when advocating with sheikhs because many sheikhs still see women as unequal to and less than men:

[54] See, e.g., Saba Mahmood, *Politics of Piety: The Islamic Revival and the Feminist Subject* (Princeton, NJ: Princeton University Press, 2005), discussing how women in Egypt invited men to "salons" to discuss pertinent religious issues.
[55] Follow-up interview 108 with Rashida, lawyer and government consultant in Hargeisa, Somaliland (June 2014).
[56] Interview 128 with Omera, NGO project manager in Hargeisa, Somaliland (June 2014).
[57] Interview 33 with Salaam, NGO executive director in Hargeisa, Somaliland (June 2013).
[58] Follow-up interview 139 with Fawzia, women's rights activist and former NGO executive director in Hargeisa, Somaliland (March 2019).

You can see a man . . . saying 'She is [just] a woman' like she is weak. And he is a big sheikh . . . He knows the rights that Allah says . . . But there was Khadija [the Prophet Muhammad's workplace boss and, later, his first wife] and Aisha [the Prophet's surviving spouse]. [Women] can produce and help. But now, [sheikhs] just say, 'She is just a woman.' One day things will change.[59]

Empowering Women and Girls

Civic activists use shari'a to empower women in education, politics, and sport. Activists I met promoted girls' education, for instance, by explaining how shari'a demands that both "boys and girls have the right to education."[60] With support from international NGOs and donor countries, activists have reminded people of the Islamic teaching that to educate a girl is to educate a family or a nation (Figure 6.1). Activists told me their work aims to "empower women . . . to have access to justice, to join politics, and to run for elections."[61] One NGO director said that Somali "culture," for instance, "refuse[d] to allow girls to play" sports, but such a rule is not in accord with Islam, which "gives rights to human beings." She reflected on her one-to-one advocacy with sheikhs, saying, "I use religion to say that girls should have a chance to play, separately [from boys.] I talk to religious leaders, Qur'anic teachers, and sheikhs. I ask them questions. When I am starting that sport, I ask them about Islam. They tell me [that] it is okay for young girls to participate [so long as they play] separately from boys."[62] The approval of sheikhs brought critical community support for an endeavor that could be seen as a foreign import inappropriate for girls. In the long term, activists said, if "you see [women] don't have property [or] don't have rights to [be free from] FGM or sexual- and gender-based violence, all this is related to [our] culture," not to Islam.[63] Again, those struggling for women's rights consistently relied on shari'a as a strategy, in the process showing how Somali law and society have distorted the religion they share.

Some women said that learning more about Islam helped them to understand broader issues in politics and daily life, including

---

[59] Interview 125 with Sohir, NGO executive director and women's rights activist in Hargeisa, Somaliland (June 2014).
[60] Ibid. See also Abdulai Abukari, "Education of Women in Islam: A Critical Islamic Interpretation of the Quran," 109(1) *Religious Education* (2014): 4–23.
[61] Interview 28 with Nahda, NGO project manager in Hargeisa, Somaliland (June 2013).
[62] Interview 116 with Nisreen, NGO executive director in Hargeisa, Somaliland (June 2014).
[63] Interview 125 with Sohir, NGO executive director and women's rights activist in Hargeisa, Somaliland (June 2014).

Figure 6.1 "Educate a girl, educate a nation": Using Islam to promote women's rights. Photo credit: Michael Walls.

obligations to others and the environment. Women I met told me that, according to religious tradition, men have important duties and obligations to women. A husband "has to be responsible for his family. If he takes another wife, he should stand in front of the court [to] look into the matter."[64] Similarly, women I met working in environmental protection groups also turned to Qur'anic text to justify their activities protecting the Somali coastline and forests. "We had verses of the Qur'an in our posters . . . in Somali. [Religion] encourage[s] people."[65]

Increasing Women's Participation in Politics

When I asked one activist why she was trying to advocate for women's rights, she spoke of the importance of using the Qur'an as a source of authority to get women into government. She said, "We need representation. The people who vote for men are women! [We need] to change their attitudes. They have to know their rights in the Qur'an. This [allowing women to participate fully in parliament] is Islamic! They have seen women ministers, role models, in parliament."[66] Why do activists want more women to vote and stand for election? "I don't think [people] understand that having women in high-level positions is

---

[64] Interview 55 with Fawzia, women's rights activist and former NGO executive director, in Hargeisa, Somaliland (June 2013).
[65] Interview 122 with Xidig, government minister in Hargeisa, Somaliland (June 2014).
[66] Interview 125 with Sohir, NGO executive director and women's rights activist in Hargeisa, Somaliland (June 2014).

better for society as a whole. If we simply let men run everything and follow them like sheep, we'll have fiascos all the time," said one activist.[67] Nevertheless, people see these efforts as "Westernized," which has become a tenet of Somali "culture . . . difficult to break."[68]

Activists seek to construct a public narrative of shari'a that reflects the concerns of women's NGOs. To do so, they have tried to earn the support of sheikhs willing to say publicly that what the women were fighting for was consistent with shari'a. But the activists were, at best, receiving mixed messages from the sheikhs. In some cases, women told me, while they felt the sheikhs "have . . . more knowledge of religion, they try to confuse us." That is, these sheikhs have said that Islam does not give women the political rights they are seeking, even though activists thought that Islam provides "rights . . . for women to be in government," or at least does not prohibit it.[69]

To gain support for their advocacy to improve women's political participation, or for a quota setting a minimum number of women members of parliament, women's groups have organized forums for sheikhs. "We invited different sheikhs and asked them, 'is it possible . . . to tell the people if it is right for women to [be] ministers [and members of] parliament?' The sheikhs said, 'yes, you . . . women can do these things.' When they are in one room in a meeting, they can accept it. But they don't like to tell the public" that Islam does not prevent women from having these rights.[70] Because many men who are not sheikhs have trouble supporting the idea of electing women to parliament, activists told me, they hoped that sheikhs might change the minds of men across society. "It is patriarchy, not Islam," an activist told me, that says women should not participate in politics.[71] These women separate Islam from patriarchy in a way that many men do not.

I was told that sheikhs were unwilling to speak publicly about issues that women cared about most. In other cases some sheikhs, women felt, were "so rude" by not giving a fuller or complete interpretation of a Qur'anic verse or statement of the Prophet Muhammad.[72] At trainings or debates sponsored by women's NGOs, for instance, religious

---

[67] Interview 128 with Omera, NGO project manager in Hargeisa, Somaliland (June 2014).
[68] Interview 29 with Daahir, NGO project manager in Hargeisa, Somaliland (June 2013).
[69] Interview 130 with Ladan, women's rights activist in Hargeisa, Somaliland (June 2014).
[70] Interview 125 with Sohir, NGO executive director and women's rights activist in Hargeisa, Somaliland (June 2014).
[71] Follow-up interview 140 with Sohir, NGO executive director and women's rights activist in Hargeisa, Somaliland (March 2019).
[72] Interview 128 with Omera, NGO project manager in Hargeisa, Somaliland (June 2014).

leaders "sometimes ... take the first part of the [Qur'anic] verse or Hadith that suits them, but they omit the rest."[73] In one example, Somalis have used an evidentiary rule – that two female witnesses to a crime are equivalent to one male witness – to say all women are worth only "half of a man."

> [But] they leave out the part which says two women [are needed] in case one of them forgets something, the other one will support her because of the overload [women] have. Sometimes women are pregnant or sick ... The [religious leaders] leave all that out. They [also] don't ask why diyya [blood money] is 50 camels for women [who are killed] and 100 for men ... [It is] because the man is ... responsible for his wife and his unmarried sisters ... But they make it like 'You as a woman are half.' And they don't give an explanation.[74]

Women activists have worked to counter sexist interpretations of the sources of shari'a. But, according to community leaders I met, the sheikhs simply "feel irritated" when they are called upon to support women's issues or to give the public a richer or more complex view of shari'a.[75] Thus, activists told me, ordinary people remain "ignorant" and women informally "advise them to study the texts and Hadith" on their own wherever possible, rather than adopting uninformed views.[76]

Stopping Female Genital Mutilation

Civic activists I met said that they have not reached their goal of eliminating the practice of FGM because "Sheikhs are not with us." They "have different versions of" shari'a, activists told me. So how do those seeking to stop the practice of FGM engage with sheikhs? "You have to start by talking about the Qur'an and Sunnah," and only after speaking about religious texts do civic groups turn to "present[ing] the facts regarding [women's] health."[77] One civic group I met had conducted "trainings of trainers" that involved facilitating workshops for hundreds of sheikhs, men mostly in their twenties and thirties, on issues related to the lives of women. Business leaders and staff from the ministry of education, the ministry of justice, and similar ministries that confront problems tied to the rights of women also attended. The

[73] Interview 62 with Bilan, NGO executive director in Hargeisa, Somaliland (July 2013).
[74] Ibid.
[75] Interview 37 with Sultan Mansoor, sultan in Hargeisa, Somaliland (June 2013).
[76] Interview 62 with Bilan, NGO executive director in Hargeisa, Somaliland (July 2013).
[77] Interview 138 with Asha, university lecturer and independent consultant in Hargeisa, Somaliland (March 2019).

organizers hoped that those sheikhs, business leaders, and government employees would then educate others about what they have learned. These are not always Somaliland's wealthiest or most influential leaders, but some of them are already somewhat supportive of women's rights, as they do voluntarily "come to learn."[78]

This NGO had met with so many people, particularly sheikhs, to promote awareness of shari'a that people labeled the NGO *hayadii diinta* (Somali: roughly, "the religion NGO"). Managers from the NGO also privately "engag[ed] women sheikhs," whom male sheikhs "would [not] accept as their own."[79] These women scholars, like Asha, have enough knowledge of Islam to educate others about women's rights in the Qur'an and Hadith. They are dismissed either as not really scholars or as fronts for Western groups; people "just presume" the women sheikhs are promoting a Western agenda "because the supporters are [international NGOs and UN agencies] using international law."[80] Activists have been careful to avoid being seen as denigrating Islam and careful to avoid criticizing sheikhs themselves; if anything, they actively promote Islam and work with sheikhs rather than against them. I was told of a Somali woman in the UK who had spoken out against sheikhs online but was quickly and deeply criticized, leading many Somalis to distance themselves from her, and of a woman who faced vocal opposition from sheikhs after she tried to open a madrasa (Arabic: religious school).

Any legislation passed in Somaliland, people told me, must have an Islamic foundation because "Those in parliament . . . know the sheikhs will become angry" if the legislation has a different foundation, such as international human rights law.[81] But sheikhs, though they all practice Islam, disagree on how to interpret shari'a. For instance, the practice of FGM has long been common in the Horn of Africa, where some estimates suggest nearly all women have been circumcised. Women activists I met have been trying to stop the practice by getting sheikhs to disavow it publicly as impermissible under Islamic law. Some sheikhs have spoken out to end it. But many of them have been silenced by more powerful or influential sheikhs, leading others to refrain from

---

[78] Follow-up interview 140 with Sohir, NGO executive director and women's rights activist in Hargeisa, Somaliland (March 2019).

[79] Interview 141 with Bourhan, NGO project coordinator in Hargeisa, Somaliland (March 2019).

[80] Follow-up interview 140 with Sohir, NGO executive director and women's rights activist in Hargeisa, Somaliland (March 2019).

[81] Follow-up interview 139 with Fawzia, women's rights activist and former NGO executive director in Hargeisa, Somaliland (March 2019).

speaking out, and still others to suggest that the practice is permissible or even required by Islamic law. Some sheikhs have promoted only the "Sunna" form of FGM, which involves removal of the clitoral hood. (The Sunna method is seen as less invasive than infibulation, or pharaonic method, involving removal of the labia and a near-total closure of the vagina, except for a small hole for the urine stream.) Women I met had gone to great effort to draft an anti-FGM policy for the Somaliland government but were disturbed that sheikhs could not agree to ban FGM.

According to one researcher, a legislative ban on FGM would be at best only a partial victory. Even if parliament passed laws against FGM, the practice would not cease unless prominent sheikhs spoke out against it. Political leaders "just say that" FGM is an outrage "to please the international community," one observer told me. She continued that the government does not have "power to [enforce] any ... [anti-FGM] laws ... [Anti-FGM laws are] just a fantasy to please donors," particularly when sheikhs have the power to stop it.[82] After many sheikhs claimed that the Sunna type of FGM was permissible under shari'a, women told me, "We [still] called [the sheikhs] from time to time" to advocate for a change in their views.[83] In these cases, women walk a fine line between entirely avoiding the sheikhs or reluctantly engaging with them.

In 2018, things took a turn for the worse for activists when sheikhs working in Somaliland's Ministry of Religious Affairs issued a fatwa that ruled additional forms of FGM acceptable. Members of one advocacy group told me they thereafter stopped their anti-FGM activism to avoid prompting the religious leaders who delivered the fatwa to speak out against their group. Instead, they began "low-profile" advocacy, such as one-to-one conversations with sheikhs, to try to change the fatwa "that is not supporting us."[84] The activists' "intentional invisibility" is authentic, strategic, and risk-averse, and helps them navigate the cultural landscape and avoid potential backlash.[85]

[82] Interview 133 with Stephanie, researcher and author in London, England (July 2014).
[83] Interview 33 with Salaam, NGO executive director in Hargeisa, Somaliland (June 2013).
[84] Interview 141 with Bourhan, NGO project coordinator in Hargeisa, Somaliland (March 2019).
[85] Swethaa Ballakhrishnen, Priya Fielding-Singh, and Devon Magliozzi, "Intentional Invisibility: Professional Women and the Navigation of Workplace Constraints," 62(1) *Sociological Perspectives* (2019): 23–41.

Ending Child Marriage

Like FGM and women's political participation, child marriage (some-times called early marriage) has been a difficult topic for sheikhs to agree upon publicly. Many community and religious leaders in Somaliland promote early marriage as a way to deal with boys and girls having sexual relations prior to marriage. Women activists told me of their failed attempts to bring sheikhs together to discuss a ban on child marriage. In one workshop, "It took three days to get [a sheikh] on board. We had to keep going back to him" to convince him with case studies. These case studies included that of a young girl whose pelvis had been broken by childbirth, and that of another child who "went crazy and drank bleach" to avoid a forced marriage.[86] That is, instead of advocating directly for a fatwa against child marriage, civic activists and NGOs have brought religious leaders together to explain to them the specific problems that often result from a young girl's marriage. Doing so helps religious leaders learn about the girls' experiences, potentially building sheikhs' empathy for these girls: "When we [talk about health-related problems in child marriage], even the sheikhs accept it, because Islam always promotes the person, health, and dignity . . . The religion doesn't accept any problem with those things, so we just identify the specific [issues] that come from early marriage."[87]

But empathy did not go far in helping activists achieve their goals. The sheikhs "were livid, not happy at all with this project" of stopping child marriage. A sheikh put in charge of a one-day workshop was given a facilitator's fee and asked to write a report on Islam and women, but when he realized the organization was against child marriage, he exclaimed, "What? I'm not doing that!" He asked the women activists if they wanted "to stop marriage" entirely. The activists clarified that they wanted to stop the practice of child marriage, not adult marriage. They hoped some sheikhs who agreed with them would "make friends with [other] religious leaders [and then] convince these guys . . . who carry out the [child marriage] ceremonies" to stop, not least to prevent the dangers to young girls.[88]

At another workshop, however, men in attendance "saw the logo" of a prominent women's organization and noticed the women sitting on the edges of the room. Realizing that the workshop was actually

---

[86] Interview 128 with Omera, NGO project manager in Hargeisa, Somaliland (June 2014).

[87] Follow-up interview 140 with Sohir, NGO executive director and women's rights activist in Hargeisa, Somaliland (March 2019).

[88] Interview 128 with Omera, NGO project manager in Hargeisa, Somaliland (June 2014).

organized by a women's rights NGO – and not by the leading sheikh and Islamic studies professor facilitating it – the participants became "really aggressive." They "stood up and shouted, 'this is Western ideologies taking over our Muslim identity. This is the last one-hundred percent Muslim country!'" It was "mayhem," according to attendees of the meeting whom I later met. The sheikhs perceived the workshop to be an attack on marriage in general, claiming that the organizers "openly oppose[d] culture, religion, tradition" by not supporting child marriage.[89]

Preventing Sexual Assault

The issue of sexual violence is particularly vexing, activists told me, because many elders have forced women to marry their assaulters, which activists see as directly contravening shari'a. Forced marriages lead to perverse incentives, such as prompting a man to rape a woman whom he wishes to marry – or, in one egregious case, incentivizing gang rape as a group of young men sexually assaulted a woman together to make it impossible to prove which one of them should be forced to marry her as his "punishment."[90] Forcing a woman to marry the perpetrator reduces and "simplifies" the punishment for *zinna* (the Islamic crime of unlawful sexual conduct) by prioritizing peace between the families or clans involved, despite the obvious injustice of such resolutions for the assault survivor.[91]

As in the battle against FGM, feminist civic groups have tried to get sheikhs and their counterparts – "cultural leaders, the sultans, and aqils" – on their side, so that these leaders would then show how local practices pervert Islamic rules.[92] Civic activists against sexual violence realized that the elders who enforce xeer would not want to behave inconsistently with Islam, and they wanted to stop any distortions of Islam. "They are not using the right [shari'a]," an activist told me of the multiple interpretations of zinna. The "right" shari'a, she exclaimed, "says to kill the rapist. But they [sheikhs and sultans] don't do that. They just talk about [the rape causing a] conflict . . . between the clans."[93] While women I met

---

[89] Ibid.
[90] Interview 82 with Mille, expatriate aid worker in Mogadishu, Somalia (conducted in Nairobi, Kenya) (August 2013).
[91] Follow-up interview 98 with Tahir, NGO executive director in Hargeisa, Somaliland (June 2014).
[92] Interview 128 with Omera, NGO project manager in Hargeisa, Somaliland (June 2014).
[93] Interview 125 with Sohir, NGO executive director and women's rights activist in Hargeisa, Somaliland (June 2014).

did not advocate publicly for the execution of rapists, they did try to open debate on the diversity of punishments for rape, pointing out how local practices overemphasize what elders see as their communities' needs at the expense of the needs of the survivors of assault and the rules of Islam.

Feminist activists focused on developing an argument that shari'a is purposefully misinterpreted to enforce patriarchy and oppress women. Some men, activists told me, "use religion to deter women" from advocacy, even though activists know "the religion [and] the [words and actions] of the Prophet" do not support these actions. Consequently, women want people to learn that men should not "change [shari'a] just to bring down women . . . [Men] use traditional [practices] and shari'a . . . to help the men. But the way it is written in the Qur'an is different."[94] Another expressed frustration that men were not following the example of "the Prophet [who] was very good to his wife." She continued that, in her work, "We . . . always take what is within the Qur'an and Hadith [that promotes] justice."[95] For these reasons, activists turn to sheikhs to discuss the scriptural basis for an end to sexual assault, despite the recalcitrance women face from many religious men.

One activist told me that she saw violence against women as a more important issue than equal inheritance rights because "It's something so clear[ly] written in the Qur'an, and men are violating" it by physically harming women and girls. Both shari'a and international law do not support violence against women, activists told me, but they found invoking shari'a to be a more useful strategy, because it helps them to emphasize that their advocacy does not intend to "contradict the sheikhs and shari'a."[96]

The primary source of shari'a is the Qur'an, and Somaliland's constitution makes Islam the primary source of law. So why would women not speak about scripture openly, instead of leaving that task to male sheikhs? After all, women played an important role in Islam's earliest history: many of the oral preservers of the Qur'an and most trustworthy and notable *muhaditheen* (Arabic: scholars of Hadith) were women. While some women do speak openly in forums, "The custodians of law were always men," I was told.[97] That is, the dominant culture expects religious leaders to be men. In the view of one longtime women's rights activist and former senior government minister, "This is a patriarchal

[94] Ibid.
[95] Follow-up interview 139 with Fawzia, women's rights activist and former NGO executive director in Hargeisa, Somaliland (March 2019).
[96] Follow-up interview 139 with Fawzia, women's rights activist and former NGO executive director in Hargeisa, Somaliland (March 2019).
[97] Interview 80 with Gul, aid worker in Nairobi, Kenya (August 2013).

society. If women need something, men would have to defend them. But they never would. They say, 'You women stay at home'."[98]

Shari'a as Strategy

Activists fighting a long tradition of patriarchy justified through simplistic interpretations of religious discourse are caught between knowing – from their private study or meetings with sheikhs – that shari'a does not have to be sexist and being unable to convince sheikhs to speak publicly about that. These sheikhs, in turn, fear distancing themselves from Somali culture or even from Islam. After an NGO organized a dialogue with religious leaders, sheikhs "accused us of promoting an alien agenda from the West. Once we realized they are against us, we decided not to engage with them."[99] The activists realized they were giving power to the sheikhs, which led them to consider alternative options, including trying to find a foreign (non-Somali) Muslim scholar who could support the women's version of shari'a. "Our sheikhs ... hide [so] we need a sheikh [who will] speak publicly" about how shari'a protects women.[100] In one case, activists told me they had hoped to hire a Black American Muslim, regardless of whether or not he had a Somali background or spoke Somali. They sought out international scholars – sheikhs – to validate what activists were trying to show about women, rights, and religion. When Somali sheikhs were unable or unwilling to speak out in support of the concerns of women's NGOs, these NGOs began looking for foreign sheikhs to do it, pinning their hopes on their feminist interpretations of shari'a. When I asked how people would respond to a Muslim American interpreting shari'a, activist leaders seemed unconcerned about such a scholar being from a Western country: "But he is Muslim," I was told. "We need an Islamic scholar from wherever in the world."[101]

Despite their focus on shari'a and bringing religious men to speak out in support of women's rights, activists do not ignore foreign and international law. They see that "traditional systems are patriarchal" and that foreign "law, starting in the West fifty

---

[98] Interview 17 with Amburo, former senior government minister and United Nations official in Hargeisa, Somaliland (June 2013).

[99] Interview 33 with Salaam, NGO executive director in Hargeisa, Somaliland (June 2013).

[100] Interview 125 with Sohir, NGO executive director and women's rights activist in Hargeisa, Somaliland (June 2014).

[101] Interview 125 with Sohir, NGO executive director and women's rights activist in Hargeisa, Somaliland (June 2014).

years ago" discusses "equality [and] positive discrimination ... giv-[ing] them more justice and rights."[102] One NGO executive direc-tor told me her organization, like other civil society groups, brought international treaties into their work.[103] The NGO held workshops discussing CEDAW, even though Somaliland – not fully recognized as a state – cannot ratify it. But just as they strategically sideline state feminism because of the legacy of Siad Barre's rule, they also sideline CEDAW because of the legacy of foreign inter-vention. They mention it, but they focus their strategies on pro-moting shari'a instead, to which they see state leaders bound for legal, religious, and moral reasons. United Nations agencies and international NGOs happily support the efforts of women's rights groups, but only if they also discuss international law. As activists told me, foreigners "were never opposed to women doing Islam-oriented work as long as they were also teaching people about ... international conventions."[104]

Activists struggling for women's rights do not see shari'a existing in isolation, but co-existing alongside discourses of rights in interna-tional and domestic law. Activists I met were pleased that Somaliland's 2005 inheritance law protected the rights of women, but the state's process of passing the law, which women told me had anyway been "kick-started by Siad Barre," was long and "more gradual."[105] Women activists also wanted Somalis to speak out about men who do not support women fully, including financially, and say that such men are actually acting contrary to shari'a and forcing women to find work:

> Sixty percent of people in Somaliland are women. They are breadwin-ners. They are working in the market [and] tea shops, selling qat, [doing] small jobs. So why can [people] say that women must stay in the home, when [women] are doing these things? In Islam, you should say 'I am a man, I am responsible for you.'[106]

This approach – giving space to state law and international law, but primacy to shari'a – has slowly worked to improve some women's status. According to activists, Somaliland has seen an "increase in enrollment

---

[102] Interview 80 with Gul, aid worker in Nairobi, Kenya (August 2013).
[103] Interview 47 with Jamila, NGO executive director in Hargeisa, Somaliland (July 2013).
[104] Interview 62 with Bilan, NGO executive director in Hargeisa, Somaliland (July 2013).
[105] Interview 130 with Ladan, women's rights activist in Hargeisa, Somaliland (June 2014).
[106] Interview 125 with Sohir, NGO executive director and women's rights activist in Hargeisa, Somaliland (June 2014).

of education for young girls. We now have women in the police force . . . and women lawyers . . . at the forefront of fighting for women's rights in individual cases."[107] Many of these women joined after they and their families understood that Islam permitted these things. Others told me that since the 1990s, "There [has been] change. Now [there are] more women lawyers and graduates."[108] It is not that activists are trying to get Somalis to see Islam's "capacity for evolution," as Ignác Goldziher, a scholar of Islamic jurisprudence, once put it,[109] but that they are trying to show that Islam never opposed women's rights. Instead, they argue that Somali practices evolved away from Islam, which has long advanced women's rights.

CONCLUSION

This chapter has uncovered how persistently and thoroughly activism for women's rights in Somaliland invokes, interprets, and relies on shari'a. Since Somaliland's 1991 declaration of independence from Somalia, women's civic groups have made strides toward becoming professional organizations while promoting grassroots order and equality principles. While aid efforts have often been predicated on the notion that shari'a is bad for women, Somali women activists instead have used it to promote women's rights. The fact that these activists continue to adopt this strategy – in the face of centuries of patriarchy that also invokes shari'a – renders shari'a malleable, even as some activists see shari'a as resolute in its support of gender equality. The psychological gains of knowing that faith is on their side, not against them, are real. As one woman activist told me, "Patriarchy will not end unless we promote how we are all . . . Muslim."[110] Just as state officials, elders, religious leaders, and militants have used religion as their ordering principle throughout Somali history – turning Islam into a tool of patriarchy – civic activists have remade these very symbols of repression into sources of hope,

---

[107] Interview 131 with Shamsi, women's rights activist in Hargeisa, Somaliland (June 2014).

[108] Interview 125 with Sohir, NGO executive director and women's rights activist in Hargeisa, Somaliland (June 2014).

[109] Ignác Goldziher, *Introduction to Islamic Theology and Law*, trans. Andras Hamori and Ruth Hamori (Princeton, NJ: Princeton University Press, 1981), 52 [originally published as *Vorlesungen über den Islam* (Heidelberg, 1910)].

[110] Follow-up interview 140 with Sohir, NGO executive director and women's rights activist in Hargeisa, Somaliland (March 2019).

redemption, and salvation. If this project is to succeed over the long term, the social transformation that activists envision will emerge from the new meanings they give to the discourses that male elites have used to hold onto power.

When I asked a Somali activist about the evolution of women's rights in the region, she looked away, sighed, and said that "Women had more rights under Siad" Barre. She was still longing for equality, even if from a dictator ruling by decree. Siad Barre, in her words, "made women and men equal."[111] A dictator's power has enduring consequences, and Siad Barre's approach contaminated the goal of equality and still tarnishes contemporary efforts to achieve it. His legacy, linked to a spurious form of state feminism that accompanied the execution of religious leaders, guided feminist activists a generation later to reconfigure women's rights as a core concern of Islam. These feminist activists continue to endure a vicious cycle in which aid organizations are seen as anti-Muslim because they support feminist causes, and because aid organizations are seen as anti-Muslim they hurt the feminist causes they support. Feminist activists have thus found themselves in an impossible position because of their relationships to international aid groups and perceptions of feminism itself as a tool of state domination or neocolonial oppression. They must try to navigate a narrow channel between challenging patriarchy and not seeming to challenge religion.

Just as Somalis have turned to shari'a to resolve disputes with one another, feminist activists have turned to shari'a to promote women's rights. Whether or not this strategy will succeed in dismantling patriarchy, women activists continue to devote resources, time, and energy to it, suggesting that they believe change and progress depend on it. For civic activists, shari'a is not just a rallying cry; it is also a guide for interpreting daily life and, inshallah, for tearing down patriarchy. Given activists' dedication, I was not surprised when some of them told me they would favor a state governed more closely by shari'a, or at least their version of it. They worried, however, that in an Islamic state some sheikhs would use shari'a as an excuse to "oppress women in the name of the Qur'an. But if the sheikhs studied [shari'a] out of love and

---

[111] Interview 77 with Khadra, United Nations official in Nairobi, Kenya (July 2013).

286

tolerance, then I wouldn't have a problem" with an Islamic state, one activist told me.[112]

Civic activists fighting male domination in Somaliland have been working hard to get Somalis to see shari'a and its sources differently, from the ground up, while disentangling women's rights from the West, from Somalia's own history of authoritarian rule under Siad Barre, and from sheikhs who see Islam narrowly as unsupportive of women's rights. But when activists launched these projects, they were accused of "openly opposing Islam" and some were told that they were "no longer Muslims," leading them to seek alliances with male religious leaders who, because of their status, could render feminist knowledge intelligible to local communities.[113] The work of these civic activists uncovers the democratic potential of Islamic activism. "You cannot say that it's 'un-Islamic' to be democratic," a former NGO director told me when we met in Hargeisa in 2019. She said that any state – Islamic or otherwise – that has a long history of men serving nearly exclusively as the "custodians of law" is likely to harm women.[114]

Summarizing colonial and state law in Somali history, one civic activist I met said simply, "Men use ... law [first] to suppress [women] and [then] to set themselves above the law," which has led women to shari'a.[115] Advocacy for the rights of women means confronting a paradox: building values related to human rights without being seen as promoting a Western agenda and without resurrecting the nation's struggle with authoritarianism. The approach to Islam among the women activists I met in Somaliland emerged not only out of their ethical formation and religious piety, but also out of hope and strategy, as it does for many others who use shari'a as a form of legal politics. Islam offers scriptural resources for dismantling patriarchy, but the doors to discourses of state-sponsored feminism and Western-style human rights remain largely closed. Shari'a gives activists a toolkit of discourses in a place where the standard tools are

---

[112] Follow-up interview 139 with Fawzia, women's rights activist and former NGO executive director in Hargeisa, Somaliland (March 2019).

[113] Interview 128 with Omera, NGO project manager in Hargeisa, Somaliland (June 2014).

[114] Follow-up interview 139 with Fawzia, women's rights activist and former NGO executive director in Hargeisa, Somaliland (March 2019).

[115] Interview 80 with Gul, aid worker in Nairobi, Kenya (August 2013).

unavailable or mistrusted. But when put into practice in political and social life, particularly in the carefully orchestrated debates between women's rights advocates and sheikhs, shari'a and its interpretations may be just as diverse, unstable, and fragmented as the Somali state itself.

CHAPTER SEVEN

THE RULE OF LAW, INSHALLAH

We have been colonized [and] denigrated. But we never lost our humanity.

Somali aid worker in Nairobi[1]

The only weapon we have is Allah.

Sheikh in Hargeisa[2]

Walking the narrow, crowded aisles of Hargeisa's central market, one cannot miss the moneychangers. These young men sit on plastic stools behind tall stacks of unguarded cash, shifting their gazes between their mobile phones and nearby shopkeepers. I have seen moneychangers relax their postures and gently shut their eyes for a while, without any noticeable fear of getting robbed. "There must be a rule of law somewhere," a Somali researcher once told me. He paused, reflecting on the comment, and continued. "It's the people."[3]

The president of Afghanistan, Ashraf Ghani, has called the rule of law the glue that binds state and society together.[4] But this glue erodes easily. As the previous chapters have shown, practices and institutions associated with the rule of law are as broken, inconsistent, and discordant as the Horn of Africa's many Islamic states and their colonial, authoritarian, and democratic architects have been. Throughout the

---

[1] Interview 85 with Ibrahim, NGO program adviser in Nairobi, Kenya (August 2013).
[2] Interview 127 with Sheikh Oweis, sheikh and senior university administrator in Hargeisa, Somaliland (June 2014).
[3] Interview 59 with Kalim, former NGO executive director in Hargeisa, Somaliland (July 2013).
[4] Ashraf Ghani and Clare Lockhart, *Fixing Failed States: A Framework for Rebuilding a Fractured World* (Oxford: Oxford University Press, 2008), 125.

Horn of Africa's history, political elites – colonial administrators, democratically elected officials, authoritarian rulers, aqils, sultans, sheikhs, international lawyers, and foreign aid workers – have sought to resolve people's disputes, write constitutions, draft laws, construct law schools, build prisons, and reform courts. Similar tools of legal politics have also been essential in attempts to rebuild the Somali state since its 1991 collapse.

But, as this book has demonstrated, one cannot disentangle legal politics from religious politics, for political and legal actors have long co-opted shari'a's power. Historically and still today, they put differing varieties of Islam in the service of their own governance and development projects. They justified their work by promoting their own versions of shari'a and by hiding or disarming other versions. Women's rights activists, too, invoked their own version of shari'a. Just as United Nations agencies' views of the rule of law differ from those of many Somalis, so too do Somalis' understandings of shari'a differ. Shari'a is a concept flexible enough to support the rule of law on one hand even as militants invoke their version of it on the other hand. State actors, institutions, and political elites all breathe meaning into shari'a, revealing its diversity and ability to be different things to different people. In the Horn of Africa, religious faith has not only been used to perpetrate violence. It has also been used to nurture peace, dignity, gender equality, and the rule of law. But the process of coding shari'a as law then merging it with the state – the secularization process – has tended to create rather than to resolve social conflict.

Legal institutions that have labeled Islam a threat are often the same ones that have embedded a different version of Islam, or of some other faith, into their work. In Somalia and Somaliland, as in the colonial and postcolonial history of the US and other nations, religion has not only reinforced the state's rules and norms, but also generated them. In that sense, religion is not separate from the state. It is embedded in the state's foundation, even – and especially – in states that call themselves secular. The question for believers in the rule of law is not so much how to ensure the freedom of religion in secular states as how to ensure religious belief continues to provide the source material for political freedom itself. In this context, shari'a offers hope.

This concluding chapter amplifies three bold propositions about religion and the rule of law:

(1) The rule of law has its roots in religion when political elites use religious principles to build peace and stable states (examined in the next two sections, "Religion and Law" and "Shari'a as the Rule of Law").

(2) Religion does not always promote the rule of law, precisely because political elites invoke religious discourse or God's will instrumentally as tools of legal politics (examined in the third section, "Shari'a Politics as Legal Politics").

(3) The rule of law offers its own systematically developed and internally coherent theory of a higher power, which – to the pious – makes it an alternative form of theology (examined in the final section, "The Rule of Law as Theology").

RELIGION AND LAW

My investigation of Somalia and Somaliland provides insight into the ways in which religion, law, and politics intersect in other contexts and times. These findings are as critical to understanding how colonies and dictatorships suppress dissent as they are to understanding how democracies struggle under pandemic, populism, and racism. Like the law, religion provides symbols, meanings, and idioms to those who use it to achieve their political, economic, and social goals. People in many places turn toward, rather than away from, religious values to shape law and politics. For those who believe in human rights and the rule of law, trouble begins when political elites invoke religion in order to put down dissent, constrain activism, or mistreat minorities. But religion – even the religion of a majority – can sometimes serve as a check on power and a source of strategy and hope for activists who work on behalf of marginalized populations.

Political elites have used and manipulated religious principles for centuries. The pagan religions of antiquity gave birth to Roman law and the "concept of *ius*, from which justice, jurisprudence, judge, and judiciary come."[5] From Roman law arose Western legal cultures and canon law. In pre-modern settings, judges accounted for their verdicts before God.[6] In early modern Europe and North America, political

---

[5] Rafael Domingo, *God and the Secular Legal System* (Cambridge: Cambridge University Press, 2017), 3.

[6] Mirjan Damaška, *Evaluation of Evidence: Pre-Modern and Modern Approaches* (Cambridge: Cambridge University Press, 2019).

291

elites building new states used what they called Christian law and ethics to develop legal systems and compel obedience to the rule of law. Christianity was, in the words of political historian Francis Fukuyama, "intimately bound up with the development of the ... European state and with the emergence of ... the rule of law."[7] This book has shown that the widespread and longstanding assumptions that people trying to build Islamic states do not follow this pattern, and that Islam is antithetical to the rule of law, do not hold.

Eventually Islam, like Christianity, can become the root of state law and the foundation upon which to build the rule of law. Rights-oriented, militant, and other versions of shari'a are not new; each reiterates an older version, making theology, like politics and law, a lived tradition. It continually changes as people reinterpret God's will for their own places and times. As people build social worlds they would like to inhabit, they confront, entangle, and pull apart law and theology. Examining a state legal system's historical emergence and logic (such as it is) requires going "inside the system" to understand the diversity of legal actors and the tools they use.[8] My investigation of the modern history of the Horn of Africa reveals that shari'a, even when it seems absent, powerfully informs how people shape states, societies, and their laws.

Classical sociologists of law have speculated that human thought, industry, and law derive from God; this book has shown how people build societies into states either out of the belief that they are doing God's will or, cynically, by exploiting or disregarding God's will for personal and political power.[9] Using religion to build states, and then separating law from religion, is a colonial project. British legal philosophers Hale and Blackstone long ago saw how Christianity pervaded British state law; later, colonial officials – among others, the British in Sudan and the Portuguese in Guinea-Bissau – constructed mosques to prop up religious institutions in order to surveil their political activities. This interpenetration of law and religion is a primary sign of

---

[7] Francis Fukuyama, *The Origins of Political Order: From Prehuman Times to the French Revolution* (London: Profile Books, 2012), 241.

[8] Marina Kurkchiyan and Agnieszka Kubal, "Administerial Justice," in *A Sociology of Justice in Russia*, eds. Marina Kurkchiyan and Agnieszka Kubal (Cambridge: Cambridge University Press, 2018), 276.

[9] See, for example, Émile Durkheim, *The Elementary Forms of the Religious Life*, trans. Joseph Ward Swain (Mineola, NY: Dover Publications, [1915] 2008); Henry Sumner Maine, *Ancient Law: Its Connection with the Early History of Society, and its Relation to Modern Ideas* (London: John Murray, 1861).

modernism, and can still be found around the world in appeals to Hinduism in Indian law, Judaism in Israeli law, Eastern Orthodox Christianity in Russian law and politics, Buddhism in Sri Lanka's and Myanmar's legal systems, Catholicism in Latin American courts and legislation, and Protestant Christianity in US and European law and politics. Too often, though, the most vocal defenders of faith seek to restrict, rather than to promote, political freedoms. But, while they use statements of religious faith or dogma to oppress, others use theological principles to dissent. They turn to their faith to create, abide by, and support principles that liberal lawmakers associate with peacebuilding, international law, and the protection of human rights.

But religion is not merely a colonial or postcolonial political fantasy. It is also a cultural thread woven into daily life. As legal scholar Rafael Domingo has argued, "God has ... legal relevance that cannot be ignored [even] by secular legal systems."[10] In some places, majorities of citizens do not see religion as problematic because their religions represent the dominant political culture. Catholicism in Ireland, Hindutva (or Hindu nationalism) in India,[11] Judaism in Israel, and Buddhism in Bhutan fit this description; in Pakistan, state leaders have portrayed Pakistanis as united by faith (Islam) and language (Urdu).[12] In these places, religious, ethnic, and linguistic minorities continue to fight for their security. But faith has also guided political resistance, as people align their faith with many ideals, not only conservative and restrictive but also moderate and progressive.[13]

In India, a superficially secular apparatus that disguises Hindu nationalism has also based its survival in part on ensuring that Muslim minorities resolve family disputes in religious courts, called *dar ul qazaas*. The result is that "Indian state secularism *needs* the

[10] Domingo (2017), 10.
[11] Thomas Blom Hansen, *The Saffron Wave: Democracy and Hindu Nationalism in Modern India* (Princeton, NJ: Princeton University Press, 1999); Angana P. Chatterji, Thomas Blom Hansen, and Christophe Jaffrelot, eds. *Majoritarian State: How Hindu Nationalism is Changing India* (London: Hurst, 2019).
[12] Maryam S. Khan, "Ethnic Federalism in Pakistan: Federal Design, Construction of Ethno-Linguistic Identity & Group Conflict," 30 *Harvard Journal of Racial and Ethnic Justice* (2014): 77–129.
[13] Interpretations of Christian ethics emanate from "evangelical, Pentecostal, new Christian conservative, liberal, Black, liberationist, creationist, feministic, [and] syncretic" views, among others. Cecelia M. Lynch, *Wrestling with God: Ethical Precarity in Christianity and International Relations* (Cambridge: Cambridge University Press, 2020), 240–241. On Jewish commitments to social justice, see David N. Myers, ed., *The Eternal Dissident: Rabbi Leonard I. Beerman and the Radical Imperative to Think and Act* (Oakland, CA: University of California Press, 2018).

Islamic non-state" to survive.[14] The state has ceded some of its functions to judges of these tribunals, who themselves are nonstate actors. In Egypt and Turkey, the state has regulated, surveilled, and exerted control over religious leaders and institutions. In Nigeria, concern over shari'a likewise was essential to producing the country's "second republic" in the 1980s. Shari'a remains important throughout the country, especially in Nigeria's Muslim-majority north, where people see it as embodying an idealized, utopian past and think that, if only shari'a were implemented properly, it would rectify present-day social injustices.[15] By coding shari'a as law – as British colonial officials and Somali political elites have done in the Horn of Africa – these states have made their legal systems look inclusive. This action has also enabled them to use shari'a as they wished. They saw Islam as potentially defeating the state, so they subsumed it and then built another system over it, never giving it much of a chance.

The struggle to understand God's will can lead to equally harmful or helpful results. It has produced, in the words of political scientist Cecelia Lynch, "the cruelest kinds of human bondage."[16] Pope Urban II, for instance, used the Latin phrase, *Deus vult* (God wills it) in 1095 to launch the Crusades against Muslims. But religious discourse has also been the foundation of local peacebuilding initiatives and attitudes favorable to liberal democracy in the world's highest-conflict regions.[17]

Religious faith has advanced human rights and social change in the US too. Christianity, Islam, Judaism, and other faith traditions have motivated many American activists to speak out against racial discrimination and police violence, in the Civil Rights Movement of the 1950s and 1960s and in the Black Lives Matter movement of the 2010s and 2020s.[18] When national and state laws have failed to live up to

---

[14] Jeffrey A. Redding, *A Secular Need: Islamic Law and State Governance in Contemporary India* (Seattle, WA: University of Washington Press, 2020), 4.

[15] Ebenezer Odabare, *Pentecostal Republic: Religion and the Struggle for State Power in Nigeria* (London: Zed Books, 2018); Sarah Eltantawi, *Shari'ah on Trial: Northern Nigeria's Islamic Revolution* (Oakland, CA: University of California Press, 2017); see also David D. Laitin, "The Sharia Debate and the Origin of Nigeria's Second Republic," 20(3) *Journal of Modern African Studies* (1982): 411–430.

[16] Lynch (2020), 234.

[17] David R. Smock, ed. *Religious Contributions to Peacemaking: When Religion Brings Peace, Not War*, Peaceworks No. 55 (Washington, DC: United States Institute of Peace, 2006); Robert A. Dowd, *Christianity, Islam, and Liberal Democracy: Lessons from Sub-Saharan Africa* (Oxford: Oxford University Press, 2015).

[18] Biko Mandela Gray, "Religion in/and Black Lives Matter: Celebrating the Impossible," 13(1) *Religion Compass* (2019): 1–9; Vincent Lloyd, ed., *Religion, Secularism, and Black Lives Matter*, The Immanent Frame (New York: Social Sciences Research Council), 2016, available: https://bit.ly/39YfZu7.

religious ethics and morality, civil rights defenders have fought back against those laws, in some cases submitting to arrest and imprisonment. Jehovah's Witnesses have taken cases to the US Supreme Court to expand American free speech protections. Progressive Christian denominations have promoted equality on the basis of gender identity. More recently, Muslims in the US have responded to domestic anti-shari'a legislation and anti-Muslim hate by merging US constitutional law with shari'a to promote social and economic justice for minorities and the poor.[19]

Morocco, Tunisia, and Pakistan each expanded constitutional rights to gender equality through shari'a, using progressive feminist interpretations of Islam to reform key laws. Catholic theology contributed to the development of human rights law in the mid-twentieth century and the repudiation of communist regimes in Eastern Europe in the late twentieth century.[20] To help change cultural values and create new laws, Orthodox Christian Patriarch Bartholomew I of Constantinople defined environmental harm as sin, asserting that nations that "degrade the integrity of the earth and contaminate the planet's waters, land and air" offend God. In Israel, some Jews have fought the rise of populist nationalism and a "clear movement towards authoritarianism" by using Hebrew law to promote tolerance and oppose systematic discrimination against Arab minorities.[21]

In Muslim-majority states, the problem is not shari'a, it is what people have done with it. Shari'a, like other forms of religious law, can be both the foundation of the legal system and an ethical guide to challenging and reforming the law, an important "check on political power."[22] Even the occupying US administration in Iraq allowed Iraqis to write Islam into their constitution in 2005, subsuming legal pluralism, helping to create a unified state authority, and making religion a constitutional anchor for civil rights. The leaders of Sudan's 2019 revolution, after toppling the thirty-year authoritarian regime of President Omar Hassan al-Bashir, reminded the country's Muslim

---

[19] Mark Fathi Massoud and Kathleen M. Moore, "Shari'a Consciousness: Law and Lived Religion among California Muslims," 45(3) *Law & Social Inquiry* (2020): 787–817.

[20] Leonard Francis Taylor, *Catholic Cosmopolitanism and Human Rights* (Cambridge: Cambridge University Press, 2020).

[21] Paul Scham, "'A Nation that Dwells Alone': Israeli Religious Nationalism in the 21st Century," 23(3) *Israel Studies* (2018): 207–215, 212; Gideon D. Sylvester, "Social Justice Lies at the Heart of the Jewish People," *Haaretz*, June 30, 2012, available: https://bit.ly/33UOVYX; Nir Kedar, "The Rule of Law in Israel," 23(3) *Israel Studies* (2018): 164–171.

[22] Fukuyama (2012), 241.

religious leaders that it was their "sacred duty" to promote harmony and compassion, emphasizing that "We were created from the same soul, so we must protect this soul in order to protect" the democratic transition.[23]

Like Sudan's revolutionary leaders, women in Afghanistan after the Taliban's 2001 collapse also laid claim "to a hegemonic religious discourse that has historically excluded them."[24] In particular, and much like women in the Horn of Africa, they have consistently rendered their knowledge legible in Islamic terms. But, as with foreign donors in Somalia and Somaliland, donors in Afghanistan gave shari'a "startlingly little attention" as they tried "to foster civil society without offending religious sensibilities . . . Islam [remains] the elephant in the NGO seminar rooms."[25] Such donors still treat religion as an impediment to building the rule of law.

Reflecting on decades of research on the legal profession, including his own, sociologist Terry Halliday explained, "An unexpected finding recurred. When we went looking for lawyers and liberalism, we . . . found religion. When we observed barristers, we saw priests . . ., ministers and imams. When we studied bar associations, we encountered churches and mosques. When we analyzed jurisprudence, we were . . . confronted with theology."[26] As Terry Halliday found in his own work, this study of legal politics and my own search for the rule of law in the Horn of Africa has revealed the enduring reach of shari'a. Religious persons, faith, and discourses constructed – not just destroyed – peace, states, and legal systems. The twists and turns of Somali history – through customary law, colonialism, religious resistance to Siad Barre's dictatorship, and peacebuilding efforts in Somalia and Somaliland – illuminate how shari'a thrives in the struggle to build legal and social order. Political leaders, militants, feminist activists, and aid workers have all engaged with God, even in times of disorienting political violence when God was hard to find. Collectively these persons have invoked shari'a, compartmentalized it, hidden it, sought

[23] Sudan Professionals Association, "Forces of Freedom and Change (FCC) Speech, on Signing the Agreement," August 17, 2019, available: https://bit.ly/3qL7MPO (accessed January 1, 2021).

[24] Sonia Ahsan, "When Muslims Become Feminists: Khana-yi Aman, Islam, and Pashtunwali," in *Afghanistan's Islam: From Conversion to the Taliban*, ed. Nile Green (Oakland, CA: University of California Press, 2017), 225–241, p. 226.

[25] Nile Green, "Introduction," in *Afghanistan's Islam: From Conversion to the Taliban*, ed. Nile Green (Oakland, CA: University of California Press, 2017), 1–40, p. 26.

[26] Terence C. Halliday, "The Conscience of Society? The Legal Complex, Religion, and the Fates of Political Liberalism," in *The Paradox of Professionalism: Lawyers and the Possibility of Justice*, ed. Scott L. Cummings (Cambridge: Cambridge University Press, 2011), 50–67, p. 51.

to impose some version of it, integrated it into political systems, justified decisions with it, or fought for freedom with it. As they struggled to achieve their own version of a good society, shari'a became a source not only of their anguish but also of their hope.

SHARI'A AS THE RULE OF LAW

Shari'a informs and exists alongside other ethical and legal systems that compete for people's attention and trust. It has come to matter in domestic politics not because extremists use it as a pretext for violence but because legal professionals use it as a mechanism to deliver justice and create limited governments. Somali history shows how some people have tried to hold their communities and governments together through a shared submission to God's will, or at least a shared assertion that their political positions are consistent with what God has willed. Semantically and practically, these people unify the values of the rule of law with the values of shari'a. For them, the rule of shari'a *is* the rule of law.

Shari'a can break states. It can also make them. In times when the ideal of the rule of law, and even the state itself, was absent, piety provided the moral accountability that state law could not. Somali society functioned, and moneychangers continued to work without fear of being robbed "because [we] are Muslim and ... must accept shari'a," as one lawyer told me.[27] Because some interpretations of shari'a fit readily into global constitutional norms, shari'a can constitute the rule of law rather than subvert it. In the Horn of Africa, as one American observer of the region told me, shari'a may look "illiberal and against human rights. But it's all they've got."[28] Obedience to the rule of law and to God's will, two interlaced higher powers, makes it easier to contest unlimited political authority.

Under what conditions do people align shari'a with values associated with the rule of law, such as challenging arbitrary authority or promoting limited government? On a practical level, Somalis have invoked shari'a – not the rule of law – precisely when they pursue these values. As recounted in Chapter 2, in the early twentieth century, Sheikh Mohamed Abdullah Hassan used shari'a to challenge British colonial intervention in the Horn of Africa, fundamentally disrupting the

---

[27] Interview 60 with Tariq, legal aid attorney in Hargeisa, Somaliland (July 2013).
[28] Interview 16 with Todd, expatriate consultant and professor, in Hargeisa, Somaliland (June 2013).

British colonial presence. Like the British administration, he also formed an army and amassed Somali followers. But to discredit the religious fervor that drove his vision of an independent society free from colonial intervention, colonial communications and media reports labeled him the "Mad Mullah."

Later, the sheikhs described in Chapter 3 fought Siad Barre's dictatorship by setting obedience to God's will as the limit on their dictator's authority. But they paid with their lives for their dissent and for understanding shari'a differently from the regime. As Chapter 4 shows, Somalia's "stateless" years demonstrate how shari'a courts – like the courts that sprang up in the early history of democracies – can become the seedlings from which peace and the rule of law grow. After Siad Barre's ouster and Somalia's collapse in 1991, warlords began patrolling the thoroughfares. Judges in Mogadishu stabilized their neighborhoods by relying on their own understanding of shari'a to punish criminals. They ousted warlords, allowing people to leave their homes and feel safe for the first time in years. Because Islam was one of the only credible institutions left in Somalia, it was no accident that the courts that took shape were inspired and justified by shari'a. When these courts merged into the Islamic Courts Union and became more vocal about national politics, they succumbed to the US-backed Ethiopian military intervention of 2006–2007, underscoring how warlords and Western governments alike fear the power of fusing law and religion by invoking shari'a.

Political elites in Somalia and Somaliland wrote Islam into their constitutions – that is, they constructed their own Islamic states – in part to stave off extremist threats. Few have done more to promote rule-of-law principles in the Horn of Africa than the founders of Somaliland in the 1990s, as Chapter 5 demonstrates. To those unaware of Somali history or the varied ways in which people use shari'a in politics, these men might at first seem to be shari'a's unlikeliest allies. They began as rebels amassing weapons against a government. But they were not trying to build a dictatorship so much as to topple one and replace it with constitutional democracy. From the start, Somaliland's state-builders saw shari'a as a source of hope from God for political change.

Somalis today continue to turn to sheikhs for help resolving disputes, particularly when they consider state courts untrustworthy or slow. In places rife with mistrust of both the state and foreign aid workers, I have met activists trying to build societies consistent with their understanding of Islamic values. As Chapter 6 shows, women activists have invoked shari'a to persuade sheikhs, and society as a whole, to see women's rights as Islamic rights. To these persons, Islam provides the moral accountability, trust, strategy, and faith – in short, the hope – that state leaders, aid workers, and their promises of the rule of law do not offer them.

While many political elites throughout modern Somali history have used shari'a to build values associated with the rule of law, aid workers from foreign governments, UN agencies, and international NGOs have consistently evaded religion not because they did not know it was there – it is hard to miss – but because they did not know what to do with it. Their silence about shari'a, alongside their active promotion of the rule of law, signals that they see these two concepts in opposition to each other, which in turn generates problems in the public perception of aid work and foreigners. Like colonial administrators long before them, contemporary aid workers and international lawyers worry about unearthing and legitimizing versions of religious law that they cannot control or that go beyond the bounds of their conscience. But their silence has facilitated the proliferation of a singular understanding of shari'a, connected to extremism, just as their practices have also shaped the meaning of democracy or development or the rule of law itself as disconnected from extremism.

Aid groups promote non-Islamic law in part out of the fear that shari'a could dilute or defeat the state's authority. Unable to react properly to people's faith in the importance of God's will – and shari'a as its vehicle – they have supported legal aid, legal education, and legal reform projects to secularize the state and minimize religion. These well-meaning international legal projects sometimes cultivate and institutionalize the very problems they seek to resolve. During my visit to Hargeisa in 2019, an aid worker who had just arrived from Europe asked me what English-language materials he should consult to learn about Somali law. I pointed across the room to the Somali lawyers, activists, and intellectuals working at their desks, reminding him that his colleagues and their experiences ought to be his primary sources of knowledge. Somali students I met, meanwhile, were making good-faith efforts to learn about the human rights law that such aid workers promoted, in law schools and legal aid programs set up by those aid workers. As aid workers encouraged Somali political leaders to regulate religion – for instance, by designating sheikhs as state employees, a practice instigated by British colonial officials – their actions further fragmented and pluralized the law.

The legal histories of Somalia and Somaliland reveal that in contexts where religion seems to dictate law's power and politics, religious law may stand in a better position than international law to institute peace, stability, and the values associated with the rule of law. But aid workers' projects promoting the rule of law – building state legal systems and their courts, prisons, law schools, and legal aid programs – have detached religion from law and purged law of religion's influence, even though religion may actually be doing the work of promoting the rule of law. Severing religion from the rule of law disempowers and stigmatizes the faithful, sapping them of their humanness. As Jewish theologian Martin Buber wrote, humanity and faith "are not separate realms ... Our faith has our humanity as its foundation and our humanity has ... faith as its foundation."[29] Most pernicious about colonial and postcolonial attempts to impose secularism in Muslim-majority societies – separating Islam from law or containing and co-opting shari'a – is the way they attack humanity, corroding or even cracking the foundation of the rule of law itself.

The rule of law is as riven with indeterminacy as shari'a is. Like any discourse or ideal introduced into politics, shari'a and the rule of law are not without problems. However perfect as ideals, shari'a and the rule of law make imperfect tools of legal politics. Political tools are as faulty as those who use them, and promoting the rule of law – like promoting shari'a – has come to symbolize both what is sacred to politics and what corrupts politics. In practice, people's social position – their gender, ethnicity, wealth, educational attainment, marital or disability status, skin color, and other characteristics – influences the extent to which they may benefit from the rule of law's promises. For the world's Christians and Jews, too, not just for Muslims, one's identity character-istics, precarity, suffering, commitments, and wrestling with God form the "lifeblood" of ethics.[30]

Shari'a remains central to the political development of the Horn of Africa. From the British and Italian colonial administrations through the Siad Barre dictatorship and beyond, political regimes in the Horn of Africa – colonial, democratic, and authoritarian – rewrote laws while struggling against the majority of Somalis who judged those laws by

[29] Paul Mendes-Flohr, *Martin Buber: A Life of Faith and Dissent* (New Haven, CT: Yale University Press, 2019), 290–291, citing Martin Buber, *A Believing Humanism: My Testament, 1902–1965*, trans. Maurice Friedman (New York:Simon & Schuster, 1967), 117. On the ways that US law masks humanity, see John T. Noonan, *Persons and Masks of the Law: Cardozo, Holmes, Jefferson, and Wythe as Makers of the Masks* (Oakland, CA: University of California Press, [1976] 2002).
[30] Lynch (2020), 234.

God's will. Politicians sought to control religion, but the pious used religion to set boundaries on political leaders' behavior. The debate is not about whether to have an Islamic state. That debate ended long ago. The debate is about how to have an Islamic state that strives toward the ideal of the rule of law. The politics of the Horn of Africa remain, like politics anywhere, imperfect. But many people are committed to peace, and they often draw inspiration from shari'a. In this context, people disagree with what God wills and what they feel God's will entitles them to do to others.

SHARI'A POLITICS AS LEGAL POLITICS

Throughout Somali history people have invoked shari'a to promote values associated with the rule of law. The bravery, fealty, humility, restraint, and altruism with which people have fought for the rule of law are unqualified human goods, even if others have not used their faith to promote these values. While this book has shown that the interpretation and use of shari'a is a Somali project, it has also shown that using shari'a – like using the rule of law – is a political project of elites who wish to create states and legal systems and to lead them. Throughout modern Somali history, the rule of law and shari'a have been promoted side by side, largely among educated Somalis, foreigners, and observers – colonial administrators, military dictators, rebel leaders, activists, and aid workers. They all hoped that submission to religious faith or to the rule of law would save them and their societies. When seen across time, they seem to have cloaked shari'a in as many rhetorical characteristics as the rule of law can be cloaked in – dogma, law, practice, surrender, hope, and more.

When political elites try to build law or legal institutions and use those laws and institutions to achieve their goals – in short, when they engage in legal politics – they also use and transform religion. Somalia's and Somaliland's political architects, from colonial administrators to contemporary politicians, all co-opted shari'a's power. To achieve their goals, they invoked, used, and transformed their own versions of shari'a – and suppressed or disarmed other versions. These actions left fingerprints on state legal institutions, and on shari'a itself, inextricably linking shari'a with politics.

As documented in Chapter 2, administrators of British Somaliland and Italian Somalia forced Islamic and colonial laws into an uneasy codependence, bringing colonial law and Islamic theology together to

enhance foreign claims to legitimacy and occupation. British colonization rewrote and reinterpreted Islam for Somalis by importing views of
shari'a from Mecca and London. Colonial officials saw how, just as
religion changes the law, law can change religion. They sidelined,
confined, and managed religion under the law to the point that religion
could come to be seen as nearly absent from the state: the active but
well-diluted ingredient of colonialism's homeopathic solution for the
ills of the uncivilized.

Unlike in Britain's colonies in Sudan, Uganda or South and
Southeast Asia, the British administration in Somaliland did not establish colleges, training schools, or other spaces to educate people about
democracy in any meaningful way. They seemed to know that the less
they interfered, the more they could penetrate. They built a state that
separated religion from politics, and then they invoked it for their own
political purposes. Aqils and sultans enforced a politically palatable
version of shari'a, becoming colonialism's political and religious professional class. Colonial officials also waged a war of weapons and words
against Somalis who used God's will to resist the administration's will.
While British invocations of shari'a may seem striking, they make sense
given the blurred ways in which religion and law intersected for colonial officials and those subjected to their rule. Administrators of Italian
Somalia acted no differently when they, too, recognized shari'a in
restricted ways and tried to limit its potential to damage the colonial
enterprise.

Postcolonial elites, like colonial officials before them, also used
shari'a instrumentally. They tried to maintain legal pluralism rather
than risk empowering a version of shari'a that they could not control.
Their efforts underscore how postcolonial states are not quite "post," for
the processes that colonial officials set into motion endure long past
their departure. The colonial legacy of legal pluralism in the Horn of
Africa was a complex brew of English common law, Italian law, different forms of xeer, and prior local versions of shari'a, all of which
colonialism transformed. As Chapter 3 discussed, the 1950s pre-
independence containment of shari'a continued after the 1960 independence, when the democratic government of the Somali Republic
closed the British-instituted Islamic courts and integrated shari'a into
the judiciary. Italian and American lawyers trying to develop a Somali
democracy co-opted Islamic styles of argument to dilute religious law's
impact on the state's legal system. All the while, political leaders
drafted constitutional provisions and new laws to cement the nascent

state's authority over what they hoped to make a single, unified legal system.

The authoritarian regime in Somalia differed little from its colonial and democratic predecessors in its attempts to stifle the power of religion and build a legal system in its own image, out of its own righteousness. As described in Chapter 3, Mohamed Siad Barre, Somalia's dictator from 1969 to 1991, revamped the legal system and dressed it up in a version of shari'a that suited nondemocratic rule. Similarly, political elites in Somalia and Somaliland since 1991 have used shari'a to construct their own Islamic states, writing Islam into their constitutions in part to stave off threats from al-Shabaab. They all tried to contain, rather than abolish, shari'a.

Like the generation that preceded Somalia's 1991 collapse, the generation that followed never saw a robust rule of law. But, determined not to repeat Siad Barre's authoritarian rule, different leaders in Somalia and Somaliland since his ouster – elders, sheikhs, government officials, and militants – have emboldened themselves with shari'a, writing Islam into their constitutions, judgments, and laws. As Chapter 6 revealed, feminist activists, too, have invoked shari'a – usually a symbol of their repression – as a source of their redemption. Combining piety and strategy, they have used anti-sexist interpretations of Quranic text and Hadith to advocate with sheikhs for better access to education, politics, and health, and for an end to sexual violence, because God demands these things for women. While aid groups have lauded and supported women's organizations' human rights goals, they also have largely shunned the discursive power and political potential of framing women's concerns as willed by God. In so doing, these groups disregard the wisdom of women activists they support financially and purport to assist.

People invoke shari'a in quite different ways even within al-Shabaab. After the fall of the Islamic Courts Union, people putting their faith in al-Shabaab used shari'a to justify extreme and often opposing ends. Some in al-Shabaab benefitted financially from piracy and terror, while others spoke out against piracy and terror as crimes that did not accord with God's will. Some in al-Shabaab instilled fear in those who did not support the organization, while others created space for people to work out their problems. In 2018, some al-Shabaab operatives were organizing suicide attacks, while others were instituting an environmental protection ban on single-use plastic bags. These choices, incompatible to outsiders, came from obedience to God's unknowable will. Put a different way, religion both undergirds the law and facilitates dissent from it; and law lies more outside the state's control than state leaders might hope, precisely because religion and people's beliefs shape the law.

In my research for *Shari'a, Inshallah*, as in Sudan while researching for *Law's Fragile State*, I saw time and again how political elites used law both to serve and to harm others. Laws in Somalia and Somaliland, as in many places struggling with legacies of political violence, have become weapons in the arsenal of politics, to be wielded this way and that. In these places I also witnessed activists use different laws – those of human rights – to challenge orthodoxy. The invocation of an unqualified rule of law – like the release of a religious passion – can hamper or support the achievement of the ideal itself, depending on the contexts in which it is invoked and the goals of those who invoke it.

THE RULE OF LAW AS A THEOLOGY

I have distinguished between the rule of law as a kind of legal belief and theology as a kind of religious belief. But the concepts merge and are actually quite similar. This section illuminates this book's final proposition – that is, that the rule of law and theology bear striking conceptual, genealogical, and empirical commonalities. States constitute legal systems as having their own wills, which emanate from or compete with divine will. Like a parallel god, law demands that citizens submit to its will. Activists, like the state authorities they resist, also submit to their own interpretations of God's will to achieve their own goals.

Religion and law constitute and shape one another, state politics, and civic activism. Across time, religion drifts into and out of law so that, when viewed at any single moment, legal and religious traditions seem to share a single origin. Analyzing law and religion in a single space across time, as *Shari'a, Inshallah* has done, is an historical and social scientific exercise in parsing the relations among overlapping normative systems. Each civic activist or member of the political elite revives religion as a living tradition to justify what they seek from the law. They then merge law and religion to achieve their goals of building nations or promoting rights. Religious traditions metamorphose and diffuse into society as they become sealed into stable, national "law." As adversaries fight – physically in wars and discursively in courts or in communications with one another – over their interpretations of shari'a and its relationship with the law, they all take God's unknowable will, time and again, into battle.

Documenting the rule of law's ongoing relationship with religion is important for understanding not only religious law's place in Western political history, but also its potential in non-Western societies confronting the legacies of colonial and postcolonial politics.

The rule of law offers its own set of internally coherent beliefs, which in practice look like an alternative theology. What do these striking parallels between theology and the rule of law reveal? They imply that building the state is an attempt to build an alternative to theology. They show that law is inseparable not only from politics but also from lived religious experience. Law's moral accountability comes from its connection to people's trust in the state or from its connection to godliness. Shari'a has as many meanings in practice as people have given to other objects of their work: democracy, development, and the rule of law. Each can be achieved through violent or nonviolent means, through direct political engagement, or through personal reflection and collective prayer.

Like shari'a, the rule of law demands a radical faith that its principles will lead to peace, justice, and social and political order. Belief in the rule of law requires hope that political leaders will submit to its message. Hope, however, demands subjects willing to have faith. Law and religion constitute power not just through their doctrines, but also through people's faith that law and religion can ease their suffering. Like theology, the rule of law demands interpretation of traditions. Such an interpretive and critical sensibility makes centuries-old principles relevant to and transformative in contemporary contexts. But these interpretive acts, when repeated across generations and places, risk separating people into believers and disbelievers, over the long term transforming a crisis of theology into a crisis in the rule of law.

The social theorist Martin Krygier labeled himself "someone with a soft spot for the rule of law."[31] I, too, hope for the rule of law, while recognizing the colonial history in which this hope has been deployed and the postcolonial history that it has helped shape. Even in the rule of law's absence, like a god it remains. The fact that some elites do not believe or do not practice does not mean it does not exist. On the contrary, it remains hidden in the aspirations that guide activists' choices of which battles to fight and how hard to fight them. The fate of the rule of law, like the fate of religion in the colonial world, depends

---

[31] Martin Krygier, "The Rule of Law between England and Sudan: Hay, Thompson, and Massoud," 41(2) *Law & Social Inquiry* (2016): 480–488.

on what people do with it and the meanings they give it in politics – from grassroots activists' attempts to construct it from the ground up to political elites' attempts to impose it from the top down. Like religious values, the values of the rule of law may be achieved, destroyed, or reconfigured through cycles of violence and peacebuilding. Like the rule of law, shari'a has hegemonic and non-hegemonic qualities. Like shari'a, the rule of law can create hegemony and undo it.

The paradox of law is very much like the paradox of religion: both rely on the operative concept that people must submit to nonhuman entities that can and should limit human behavior. Put another way, law and religion are two different horizons of the human, created by the human, that also take us beyond the human. They both require a radical, inexplicable, and unknowable faith. What unites the legal, theological, and spiritual aspects of Islam (*islam*, *iman*, and *ihsan*, from the Hadith of the Angel Gabriel, described in Chapter 1) is the powerful notion that people must act toward others and toward the earth as if God is constantly watching and judging.

The authority of the law and the authority of God, if they exist in any society, derive from people's faith in them, either in the stability they provide or in the transformative potential they promise. These forms of authority also inhere in the fear of consequences in this life or the next. Standing on a precarious ledge – as the Marxist historian E. P. Thompson did long ago when he labeled the rule of law an unqualified human good – if we were to say that the rule of law is not only a human good but also a gift from a higher power, then would political leaders be more likely to care for it? Would we as scholars be more willing to fight for it in our papers and lectures? Would lawyers take more care in planning activities that promote it? Or would our fervent prayers for the rule of law cause us to see ourselves as God's chosen, ascribe excessive authority to our plans, and save ourselves while the poor wonder why we worship our idol so zealously?

My study of law in Somali political history has taught me how religious faith and experience generate legal systems – be they colonial, authoritarian, democratic, or even collapsed legal systems. I have also learned how cosmopolitanism, while not requiring faith in God, requires embracing the faithful and their struggle to submit to God's will. It also requires deep and meaningful moral convictions or, at least, in the words of legal philosopher Ronald Dworkin, a "religious attitude to life . . . believing we have made something good in [the face of death]."[32] Such a theological sensibility about the rule of law involves believing, as Dworkin wrote months prior to his own death, that we are "filling the world with value and purpose."[33] It illuminates how dictatorial, populist, and patriarchal powers belong not to humans, nor to God, nor to religion.

Insofar as we each will into our lives a higher power – a spouse or parent, the rule of law, or God – we constrain our own will by trying to understand that higher power's will for us. Submission to God, like obedience to the rule of law, is not merely an object of study. It is a lived, practiced, and real experience. It is a form of personal devotion, and it is a political strategy. In Somalia and Somaliland, as in many other places, it makes sense that shari'a – a legal, political, social, and ethical guide that predated a chaotic and divisive colonial and postcolonial history and that has been integrated with local customs – has functioned as people's shared reference point. When a political leader limits their power by submitting to what they believe is a higher, nonhuman power, their recognition of that greater power involves following principles that observers associate with the rule of law. The rule of law relies upon collective acceptance that such a nonhuman power – either God or the law – is in control. For those who have struggled against colonialism, dictatorship, extremism, and foreign intervention, God's will creates agency precisely through one's submission to it. Acceptance of a higher power – be it God's power, law's power, or both – creates space for the humility leaders need to recognize that their authority is not arbitrary and that it has limits.

The fact that people building countries in such seemingly disparate places as the Horn of Africa, North America, and Western Europe all engaged with religious thought to construct their legal institutions means that, for them, law and religion were inseparable from one another and from politics. It does not mean that the rule of law and religion are compatible in some places and not others. Religion's imprint is part of the foundation of legal institutions, and people tearing down those institutions or rebuilding them reshape both the rule of law and religion. As religion forms the root of state law, it also becomes the

---

[32] Ronald Dworkin, *Religion without God* (Cambridge, MA: Harvard University Press, 2013), 155, 158.
[33] Ibid., 1.

foundation of the rule of law, rendering law, politics, religion, and morality inseparable.

With some trepidation I write these reflections about the Horn of Africa from my desk far away in California, amidst a barrage of reports of political leaders who stoke my innermost fears of unfettered authority. The pathologies of their projects caused my family to seek refuge from Sudan decades ago, carrying with us little but faith in a better life. In the intervening years, many Somali faithful have attempted the same journey. My fortunes – surviving dictatorship, emigrating, learning, and teaching – have allowed me to investigate the politics of law and to challenge the orthodoxy that law, religion, and politics are separate, when they only seem so because we study them separately. From my privileged place I mourn the erosion of a global commitment to the revolutionary concept underlying the rule of law, the same concept underlying God, as I watch politicians use religion, public health, public order, and other pretexts to consolidate power and stretch political and legal systems past their breaking points. In times of fragility and fearfulness, faith remains, as it did long ago during my journey out of Sudan. It is faith for courage in the face of fear, faith for comfort in the face of uncertainty, and faith in the radical notion that we can dissent from those in power by surrendering to a different power. Surrendering to a different higher power – God, the rule of law, democratic constitutionalism, or whatever we choose – guides us into faith that even under the most intractable regimes or during crises, change can still come.

The complex and often misunderstood role of religion is as real in fragile or authoritarian states as it is in Western democracies where, as Richard Abel has warned, the rule of law remains under grave threat.[34] International lawyers, aid workers, and other modern defenders of the rule of law must consider their faith not only in legal tools but also in religious ones.

Ending my interview with him in Hargeisa, an imam told me he felt free because "the white man left Africa." When I asked for clarification, he paused, and continued: "When the white man also takes his thoughts, his culture, his legal system, his economic domination, and his political influence – on that day, I will finally

---

[34] Richard Abel, *Law's Wars: The Fate of the Rule of Law in the US "War on Terror"* (Cambridge: Cambridge University Press, 2018).

be independent."[35] Somali political history reveals that true independence demands faith, that faith in shari'a thrives in the construction of legal and social order, that faith in shari'a advances rule of law principles, and that faith in shari'a provides people hope that, inshallah, our actions serve a will higher than our own.

---

[35] Interview 127 with Sheikh Oweis, sheikh and senior university administrator in Hargeisa, Somaliland (June 2014).

Appendix A

METHODOLOGICAL DETAIL

This appendix supplements the methodological description found in the Introduction. Here, I provide further detail on the archival, ethnographic, interview, and data-analysis components of this study, particularly for scholars and students considering projects that involve comparative and historical research on law and religion in Somalia, Somaliland, or elsewhere.[1]

ARCHIVAL RESEARCH

Archival records on the colonial period, particularly materials from the British Somaliland Protectorate, are scattered across multiple cities in England and East Africa. I conducted archival research in the United Kingdom (Cambridge, Durham, London, and Oxford); Somaliland (Hargeisa), and Kenya (Nairobi). Together these six cities hold the largest collection of English-language documents on British Somaliland, its transitions to independence, and post-independence periods. The list summarizing the archives and libraries visited for this book follows in Appendix B.

---

[1] On conducting empirical research in conflict and post-conflict settings, see Mark Fathi Massoud, "Field Research on Law in Conflict Zones and Authoritarian States," 12 *Annual Review of Law and Social Science* (2016c): 85–106; Sarah Nouwen "'As You Set Out for Ithaka': Practical, Epistemological, Ethical, and Existential Questions about Socio-Legal Empirical Research in Conflict," 27(1) *Leiden Journal of International Law* (2014): 227–260.

United Kingdom
In the UK, I investigated how and why British colonial officials formalized shari'a by creating qadi courts and formalized Somali customs (*xeer*) by bringing local authorities into the British administration as dispute resolvers. I accessed original documents from the British Somaliland Protectorate (1884–1960), including memoirs of colonial officials and correspondences with the Foreign Office and their families, from the British Library, SOAS University of London, and the Royal Anthropological Institute in London; the Cambridge University Centre for African Studies; and the Oxford University African and Commonwealth Library, formerly at Rhodes House.

Somaliland and Kenya
Archival records and libraries I consulted in Hargeisa include the libraries of the University of Hargeisa and the Academy for Peace and Development, the resource center of the Institute of Peace and Conflict Studies, and the records offices of the Ministry of Planning, Ministry of Justice, and Ministry of Islamic Affairs. In Nairobi, I consulted archival materials kept at the Rift Valley Institute and the British Institute for Eastern Africa.

In addition to scouring these records, I accessed government documents from Somaliland to provide evidence for the argument that shari'a plays a critical role in state development. This includes compiling the registered lawyers, courts, clan chiefs, and non-state Islamic tribunals (*macduum*) from government ministries, including the Somaliland Ministry of Interior (which licenses *aqils*, or clan elders); the Ministry of Justice (which records the number and location of state courts and judges); and international and local aid groups active in the Horn of Africa, which have conducted legal assessments for their proposals to international donors. Organizations include the United Nations Development Programme (UNDP) Somalia, the Observatory for Conflict and Violence Prevention, and the University of Hargeisa Faculty of Law.

ETHNOGRAPHIC OBSERVATIONS

Understanding the role of Islamic legal politics in Somalia and Somaliland necessitates observations of law in action. In Hargeisa, I observed three key legal arenas: state courts; legal aid centers; and workshops and conferences designed and implemented by local or international aid groups. I was unable to sit in on non-state shari'a tribunals (macduum), which feature in the later chapters of this study, and customary tribunals involving clan elders (sultans and aqils), though sheikhs, sultans, aqils, and others whom I met and interviewed shared with me many stories from these venues.

State courts. In 2013 and 2014, with the assistance of a translator, I observed multiple proceedings of the district (shariʻa) and regional (non-shariʻa) courts of Hargeisa, to understand how people use religious discourse and rights discourse in state courts and the relationship between state law and religious legal principles in these places.

Legal aid centers. Somaliland's first law school opened in 2002 at the University of Hargeisa. A cohort of law graduates each year serves required one-year internships in one of the many legal aid centers throughout the country, including the University of Hargeisa Legal Aid Clinics (in Hargeisa, Berbera, and Burao), the Somaliland Lawyers Association Legal Aid Clinics, and the Somaliland Women Lawyers Association Legal Aid Clinics (in Hargeisa, Borama, and Burao). In the legal aid clinics I shadowed local lawyers and paralegals as they documented disputes and represented clients who otherwise would be unable to afford a private attorney.

Human rights workshops and conferences. Aid groups, primarily UN agencies or NGOs from Europe and North America, promote legal progress by holding educational workshops for government officials, religious leaders, and others to discuss law and development in the Horn of Africa. Many Somalis I met actively debated the relationship between principles of international law and human rights, largely drafted and taught by outsiders, and the customary norms and religious principles to which they adhere. I observed these activities and spoke with participants during the breaks and after the workshops.

INTERVIEWS

During the first two extended visits to the Horn of Africa for this project, in summer 2013 and summer 2014, I conducted more than 130 interviews in Somaliland, Kenya, and Ethiopia. In 2015 and 2016 I conducted three additional telephone interviews with foreign lawyers who had lived or worked in Mogadishu and, in 2019, I conducted six additional in-person interviews in Hargeisa, totaling 142 interviews between 2013 and 2019.

Most interviews were in a combination of Arabic and English. A research assistant was present as a translator for interview 114, in which the respondent spoke Somali. My interview guide was initially wide-ranging across legal topics, which allowed me to focus on more specific issues during my second period of fieldwork one year later. I developed a clear set of interview questions based on defined themes I wanted to discuss, relating to interviewees' perceptions of shari'a, customary law, and state courts. The semi-structured format I adopted allowed for flexibility in response to each interviewee's statements. This format also allowed me, in the course of a single interview, to assess how people's behaviors and perspectives have changed across their careers – for instance, as university lecturers become judges, activists join aid agencies, and administrators become government officials.

To protect confidentiality, I translated Arabic into English on my own. I kept data in encrypted, password-protected files. The interview list follows in Appendix C.

ANALYSIS AND CODING

I coded interview transcripts using a qualitative analysis software program, Text Analysis Markup Software (TAMS) Analyzer. Coding software like TAMS Analyzer allows scholars to find common themes emerging across the data and then to tag and categorize text according to those common themes or keywords. I developed, checked, and used more than 230 codes and subcodes. For instance, the code "law>pluralism>colonial" allowed me to evaluate how different interviewees spoke about the multiple legal orders that existed in the colonial environment. Another code, "NGO>strategies>legal" allowed me to analyze how NGOs adopted legal strategies to promote social change. I also developed "metacodes" to allow me to search transcripts by demographic data.

Analysis involved searching common themes across interview transcripts, field notes, and historical materials, to understand how patterns emerged, and then to think about those patterns in relation to theories I have considered in the law and society literature addressing the interplay between religion and the rule of law.

Appendix B

ARCHIVES AND LIBRARIES VISITED

United Kingdom (Cambridge, Durham, London, and Oxford)
African and Commonwealth Library (formerly Rhodes House), Oxford
    University
Bodleian Library, Oxford University
British Library, London
Centre for African Studies, Cambridge University
Foreign Office Confidential Prints, Oxford University Faculty of Law
Royal Anthropological Institute, London
SOAS University of London
Sudan Archive, Palace Green Library, Durham University

Somaliland (Hargeisa)
Institute for Peace and Conflict Studies, University of Hargeisa
Somaliland Ministry of Interior
Somaliland Ministry of Justice
Observatory for Conflict and Violence Prevention
United Nations Development Programme (UNDP) Somalia

Kenya (Nairobi)
British Institute for East Africa

Appendix C

INTERVIEW LIST

Note: The author conducted all interviews, except numbers 72–76 in this list, which were conducted by a research assistant under the author's supervision. All interviews by the author were in a combination of English and Arabic, except number 114, which was in Somali with a research assistant present as a translator. Eighteen of these 142 interviews are repeat interviews, listed accordingly. Unless otherwise indicated, each interview in this list describes the interviewee's workplace at the time of the interview and interview location, if different. All names are pseudonyms.

1. Interview with Hanson, professor in London, England (June 2013).
2. Interview with Noori, independent researcher in London, England (June 2013).
3. Interview with Sam, professor in London, England (June 2013).
4. Interview with Adnan, law graduate from Somaliland in London, England (June 2013).
5. Interview with Na'im, lawyer and legal consultant in England (conducted by telephone from London, England) (June 2013).
6. Interview with Rashida, lawyer and government consultant in Hargeisa, Somaliland (conducted by telephone from London, England) (June 2013).
7. Interview with Faris, professor and government official in Hargeisa, Somaliland (June 2013).
8. Interview with Abdullahi, independent researcher in Hargeisa, Somaliland (June 2013).

9. Interview with Naqeeb, professor at the University of Mogadishu, Somalia (conducted in person in Hargeisa, Somaliland) (June 2013).

10. Interview with Tahir, NGO executive director in Hargeisa, Somaliland (June 2013).

11. Follow-up interview with Faris, professor and government official in Hargeisa, Somaliland (June 2013).

12. Interview with Daniel, expatriate lawyer and NGO program manager in Hargeisa, Somaliland (June 2013).

13. Interview with Farooq, NGO program manager in Hargeisa, Somaliland (June 2013).

14. Interview with Maxamed, independent researcher and consultant in Hargeisa, Somaliland (June 2013).

15. Interview with Evelyn, United Nations official in Garowe, Puntland (conducted by telephone from Hargeisa, Somaliland) (June 2013).

16. Interview with Todd, expatriate consultant and professor, in Hargeisa, Somaliland (June 2013).

17. Interview with Amburo, former senior government minister and United Nations official in Hargeisa, Somaliland (June 2013).

18. Interview with Bashir, university administrator in Hargeisa, Somaliland (June 2013).

19. Interview with Jeff, aid worker and consultant in Hargeisa, Somaliland (June 2013).

20. Interview with Akifah, lawyer and university lecturer in Hargeisa, Somaliland (June 2013).

21. Interview with Ra'ed, writer and consultant in Hargeisa, Somaliland (June 2013).

22. Interview with Shahab, expatriate consultant in Hargeisa, Somaliland (June 2013).

23. Interview with Rafiq, expatriate consultant in Hargeisa, Somaliland (June 2013).

24. Interview with Faraax, NGO program manager and government agency staff member in Hargeisa, Somaliland (June 2013).

25. Interview with Raouf, senior United Nations official in Hargeisa, Somaliland (June 2013).

26. Interview with Amina, independent researcher in Hargeisa, Somaliland (June 2013).

27. Interview with Leslie, expatriate aid worker in Hargeisa, Somaliland (June 2013).

28. Interview with Nahda, NGO project manager in Hargeisa, Somaliland (June 2013).
29. Interview with Daahir, NGO project manager in Hargeisa, Somaliland (June 2013).
30. Interview with Zack, expatriate lawyer in Hargeisa, Somaliland (June 2013).
31. Interview with Fadl, lawyer in Hargeisa, Somaliland (June 2013).
32. Interview with Axmed, lawyer and university lecturer in Hargeisa, Somaliland (June 2013).
33. Interview with Salaam, NGO executive director in Hargeisa, Somaliland (June 2013).
34. Interview with Cabdi, former political prisoner and retired NGO executive director in Hargeisa, Somaliland (June 2013).
35. Interview with Cabdulmajid, senior government official in Hargeisa, Somaliland (June 2013).
36. Interview with Yasir, senior government official in Hargeisa, Somaliland (June 2013).
37. Interview with Sultan Mansoor, sultan in Hargeisa, Somaliland (June 2013).
38. Interview with Fatima, lawyer and aid worker in Hargeisa, Somaliland (July 2013).
39. Interview with Samira, lawyer and paralegal in Hargeisa, Somaliland (July 2013).
40. Interview with Gasim, NGO program manager in Hargeisa, Somaliland (July 2013).
41. Interview with Khalid, lawyer and university lecturer in Hargeisa, Somaliland (July 2013).
42. Interview with Faisal, senior government official in Hargeisa, Somaliland (July 2013).
43. Interview with Khadija, legal aid attorney in Hargeisa, Somaliland (July 2013).
44. Interview with Yusuf, corporate executive in Hargeisa, Somaliland (July 2013).
45. Interview with Aqil Zaki Yasim, aqil and senior government official in Hargeisa, Somaliland (July 2013).
46. Interview with Xabiib, senior government official in Hargeisa, Somaliland (July 2013).
47. Interview with Jamila, NGO executive director in Hargeisa, Somaliland (July 2013).

48. Interview with Asma, senior legal aid attorney in Hargeisa, Somaliland (July 2013).
49. Interview with Babiker, university administrator and lecturer in Hargeisa, Somaliland (July 2013).
50. Interview with Caziz, lawyer and human rights activist in Hargeisa, Somaliland (July 2013).
51. Interview with Jalal, former judge and law professor in Mogadishu, Somalia (conducted in Hargeisa, Somaliland) (July 2013).
52. Interview with Sheikh Zaki, sheikh and former senior judiciary official in Hargeisa, Somaliland (July 2013).
53. Interview with Talal, paralegal in Hargeisa, Somaliland (July 2013).
54. Follow-up interview with Faisal, senior government official in Hargeisa, Somaliland (July 2013).
55. Interview with Fawzia, women's rights activist and former NGO executive director in Hargeisa, Somaliland (July 2013).
56. Interview with Kabir, lawyer and senior university administrator in Hargeisa, Somaliland (July 2013).
57. Interview with Aisha, legal aid attorney in Borama, Somaliland (conducted by telephone from Hargeisa, Somaliland) (July 2013).
58. Interview with Hussein, university lecturer and former judge in Hargeisa, Somaliland (July 2013).
59. Interview with Kalim, former NGO executive director in Hargeisa, Somaliland (July 2013).
60. Interview with Tariq, legal aid attorney in Hargeisa, Somaliland (July 2013).
61. Interview with Mire, legal aid attorney in Hargeisa, Somaliland (July 2013).
62. Interview with Bilan, NGO executive director in Hargeisa, Somaliland (July 2013).
63. Interview with Da'ood, NGO executive director in Hargeisa, Somaliland (July 2013).
64. Follow-up interview with Khalid, lawyer and university lecturer in Hargeisa, Somaliland (July 2013).
65. Interview with Jen, expatriate aid worker in Nairobi, Kenya (conducted by telephone from Hargeisa, Somaliland) (July 2013).
66. Interview with Aaliyah, independent researcher and former government attorney in Hargeisa, Somaliland (July 2013).

67. Interview with Omar, senior government official in Hargeisa, Somaliland (July 2013).
68. Follow-up interview with Faisal, senior government official in Hargeisa, Somaliland (July 2013).
69. Follow-up interview with Axmed, lawyer and university lecturer in Hargeisa, Somaliland (June 2013).
70. Follow-up interview with Kabir, lawyer and senior university administrator in Hargeisa, Somaliland (July 2013).
71. Interview with Souad, women's health activist in Hargeisa, Somaliland (July 2013).
72. Interview with Taban, legal aid attorney in Hargeisa, Somaliland (July 2013).
73. Interview with Filsan, legal aid attorney in Hargeisa, Somaliland (July 2013).
74. Interview with Ibtisam, legal aid attorney in Hargeisa, Somaliland (July 2013).
75. Interview with Kamal, United Nations staff member in Hargeisa, Somaliland (July 2013).
76. Interview with Iman, government attorney in Hargeisa, Somaliland (July 2013).
77. Interview with Khadra, United Nations official in Nairobi, Kenya (July 2013).
78. Interview with Majda, lawyer and human rights activist in Mogadishu and Hargeisa (conducted in Nairobi, Kenya) (July 2013).
79. Interview with Karim, aid worker in Nairobi, Kenya (August 2013).
80. Interview with Gul, aid worker in Nairobi, Kenya (August 2013).
81. Interview with Warsame, lawyer and adviser to the Transitional Federal Government of Somalia (conducted in Nairobi, Kenya) (August 2013).
82. Interview with Mille, expatriate aid worker in Mogadishu, Somalia (conducted in Nairobi, Kenya) (August 2013).
83. Interview with Agnes, NGO executive director in Nairobi, Kenya (August 2013).
84. Interview with Edith, human rights researcher in Nairobi, Kenya (August 2013).
85. Interview with Ibrahim, NGO program adviser in Nairobi, Kenya (August 2013).

86. Interview with Barkhado, retired senior government minister in Mogadishu, Somalia (conducted in Nairobi, Kenya) (August 2013).
87. Interview with Muuse, retired senior government minister in Mogadishu, Somalia (conducted in Addis Ababa, Ethiopia) (August 2013).
88. Interview with Sheikh Tawfiiq, sheikh and senior government official in Hargeisa, Somaliland (June 2014).
89. Interview with Sheikh Abdirahman, sheikh and senior government official in Hargeisa, Somaliland (June 2014).
90. Interview with Suleiman, lawyer and paralegal in Hargeisa, Somaliland (June 2014).
91. Interview with Bassam, law student in Hargeisa, Somaliland (June 2014).
92. Interview with Tayyib, lawyer and paralegal in Hargeisa, Somaliland (June 2014).
93. Follow-up interview with Caziz, lawyer and human rights activist in Hargeisa, Somaliland (June 2014).
94. Follow-up interview with Jeff, aid worker and consultant in Hargeisa, Somaliland (June 2014).
95. Interview with Adam, independent researcher and consultant in Hargeisa, Somaliland (June 2014).
96. Follow-up interview with Adam, independent researcher and consultant in Hargeisa, Somaliland (June 2014).
97. Interview with Sadiq, NGO executive director in Hargeisa, Somaliland (June 2014).
98. Follow-up interview with Tahir, NGO executive director in Hargeisa, Somaliland (June 2014).
99. Interview with Shermarke, former senior university administrator and United Nations official in Hargeisa, Somaliland (June 2014).
100. Interview with Hassan, legal aid attorney and former militia leader and police official in Hargeisa, Somaliland (June 2014).
101. Interview with Idriss, university lecturer and independent consultant in Hargeisa, Somaliland (June 2014).
102. Interview with Cabdelcaziz, government agency director in Hargeisa, Somaliland (June 2014).
103. Interview with Garaad, political activist in Hargeisa, Somaliland (June 2014).
104. Interview with Yasmeen, legal aid attorney in Hargeisa, Somaliland (June 2014).

105. Follow-up interview with Faisal, senior government official in Hargeisa, Somaliland (June 2014).
106. Interview with Nabil, senior government official in Hargeisa, Somaliland (June 2014).
107. Interview with Roble Ali, government agency director in Hargeisa, Somaliland (June 2014).
108. Follow-up interview with Rashida, lawyer and government consultant in Hargeisa, Somaliland (June 2014).
109. Interview with Qasim, lawyer and government consultant in Hargeisa, Somaliland (June 2014).
110. Interview with Kahlil, lawyer and government consultant in Hargeisa, Somaliland (June 2014).
111. Interview with Huda, NGO program manager in Hargeisa, Somaliland (June 2014).
112. Follow-up interview with Qasim, lawyer and government consultant in Hargeisa, Somaliland (June 2014).
113. Interview with Majed, legal aid attorney in Hargeisa, Somaliland (June 2014).
114. Interview with Aqil Mustafa, senior government official and former aqil of British colonial administration (June 2014).
115. Interview with Idil, children's rights activist in Hargeisa, Somaliland (June 2014).
116. Interview with Nisreen, NGO executive director in Hargeisa, Somaliland (June 2014).
117. Interview with Badri, youth activist and artist in Hargeisa, Somaliland (June 2014).
118. Interview with Ismaciil, NGO executive director in Hargeisa, Somaliland (June 2014).
119. Interview with Abubakr, NGO finance manager in Hargeisa, Somaliland (June 2014).
120. Interview with Cadil, senior government official in Hargeisa, Somaliland (June 2014).
121. Interview with Guleed, senior government official in Hargeisa, Somaliland (June 2014).
122. Interview with Xidig, government minister in Hargeisa, Somaliland (June 2014).
123. Follow-up interview with Shermarke, former senior university administrator and United Nations official in Hargeisa, Somaliland (June 2014).

124. Interview with Najib, former senior government minister in Hargeisa, Somaliland (June 2014).
125. Interview with Sohir, NGO executive director and women's rights activist in Hargeisa, Somaliland (June 2014).
126. Interview with Dhahir, senior university administrator in Borama, Somaliland (conducted in Hargeisa, Somaliland) (June 2014).
127. Interview with Sheikh Oweis, sheikh and senior university administrator in Hargeisa, Somaliland (June 2014).
128. Interview with Omera, NGO project manager in Hargeisa, Somaliland (June 2014).
129. Interview with Xalwo, women's rights activist in Hargeisa, Somaliland (June 2014).
130. Interview with Ladan, women's rights activist in Hargeisa, Somaliland (June 2014).
131. Interview with Shamsi, women's rights activist in Hargeisa, Somaliland (June 2014).
132. Interview with Cabaas, senior government attorney and minister in Hargeisa, Somaliland (June 2014).
133. Interview with Stephanie, researcher and author in London, England (July 2014).
134. Interview with Hatim, United Nations official and adviser to the Somali constitution drafting process in Mogadishu, Somalia (reached via telephone from Princeton, New Jersey) (November 2015).
135. Interview with Matilda, international lawyer and adviser to the Somali constitution drafting process in Mogadishu, Somalia (reached via telephone from Princeton, New Jersey) (December 2015).
136. Interview with Philip, retired international lawyer who worked in the 1960s-70s in Mogadishu, Somalia (reached via telephone from San Francisco, California) (September 2016).
137. Follow-up interview with Idriss, university lecturer and independent consultant in Hargeisa, Somaliland (March 2019).
138. Interview with Asha, university lecturer and independent consultant in Hargeisa, Somaliland (March 2019).
139. Follow-up interview with Fawzia, women's rights activist and former NGO executive director in Hargeisa, Somaliland (March 2019).

140. Follow-up interview with Sohir, NGO executive director and women's rights activist in Hargeisa, Somaliland (March 2019).
141. Interview with Bourhan, NGO project coordinator in Hargeisa, Somaliland (March 2019).
142. Follow-up interview with Kabir, senior judicial official and former university administrator in Hargeisa, Somaliland (March 2019).

BIBLIOGRAPHY

BODLEIAN LIBRARIES, OXFORD UNIVERSITY

Address by Sir Harold Baxter Kittermaster. 1931. Colonial Office Confidential Prints, Bodleian African and Commonwealth Library, Oxford University, Mss. Afr. S. 2341(1).

Affairs in Somaliland, May 1908–December 1909. Colonial Office Confidential Prints, Bodleian African and Commonwealth Library, Oxford University, 926/1–144.

Churchill, Winston. 1894. "A Minute on the Somaliland Protectorate," May 5, 1894. Colonial Office Confidential Prints, Bodleian Library, Oxford University, 702/73.

1905. "Letter from Hargeisa Commissioner to Political Officer in Wadamago," March 17, 1905. Colonial Office Confidential Prints, Bodleian Library, Oxford University, 770/12.

1907. "A Minute on the Somaliland Protectorate," October 28, 1907. Colonial Office Confidential Prints, Bodleian Library, Oxford University, 896/3.

Confidential Memorandum Respecting Affairs of Somaliland, March 4, 1909. Foreign Office Confidential Prints – Colonial Office, Bodleian Library, Oxford University.

Great Britain Treaties with the Tribes on the Somali Coast (Eisa, Gadabursi, Habr-Awal, Habr Toljaala, Habr Gerhajis, and Warsangali treaties), June 1887. File 5453, Foreign Office Confidential Prints, Bodleian Law Library, Oxford University.

Letter from Somaliland Commissioner Cordeaux to Secretary of State, in "Affairs in Somaliland, May 1908–December 1909," September 11, 1909. Colonial Office Confidential Prints, Bodleian African and Commonwealth Library, Oxford University, 926/115.

Memorandum by Mr. Bertie on Questions Affecting the Somali Coast Protectorate, Harrar, and Abysssinia, August 1892 to October 1893. Foreign Office Confidential Prints, Bodleian Law Library, Oxford University, 6410/3.

Note by the Commissioner on Mr. Churchill's Confidential Minute, December 28, 1907. Colonial Office Confidential Prints 896, Bodleian Library, Oxford University. African No. 896 (African Print No. 904).

Stanton, Colonel. 1870. "Memorandum on Turkish Claims to Sovereignty over the Soumali [sic] Territory," June 3, 1870. Foreign Office Confidential Prints, Bodleian Law Library, Oxford University, Document 1949.

Untitled Manuscript. Colonial Office Confidential Prints, Bodleian Library, Oxford University, 702/26.

Untitled Manuscript. Colonial Office Confidential Prints, Bodleian African and Commonwealth Library, Oxford University, 919/1–23.

Untitled Manuscript. February 1880. Foreign Office Confidential Prints, Bodleian Law Library, Oxford University, 4099/18.

Untitled Manuscript. Foreign Office Confidential Prints, Bodleian Law Library, Oxford University, 9508/7.

Wingate, Reginald. 1909. "Lieutenant-General Sir Reginald Wingate's Special Mission to Somaliland," unpublished report, June 12, 1909, Foreign Office Confidential Prints, Bodleian Law Library, Oxford University, 9507.

SUDAN ARCHIVE, DURHAM UNIVERSITY

Africa No. 3, 1902. Wingate Collection, Sudan Archive, Durham University, 125/1.

Communication of J. L. Baird, Member of the British Parliament for Rugby and Acting Agent and Consul General in Abyssinia, 1902. Sudan Archive, Durham University, 296/1/157.

Copies of Correspondence between British Officials and Sheikh Hassan. Wingate Report of 1909. Sudan Archive, Durham University, 446/5/301–309.

Interview with the Messengers Who Took the Letter from the Mission to the Mullah, Sheikh, Somaliland, June 14, 1909. Sudan Archive, Durham University, 446/5/315.

July 1909 Letter from Sayed Mohamed Ibn Abdullah El Hashmi (Sheikh Mohamed Abdullah Hassan) to the British Government. Wingate Collection, Sudan Archive, Durham University, 288/2/109.

Letter from Wilfred G. Thesiger at the British Legation, Addis Ababa, October 11, 1917. Sudan Archive, Durham University, 125/8/21.

Letter from Hashim El Shafii El Sumii. Wingate Collection, Sudan Archive, Durham University, 288/6/122–125.

Letter from Sheikh Hassan. Sudan Archive, Durham University, 446/3/303.

Letter from Wingate (Governor-General of Anglo-Egyptian Sudan) and Slatin Pasha (Sirdar of the Army) to El Seyid Mohmamed Ibn Abdullah. Sudan Archive, Durham University, 125/6/328.

Lieutenant-General Sir Reginald Wingate's Special Mission to Somaliland, June 12, 1909. Sudan Archive, Durham University, 287/3.

Notes from the Interview with the Messengers who Took the Letter from the Mission to the Mullah, June 14, 1909. Sudan Archive, Durham University, 125/6/337.

Private Correspondence of Sir R. Wingate to Sheikh Abdel Kader in Burao, Somaliland. Sudan Archive, Durham University, 287/2/140.

Reports on Activities of the Mullah as of March 1, 1909. Wingate Collection, Sudan Archive, Durham University, 286/2/3.

Supplement to the Report on Lieutenant-General Sir Reginald Wingate's Special Mission to Somaliland, July 1909. Sudan Archive, Durham University, 125/7/2.

"The Pacification of Somaliland," *Egyptian Daily Post*, 1909. Wingate Collection, Sudan Archive, Durham University, 287/2/234.

Untitled cutting. 1909. *New York Herald*, March 15, 1909. Sudan Archive, Durham University, 286/2/26.

Untitled cutting. 1909. *Liverpool Daily Courier*, June 18, 1909. Sudan Archive, Durham University, 287/3/78.

Untitled manuscript. Sudan Archive, Durham University, 125/1/3.

Untitled manuscript. Sudan Archive, Durham University, 237/3/140.

Untitled manuscript. Sudan Archive, Durham University, 273/7/6–7.

Untitled manuscript. Sudan Archive, Durham University, 286/2/27.

Untitled manuscript. Sudan Archive, Durham University, 287/1/196.

Untitled manuscript. Sudan Archive, Durham University, 287/2/134.

Untitled manuscript. Sudan Archive, Durham University, 446/5/301.

Wingate, Reginald. 1909. "Lieutenant-General Sir Reginald Wingate's Special Mission to Somaliland," unpublished report. Wingate Collection, Sudan Archive, Durham University, box 125; also 287/3.

CASES

Aqil Gulaid Jama v. *Abdullahi Ali*, Supreme Court Full Bench Civil Appeal No. 24 of 1964, judgment by Dr. Aldo Peronaci, President, Supreme Court of the Somali Republic.

Brief of Amici Curiae Academic Experts in Somali History and Current Affairs in Support of Respondents (No. 08–155), *Mohamed Ali Samantar*

v. *Bashe Abdi Yousuf, et. al.*, Supreme Court of the United States, January 27, 2010.

Hussein Hersi and Ahmed Adan v. *Yusuf Deria Ali*, Supreme Court Civil Appeal No. 2 of 1964, judgment by Haji N. A. Noor Muhammad, Vice President, Supreme Court of the Somali Republic. 9(3) *Journal of African Law* (1965): 170–183.

Kasymakhunov and Saybatalov v. *Russia*, Applications Nos. 26261/05 and 26377/06, judgment of March 13, 2013, European Court of Human Rights.

Refah Partisi and Others v. *Turkey*, Application No. 41340/98, judgment of February 13, 2003, European Court of Human Rights.

Somali National Congress v. *the State*, November 5, 1963, judgment by Dr. Giuseppe Papale, President, Supreme Court of the Somali Republic.

LAWS

Amendment to Judiciary Law, June 8, 1958, United Nations Trust Territory of Somalia.

Constitution of the Republic of Somaliland, 2001.

Constitution of the Somali Republic, 1960, as amended in 1963.

Customs regulations of 1902, British Somaliland Protectorate. Foreign Office Confidential Prints, Bodleian Library, Oxford University.

Fire-arms Regulations of 1899, British Somaliland Protectorate. Foreign Office Confidential Prints, Bodleian Library, Oxford University.

Judicial Regulations, Decree No. 1638 of June 20, 1935, British Somaliland Protectorate.

Law No. 5 of January 31, 1961, Somali Republic.

Law No. 9 of February 19, 1958, British Somaliland Protectorate.

Law No. 10 of February 20, 1958, British Somaliland Protectorate.

Law No. 20 of January 15, 1973, Somali Democratic Republic.

Law No. 67 of November 1, 1970, Somali Democratic Republic.

Law on the Organization of the Judiciary, Legislative Decree No. 3 of June 12, 1962, Somali Republic.

Law on the Organization of the Judiciary of 1956, United Nations Trust Territory of Somalia.

Law on the Organization of the Judiciary, Royal Decree No. 937 of June 11, 1911, British Somaliland Protectorate.

The Laws of the Somaliland Protectorate: Containing the Ordinances, Orders in Council and Orders of the Secretary of State in Force on the 1st Day of January 1950, prepared by Sir Henry Webb (London: Waterlow & Sons, 1950), Volumes 1–3.

Ordinance No. 5 of 1901. Foreign Office Confidential Prints 7603, Bodleian Library, Oxford University.

Penal Code of 1962, Somali Republic.
Preservation of Game Ordinance, July 10, 1901. Foreign Office Confidential Prints 7665, Bodleian Library, Oxford University.
Provisional Constitution of the Federal Republic of Somalia, 2012.
Public Order Law of 1963, Somali Republic.
Regulations for the Employment of Officers in the British Protectorate on the Somali Coast. September 1, 1902. Foreign Office Confidential Prints 7762, Bodleian Library, Oxford University.
Regulations for the Qadis (Administration of Justice) of 1893. Compagnia Italiana per la Somalia.
Somaliland Law No. 24 of 2003, Republic of Somaliland.
Sporting Regulations, January 1, 1902, British Somaliland Protectorate. Foreign Office Confidential Prints 7640, Bodleian Library, Oxford University.
Subordinate Courts Ordinance of July 1, 1944, British Somaliland Protectorate.
Transitional Federal Charter of the Somali Republic, 2004.
United Nations Draft Trusteeship Agreement for the Territory of Somaliland under Italian Administration, Fifth Session of the General Assembly, Supplement No. 10 (A/1294), January 27, 1950.
United Nations Trusteeship Agreement for the Territory of Somaliland under Italian Administration, General Assembly Resolution 442.V, December 2, 1950.

ARTICLES, BOOKS, AND REPORTS

Abdi, Cawo Mohamed. 2018. "Somalia," in Suad Joseph, ed., *Arab Family Studies: Critical Reviews*. Syracuse, NY: Syracuse University Press, pp. 96–110.
Abdulkadir Mohamed, Iman. 2015. "Somali Women and the Socialist State," *Journal of the Georgetown University-Qatar Middle Eastern Studies Student Association*.
Abdullahi, Abdurahman M. 2007a. "Perspectives on the State Collapse in Somalia," in Abdulahi A. Osman and Issaka K. Souaré, eds., *Somalia at the Crossroads: Challenges and Perspectives in Reconstituting a Failed State*. London: Adonis & Abbey, pp. 4–57.
Abdullahi, Abdurahman M. 2007b. "Recovering the Somali State: The Islamic Factor," in Abdulkadir Osman Farah, Mammo Muchie, and Joakim Gundel, eds., *Somalia: Diaspora and State Reconstruction in the Horn of Africa*. London: Adonis & Abbey, pp. 196–208.
Abel, Richard. 2018. *Law's Wars: The Fate of the Rule of Law in the US "War on Terror"*. Cambridge: Cambridge University Press.

Abou-Elyousr, Khaled. 2016. "Understanding the Somalia Justice Systems: Challenges and the Way Forward," unpublished paper, December 2016. Copy on file with author.

Abukari, Abdulai. 2014. "Education of Women in Islam: A Critical Islamic Interpretation of the Quran," 109(1) *Religious Education*: 4–23.

Agrama, Hussein Ali. 2012. *Questioning Secularism: Islam, Sovereignty, and the Rule of Law in Egypt*. Chicago, IL: University of Chicago Press.

Ahmed, Ali Hirsi. 2014. "Constitution-Making in Somalia: A Critical Analysis, 1960–2013." MA Thesis, Institute of Diplomacy and International Studies. Nairobi: University of Nairobi.

Ahmed, Shahab. 2015. *What Is Islam? The Importance of Being Islamic*. Princeton, NJ: Princeton University Press.

Ahsan, Sonia. 2017. "When Muslims Become Feminists: Khana-yi Aman, Islam, and Pashtunwali," in Nile Green, ed., *Afghanistan's Islam: From Conversion to the Taliban*. Oakland, CA: University of California Press, pp. 225–241.

Aideed, H. A. A. 2004. "The Siyad Barre Regime's Genocide of the Somaliland People," in R. Ford, H. Adam, and E. Ismail, eds., *War Destroys, Peace Nurtures: Somali Reconciliation and Development*. Lawrenceville, NJ: Red Sea Press.

Al-Bajuri, Shaykh Muhammad Al-Khudari Bak. 2012. *The History of the Four Caliphs (Itmam al-Wafa'fi Sirat al-Khulafa)*. London: Turath Publishing.

Alpozzi, Alberto. 2015. *Il Faro di Mussolini: L'opera Colonial più Controversa e il Sogno dell'Impero nella Somalia Italiana, 1889–1941*. Turin: 001 Edizioni.

"Al-Shabaab in Somalia: US Air Strike 'Kills 60 Militants'," *BBC News*, October 16, 2018. Available: https://bbc.in/2MoRQmP (accessed January 1, 2021).

Amadi, Sam. 2004. "Religion and Secular Constitution: Human Rights and the Challenge of Sharia," unpublished research paper, Carr Center for Human Rights Policy, Harvard Kennedy School.

Amnesty International. 1994. "Report – Somalia (1 January 1994)." Available: https://bit.ly/3rJZWXa (accessed January 1, 2021).

An-Na'im, Abdullahi, ed. 2002. *Islamic Family Law in a Changing World: A Global Resource Book*. London: Zed Books, 2002.

An-Na'im, Abdullahi. 2008. *Islam and the Secular State: Negotiating the Future of Shari'a*. Cambridge, MA: Harvard University Press.

Archer, Sir Geoffrey Francis. 1963. *Personal and Historical Memoirs of an East Africa Administrator*. Edinburgh: Oliver & Boyd.

Areshidze, Girogi. 2017. "Taking Religion Seriously? Habermas on Religious Translation and Cooperative Learning in Post-secular Society," 111(4) *American Political Science Review*: 724–737.

Asad, Talal. 2003. *Formations of the Secular: Christianity, Islam, Modernity*. Stanford, CA: Stanford University Press.

Bail, Christopher. 2015. *Terrified: How Anti-Muslim Fringe Organizations Became Mainstream*. Princeton, NJ: Princeton University Press.

Bakonyi, Jutta. 2018. "Seeing Like Bureaucracies: Rearranging Knowledge and Ignorance in Somalia," 12(3) *International Political Sociology*: 256–273.

      2019. "Failing States and Statebuilding," in Klaus Larres and Ruth Wittlinger, eds., *Understanding Global Politics: Actors and Themes in International Affairs*. New York: Routledge, pp. 313–328.

Bâli, Aslı Ü. and Hanna Lerner, eds. 2017. *Constitution Writing, Religion and Democracy*. Cambridge: Cambridge University Press.

Ballakhrishnen, Swethaa, Priya Fielding-Singh, and Devon Magliozzi. 2019. "Intentional Invisibility: Professional Women and the Navigation of Workplace Constraints," 62(1) *Sociological Perspectives*: 23–41.

Banner, Stuart. 1998. "When Christianity Was Part of the Common Law," 16 (1) *Law and History Review*: 27–62.

Barnes, Cedric and Harun Hassan. 2007. *The Rise and Fall of Mogadishu's Islamic Courts*. Chatham House Africa Programme Briefing Paper. London: Chatham House.

Barr, Michael D. 2000. "Lee Kwan Yew and the 'Asian Values' Debate," 24(3) *Asian Studies Review*: 309–334.

Battera, Federico and Alessandro Campo. 2001. "The Evolution and Integration of Different Legal Systems in the Horn of Africa: The Case of Somaliland," *Global Jurist Topics*, April 20. Available: https://bit.ly/2 XOoRry (accessed January 1, 2021).

Bayraklı, Enes and Farid Hafez. 2019 *Islamophobia in Muslim Majority Societies*. New York: Routledge.

Beachey, Ray. 1990. *The Warrior Mullah: The Horne Aflame 1892–1920*. London: Bellew Publishing.

Bell, James et al. 2013. *The World's Muslims: Religion, Politics, and Society*. Washington, DC: The Pew Forum on Religion and Public Life.

Bendaña, Alejandro and Tanja Chopra. 2013. "Women's Rights, State-Centric Rule of Law, and Legal Pluralism in Somaliland," 5(1) *Hague Journal on the Rule of Law*: 44–73.

Benford, Robert D. and David A. Snow. 2000. "Framing Processes and Social Movements," 26 *Annual Review of Sociology*: 611–639.

Berman, Harold J. 1983. "Religious Foundations of Law in the West: A Historical Perspective," 1(1) *Journal of Law and Religion*: 3–43.

Berridge, W. J. 2017. *Hasan al-Turabi: Islamist Politics and Democracy in Sudan*. Cambridge: Cambridge University Press.

Bhalla, Nita. 2018. "Somaliland Elders Approve 'Historic' Law Criminalising Rape," *Reuters*, April 9. Available: https://reut.rs/2K8tLiU (accessed January 1, 2021).

Bharath, Deepa. 2018. "Appeal Filed over 'Appalling, Islamophobic' Teaching Material Distributed in 7th-Grade Social Studies Class," *The Press-*

Enterprise, January 11. Available: https://bit.ly/39SRcaS (accessed January 1, 2021).

Bickel, Alexander M. 1986. *The Least Dangerous Branch: The Supreme Court at the Bar of Politics*. New Haven, CT: Yale University Press.

Bowden, Mark. 1999. *Black Hawk Down: A Story of Modern War*. New York: Grove Press.

Bradbury, Mark. 2008. *Becoming Somaliland*. Bloomington: Indiana University Press.

Brankamp, Hanno. 2013. "Somalia: Not Just Islam – How Somalia's Union of Islamic Courts Used Local Customs," *ThinkAfricaPress*, July 22. Available: https://bit.ly/38VD2no (accessed January 1, 2021).

Brown, Jonathan A. C. 2017. *Stoning and Hand Cutting: Understanding the Huduud and Shariah in Islam*. Irving, TX: Yaqeen Institute for Islamic Research.

Bruton, Bronwyn E. 2010. "Somalia: A New Approach," *Council on Foreign Relations Special Report No. 52*. New York: Council on Foreign Relations.

Buber, Martin. 1967. *A Believing Humanism: My Testament, 1902–1965*, trans. Maurice Friedman. New York: Simon & Schuster.

Burak, Guy. 2015. *The Second Formation of Islamic Law: The Hanafi School in the Early Modern Ottoman Empire*. Cambridge: Cambridge University Press.

Calvin, John. 1960 [1536]. *Institutes of the Christian Religion*, ed. J. T. McNeill, trans. F. L. Battles. Philadelphia, PA: Westminster Press.

Cavedon, Matthew. 2014. "Men of the Spear and Men of God: Islamism's Contributions to the New Somali State," 28 *Emory International Law Review* 473–508.

Cawthorne, Andrew. 2006. "US Says al Qaeda behind Somali Islamists," *Reuters*, December 15.

Chatterji, Angana P., Thomas Blom Hansen, and Christophe Jaffrelot, eds., 2019. *Majoritarian State: How Hindu Nationalism is Changing India*. London: Hurst.

Cheesman, Nick. 2015. *Opposing the Rule of Law: How Myanmar's Courts Make Law and Order*. Cambridge: Cambridge University Press.

2018. "Rule-of-Law Ethnography," 14 *Annual Review of Law and Social Science* 167–184.

Chiesi, Gustavo. 1909. *Law Colonizzazione Europea dell'Est Africa*. Turin: Unione Tipografica Torinese.

Choi, Seung-Whan. 2010. "Fighting Terrorism through the Rule of Law?" 54 (6) *Journal of Conflict Resolution*: 940–966.

Choudhury, Cyra Akila. 2015. "Beyond Culture: Human Rights Universalisms Versus Religious and Cultural Relativism in the Activism for Gender Justice," 30 *Berkeley Journal of Gender, Law & Justice* 226–267.

Chua, Lynette J. 2014. *Mobilizing Gay Singapore: Rights and Resistance in an Authoritarian State*. Philadelphia, PA: Temple University Press.

2019. *The Politics of Love in Myanmar: LGBT Mobilization and Human Rights as a Way of Life*. Stanford, CA: Stanford University Press.

Clarke, Morgan. 2018. *Islam and Law in Lebanon: Sharia within and without the State*. Cambridge: Cambridge University Press.

Collins, Robert O. 2008. *A History of Modern Sudan*. Cambridge: Cambridge University Press.

Committee to Protect Journalists. 2016. "Somalia: Journalist Shot and Killed in Mogadishu," June 6. Available at: https://bit.ly/3aY5TK4 (accessed January 1, 2021).

Cotterrell, Roger. 2020. "Still Afraid of Legal Pluralism? Encountering Santi Romano," 45 (2)*Law & Social Inquiry* 539–558.

Cover, Robert M. 1986. "Violence and the Word," 95 *Yale Law Journal* 1601–1629.

Crouch, Melissa, ed. 2016. *Islam and the State in Myanmar: Muslim-Buddhist Relations and the Politics of Belonging*. Oxford: Oxford University Press.

Dahl, Robert A. 1957. "Decision-Making in a Democracy: The Supreme Court as a National Policy Maker," 6 *Journal of Public Law*: 279–295.

Damaška, Mirjan. 2019. *Evaluation of Evidence: Pre-Modern and Modern Approaches*. Cambridge: Cambridge University Press.

Darnton, John. 1977. "Somalia Trys [sic] to Live by Both the Koran and 'Das Kapital,'" *New York Times*, October 11. Available: https://nyti.ms/2Lpl5 Fy (accessed January 1, 2021).

1978. "For Many Somalis, It Was a War That Wasn't," *New York Times*, March 19. Available: https://nyti.ms/2WdHYOx (accessed January 1, 2021).

De Waal, Alex. 2015. *The Real Politics of the Horn of Africa: Money, War and the Business of Power*. Cambridge, UK: Polity Press.

Deforche, Robrecht. 2013. "Stabilization and Common Identity: Reflections on the Islamic Courts Union and Al-Itihaad," 13 *Bildhaan: An International Journal of Somali Studies* 102–120.

Domingo, Rafael. 2017. *God and the Secular Legal System*. Cambridge: Cambridge University Press.

Dowd, Robert A. 2015. *Christianity, Islam, and Liberal Democracy: Lessons from Sub-Saharan Africa*. Oxford: Oxford University Press.

"Dozens Killed in Attacks in Somali Capital: Al-Qaeda-linked al-Shabab Claims Responsibility for Two Attacks in Mogadishu That Left More Than 30 People Dead," *Al-Jazeera News*, April 14, 2013. Available: https://bit.ly/3qH8VrD (accessed January 1, 2021).

"Draft Interim Constitution Handed to Howe; Unosom [sic] to Stay in Interim Period," *BBC Summary of World Broadcasts*. London: British Broadcasting Corporation, November 13, 1993.

Dua, Jatin. 2015. "After Piracy: Mapping the Means and Ends of Maritime Predation in the Western Indian Ocean," 9(3) *Journal of Eastern African Studies*: 505–521.

2019. *Captured at Sea: Piracy and Protection in the Indian Ocean.* Oakland, CA: University of California Press.

Dua, Jatin and Ken Menkhaus. 2012. "The Context of Contemporary Piracy: The Case of Somalia," 10(4) *Journal of International Criminal Justice:* 749–766.

Dualeh, Hussain Ali. 1994. *From Barre to Aideed – Somalia: The Agony of a Nation.* Nairobi, Kenya: Stellagraphics.

Durkheim, Émile. [1915] 2008. *The Elementary Forms of the Religious Life,* trans. Joseph Ward Swain. Mineola, NY: Dover Publications.

Dworkin, Ronald. 2013. *Religion without God.* Cambridge, MA: Harvard University Press.

Egal, Mohamed Haji Ibrahim. 1968. "Somalia: Nomadic Individualism and the Rule of Law," 67(268) *African Affairs:* 219–226.

Ehret, Christopher. 1995. "The Eastern Horn of Africa, 1000 B.C. to 1400 A.D.: The Historical Roots," in Ali Jimale Ahmed ed., *The Invention of Somalia.* Lawrenceville, NJ: Red Sea Press, pp. 233–256.

Ellis, Richard. 1993. "Muslim 'police' crack down on vice in Somalia," *The Sunday Times* (London), June 27.

Elsheikh, Elsadig, Basima Sisemore, and Natalia Ramirez Lee. 2017. "Legalizing Othering: The United States of Islamophobia," Report of the UC Berkeley Haas Institute for a Fair and Inclusive Society. Available: https://bit.ly/39ZVu0e (accessed January 1, 2021).

Eltantawi, Sarah. 2017. *Shari'ah on Trial: Northern Nigeria's Islamic Revolution.* Oakland, CA: University of California Press.

Emon, Anver. 2012. *Religious Pluralism and Islamic Law: Dhimmis and Others in the Empire of Law.* Oxford: Oxford University Press.

Englard, Izhak. 1987. "Law and Religion in Israel," 35(1) *American Journal of Comparative Law:* 185–208.

Epstein, Lee, William M. Landes, and Richard A. Posner. 2013. *The Behavior of Federal Judges: A Theoretical and Empirical Study of Rational Choice.* Cambridge, MA: Harvard University Press.

Erie, Matthew. 2016. *China and Islam: The Prophet, the Party, and Law.* Cambridge: Cambridge University Press.

2018. "Shari'a as Taboo of Modern Law: Halal Food, Islamophobia, and China," 33(3) *Journal of Law & Religion:* 390–420.

Eslava, Luis. 2015. *Local Space, Global Life: The Everyday Operation of International Law and Development.* Cambridge: Cambridge University Press.

"Ethiopia Says Somalia 'a Threat'," *BBC News,* June 28, 2006. Available: https://bbc.in/3pwPHnc (accessed January 1, 2021).

Ewick, Patricia and Susan S. Silbey. 1998. *The Common Place of Law: Stories from Everyday Life.* Chicago, IL: University of Chicago Press.

Feener, R. Michael. 2013. *Shari'a and Social Engineering: The Implementation of Islamic Law in Contemporary Aceh, Indonesia*. Oxford: Oxford University Press.

Fergusson, James. 2013. *The World's Most Dangerous Place: Inside the Outlaw State of Somalia*. Boston, MA: Da Capo Press.

Fernando, Mayanthi. 2014. *The Republic Unsettled: Muslim French and the Contradictions of Secularism*. Durham, NC: Duke University Press.

Finazzo, Giuseppina. 1966. *L'Italia nel Benadir: L'azione di Vincenzo Filonardi, 1884–1896*. Rome: Ateneo.

Forni, Elisabetta. 1980. "Women's Role in the Economic, Social and Political Development of Somalia," 19 *Africa Spectrum* 19–28.

Fragile States Index, The Fund for Peace. Available: http://fragilestatesindex.org/.

Friedman, Lawrence M. 1993. *Crime and Punishment in American History*. New York: Basic Books.

Fukuyama, Francis. 2012. *The Origins of Political Order: From Prehuman Times to the French Revolution*. London: Profile Books.

Fuller, Lon. 1964. *The Morality of Law*. New Haven, CT: Yale University Press.

Gaffney, Frank Jr. 2020. "Beware the Other Pandemic: Sharia-supremacism." *Center for Security Policy*, March 12. Available: https://bit.ly/2IAe7wp (accessed January 1, 2021).

Gallab, Abdullahi A. 2018. *Hasan al-Turabi, the Last of the Islamists: The Man and His Times, 1932–2016*. London: Rowman & Littlefield.

Ganzglass, Martin R. 1967. "A Common Lawyer Looks at an Uncommon Legal Experience," 53(9) *American Bar Association Journal*: 815–818.

1971. *The Penal Code of the Somali Democratic Republic, with Cases, Commentary, and Examples*. New Brunswick, NJ: Rutgers University Press.

Gardner, Judith and Judy El-Bushra, eds. 2004. *Somalia – The Untold Story: The War through the Eyes of Somali Women*. London: Pluto Press.

Geertz, Clifford. 1983. *Local Knowledge: Further Essays in Interpretive Anthropology*. New York: Basic Books.

Gettleman, Jeffrey. 2006. "Islamists Calm Somali Capital with Restraint," *New York Times*, September 24. Available: https://nyti.ms/3pxX3Xu (accessed January 1, 2021).

Ghai, Yash. 1993. "Asian Perspectives on Human Rights," 23(3) *Hong Kong Law Journal*: 342–357.

Ghani, Ashraf and Clare Lockhart. 2008. *Fixing Failed States: A Framework for Rebuilding a Fractured World*. Oxford: Oxford University Press.

Giunchi, Elisa. 2010. "The Reinvention of 'Shari'a' under the British Raj: In Search of Authenticity and Certainty," 69(4) *The Journal of Asian Studies*: 1119–1142.

Glenn, H. Patrick. 2006. "Comparative Legal Families and Comparative Legal Traditions," in Mathias Reimann and Reinhard Zimmerman, eds., *The Oxford Handbook of Comparative Law*. Oxford: Oxford University Press, pp. 421–440.

Goldziher, Ignác. 1981. *Introduction to Islamic Theology and Law*, trans. Andras Hamori and Ruth Hamori (Princeton, NJ: Princeton University Press, originally published as *Vorlesungen über den Islam*, Heidelberg, 1910).

Gowder, Paul. 2016. *The Rule of Law in the Real World*. Cambridge: Cambridge University Press.

Gray, Biko Mandela. 2019. "Religion in/and Black Lives Matter: Celebrating the Impossible," 13(1) *Religion Compass*: 1–9.

Green, Nile. 2017. "Introduction," in Nile Green, ed., *Afghanistan's Islam: From Conversion to the Taliban*. Oakland, CA: University of California Press, 2017, pp. 1–40.

Gupta, Akhil. 2012. *Red Tape: Bureaucracy, Structural Violence, and Poverty in India*. Durham, NC: Duke University Press.

Hagan, John. 2003. *Justice in the Balkans: Prosecuting War Crimes in the Hague Tribunal*. Chicago, IL: University of Chicago Press.

Hallaq, Wael B. 2009a. *An Introduction to Islamic Law*. Cambridge: Cambridge University Press.

   2009b. *Sharī'a: Theory, Practice, Transformations*. Cambridge: Cambridge University Press.

   2012. *The Impossible State: Islam, Politics, and Modernity's Moral Predicament*. New York: Columbia University Press.

Halliday, Terence C. 2011. "The Conscience of Society? The Legal Complex, Religion, and the Fates of Political Liberalism," in Scott L. Cummings, ed., *The Paradox of Professionalism: Lawyers and the Possibility of Justice*. Cambridge: Cambridge University Press, pp. 50–67.

Hammond, Laura. 2011. "Obliged to Give: Remittances and the Maintenance of Transnational Networks Between Somalis at Home and Abroad," 10 *Bildhaan: An International Journal of Somali Studies* 125–151.

Hansen, Stig Jarle. 2013. *Al-Shabaab in Somalia: The History and Ideology of a Militant Islamist Group, 2005–2012*. Oxford: Oxford University Press.

Hansen, Thomas Blom. 1999. *The Saffron Wave: Democracy and Hindu Nationalism in Modern India*. Princeton, NJ: Princeton University Press.

Harding, Andrew. 2016. *The Mayor of Mogadishu: A Story of Chaos and Redemption in the Ruins of Somalia*. New York: St. Martin's Press.

Harper, Erica, ed. 2011. *Working with Customary Justice: Post-Conflict and Fragile States*. Rome: IDLO-International Development Law Organization.

Harper, Mary. 2012. *Getting Somalia Wrong? Faith, War, and Hope in a Shattered State*. London: Zed Books.

2019. *Everything You Have Told Me Is True: The Many Faces of Al Shabaab*. London: Hurst.

Hashim, Abdulkadir. 2012. "Shaping of the Sharia Courts: British Policies on Transforming the *Kadhi* Courts in Colonial Zanzibar," 38(3) *Social Dynamics*: 381–397.

Hassan, H. 1957. *Intishar al-Islam wa-al-Urubah Fima yali al-Sahra al-Kubra Sharq al-Qarra al-Ifriqiyyah wa-Gharbiha*. Cairo: Matba-at Lujnat al-Bayan al-Arabi.

Hay, Douglas. 1975. "Property, Authority, and the Criminal Law," in D. Hay, P. Linebaugh, J. G. Rule, E. P. Thompson, and C. Winslow, eds., *Albion's Fatal Tree: Crime and Society in Eighteenth Century England*. New York: Pantheon Press, pp. 17–64.

Hefner, Robert, ed. 2016. *Shari'a Law and Modern Muslim Ethics*. Bloomington: Indiana University Press.

"Help Thousands Displaced, Civil Society Urges Aid Agencies," *United Nations Integrated Regional Information Network (IRIN) News*, April 18, 2007. Available: https://bit.ly/3o3UUme (accessed January 1, 2021).

Hernandez, Wil. 2006. *Henri Nouwen: A Spirituality of Imperfection*. New York: Paulist Press, 2006.

Hess, Robert. 1966. *Italian Colonialism in Somalia*. Chicago, IL: University of Chicago Press.

Hirschl, Ran and Ayelet Shachar. 2018. "Competing Orders? The Challenge of Religion to Modern Constitutionalism." 85 *The University of Chicago Law Review*: 425–455.

Hoehne, Markus V. and Virginia Luling, eds. 2010. *Peace and Milk, Drought and War: Somali Culture, Society, and Politics (Essays in Honour of I. M. Lewis)*. London: Hurst Publishers.

Horwitz, Morton J. 1977. "The Rule of Law: An Unqualified Human Good?" 86 *Yale Law Journal* 561–66.

Huband, Mark. 1998. *Warriors of the Prophet: The Struggle for Islam*. Boulder, CO: Westview Press.

"Human Rights Brief: Women in Somalia," Immigration and Refugee Board of Canada, 1 April 1994. Available: https://bit.ly/2WY0pqz (accessed January 1, 2021).

Hurd, Elizabeth Shakman. 2015. *Beyond Religious Freedom: The New Global Politics of Religion*. Princeton, NJ: Princeton University Press.

Hurst, William. 2018. *Ruling Before the Law: The Politics of Legal Regimes in China and Indonesia*. Cambridge: Cambridge University Press.

Hussin, Iza. 2016. *The Politics of Islamic Law: Local Elites, Colonial Authority, and the Making of the Muslim State*. Chicago, IL: University of Chicago Press.

Ibrahim, Huawa. 2012. *Practicing Shariah Law: Seven Strategies for Achieving Justice in Shariah Courts*. Chicago, IL: American Bar Association Book Publishing.

Ibrahim, Mohamed. 2013. "Coordinated Blasts Kill At Least 20 in Somalia's Capital," *New York Times*, April 14. Available: https://nyti.ms/3gzA3Eq.

Ingiriis, Mohamed Haji. 2016. "'We Swallowed the State as the State Swallowed Us': The Genesis, Genealogies, and Geographies of Genocides in Somalia," 9 (3)*African Security* 237–258.

"Integration of the Laws in the Somali Republic: Report on the Work of the Consultative Commission for Integration from its Inception Until 31st March, 1964," 1964. 8(2)*Journal of African Law* 56–58.

International Crisis Group. 2003. *Somaliland: Democratisation and its Discontents*. Africa Report No. 66. Nairobi/Brussels: ICG.

2006. "Can the Somali Crisis Be Contained?" *Crisis Group Africa Report No. 116*. Nairobi/Brussels: ICG.

Ismail, Ismail Ali. 2010. *Governance: The Scourge and Hope of Somalia*. Vancouver: Trafford Publishing.

Jama, Mohamed. 1963. "A History of the Somal," Unpublished paper from Mogadishu, Somalia. SOAS University of London, L.VH 967.73, 218.869.

James, George. 1995. "Somalia's Overthrown Dictator, Mohammed Siad Barre, Is Dead," *New York Times*, January 3. Available: https://nyti.ms/340t8z1 (accessed January 1, 2021).

Jamestown Foundation. 2016. "Al-Shabaab Aims for 'Hearts and Minds' With Establishment of Islamic Police Force," August 19. Vol. 14, Issue 17. Available: https://bit.ly/3rLJHZY (accessed January 1, 2021).

Jaynes, Gregory. 1980. "In Somalia, Every Day's an Emergency," *New York Times*, November 3.

Judge, Rajbir Singh. 2020. "Mind the Gap: Islam, Secularism, and the Law," 29 (1) *Qui Parle*: 179–202.

Kakwenzire, Patrick Kitaburaza. 1976. "Colonial Rule in the British Somaliland Protectorate, 1905–1939." Ph.D. thesis, University of London.

Kamali, Mohammad Hashim. 2005. *Principles of Islamic Jurisprudence*, 3rd ed. Cambridge: Islamic Texts Society.

2008. *Shari'ah Law: An Introduction*. London: Oneworld Publications.

Kang'atta, Elizabeth, Christine Fowler, Abdisalam Farah, Abdullahi Yusuf Mohamed, and Magdalene Wanza Kioko. 2015. "Access to Justice Project: C.2 Project Annual Report, 2014," United Nations Development Programme Somalia.

Kaplan, Irving, Margarita K. Dobert, James L. McLaughlin, Barbara Marvin, H. Mark Roth, and Donald P. Whitaker. 1977. *Area Handbook for Somalia*. Washington, DC: US Government Printing Office.

Kapteijns, Lidwien. 2004. "I. M. Lewis and Somali Clanship: A Critique," 11 (1) *Northeast African Studies*: 1–23.

Kaufman, Michael T. 1978. "Somalia Announces Mobilization, Dispatch of Its Troops to Ogaden," *New York Times*, February 12. Available: https://nyti.ms/3m2pzOV (accessed January 1, 2021).

Kedar, Nir. 2018. "The Rule of Law in Israel," 23(3) *Israel Studies*: 164–171.

Kenya Human Rights Institute. 2007. *Interventionism and Human Rights in Somalia: Report of an Exploratory Forum on the Somalia Crisis.* Nairobi: KHRI.

Khalid, Adeeb. 2014. *Islam after Communism: Religion and Politics in Central Asia.* Oakland, CA: University of California Press, 2014.

Khan, Maryam S. 2014. "Ethnic Federalism in Pakistan: Federal Design, Construction of Ethno-Linguistic Identity & Group Conflict," 30 *Harvard Journal of Racial and Ethnic Justice*: 77–129.

Kleinfeld, Rachel. 2012. *Advancing the Rule of Law Abroad: Next Generation Reform.* Washington, DC: Carnegie Endowment for International Peace.

2018. *A Savage Order: How the World's Deadliest Countries Can Forge a Path to Security.* New York: Pantheon.

Kroncke, Jedidiah J. 2016. *The Futility of Law and Development: China and the Dangers of Exporting American Law.* Oxford: Oxford University Press.

Krygier, Martin. 2011a. "Approaching the Rule of Law," in Whit Mason, ed., *The Rule of Law in Afghanistan: Missing in Inaction.* Cambridge: Cambridge University Press.

2011b. "Four Puzzles About the Rule of Law: Why, What, Where? And Who Cares?" in J. E. Fleming, ed., *Getting to the Rule of Law: Nomos No. 50.* New York: New York University Press, pp. 64–104.

2016. "The Rule of Law between England and Sudan: Hay, Thompson, and Massoud," 41(2) *Law & Social Inquiry*: 480–488.

Kuran, Timur. 2010. *The Long Divergence: How Islamic Law Held Back the Middle East.* Princeton, NJ: Princeton University Press.

Kurkchiyan, Marina and Agnieszka Kubal. 2018. "Administerial Justice," in Marina Kurkchiyan and Agnieszka Kubal, eds., *A Sociology of Justice in Russia.* Cambridge: Cambridge University Press.

Laitin, David. 1977a. *Politics, Language, and Thought: The Somali Experience.* Chicago, IL: University of Chicago Press.

1977b. "Revolutionary Change in Somalia." 62 *Middle East Research and Information Project Reports* 6–18.

1982. "The Sharia Debate and the Origins of Nigeria's Second Republic." 20 (3) *Journal of Modern African Studies*: 411–430.

Lacey, Marc. 2006. "In Somalia, Islamic Militias Fight Culture Wars." *New York Times*, June 19. Available: https://nyti.ms/3aXnYrW (accessed January 1, 2021).

Lazarev, Egor. 2019. "Laws in Conflict: Legacies of War, Gender, and Legal Pluralism in Chechnya," 71(4) *World Politics*: 667–709.

Le Sage, Andre. 2005. *Stateless Justice in Somalia: Formal and Informal Rule of Law Initiatives*. Geneva: Centre for Humanitarian Dialogue.

2010. "Somalia's Endless Transition: Breaking the Deadlock," *Strategic Forum No. 257*. Washington, DC: Institute for National Strategic Studies, National Defense University.

Lemons, Katherine. 2019. *Divorcing Traditions: Islamic Marriage Law and the Making of Indian Secularism*. Ithaca, NY: Cornell University Press.

Lev, Daniel. 1972. *Islamic Courts in Indonesia: A Study in the Political Bases of Legal Institutions*. Oakland, CA: University of California Press.

Levinson, Sanford and Jack M. Balkin. 2011. "Morton Horwitz Wrestles with the Rule of Law," in Daniel W. Hamilton and Alfred L. Brophy, eds., *Transformations in American Legal History II: Law, Ideology, and Morals – Essays in Honor of Morton J. Horwitz*. Cambridge, MA: Harvard University Press, pp. 483–500.

Lewis, I. M. 1958a. The Somali Lineage System and the Total Genealogy: A General Introduction to the Basic Principles of Somali Political Institutions (presented March 18, 1958, to the Royal Anthropological Institute). London: RAI Archives, MS 191.

1958b. "Modern Political Movements in Somaliland, Part I," 28(3) *Africa: Journal of the International African Institute*: 244–261.

1998. *Saints and Somalis: Popular Islam in a Clan-Based Society*. Lawrenceville, NJ: Red Sea Press.

2003. *A Modern History of the Somali: Nation and State in the Horn of Africa*. London: Boydell and Brewer.

2004. "Visible and Invisible Differences: The Somali Paradox," 74 *Africa: Journal of the International Africa Institute*: 489–515.

Liberty: Magazine of the Somali National Movement. No. 1, Spring, January 9, 1986. Available: zc.9.b.1695, British Library, London.

Little, Peter D. 2003. *Somalia: Economy without a State*. Bloomington: Indiana University Press.

Lloyd, Vincent, ed. 2016. "Religion, Secularism, and Black Lives Matter." *The Immanent Frame*. New York: Social Sciences Research Council. Available: https://bit.ly/34taQXB.

Lokaneeta, Jinee. 2011. *Transnational Torture: Law, Violence, and State Power in the United States and India*. New York: New York University Press.

Lombardi, Clark. 2006. *State Law as Islamic Law in Modern Egypt: The Incorporation of the Shari'a into Egyptian Constitutional Law*. Leiden: Brill Publishers.

Lynch, Cecelia M. 2020. *Wrestling with God: Ethical Precarity in Christianity and International Relations*. Cambridge: Cambridge University Press.

Mahmood, Saba. 2005. *Politics of Piety: The Islamic Revival and the Feminist Subject*. Princeton, NJ: Princeton University Press.

2015. *Religious Difference in a Secular Age: A Minority Report.* Princeton, NJ: Princeton University Press.

Maine, Henry Sumner. 1861. *Ancient Law: Its Connection with the Early History of Society, and its Relation to Modern Ideas.* London: John Murray.

Manuel, Marcus, Raphaelle Faure, and Dina Mansour-Ille. 2017. *Somalia: Country Evaluation Brief.* Chr. Michelson Institute, Overseas Development Institute and the Norwegian Agency for Development Cooperation. Oslo: NORAD.

March, Andrew. 2009. *Islam and Liberal Citizenship: The Search for an Overlapping Consensus.* Oxford: Oxford University Press.

2015. "What Can the Islamic Past Teach Us About Secular Modernity?" 43 *Political Theory*: 838–849.

Marchal, Roland. 2004. "Islamic Political Dynamics in the Somali Civil War," in Alex de Waal, ed., *Islamism and its Enemies in the Horn of Africa.* London: Hurst, 114–145.

Marotta, Girolamo. 1974. "The Active Functions of Judges," 9 *Somali National Reports to the 9th International Congress of Comparative Law*: 15–23.

Marr, Kendra. 2011. "Santorum: Sharia 'is evil'." *Politico*, March 11. Available: https://politi.co/3a4X9l8 (accessed January 1, 2021).

Marshall, David, ed., 2014. *The International Rule of Law Movement: A Crisis of Legitimacy and the Way Forward.* Cambridge, MA: Harvard University Press.

Maru, Mehari Taddele. 2008. "The Future of Somalia's Legal System and Its Contribution to Peace and Development," 4(1) *Journal of Peacebuilding and Development*: 1–15.

Massoud, Mark Fathi. 2006. "Rights in a Failed State: Internally Displaced Women in Sudan and Their Lawyers," 21 *Berkeley Journal of Gender, Law & Justice*: 2–12.

2011. "Do Victims of War Need International Law? Human Rights Education Programs in Authoritarian Sudan," 45(1) *Law & Society Review*: 1–32.

2013a. *Law's Fragile State: Colonial, Authoritarian, and Humanitarian Legacies in Sudan.* Cambridge: Cambridge University Press.

2013b. "Legal Poverty and the Rule of Law in Strife-Torn States," 34(2) *Whittier Law Review*: 245–259.

2015. "Work Rules: How International NGOs Build Law in War-Torn Societies," 49(2) *Law & Society Review*: 333–364.

2016a. "The Politics of Islamic Law and Human Rights: Sudan's Rival Legal Systems," in Heinz Klug and Sally Engle Merry, eds., *The New Legal Realism, Volume 2: Studying Law Globally.* Cambridge: Cambridge University Press, pp. 96–112.

2016b. "Ideals and Practices in the Rule of Law," 41(2) *Law & Social Inquiry*: 489–501.

2016c. "Field Research on Law in Conflict Zones and Authoritarian States," 12 *Annual Review of Law and Social Science*: 85–106.

2018a. "How an Islamic State Rejected Islamic Law," 66 *American Journal of Comparative Law*: 579–602.

2018b. "Reflections on the Future of Global Legal Studies," 25(2) *Indiana Journal of Global Legal Studies*: 569–581.

Massoud, Mark Fathi and Kathleen M. Moore. 2015. "Rethinking *Shari'a*: Voices of Islam in California," 5(4) *Boom: A Journal of California*: 94–99.

2020. "Shari'a Consciousness: Law and Lived Religion Among California Muslims," 45(3) *Law & Social Inquiry*: 787–817.

McCann, Michael. 1994. *Rights at Work: Pay Equity Reform and the Politics of Legal Mobilization*. Chicago, IL: University of Chicago Press.

McCants, William. 2015. *The ISIS Apocalypse: The History, Strategy, and Doomsday Vision of the Islamic State*. New York: St. Martin's Press.

McGranahan, Carole. 2014. "What Is Ethnography? Teaching Ethnographic Sensibilities without Fieldwork," 4 *Teaching Anthropology*: 23–36.

Médecins Sans Frontières. 2013. *Somalia 1991–1993: Civil War, Famine Alert and a UN "Military-Humanitarian" Intervention*. Nairobi: Médecins Sans Frontières. Available: https://bit.ly/34bEZtY (accessed January 1, 2021).

Meierhenrich, Jens. 2008. *The Legacies of Law: Long-Run Consequences of Legal Development in South Africa, 1652–2000*. Cambridge: Cambridge University Press.

2014. "The Practice of International Law: A Theoretical Analysis," 76(3–4) *Law and Contemporary Problems*: 1–83.

2018. *The Remnants of the Rechsstaat: An Ethnography of Nazi Law*. Oxford: Oxford University Press.

Mendes-Flohr, Paul. 2019. *Martin Buber: A Life of Faith and Dissent*. New Haven, CT: Yale University Press.

Menkhaus, Ken and John Prendergast. 1995. "Governance and Economic Survival in Post-intervention Somalia," 172 *CSIS Africa Note* 1–10.

Menkhaus, Ken. 2002. "Political Islam in Somalia," 9(1) *Middle East Policy*: 109–123. Available: https://bit.ly/384m9HU.

2003. "State Collapse in Somalia: Second Thoughts," 97 *Review of African Political Economy*: 405–422.

2004. *Somalia: State Collapse and the Threat of Terrorism*. Oxford: Oxford University Press.

2007a. "Governance without Government in Somalia: Spoilers, State Building, and the Politics of Coping," 31(3) *International Security*: 74–106.

2007b. "There and Back Again in Somalia," *Middle East Research and Information Project (MERIP)*, February 11. Available: https://bit.ly/37ZU5VQ (accessed January 1, 2021).

Messick, Brinkley. 1993. *The Calligraphic State: Textual Domination and History in a Muslim Society*. Oakland, CA: University of California Press.

Middleton, Roger. 2008. *Piracy in Somalia: Threatening Global Trade, Feeding Local Wars*. London: Chatham House.

Millman, Brock. 2014. *British Somaliland: An Administrative History, 1920–1960*. London and New York: Routledge.

Ministry of Information and National Guidance. 1975. *Somalia Today*. Mogadishu: Ministry of Information and National Guidance, Somali Democratic Republic.

Ministry of Planning and Coordination. 1967. *Somalia in Figures*. Mogadishu: Ministry of Planning and Coordination, Somali Republic. Available at British Library, London, C.S.C. 179/10. (2.).

Mir-Hosseini, Ziba. 1999. *Islam and Gender: The Religious Debate in Contemporary Iran*. Princeton, NJ: Princeton University Press, 1999.

Miyazaki, Hirokazu. 2004. *The Method of Hope: Anthropology, Philosophy, and Fijian Knowledge*. Stanford, CA: Stanford University Press.

Mohamed, A. Ibrahim (Qoorcade). 2009. *A Nation in Tatters: Somalia (Qaran Dumay)*. Liverpool: Somali Education Trust.

Mohamed, Omar Osman. 1976. *Administrative Efficiency and Administrative Language in Somalia*. Mogadishu: Somali Institute of Development, Administration, and Management.

Moustafa, Tamir. 2007. *The Struggle for Constitutional Power: Law, Politics, and Economic Development in Egypt*. Cambridge: Cambridge University Press.

2013. "Islamic Law, Women's Rights, and Popular Legal Consciousness in Malaysia," 38(1) *Law & Social Inquiry*: 168–188.

2018. *Constituting Religion: Islam, Liberal Rights, and the Malaysian State*. Cambridge: Cambridge University Press.

Muhammad, Hassan Sheikh Ali Nur, Muhammad Danial Azman, and Roy Anthony Rogers. 2017. "Before Things Fall Apart: The Role of the Soviet Union in Somalia's Troubled Past (1969–1978)," 25(2) *Intellectual Discourse*: 409–427.

Mukhtar, Mohamed Haji. 1995. "Islam in Somali History: Fact and Fiction," in Ali Jimale Ahmed, ed., *The Invention of Somalia*. Lawrenceville, NJ: Red Sea Press, pp. 1–28.

2003. *Historical Dictionary of Somalia*. Oxford: Scarecrow Press.

2007. "Somali Reconciliation Conferences: The Unbeaten Track," in Abdulahi A. Osman and Issaka K. Souaré, eds., *Somalia at the Crossroads: Challenges and Perspectives in Reconstituting a Failed State*. London: Adonis & Abbey, pp. 123–130.

Munger, Frank. 2015. "Thailand's Cause Lawyers and Twenty-First-Century Military Coups: Nation, Identity, and Conflicting Visions of the Rule of Law," 2(2) *Asian Journal of Law and Society*: 301–22.

Mustafa, Zaki. 1971. *The Common Law in the Sudan: An Account of the "Justice, Equity, and Good Conscience" Provision*. Oxford: Clarendon Press.

Mutua, Makau. 2002. *Human Rights: A Political and Cultural Critique*. Philadelphia, PA: University of Pennsylvania Press.

Mwangi, Oscar Gakuo. 2010. "The Union of Islamic Courts and Security Governance in Somalia," 19(1) *African Security Review*: 88–94.

Myers, David N., ed. 2018. *The Eternal Dissident: Rabbi Leonard I. Beerman and the Radical Imperative to Think and Act*. Oakland, CA: University of California Press.

Nader, Laura. 2005. *The Life of the Law: Anthropological Projects*. Oakland, CA: University of California Press.

Nasr, Octavia. "Tape: Bin Laden Tells Sunnis to Fight Shiites in Iraq," *CNN*, July 2, 2006. Available: https://cnn.it/3o3VCjo (accessed January 1, 2021).

Noonan, John T. [1976] 2002. *Persons and Masks of the Law: Cardozo, Holmes, Jefferson, and Wythe as Makers of the Masks*. Oakland, CA: University of California Press.

Noor Muhammad, Haji N. A. 1969. *The Development of the Constitution of the Somali Republic*. Mogadishu: Ministry of Grace and Justice, Government of the Somali Republic.

1972. *The Legal System of the Somali Democratic Republic*. Charlottesville, VA: The Michie Company.

North, Charles M., Wafa Hakim Orman, and Carl R. Gwin. 2013. "Religion, Corruption, and the Rule of Law," 45(5) *Journal of Money, Credit, and Banking*: 757–779.

Nouwen, Henri. 1979. *The Wounded Healer: Ministry in Contemporary Society*. New York: Doubleday.

Nouwen, Sarah. 2014. "'As You Set Out for Ithaka': Practical, Epistemological, Ethical, and Existential Questions about Socio-Legal Empirical Research in Conflict," 27(1) *Leiden Journal of International Law*: 227–260.

Odabare, Ebenezer. 2018. *Pentecostal Republic: Religion and the Struggle for State Power in Nigeria*. London: Zed Books.

Orr, Deborah. 2013. "For Human Rights to Flourish, Religious Rights Have to Come Second," *Guardian*, December 27. Available: https://bit.ly/37hVmHG (accessed January 1, 2021).

Osanloo, Arzoo. 2009. *The Politics of Women's Rights in Iran*. Princeton, NJ: Princeton University Press.

Osman, Abdulahi A. 2007. "The Somali Conflict and the Role of Inequality, Tribalism and Clanism," in Abdulahi A. Osman and Issaka K. Souaré, eds., *Somalia at the Crossroads: Challenges and Perspectives in Reconstituting a Failed State*. London: Adonis & Abbey, pp. 83–109.

Osman, Abdulahi A. and Issaka K. Souaré. 2007. "Introduction," in Abdulahi A. Osman and Issaka K. Souaré, eds., *Somalia at the Crossroads: Challenges and Perspectives in Reconstituting a Failed State*. London: Adonis & Abbey, pp. 7–22.

Payton, Matt. 2016. "Japan's Top Court Has Approved the Blanket Surveillance of the Country's Muslims," *Independent*. June 29. Available: https://bit.ly/3aaTFgQ (accessed January 1, 2021).

Peletz, Michael G. 2002. *Islamic Modern: Religious Courts and Cultural Politics in Malaysia*. Princeton, NJ: Princeton University Press.

2020. *Sharia Transformations: Cultural Politics and the Rebranding of an Islamic Judiciary*. Oakland, CA: University of California Press.

Pelton, Robert Young. 2012. "Puntland Marine Police Force Enter Eyl: Force Welcomed by Mayor and Locals but not by UN Somalia-Eritrea Monitoring Group," *Somalia Report*, March 2. Available: https://bit.ly/2 K2DLdT (accessed January 1, 2021).

Peskin, Victor. 2008. *International Justice in Rwanda and the Balkans: Virtual Trials and the Struggle for State Cooperation*. Cambridge: Cambridge University Press.

Philips, Abu Ameenah Bilal. 1990. *The Evolution of Fiqh (Islamic Law and the Madh-habs)*. Riyadh: International Islamic Publishing House.

Piazza, Giovanni. 1909. "La Regione di Brava nel Benadir," *Bollettino della Societa'Italiana di Esplorazioni Geografiche e Commerciali*, Fasc. I & II 7–29.

Pierucci, Antônio Flávio. 2000. "Secularization in Max Weber: On Current Usefulness of Re-Accessing that Old Meaning." Special Issue No. 1 *Brazilian Review of Social Sciences* 129–158 (trans. Roderick Steel), published originally in 13(37) *Revista Brasileira de Ciências Sociais* (1998): 43–73.

Platteau, Jean-Philippe. 2017. *Islam Instrumentalized: Religion and Politics in Historical Perspective*. Cambridge: Cambridge University Press.

Powell, Benjamin, Ryan Ford, and Alex Nowrasteh. 2008. "Somalia after State Collapse: Chaos or Improvement?" 67(3–4) *Journal of Economic Behavior & Organization*: 657–670.

"Profile: Somalia's Islamic Courts," *BBC News*, June 6, 2006. Available: https://bbc.in/3aW6xb3 (accessed January 1, 2021).

Prunier, Gérard. 1995. *Somalia: Civil War, Intervention and Withdrawal, 1990–1995*. Geneva: United Nations High Commissioner for Refugees.

Quraishi-Landes, Asifa. 2008. "Who Says Shari'a Demands the Stoning of Women? A Description of Islamic Law and Constitutionalism," 1(1) *Berkeley Journal of Middle Eastern and Islamic Law*: 163–178.

2013. "Secular Is Not Always Better: A Closer Look at Some Women-Empowering Features of Islamic Law," Policy Brief No. 61. Washington, DC: Institute for Social Policy and Understanding.

Rabb, Intisar A. 2015. *Doubt in Islamic Law: A History of Legal Maxims, Interpretation, and Islamic Criminal Law*. Cambridge: Cambridge University Press.

Rajah, Jothie. 2012. *Authoritarian Rule of Law: Legislation, Discourse, and Legitimacy in Singapore*. Cambridge: Cambridge University Press.

Ramet, Pedro, ed. 1989. *Religion and Nationalism in Soviet and East European Politics*. Durham, NC: Duke University Press.

Redding, Jeffrey A. *A Secular Need: Islamic Law and State Governance in Contemporary India*. Seattle, WA: University of Washington Press.

"Refounding Somalia: Constitution and Islam," *Pambazuka News*, May 3, 2012. Available: https://bit.ly/3qVM5N5 (accessed January 1, 2021).

Reinhart, A. Kevin. 1983. "Islamic Law as Islamic Ethics," 11(2) *Journal of Religious Ethics*: 186–203.

Religious Literacy Project. 2020. *The Islamic Courts Union*. Cambridge, MA: Harvard Divinity School. Available: https://bit.ly/3aWsFlz (accessed January 1, 2021).

Rosen, Lawrence. 2018. *Islam and the Rule of Justice: Image and Reality in Muslim Law and Culture*. Chicago, IL: University of Chicago Press.

Rosenberg, Gerald N. 2008. *The Hollow Hope: Can Courts Bring About Social Change?* 2nd ed. Chicago, IL: University of Chicago Press.

Rowen, Jamie. 2017. *Searching for Truth in the Transitional Justice Movement*. Cambridge: Cambridge University Press.

Rubin, Lawrence. 2014. *Islam in the Balance: Ideational Threats in Arab Politics*. Stanford, CA: Stanford University Press.

Rýdlová, Barbora. 2007. "Civil War in Somalia – A Colonial Legacy?" Research report. Charles University: Institute of Political Studies.

Sachs, Jeffrey Adam. 2018. "Seeing Like an Islamic State: Shari'a and Political Power in Sudan," 52(3) *Law & Society Review*: 630–651.

Salem, Ola and Hassan Hassan. 2019. "Arab Regimes Are the World's Most Powerful Islamophobes," *Foreign Policy*. Available: https://bit.ly/2LAaAzk (accessed January 1, 2021).

Salomon, Noah. 2016. *For Love of the Prophet: An Ethnography of Sudan's Islamic State*. Princeton, NJ: Princeton University Press.

Samatar, Ahmed. 1994. "The Curse of Allah: Civic Disembowelment and the Collapse of the State in Somalia," in Ahmed Samatar, ed., *The Somali Challenge: From Catastrophe to Renewal?* Boulder, CO: Lynne Reinner Publishers.

Samatar, Said. 1982. *Oral Poetry and Somali Nationalism: The Case of Sayid Mahammad 'Abdille Hasan*. Cambridge: Cambridge University Press.

Sanjian, Gregory. 1999. "Promoting Stability or Instability? Arms Transfers and Regional Rivalries," 43(4) *International Studies Quarterly*: 641–670.

Santoro, Lara. 1999. "Islamic Clerics Combat Lawlessness in Somalia," *Christian Science Monitor*, July 13.

Scham, Paul. 2018. "'A Nation that Dwells Alone': Israeli Religious Nationalism in the 21st Century," 23(3) *Israel Studies*: 207–215.

Schonthal, Benjamin, Tamir Moustafa, Matthew Nelson, and Shylashri Shankar. 2015. "Is the Rule of Law an Antidote for Religious Tension? The Promise and Peril of Judicializing Religious Freedom," 60 (8) *American Behavioral Scientist* 966–986.

Schonthal, Benjamin. 2016. *Buddhism, Politics and the Limits of Law: The Pyrrhic Constitutionalism of Sri Lanka*. Cambridge: Cambridge University Press.

Selznick, Philip. 2008. *A Humanist Science: Values and Ideals in Social Inquiry*. Stanford, CA: Stanford University Press, 2008.

Shahar, Ido. 2008. "Legal Pluralism and the Study of Shari'a Courts," 15 *Islamic Law and Society*: 112–141.

Shank, Michael. 2007. "Understanding Political Islam in Somalia," 1(1) *Contemporary Islam*: 89–103.

Shanmugasundaram, Swathi. 2018. "Anti-Sharia Law Bills in the United States," *Southern Poverty Law Center*, February 5. Available: https://bit.ly/3qV1vkB (accessed January 1, 2021).

Sharkey, Heather J. 1994. "Ahmad Zayni Dahlan's Al-Futuhat Al-Islamiyya: A Contemporary View of the Sudanese Mahdi," 5 *Sudanic Africa*: 67–75.

Shay, Saul. 2017. *Somalia between Jihad and Restoration*. London: Routledge.

Shelley, Fred M. 2015. *Governments around the World: From Democracies to Theocracies*. Santa Barbara, CA: ABC-CLIO.

Shklar, Judith. 1964. *Legalism: Law, Morals, and Political Trials*. Cambridge, MA: Harvard University Press.

Simons, Anna. 1996. *Network of Dissolution: Somalia Undone*. Boulder, CO: Westview Press.

Singh, Iqbal and Mohamed Hassan Said. 1973. *Commentary on the Criminal Procedure Code (Published under the Authority of the Ministry of Justice and Religion)*. Mogadishu: Wakaladda Madbacadda Qaraka – Xamar.

Slackman, Michael. 2008. "With a Word, Egyptians Leave It All to Fate," *New York Times*, June 20. Available: https://nyti.ms/3huY93u (accessed January 1, 2021).

Smith, David. 2018. "'Are You Concerned by Sharia Law?': Trump Canvasses Supporters for 2020." *Guardian*, March 3. Available: https://bit.ly/3ai2DsC (accessed January 1, 2021).

Smith, Nicholas Rush. 2019. *Contradictions of Democracy: Vigilantism and Rights in Post-Apartheid South Africa*. Oxford: Oxford University Press.

Smock, David R., ed. 2006. *Religious Contributions to Peacemaking: When Religion Brings Peace, Not War*, Peaceworks No. 55. Washington, DC: United States Institute of Peace.

Snow, David A. and Robert D. Benford. 1992. "Master Frames and Cycles of Protest," in Aldon D. Morris and Carol McClurg Mueller, eds., *Frontiers in Social Movement Theory*. New Haven, CT: Yale University Press, pp. 133–155.

Somali Delegation to the Third Session of the United Nations. 1949. "Memoranda and Petition from the Somali Peoples on the Future of ex-Italian Somaliland and the Unification of all Somali Territories under UN Trusteeship."

Somali Institute for Public Administration. 1968. *Perspectives on Somalia: Orientation Course for Foreign Experts Working in Somalia*. Mogadishu, Somalia: Somali Institute of Public Administration.

"Somalia Calling: An Unlikely Success Story," *The Economist*, December 20, 2005. Available: https://econ.st/2KQs3Dx (accessed January 1, 2021).

"Somalia: Escalation and Human Rights Abuses," *AfricaFocus*, April 9, 2007. Available: https://bit.ly/2WY1ZJ1 (accessed January 1, 2021).

"Somalia: Mogadishu Islamic Leaders Claim Victory Over Rivals," *United Nations Integrated Regional Information Network (IRIN) News*, June 5, 2006. Available: https://bit.ly/3mpezLW (accessed January 1, 2021).

"Somalia: Puntland Court Sentences Al Shabaab Chief Godane and 11 Others to Death," *Garowe Online*, February 27, 2013. Available: https://bit.ly/2Xc6zDT (accessed January 1, 2021).

Somalia Police Force. "History." Available: https://bit.ly/38IlD12 (accessed January 1, 2021).

"Somaliland Legal Profession," Somaliland Law. 2019. Available: https://bit.ly/34YeSai (accessed January 1, 2021).

Souaré, Issaka K. 2007. "Conclusions: Towards a Revived Somali State," in Abdulahi A. Osman and Issaka K. Souaré, eds., *Somalia at the Crossroads: Challenges and Perspectives in Reconstituting a Failed State*. London: Adonis & Abbey, pp. 207–213.

Stanford University Center for International Security and Cooperation (CISAC). 2016. *Mapping Militant Organizations: Islamic Courts Union*. Stanford, CA: CISAC.

"Statement by the Minister of Finance, H. E. Hagi Farah Ali Omar, on the Budget Estimates for Financial Year 1968." *Bollettino Ufficiale Della Repubblica Somalia*, 1968.

Stern, Rachel E. 2013. *Environmental Litigation in China: A Study in Political Ambivalence*. Cambridge: Cambridge University Press.

Stilt, Kristen. 2010. "Islam Is the Solution: Constitutional Visions of the Egyptian Muslim Brotherhood," 46 *Texas International Law Journal* 74–108.

　　2012. *Islamic Law in Action: Authority, Discretion, and Everyday Experiences in Mamluk Egypt*. Oxford: Oxford University Press.

2014. "Constitutional Islam: Genealogies, Transmissions and Meanings," in Brian T. Edwards, ed., *On the Ground: New Directions in Middle East and North African Studies*. Doha: Akkadia Press.

Sudan Professionals Association. 2019. "Forces of Freedom and Change (FCC) Speech, on Signing the Agreement," August 17. Available: https://bit.ly/3nkZbRI (accessed January 1, 2021).

Sullivan, Winnifred Fallers. 2018. *The Impossibility of Religious Freedom*, 2nd ed. Princeton, NJ: Princeton University Press.

Sunder, Madhavi. 2003. "Piercing the Veil," 112 *Yale Law Journal*: 1399–1472.

Swart, Gerrie. 2007. "Somalia: A Failed State Governed by a Failed Government?" in Abdulahi A. Osman and Issaka K. Souaré, eds., *Somalia at the Crossroads: Challenges and Perspectives in Reconstituting a Failed State*. London: Adonis & Abbey, pp. 109–122.

Swidler, Ann. 2013. "African Affirmations: The Religion of Modernity and the Modernity of Religion," 28(6) *International Sociology*: 680–696.

Sylvester, Gideon D. 2012. "Social Justice Lies at the Heart of the Jewish People," *Haaretz*, June 30. Available: https://bit.ly/3r3vd7p (accessed January 1, 2021).

Tanner, Henry. 1975. "Soviet Giving a Lift to Marxist Junta Trying to Pull Somalis Out of Poverty," *New York Times*, July 15. Available: https://nyti.ms/37fB81c (accessed January 1, 2021).

Taylor, Leonard Francis. 2020. *Catholic Cosmopolitanism and Human Rights*. Cambridge: Cambridge University Press.

Thompson, E. P. 1975. *Whigs and Hunters: The Origin of the Black Act*. New York: Pantheon Books.

Touval, Saadia. 1963. *Somali Nationalism: International Politics and the Drive for Unity in the Horn of Africa*. Cambridge, MA: Harvard University Press.

"UN Ruling: Islamic Sharia Taboo in Human Rights Council Debates." 2008. *UN Watch*. Available: https://bit.ly/3n4I85u (accessed January 1, 2021).

UNESCO. *Public Education in Somalia*. 1960. Geneva: UNESCO.

UNICEF and Academy for Peace and Development. 2002. *Women's Rights in Islam and Somali Culture*.

United Kingdom Central Office of Information. Undated. "The Somaliland Protectorate." London: UK Government Overseas Services.

United Nations Development Programme. 2005. "Quarterly Update – July 2005," Report of UNDP Somalia. Available: https://bit.ly/3a8caT5 (accessed January 1, 2021).

United Nations General Assembly. 2012. "World Leaders Adopt Declaration Reaffirming Rule of Law as Foundation for Building Equitable State Relations, Just Societies," Sixty-seventh General Assembly, GA/11290. Available: https://bit.ly/3huArEL (accessed January 1, 2021).

United Nations Habitat. 2015. "Harmonization of the Legal Systems Resolving Land Disputes in Somaliland and Puntland: Report and Recommendations," HS/007/16E.

United Nations Office of the High Commissioner for Human Rights. 2012. "Addressing Impunity in Somalia," April 13. Available: https://bit.ly/3a9CPPu (accessed January 1, 2021).

United Nations Security Council. 2006. "Security Council Approves African Protection, Training Mission in Somalia, Unanimously Adopting Resolution 1725 (2006)." United Nations Security Council Press Release SC/8887, December 6. Available: https://bit.ly/3rCF9F7 (accessed January 1, 2021).

"U.S. Bans Contact with Islamist Leader in Somalia." 2006. Reuters, June 26. Available: https://bit.ly/3gMfkNB (accessed January 1, 2021).

US Department of State. 2010. *Country Reports on Human Rights Practices for 2008*. Washington, DC: Government Printing Office.

"US Troops to Help Somalia Fight al-Shabaab," *BBC News*, April 14, 2017. Available: https://bbc.in/3pzS8FJ (accessed January 1, 2021).

Vianello, Alessandra and Mohamed M. Kassim. 2006. *Servants of the Sharia: The Civil Register of the Qadis' Court of Brava, 1893–1900, Vol. 1 and 2*. Leiden: Brill.

Von Benda-Beckmann, Keebet. 1981. "Forum Shopping and Shopping Forums: Dispute Processing in a Minangkabau Village in West Sumatra," 13(19) *The Journal of Legal Pluralism and Unofficial Law*: 117–159.

Wabala, Dominic. 2012. "East Africa: Al Qaeda Criticises Al Shabaab Over 'Heinous and Anti-Islamic' Activities," *STAR*, September 7. Available: https://bit.ly/37YPRhk (accessed January 1, 2021).

Walker, Samuel. 1980. *Popular Justice: A History of American Criminal Justice*. Oxford: Oxford University Press.

Wedeen, Lisa. 1996. *Ambiguities of Domination: Politics, Rhetoric, and Symbols in Contemporary*. Chicago, IL: University of Chicago Press.

Weldemichael, Awet Tewelde. 2019. *Piracy in Somalia: Violence and Development in the Horn of Africa*. Cambridge: Cambridge University Press.

Williams, Paul D. 2018. *Fighting for Peace in Somalia: A History and Analysis of the African Union Mission (AMISOM), 2007–2017*. Oxford: Oxford University Press.

Witte, Jr., John and M. Christian Green, eds. 2012. *Religion and Human Rights: An Introduction*. Oxford: Oxford University Press.

Wintersteen, A. H. 1890. "Christianity and the Common Law," 29 *American Law Register*: 273–285.

Woldemariam, Michael. 2018. *Insurgent Fragmentation in the Horn of Africa: Rebellion and Its Discontents*. Cambridge: Cambridge University Press.

Woodward, Peter. 1996. *The Horn of Africa: State Politics and International Relations*. New York: Tauris Academic Studies.

Zaki, Hind Ahmed. 2017. "Law, Culture, and Mobilization: Legal Pluralism and Women's Access to Divorce in Egypt," 14(1) *Muslim World Journal of Human Rights*: 1–25.

Zimmermann, Lisbeth. 2017. *Global Norms with a Local Face: Rule-of-Law Promotion and Norm-Translation*. Cambridge: Cambridge University Press.

INDEX

Page numbers with *italics* indicate figures, maps, notes, and tables. Surnames and terms beginning with *al-* are alphabetized by the subsequent part of the name.

blood money. *See diyya*
British colonialism and British Somaliland. *See* colonial legal politics
Buber, Martin, 300
Buddhism: as dominant culture in Bhutan, 293; legal appeals to, 293

Cabdulqaadir Mosque, Mogadishu, 148
Calvin, John, 160
Camel Corps, 87
CEDAW (Convention on the Elimination of All Forms of Discrimination Against Women), 147, 267, 284
Center for Security Policy, 4
child marriage, 280–281
Choi, Seung-Whan, 39
Christianity: *ah al-kitaab* (Jews and Christians; people of the book), treatment of, 66; anticolonialism and, 133; Berbera, colonial Roman Catholic mission in, 79, 100; legal appeals to, 293; legal systems, development of, 176, 292; religion and law, connection between, 301–304; varied political interpretations of ethics in, 293, 294
Churchill, Winston, 81
civic groups, as political elites, *14*
Civil Rights Movement, 294
civil war in Somalia, 18–20; archetype of disaster, Somali political and legal culture viewed as, 57–58; constitutional shari'a, 197, 199–205; economy during, 57; ICU (Islamic Courts Union), 19–20, 37, 159, 163–164, 179–189, 298; IFCC (Independent Federal Constitution Commission), 183; judiciary, TFG attempting to reestablish, 179, 195–199; life expectancy during, 180; map of Somalia during, *159*; piracy during, 182, 190, 193–194; political and social organizations during, 162, 166–168, 170; post-ICU efforts to establish political authority (2007–2021), 189–205; religion as means of restoring law, 160–165, 303; rule of law, shari'a courts/ICU building, 180–186; al-Shabaab, 163–165, 183, 188, 189–196, 200–207, 208, 303; Somali legal order[s] during, 58–61; "stateless" period in Somalia (1991–2001), 166–169; TFG (Transitional Federal Government), 159, 164–165, 175, 178–179, 183–185, 186–188, 189–190, 192, 195–206; TNG (Transitional National Government), 164–165, 175, 176–177; transitional governments during, 20, 37, 57, 164–165, 169, 175; UNISOM and UNITAF, 168–169; US-backed Ethiopian invasion and collapse of ICU (2006/2007), 19, 37, 163, 186–189, 298; warlords during, 18–20,

57, 162, 168, 169, 172, 173–174, 183–184, 298; women, self-help groups formed by, 262. *See also* shari'a courts
clan system: al-Shabaab and, 192; shari'a courts and, 170–171, 174, 178, 181; in Somalia and Somaliland, 55–56; TFG and, 178, 179
Cold War, 152
colonial legal politics (1884–1960), 17–18, 65–109; Anglo-Italian Protocol (1890s), 79; anticolonial response to, 94; Berbera, Roman Catholic mission in, 79, 100; Christian missions, British control of, 79; courts, civil and Islamic, 87–90; disagreements over prevailing law in, 66–69; dispute resolution processes, coopting, 80–82; European settlements in Somalia, British not allowing, 79; formal legal agreements and treaties between Somalis and British, 75–80, 78; geopolitical districts, establishment of, 87; Sheikh Hassan, war against (1899–1920), 17, 36, 65, 68, 69, 95–107, 109, 174, 217, 297; independent Somaliland, continuing operation of colonial process in, 231–232, 241, 246–248; law, building colony through, 75–95, 108; legacy in Somali legal culture, 54; legal pluralism and, 67–68; map of European colonial administrations, 65; modern Somali opinions of, 107; multiple colonial legacies in Horn of Africa, 69–75, 74, 107; political/legal elites, creating new classes of, 82–87, 84; pre-colonial law in Horn of Africa, 73; religion and, 66, 88, 95–96, 108–109; rule of law, separation of religion and law, and secularization, 11, 41–42; shari'a, British use of, 3, 17, 36, 66, 72, 101–107, 301–302; women, treatment of, 260, 264; *xeer*, use of, 80–81; *xeer* and shari'a, British separation of, 75, 85. *See also* French Somaliland; Italian Somalia
Committee for the Protection of Journalists, 198
common law: American association of Christianity with, 161; Catholic development of legal systems and, 176; shari'a-trained judges, analogical methodology of, 128; *xeer* as form of, 80–81, 111, 115. *See also* English common law
Conference on National Reconciliation (1993), 168
constitution of independent Somaliland (2001), 20, 208, 209, 229–234, 249, 269–271, 298
constitution of Somalia (2012), 197, 199–205, 269–271, 298

145, 146, 152; family law under, 146–152, 261; "famous call" (1969), 141; First and Second Charters of the Revolution, 138; first Somali script and legal language, creation of, 144; independent Somaliland's reaction against, 20, 208, 212, 215, 222, 223–224, 245, 253; legal pluralism under, 141; national security courts, 142, 143, 149, 153, 154, 155, 208, 223, 245; popular feeling about, 137, 154; postcolonial legal politics and, 36, 57, 62, 112–113; rebuilding of legal system under, 139, 140–145, 142; religious leaders under, 205; resistance to, 143, 144, 145–155, 298; shari'a under, 136, 139, 145–155, 303; sheikhs, execution of, 146, 148–151; socialism under, 18, 62, 112, 135–136, 139, 144, 171; SRC (Supreme Revolutionary Council) under, 135, 138, 140, 155; US aid to, 162; women/women activists under, 143, 259, 261–263, 286; xeer under, 140

Simons, Anna, 57

Sisters in Islam, 258

slavery: British treaties on, 77; Islamic social justice and, 47; prohibition in Italian Somalia, 91

SNM (Somali National Movement), 153, 215, 217, 223–225, 263

social justice, in Islam, 47

socialism in Somalia (1969–1991), 18, 62, 112, 135–136, 139, 144, 171

socio-legal approach to shari'a, 51–53

Somali language, xvi–xvii, 144

Somali legal politics, 1–30; aims and motivations for studying, 28–30; archetype of disaster, viewed as, 57–58; clan system, 55–56; concept of legal politics, xii; extremism, fear of, 30, 52, 189, 199; fragile or failed state, Somalia viewed as, 13; historical overview, 16–22; inshallah, concept of, 2; law and religion, as concepts, 3–4; legal pluralism and, 31–36, 40–44, 58–61, 60; map of horn of Africa, xviii; political elites in Somalia and Somaliland, 14, 14–15; political geography of Somalia, Somaliland, and Puntland, xvi; populations identifying as Somali in Djibouti, Kenya, and Ethiopia, xvi; pre-colonial law in Horn of Africa, 73; religion, legal politics of, xi–xii, 53–61; separation of religion and law, and secularization, 9–12. See also civil war in Somalia; colonial legal politics; independent Somaliland; postcolonial legal politics; research methods; rule of law; women and women activists

Somali National Congress v. the State (1963), 132

Somali National Movement (SNM), 153, 215, 217, 223–225, 263

Somali National University (formerly Higher Institute of Legal, Economic and Social Studies, and University Institute of Law and Economics), 119, 119–120, 134, 145

Somali Republic. See postcolonial legal politics

Somali script, creation of, 144

Somalia. See civil war in Somalia; colonial legal politics; postcolonial legal politics; Siad Barre, Mohamed, dictatorship of; Somali legal politics

Somaliland. See independent Somaliland; Somali legal politics

Somaliland Lawyers Association, 244

Somaliland Women Lawyers Association, 244

Souaré, Issaka K., 186, 206

Southern Poverty Law Center, 5

sovereignty: former British Somaliland's five days of (in 1960), xvi, 20, 74, 208; international nonrecognition of, for independent Somaliland, 213, 214, 235, 267; reassertion of, by independent Somaliland, 18, 20, 58, 208

Soviet Union: Ethiopia's alliance with, 152; religion and Bolshevik revolution in, 66; Siad Barre and, 135, 146, 152; US aid following Siad Barre's renunciation of allegiance to, 162

Special Representative of the Secretary General (SRSG), 202

sports for women and girls, 274

SRC (Supreme Revolutionary Council), 135, 138, 140, 155

Sri Lanka, legal appeals to Buddhism in, 293

SRSG (Special Representative of the Secretary General), 202

state, defined, 6

state courts: attacks on, in Mogadishu, 187, 195, 205; ethnographic observation in, 312; fatwas, state courts in independent Somaliland issuing, 221

"stateless" period in Somalia (1991–2001), 166–169

statelessness, concept of, 33

Sudan: Sheikh Hassan, envoys sent to, 104; al-Itihaad al-Islamiyya, aid sent to, 168; legal appeals to Islam in, 295; Mahdi, Islamic revolution under, 70, 102; postcolonial period, law and shari'a in, 111; women and women's activism in, 147

Suez Canal, 1967 closure of, 134

Sufis and Sufism, 167, 168, 182, 196, 253

sultans: in colonial Somalia, 70, 71, 76, 77, 83, 84, 85; in independent Somaliland, 209, 219, 250; as political elites, 14; women/women activists and, 264; xeer, use of, 31

CAMBRIDGE STUDIES IN LAW AND SOCIETY

Printed in the USA
CPSIA information can be obtained
at www.ICGtesting.com
LVHW062030200823
755748LV00001B/31

9 781108 965705